DISCARD

# Langenscheidt

## Universal-Chinese Dictionary

### Chinese – Englisch
### Englisch – Chinese

edited by the
Langenscheidt editorial staff

Langenscheidt

Berlin · Munich · Vienna · Zurich
London · Madrid · New York · Warsaw

Neither the presence nor the absence of a designation indicating that any entered word constitutes a trademark should be regarded as affecting the legal status thereof.

compiled by LEXUS with

**吴乐军 (Emma Lejun Wu)**
**张晨阳 (Lulu Langtree)**
Jim Weldon
Gaius Moore

# Contents

11010 (98184)

# Preface

This Chinese Dictionary focuses on modern usage in English and Chinese.

The Chinese is Mainland Chinese, written in simplified characters, with pinyin pronunciation.

The two sides of the book, the Chinese-English dictionary and the English-Chinese dictionary, are different in structure and purpose. The Chinese-English is a decoding dictionary, designed to enable the native speaker of English to understand Chinese. The English-Chinese is designed for productive usage, for self-expression in Chinese.

A system of signposting helps the user find the correct translation.

Grammar labels (*n*, *adj*, *v/t*) are given when it is necessary to identify *which* use or uses of an English word are being translated.

Indicators in italics (typical objects of verbs, synonyms of nouns etc) and subject area labels are given to clarify *which* sense or area of usage of a headword is being translated.

In the Chinese-English dictionary the Chinese headwords are alphabetically ordered according to their pinyin pronunciation. When the pinyin spelling of different words is the same, the words are then ordered by their tone and in the sequence: first, second, third, fourth tone.

White lozenges (◊) are used in the Chinese-English to separate out different English grammatical categories, when all of these correspond to one single Chinese word.

# The pronunciation of Chinese

All Chinese characters in this dictionary are accompanied by a romanized script known as pinyin. Not all pinyin letters, or groups of letters, are pronounced as you would normally expect them to be in English. The following is a guide to the pronunciation of pinyin.

## Initial consonants

| | |
|---|---|
| b | more abrupt than English, like p in s*p*are |
| c | like ts in be*ts* |
| ch | like ch in *ch*urch, pronounced with the tip of the tongue curled back |
| d | more abrupt than English, like t in s*t*are |
| g | more abrupt than English, like c in s*c*are; always hard as in *g*o or *g*irl |
| h | like the Scottish pronunciation of lo*ch*, with a little friction in the throat |
| j | like j in *j*eep, pronounced with the lips spread as in a smile |
| k | pronounced with a slight puff of air as in *c*op |
| p | pronounced with a slight puff of air as in *p*op |
| q | like ch in *ch*eap, pronounced with the lips spread as in a smile |
| r | like r in *r*ung, pronounced with the tip of the tongue curled back |
| sh | like sh in *sh*irt, pronounced with the tip of the tongue curled back |
| t | pronounced with a slight puff of air as in *t*op |
| x | like sh in *sh*eep, pronounced with the lips spread as in a smile |
| z | like ds in be*ds* |

| zh | like j in *judge*, pronounced with the tip of the tongue curled back |
|---|---|

## Finals

| a | as in *father* |
|---|---|
| ai | as in *aisle* |
| an | as in *ran* (with the *a* slightly longer as in *ah*); but: yan as in *yen* |
| ang | as in *rang* (with the *a* slightly longer as in *ah*) |
| ao | like ow in *how* |
| e | as in *her* |
| ei | as in *eight* |
| en | as in op*en* |
| eng | like *en* in op*en* and g |
| er | like *err* – but with the tongue curled back and the sound coming from the back of the throat |
| i | (1) as in *magazine* |
| | (2) after c, ch, r, s, sh, z and zh like the i in b*i*rd |
| ia | like ya in *yard* |
| ian | similar to *yen* |
| iang | *i* (as in *magazine*) merged with *ang* (above) – but without lengthening the *a* |
| iao | as in *yowl* |
| ie | like ye in *yes* |
| in | as in th*in* |
| ing | as in th*ing* |
| iong | *i* (as in *magazine*) merged with *ong* (below) |
| iu | like yo in *yoga* |
| o | as in *more* |
| ou | as in d*ough* |
| ong | *oong* with oo as in *soon* |

| u | (1) as in r*u*le |
| | (2) after j, q and x like the 'u' sound in French t*u* or German *ü*ber |
| ua | w followed by *a* (above) |
| uai | similar to *why* |
| uan | w followed by *an* (above) |
| uang | w followed by *ang* (above) |
| ue | u (above) followed by e as in l*e*t |
| ui | similar to *way* |
| un | like uan in tr*uan*t |
| uo | similar to *war* |
| ü | as in French t*u* or German *ü*ber |
| üe | ü followed by e as in g*e*t |

## Tones

**First tone,** as in 科 **kē** (department): a high, level tone with the volume held constant.

**Second tone,** as in 壳 **ké** (shell): rises sharply from middle register and increasing in volume, shorter than the first tone; like a surprised 'what?'

**Third tone,** as in 渴 **kě** (thirst ◊ thirsty): starts low, then falls lower before rising again to a point slightly higher than the starting point; louder at the beginning and end than in the middle; slightly longer than the first tone.

**Fourth tone,** as in 客 **kè** (guest): starts high then drops sharply in pitch and volume; like saying 'right' when agreeing to an instruction.

# Abbreviations

| | | | |
|---|---|---|---|
| *adj* | adjective | MUS | music |
| *adv* | adverb | NAUT | nautical |
| ANAT | anatomy | *pej* | pejorative |
| BIO | biology | PHOT | photography |
| BOT | botany | PHYS | physics |
| *Br* | British English | POL | politics |
| CHEM | chemistry | *prep* | preposition |
| COM | commerce, business | *pron* | pronoun |
| COMPUT | computers, IT term | PSYCH | psychology |
| | | RAD | radio |
| *conj* | conjunction | RAIL | railroad |
| EDU | education | REL | religion |
| ELEC | electricity, electronics | S.O. | someone |
| | | SP | sports |
| F | familiar, colloquial | sth | something |
| | | TECH | technology |
| *fig* | figurative | TELEC | telecommunications |
| FIN | financial | | |
| GRAM | grammar | THEA | theater |
| *interj* | interjection | TV | television |
| LAW | law | *v/i* | intransitive verb |
| MATH | mathematics | *v/t* | transitive verb |
| MED | medicine | → | see |
| MIL | military | ® | registered trademark |
| MOT | motoring | | |

# A

阿富汗 Āfùhàn Afghanistan ◊ Afghan

哀 āi sorrow; mourning

挨 āi be next to

唉 āi alas

癌 āi cancer

挨 āi undergo

矮 ǎi short *person*; low

爱 ài love

碍 ài block; hinder; obstruct

爱称 àichēng diminutive

挨打 āidǎ get a beating

挨饿 ái'è starve

爱管事 ài guǎnshì bossy

爱国 àiguó patriotic

爱国者 àiguózhě patriot

爱好 àihào hobby

爱护 àihù take care of

挨近 āijìn approach

爱情 àiqíng love

哀求 āiqiú implore

爱人 àirén husband; wife

哀伤 āishāng grieved

爱上 àishàng fall in love with

唉声叹气 āishēng-tànqì sigh

哀乐 āiyuè lament (*music*)

癌症 áizhèng cancer

矮子 ǎizi dwarf

艾滋病 àizībìng Aids

鞍 ān saddle

按 àn press ◊ according to

岸 àn shore

案 àn (legal) case; file

暗 àn dark; secret

案板 ànbǎn chopping board

暗淡 àndàn gloomy

安定 āndìng settle down

昂贵 ángguì expensive

肮脏 āngzāng dirty

安家 ānjiā set up home

暗礁 ànjiāo reef; (*fig*) hidden danger

按揭贷款 ànjiē dàikuǎn mortgage

安静 ānjìng calm ◊ quiet; peaceful ◊ calm down

按扣 ànkòu snap fastener

按喇叭 **àn lǎba** honk the horn

按铃 **ànlíng** ring the bell

安眠药 **ānmiányào** sleeping pill

按摩 **ànmó** massage

按钮 **ànniǔ** button (*on machine*)

安排 **ānpái** arrange ◊ arrangement

安全 **ānquán** safe ◊ safely ◊ safety; security

安全带 **ānquándài** seat belt

暗杀 **ànshā** assassinate ◊ assassination

按时 **ànshí** on time

暗示 **ànshì** hint ◊ imply

安慰 **ānwèi** comfort

安心 **ānxīn** reassured

安葬 **ānzàng** bury *the dead*

按照 **ànzhào** according to

安装 **ānzhuāng** install ◊ installation

熬 **áo** endure; boil

傲 **ào** arrogant

澳大利亚 **Àodàlìyà** Australia ◊ Australian

懊悔 **àohuǐ** regret

奥林匹克运动会 **Àolínpǐkè Yùndònghuì** Olympic Games

傲慢 **àomàn** arrogance ◊ arrogant

澳门 **Àomén** Macao ◊ Macanese

奥秘 **àomì** profound mystery

懊丧 **àosàng** morose

熬夜 **áoyè** stay up late

奥运会 **Àoyùnhuì** Olympics

阿姨 **āyí** aunt

# B

八 **bā** eight

疤 **bā** scar

拔 **bá** pull out

靶 **bǎ** target

把 **bǎ** *measure word for knives, umbrellas, things with handles*

爸 **bà** dad

坝 **bà** dam

把 **bǎ** handle

罢 **bà** stop, cease

吧 **ba** *used to make*

*suggestions*

爸爸 **bàba** dad

拔出 ◊ **báchū** extract, pull
out ◊ extraction

霸道 **bàdào** domineering

罢工 **bàgōng** strike *(of
workers)*

白 **bái** white

百 **bǎi** hundred

摆 **bǎi** put

败 **bài** defeat; fail

拜 **bài** congratulate

拜拜 **bàibai** bye-bye

百倍 **bǎibèi** hundredfold

白菜 **báicài** Chinese cabbage

白痴 **báichī** idiot

白饭 **báifàn** boiled rice

摆放 **bǎifàng** set out *goods*

拜访 **bàifǎng** visit

百分比 **bǎifēnbǐ** percentage

百分之百 **bǎifēn zhī bǎi**
one hundred percent

白宫 **Báigōng** White House

白喉 **báihóu** diphtheria

败坏 **bàihuài** spoil

百货商店 **bǎihuò shāng-
diàn** department store

摆架子 **bǎi jiàzi** put on airs

白酒 **báijiǔ** clear grain spirit

白开水 **báikāishuǐ** boiled
water

百科全书 **bǎikē quánshū**
encyclopedia

白兰地 **báilándì** brandy

白领工人 **báilǐng gōngrén**
white-collar worker

败露 **bàilù** emerge

拜年 **bàinián** pay New Year
visit; wish happy New Year

百日咳 **bǎirìké** whooping
cough

白日梦 **báirì mèng**
daydream

白肉 **báiròu** white meat;
boiled pork fat

白色 **báisè** white

白糖 **báitáng** white sugar

白天 **báitiān** in the daytime

摆脱 **bǎituō** get rid of

拜托 **bàituō** request

百万 **bǎiwàn** million

百万富翁 **bǎiwànfùwēng**
millionaire

摆碗筷 **bǎi wǎnkuài** lay
the table

白银 **báiyín** silver

柏油 **bǎiyóu** asphalt

柏油马路 **bǎiyóu mǎlù**
bitumen road

拔尖儿 **bájiānr** excellent

八角 **bājiǎo** star anise

巴基斯坦 **Bājīsītǎn**

bāléiwǔ

Pakistan ◊ Pakistani

芭蕾舞 **bāléiwǔ** ballet
班 **bān** class; shift (*at work*)
搬 **bān** move
斑 **bān** stain
扳 **bān** pull
板 **bǎn** board
版 **bǎn** edition
瓣 **bàn** segment; petal
半 **bàn** half
拌 **bàn** mix
绊 **bàn** trip up
扮 **bàn** play the role of
办 **bàn** do; deal with
版本 **bǎnběn** edition; version
搬出 **bānchū** move out
班船 **bānchuán** liner (*ship*)
半岛 **bàndǎo** peninsula
办到 **bàndào** manage to do sth
板凳 **bǎndèng** stool
斑点 **bāndiǎn** spot
办法 **bànfǎ** method; means
帮 **bāng** help ◊ gang
绑 **bǎng** bind
榜 **bǎng** official announcement
磅 **bàng** pound (*weight*)
棒 **bàng** stick ◊ excellent
半个小时 **bànge xiǎoshí**

half an hour

绑架 **bǎngjià** kidnap
邦交 **bāngjiāo** diplomatic relations
帮忙 **bāngmáng** help
办公楼 **bàn'gōnglóu** office (*building*)
办公室 **bàn'gōngshì** office
办公时间 **bàn'gōng shíjiān** office hours
棒球 **bàngqiú** baseball
帮手 **bāngshǒu** helper
傍晚 **bàngwǎn** dusk
帮凶 **bāngxiōng** accomplice
榜样 **bǎngyàng** role model
棒子 **bàngzi** stick; pole
版画 **bǎnhuà** engraving; print
班级 **bānjí** class; grade
搬家 **bānjiā** move
绊脚石 **bànjiǎoshí** obstacle
搬进 **bānjìn** move in
半径 **bànjìng** radius
半决赛 **bànjuésài** semifinal
板栗 **bǎnlì** Chinese chestnut
办理 **bànlǐ** deal with
斑马 **bānmǎ** zebra
般配 **bānpèi** complement
半票 **bànpiào** half-price ticket
办签证 **bàn qiānzhèng**

apply for a visa

版权 **bǎnquán** copyright

拌色拉 **bàn sèlā** dress a salad

办事处 **bànshìchù** office, bureau

扳手 **bānshǒu** wrench (*tool*)

伴随 **bànsuí** pursue; accompany; follow

半天 **bàntiān** half a day; a long time

版图 **bǎntú** territory

扮演 **bànyǎn** portray ◊ portrayal

半夜 **bànyè** midnight

板子 **bǎnzi** board; plate

搬走 **bānzǒu** move away

包 **bāo** pack

剥 **bāo** peel

雹 **báo** hail

薄 **báo** thin

宝 **bǎo** treasure

保 **bǎo** protect; keep; guarantee

饱 **bǎo** full

堡 **bǎo** castle

包 **bāo** packet; *measure word for packages etc*

报 **bào** newspaper

豹 **bào** leopard

抱 **bào** hug

刨 **bào** plane (*tool*)

保安 **bǎo'ān** ensure public safety

报案 **bào'àn** report a case to the police

宝贝 **bǎobèi** treasure; darling

保持 **bǎochí** keep; maintain

报仇 **bàochóu** take revenge

报酬 **bàochóu** reward; remuneration

保存 **bǎocún** preserve

报道 **bàodào** report

暴发户 **bàofāhù** nouveau riche

报废 **bàofèi** scrap

暴风雨 **bàofēngyǔ** rainstorm

报复 **bàofù** pay back (*fig*); retaliate ◊ revenge

报告 **bàogào** break *news*; report ◊ presentation

饱嗝儿 **bǎogér** belch

报关 **bàoguān** customs declaration

宝贵 **bǎoguì** precious; valuable

包裹 **bāoguǒ** parcel

包含 **bāohán** comprise

饱和 **bǎohé** saturation

保护 **bǎohù** protect ◊

protection

包机 **bāojī** charter flight

保健 **bǎojiàn** health care

报价 **bàojià** quotation ◊ quote *price*

报警 **bàojǐng** raise the alarm

暴君 **bàojūn** despot; tyrant

包括 **bāokuò** include

暴力 **bàolì** violence ◊ violent

爆裂 **bàoliè** burst

保龄 **bǎolíng** bowling; bowl

保留 **bǎoliú** keep; hold; reserve ◊ reservation

暴露 **bàolù** reveal

保密 **bǎomì** keep secret

爆米花 **bàomǐhuā** puffed rice; popcorn

报名 **bàomíng** register

保姆 **bǎomǔ** nanny

报幕 **bàomù** announce a program

爆破 **bàopò** blow up

抱歉 **bàoqiàn** be sorry

宝石 **bǎoshí** precious stone

报失 **bàoshī** report a loss

保释金 **bǎoshìjīn** bail

保守 **bǎoshǒu** conservative

报税 **bàoshuì** declare tax

宝塔 **bǎotǎ** pagoda

包围 **bāowéi** encircle

保卫 **bǎowèi** defend ◊

defense

保险 **bǎoxiǎn** safe ◊ insurance

保险柜 **bǎoxiǎnguì** safe (*for valuables*)

保养 **bǎoyǎng** maintain ◊ maintenance

保佑 **bǎoyòu** bless

暴雨 **bàoyǔ** torrential rain

抱怨 **bàoyuàn** grumble

暴躁 **bàozào** hot-headed

爆炸 **bàozhà** explosion ◊ explode

保障 **bǎozhàng** guarantee

保证 **bǎozhèng** pledge; promise; guarantee

报纸 **bàozhǐ** newspaper

保重 **bǎozhòng** look after oneself ◊ take care!

包装 **bāozhuāng** pack ◊ packaging

刨子 **bàozi** plane (*tool*)

拔起 **báqǐ** pull up

八十 **bāshí** eighty

巴士 **bāshì** bus

把手 **bǎshǒu** handle

把握 **bǎwò** grasp; seize ◊ certainty

八月 **bāyuè** August

巴掌 **bāzhang** palm of the hand

杯 **bēi** cup; glass; *measure word for drinks*

背 **bēi** carry on one's back

碑 **bēi** monument; gravestone

北 **běi** north

倍 **bèi** -fold

辈 **bèi** generation; lifetime

背 **bèi** back

被 **bèi** quilt ◊ *passive indicator*

悲哀 **bēi'āi** sad

背包 **bēibāo** backpack

卑鄙 **bēibǐ** nasty; sordid

被捕 **bèibǔ** be under arrest

悲惨 **bēicǎn** tragic

北朝鲜 **Běi Cháoxiǎn** North Korea ◊ North Korean

被单 **bèidān** sheet

被动 **bèidòng** passive

北方 **běifāng** the North

被告 **bèigào** defendant; defense

悲观 **bēiguān** pessimistic; dim ◊ pessimism

背后 **bèihòu** behind ◊ behind one's back

北极 **Běijí** Arctic; North Pole

卑贱 **bēijiàn** humble

备件 **bèijiàn** spare part

北京 **Běijīng** Beijing

背景 **bèijǐng** background

北京烤鸭 **Běijīng kǎoyā** Peking duck

悲剧 **bēijù** tragedy

贝壳 **bèiké** shell (*of shellfish*)

蓓蕾 **bèilěi** bud

背面 **bèimiàn** back

背叛 **bèipàn** betray ◊ betrayal

被褥 **bèirù** quilt

悲伤 **bēishāng** sad ◊ grief

背书 **bèishū** endorse

被套 **bèitào** quilt cover

悲痛 **bēitòng** grief

碑文 **bēiwén** inscription

背心 **bèixīn** undershirt; vest; T-shirt

备用 **bèiyòng** spare

北约 **Běiyuē** NATO

倍增 **bèizēng** double

备注 **bèizhù** remarks; notes

杯子 **bēizi** cup; glass

被子 **bèizi** quilt

奔 **bēn** run fast

本 **běn** *measure word for books*

笨 **bèn** stupid

奔驰 **bēnchí** dash

笨蛋 **bèndàn** idiot

本地 **běndì** local; native

本地人 **běndìrén** local (*person*)

绷 **bēng** tighten

泵 **bèng** pump

蹦 **bèng** jump

绷带 **bēngdài** bandage

崩溃 **bēngkuì** collapse

崩塌 **bēngtā** collapse

本来 **běnlái** actually; originally

本领 **běnlǐng** ability

本能 **běnnéng** instinct ◊ instinctive

奔跑 **bēnpǎo** sprint

本钱 **běnqián** capital

本人 **běnrén** oneself; personally

本身 **běnshēn** itself; in itself

本性 **běnxìng** nature, character

本质 **běnzhì** nature ◊ fundamental

笨重 **bènzhòng** cumbersome

笨拙 **bènzhuō** clumsy

逼 **bī** force

鼻 **bí** nose

比 **bǐ** compare

笔 **bǐ** pen

闭 **bì** shut

毕 **bì** finish

币 **bì** currency

避 **bì** avoid

壁 **bì** wall

臂 **bì** arm

边 **biān** side

扁 **biǎn** flat

贬 **biǎn** devalue

辩论 **biànlùn** discuss

变 **biàn** change

辨别 **biànbié** distinguish

辩驳 **biànbó** dispute; refute

变成 **biànchéng** become

便当 **biàndāng** lunch box

变得 **biàndé** become, go

贬低 **biǎndī** belittle

变动 **biàndòng** change; upheaval

扁豆 **biǎndòu** green bean

蝙蝠 **biānfú** bat

编号 **biānhào** number ◊ serial number

辩护 **biànhù** plead; defend

变化 **biànhuà** change

辩护人 **biànhùrén** defense lawyer

编辑 **biānjí** edit ◊ editor ◊ editorial

编辑部 **biānjíbù** editorial department

边界 **biānjiè** border

边疆 **biānjiāng** frontier

便利 **biànlì** convenient

辩论 **biànlùn** debate

便秘 **biànmì** constipation

鞭炮 **biānpào** firework

便盆 **biànpén** chamber pot

变迁 **biànqiān** change

辨认 **biànrèn** identify

变态 **biàntài** abnormal; kinky ◊ metamorphosis

扁桃腺 **biāntáoxiàn** tonsil

便条 **biàntiáo** note; compliments slip

变通 **biàntōng** flexible

便鞋 **biànxié** slippers

编织 **biānzhī** knit; weave ◊ knitting; weaving

贬值 **biǎnzhí** devalue ◊ devaluation

变质 **biànzhì** spoil; deteriorate

便装 **biànzhuāng** civilian dress

鞭子 **biānzi** whip

辫子 **biànzi** braid

表 **biǎo** table; form; meter; watch

表达 **biǎodá** express

表带 **biǎodài** watch strap

表弟 **biǎodì** cousin

标点 **biāodiǎn** punctuation

表哥 **biǎogē** cousin

表格 **biǎogé** form; table

标记 **biāojì** sign; symbol

表姐 **biǎojiě** cousin

表决 **biǎojué** decide by vote

表妹 **biǎomèi** cousin

表面 **biǎomiàn** surface

表明 **biǎomíng** indicate

标签 **biāoqiān** label

标枪 **biāoqiāng** javelin

表情 **biǎoqíng** expression (facial)

标题 **biāotí** heading

表演 **biǎoyǎn** act; perform ◊ acting; performance

表扬 **biǎoyáng** praise

标语 **biāoyǔ** slogan

标准 **biāozhǔn** standard

臂膀 **bìbǎng** arm

弊病 **bìbìng** disadvantage

壁柜 **bìguì** cabinet

彼此 **bǐcǐ** each other

必定 **bìdìng** must; definitely

弊端 **bìduān** corrupt practices

别 **bié** other ◊ don't ◊ leave; part

瘪 **biě** shriveled; flat *tire*

别离 **biélí** leave; part from

别人 **biérén** someone else;

other people

别墅 biéshù villa

别针 biézhēn safety pin

庇护 bìhù asylum; refuge; shelter

笔画 bǐhuà stroke (*in writing*)

壁画 bìhuà fresco

笔迹 bǐjì handwriting

笔记 bǐjì write down ◊ notes

比价 bǐjià price ratio

比较 bǐjiào compare ◊ comparison ◊ comparative

笔记本 bǐjìběn notebook

毕竟 bìjìng after all

鼻孔 bíkǒng nostril

壁炉 bìlú fireplace; hearth

比率 bǐlǜ rate

闭路电视 bìlù diànshì closed-circuit television

避免 bìmiǎn avoid

闭幕式 bìmùshì closing ceremony

宾 bīn guest

冰 bīng ice

兵 bīng soldier

饼 bǐng pancake

病 bìng illness ◊ sick

并 bìng combine ◊ *negative intensifier* ◊ and

冰雹 bīngbáo hail

冰川 bīngchuān glacier

冰冻 bīngdòng freeze

病毒 bìngdú virus ◊ viral

病房 bìngfáng room (*in hospital*)

饼干 bǐnggān cookie; cracker

冰棍儿 bīnggùnr Popsicle®

病假 bìngjià sick leave

并肩 bìngjiān side by side

冰冷 bīnglěng ice-cold

兵力 bīnglì troops

兵马俑 bīngmǎyǒng terracotta warriors

并且 bìngqiě and; besides

冰淇淋 bīngqílín ice cream

病人 bìngrén patient (*sick person*)

冰糖 bīngtáng candy sugar

宾馆 bīnguǎn hotel

冰箱 bīngxiāng refrigerator; freezer

冰鞋 bīngxié ice-skates

兵役义务 bīngyì yìwù military service

冰镇 bīngzhèn chilled

逼迫 bīpò force

壁球 bìqiú squash (*game*)

必然 bìrán inevitable ◊ inevitably

比如 bǐrú for example

比赛 **bǐsài** competition; match

毕生 **bìshēng** whole life

鄙视 **bǐshì** despise

壁毯 **bìtǎn** tapestry

鼻涕 **bítì** snot

笔芯 **bǐxīn** pencil lead; pen refill

必修 **bìxiū** compulsory *course*

必须 **bìxū** must ◊ obligatory

必需 **bìxū** necessary

必要 **bìyào** necessary

必要性 **bìyàoxìng** necessity

毕业 **bìyè** graduate ◊ graduation

笔友 **bǐyǒu** penpal

避孕 **bìyùn** birth control; contraception

避孕套 **bìyùn tào** condom

避孕药 **bìyùn yào** contraceptive (*pill*), the pill

比喻 **bǐyù** ◊ analogy ◊ figurative

逼真 **bīzhēn** true to life

笔直 **bǐzhí** straight; upright

币值 **bìzhí** currency value

壁纸 **bìzhǐ** (wall)paper

币制 **bìzhì** monetary system

鼻子 **bízi** nose

闭嘴 **bìzuǐ** be quiet

拨 **bō** dial *number*

播 **bō** sow seed; broadcast

波 **bō** wave

伯 **bó** uncle

博 **bó** broad

博爱 **bó'ài** universal love; fraternity

伯伯 **bóbo** uncle; *used to address a man older than one's father*

菠菜 **bōcài** spinach

驳斥 **bóchì** refute; disprove

驳船 **bóchuán** barge

波动 **bōdòng** fluctuate ◊ fluctuation

搏斗 **bódòu** battle

波段 **bōduàn** frequency (*radio*)

伯父 **bófù** uncle

脖颈儿 **bógěngr** (nape of) neck

薄荷 **bòhe** peppermint

簸箕 **bòji** dustpan

波浪 **bōlàng** wave

博览会 **bólǎnhuì** trade fair

玻璃 **bōli** glass

玻璃杯 **bōlibēi** glass (*for drinking*)

菠萝 **bōluó** pineapple

博士 **bóshì** doctor (*PhD*)

波涛 **bōtāo** wave

博物馆 **bówùguǎn** museum

跛行 **bǒxíng** limp

剥削 **bōxuē** exploit ◊ exploitation

博学 **bóxué** well-read

播音 **bōyīn** broadcast

播音员 **bōyīnyuán** radio announcer

脖子 **bózi** neck

捕 **bǔ** catch

不 **bù** no ◊ not

步 **bù** step

布 **bù** cloth

簿 **bù** book

不安 **bù'ān** uneasy

不必 **búbì** unnecessary

不便 **búbiàn** inconvenient

不变 **búbiàn** always, invariably ◊ unswerving

补偿 **bǔcháng** make up for

补车票 **bǔ chēpiào** buy ticket after boarding

补充 **bǔchōng** add to ◊ additional

不错 **búcuò** not bad; excellent

不大 **búdà** small

不大可能 **bú dà kěnéng** improbable, unlikely

不到 **bú dào** under, less

than

不得不 **bùdébù** have to, be compelled to

布丁 **bùdīng** pudding

不动产 **bùdòngchǎn** real estate

不断 **búduàn** constant

部队 **bùduì** army

步伐 **bùfá** step

部分 **bùfen** part

补付 **bǔfù** pay extra; pay later

不符 **bùfú** not be in accord with

布告 **bùgào** announcement

不公正 **bù gōngzhèng** unjust

捕获 **bǔhuò** capture

簿记 **bùjì** bookkeeping

不仅 **bùjǐn** not only

不景气 **bù jǐngqì** depression

不久 **bùjiǔ** soon

不可口 **bù kěkǒu** tasteless

不可能 **bù kěnéng** impossible

不客气¹ **bú kèqi** impolite

不客气² **bú kèqi** you're welcome

不可思议 **bùkě sīyì** unthinkable

不利 **búlì** unfavorable

不满 bùmǎn dissatisfied

部门 bùmén department

不明智 bù míngzhì unwise

不能 bùnéng not be able to

不平 bùpíng uneven

不平常 bù píngcháng unusual

不清楚 bù qīngchu unclear

不忍 bùrěn cannot bear to

哺乳 bǔrǔ breastfeed

不如 bùrú not as good as

部首 bùshǒu radicals (of Chinese characters)

补贴 bǔtiē grant

不同 bùtóng different ◊ difference

部位 bùwèi position

不小心 bù xiǎoxīn careless

不幸 búxìng unlucky

不行 bùxíng no can do ◊ impossible

步行 bùxíng walk

补牙 bǔyá filling (in tooth)

捕鱼 bǔyú catch fish ◊ fishing

哺育 bǔyù feed; bring up

部长 bùzhǎng minister POL ◊ ministerial

不只 bùzhǐ not only

布置 bùzhì fit out

不重要 bú zhòngyào unimportant

不中意 bú zhòngyì unattractive

不准 bùzhǔn forbid

捕捉 bǔzhuō catch

簿子 bùzi notebook

不足 bùzú inadequate

# C

擦 cā wipe

擦掉 cādiào wipe away

猜 cāi guess

才 cái talent ◊ only

裁 cái cut

财 cái assets; wealth

采 cǎi pick

踩 cǎi step on

菜 cài dish; vegetable

猜测 cāicè guess ◊ speculation

财产 cáichǎn property

菜单 càidān menu

菜刀 càidāo kitchen knife

彩电 cǎidiàn color TV

采访 cǎifǎng interview

裁缝 **cáifeng** tailor

财富 **cáifù** treasure; wealth

采购 **cǎigòu** buy

彩虹 **cǎihóng** rainbow

菜花 **càihuā** cauliflower

采集 **cǎijí** collect

裁减 **cáijiǎn** reduce

裁军 **cáijūn** disarm ◊ disarmament

采矿 **cǎikuàng** mining

材料 **cáiliào** materials

才能 **cáinéng** ability

裁判员 **cáipànyuán** umpire

彩票 **cǎipiào** lottery ticket; raffle ticket

菜谱 **càipǔ** recipe

彩色 **cǎisè** color

彩色胶卷 **cǎisè jiāojuǎn** color film

踩刹车 **cǎi shāchē** put on the brake(s)

财务 **cáiwù** finance ◊ financial

财务处 **cáiwùchù** accounts (department)

采用 **cǎiyòng** use

菜油 **càiyóu** vegetable oil

菜园 **càiyuán** vegetable garden

裁员 **cáiyuán** cut back; downsize ◊ layoff

财政 **cáizhèng** finance

才智 **cáizhì** wisdom

餐 **cān** meal

蚕 **cán** silkworm

惨 **cǎn** tragic; brutal

惨案 **cǎn'àn** massacre

残暴 **cánbào** cruel

餐车 **cānchē** restaurant car

蚕豆 **cándòu** broad bean

残废 **cánfèi** disabled

舱 **cāng** cabin

藏 **cáng** hide

苍白 **cāngbái** pale

仓促 **cāngcù** hasty

仓库 **cāngkù** warehouse

藏匿 **cángnì** hide

仓鼠 **cāngshǔ** hamster

参观 **cānguān** tour

餐馆 **cānguǎn** restaurant

参观者 **cānguānzhě** visitor

苍蝇 **cāngying** fly (*insect*)

残骸 **cánhái** remains

参加 **cānjiā** attend

蚕茧 **cánjiǎn** silk cocoon

餐巾 **cānjīn** napkin

残疾人 **cánjírén** disabled person

餐具 **cānjù** tableware

参考 **cānkǎo** refer to ◊ reference

残酷 **cánkù** cruel

惭愧 **cánkuì** ashamed

灿烂 **cànlàn** bright; brilliant

残缺 **cánquē** incomplete

参赛 **cānsài** play sp; take part (*in match, contest*)

餐厅 **cāntīng** dining hall; restaurant

惨痛 **cǎntòng** painful

参与 **cānyù** take part in, participate in

残余 **cányú** remainder

槽 **cáo** trough; groove

草 **cǎo** grass; straw

草地 **cǎodì** lawn

操劳 **cāoláo** work hard; struggle

操练 **cāoliàn** drill MIL

草帽 **cǎomào** straw hat

草莓 **cǎoméi** strawberry

草坪 **cǎopíng** lawn; meadow; green space

草图 **cǎotú** draft

操心 **cāoxīn** worry

槽牙 **cáoyá** molar

草药 **cǎoyào** herbal medicine

草原 **cǎoyuán** grasslands

嘈杂 **cáozá** noisy

操纵 **cāozòng** operate; control

操作 **cāozuò** operate ◊ operation

擦油 **cāyóu** apply cream

测 **cè** measure

侧 **cè** side

册 **cè** (exercise) book

测量 **cèliáng** measure ◊ measurement

策略 **cèlüè** tactics

侧面 **cèmiàn** side; profile

层 **céng** layer; story (*of building*); tier

曾经 **céngjīng** ever; once, formerly

厕所 **cèsuǒ** toilet

测验 **cèyàn** test

插 **chā** insert

叉 **chā** fork

茶 **chá** tea

搽 **chá** rub in

查 **chá** check; test

差 **chà** bad; poor (*in quality*); inferior ◊ badly ◊ lack; be short of

茶杯 **chábēi** teacup

差别 **chābié** difference

差错 **chācuò** mistake

茶点 **chádiǎn** refreshments; tea and snacks

查地图 **chá dìtú** consult a map

搽粉 **cháfěn** powder

茶馆 **cháguǎn** tea house

查号台 **cháhàotái** information TEL

茶壶 **cháhú** teapot

拆 **chāi** dismantle; demolish

柴 **chái** firewood

拆除 **chāichú** demolish

拆开 **chāikāi** take to pieces; unravel

拆卸 **chāixiè** dismantle

柴油 **cháiyóu** diesel

差劲 **chàjìn** disappointing

差距 **chàjù** gap; difference; distance

茶具 **chájù** tea service

察觉 **chájué** detect

缠 **chán** bind; wrap

蝉 **chán** cicada

铲 **chǎn** shovel

颤 **chàn** tremble

颤抖 **chàndǒu** shake

长 **cháng** long

尝 **cháng** taste

常 **cháng** frequent

肠 **cháng** intestines

厂 **chǎng** plant

场 **chǎng** place

唱 **chàng** sing

畅 **chàng** smooth; unimpeded

常常 **chángcháng** often

长城 **chángchéng** the Great Wall

长处 **chángchu** advantage; strength

长笛 **chángdí** flute

长度 **chángdù** length

长短 **chángduǎn** length

长方形 **chángfāng xíng** rectangle ◊ rectangular

唱歌 **chànggē** sing

常规 **chángguī** customary ◊ custom; routine

偿还 **chánghuán** pay back

唱机 **chàngjī** record player

长江 **Chángjiāng** Yangtze River

长颈鹿 **chángjǐnglù** giraffe

敞开 **chǎngkāi** open

厂矿企业 **chǎngkuàng-qǐyè** industrial enterprises

场面 **chǎngmiàn** scene

长跑 **chángpǎo** long-distance running

唱片 **chàngpiàn** record (*LP*)

长期 **chángqī** long-term

厂商 **chǎngshāng** commercial and industrial enterprises

昌盛 **chāngshèng** flourishing

常识 **chángshí** general

knowledge

尝试 **chángshì** try; taste

长寿 **chángshòu** long life

场所 **chǎngsuǒ** place

畅通 **chàngtōng** unobstructed

长统袜 **chángtǒngwà** stocking

长途电话 **chángtú diànhuà** long-distance call

畅销 **chàngxiāo** in demand; selling well

肠炎 **chángyán** enteritis

长椅 **chángyǐ** bench

常用 **chángyòng** in daily use

厂长 **chǎngzhǎng** factory director

忏悔 **chànhuǐ** repent; confess

掺假 **chānjiǎ** adulterate

产量 **chǎnliàng** production; capacity; output; yield; turnover ◊ turn over

阐明 **chǎnmíng** explain; interpret

产品 **chǎnpǐn** produce; product

产生 **chǎnshēng** produce; emerge

阐述 **chǎnshù** explain

铲子 **chǎnzi** shovel

抄 **chāo** transcribe; plagiarize

巢 **cháo** nest

朝 **cháo** toward

潮 **cháo** tide ◊ damp

炒 **chǎo** cook; stir fry

吵 **chǎo** argue

炒菜 **chǎo cài** cook ◊ stir-fried dish

炒菜锅 **chǎocàiguō** wok

超车 **chāochē** overtake

朝代 **cháodài** dynasty

炒饭 **chǎofàn** fried rice ◊ fry rice

超过 **chāoguò** exceed ◊ over

吵架 **chǎojià** argue ◊ argument

炒面 **chǎomiàn** fried noodles ◊ fry noodles

钞票 **chāopiào** bank note

潮湿 **cháoshī** damp

潮水 **cháoshuǐ** tide

朝鲜 **Cháoxiǎn** Korea ◊ Korean

嘲笑 **cháoxiào** laugh at

巢穴 **cháoxué** den

超重 **chāozhòng** overload; overweight

插头 **chātóu** plug ELEC

插图 **chātú** illustration

查询 **cháxún** enquire

茶叶 **cháyè** tea (leaves)

诧异 **chàyì** amazed

查阅 **cháyuè** look up

插座 **chāzuò** outlet ELEC

车 **chē** vehicle

扯 **chě** pull; bear; tell lies;
talk nonsense

撤 **chè** withdraw

车次 **chēcì** train/bus number

彻底 **chèdǐ** thorough ◊
completely

撤回 **chèhuí** withdraw

车祸 **chēhuò** traffic accident

车间 **chējiān** workshop

车库 **chēkù** garage

车辆 **chēliàng** vehicle

车轮 **chēlún** wheel

沉 **chén** sink

晨 **chén** morning

衬垫 **chèndiàn** lining

撑 **chēng** support; hold up

乘 **chéng** by ◊ multiply

橙 **chéng** orange

诚 **chéng** honest

城 **chéng** city; wall

秤 **chèng** scales

城堡 **chéngbǎo** castle

惩处 **chéngchǔ** punish;
penalize

承担 **chéngdān** undertake

呈递 **chéngdì** submit; hand

over

程度 **chéngdù** degree;
measure

成堆 **chéngduī** in piles;
loads of

承兑 **chéngduì** cash; accept
check

惩罚 **chéngfá** punish ◊
punishment

成分 **chéngfèn** component

成功 **chénggōng** succeed
◊ success ◊ successful ◊
successfully

成果 **chéngguǒ**
achievement; success

称号 **chēnghào** title;
designation

称呼 **chēnghu** form of
address

成绩 **chéngjī** achievement;
results

成见 **chéngjiàn** prejudice

成交！ **chéngjiāo!** it's a
deal!

成就 **chéngjiù** achievement

撑开 **chēngkāi** open
umbrella

乘客 **chéngkè** passenger

诚恳 **chéngkěn** sincere

成立 **chénglì** establish ◊
foundation

成年 **chéngnián** come of age

承诺 **chéngnuò** promise; commit; pledge

澄清 **chéngqīng** clarify

成人 **chéngrén** adult

诚实 **chéngshí** honest ◊ honesty

城市 **chéngshì** city

成熟 **chéngshú** mature

成套 **chéngtào** complete set

成为 **chéngwéi** become

乘务员 **chéngwùyuán** conductor; ticket collector

成效 **chéngxiào** effect

程序 **chéngxù** procedure; program

诚意 **chéngyì** honesty; sincerity

成员 **chéngyuán** member

称赞 **chēngzàn** praise

成长 **chéngzhǎng** grow ◊ growth

橙汁 **chéngzhī** orange juice

诚挚 **chéngzhì** sincere ◊ sincerely

称重量 **chēng zhòngliàng** weigh

橙子 **chéngzi** orange (*fruit*)

陈旧 **chénjiù** outmoded

陈列 **chénliè** display ◊ be on display

沉闷 **chénmèn** close *weather*; dejected; reserved *character*

沉默 **chénmò** silent ◊ silence

沉默寡言 **chénmò guǎyán** silent; taciturn

衬衫 **chènshān** shirt; blouse

沉思 **chénsī** thoughtful ◊ muse

沉痛 **chéntòng** deeply distressed

晨曦 **chénxī** daybreak

称心 **chènxīn** be satisfied

沉重 **chénzhòng** heavy *loss*; oppressive *weather*

沉着 **chénzhuó** level-headed

车皮 **chēpí** freight car

车票 **chēpiào** ticket

车胎 **chētāi** tire

车厢 **chēxiāng** car (*of train*)

撤销 **chèxiāo** cancel; get rid of

车站 **chēzhàn** bus stop; station

车子 **chēzi** bicycle; car

吃 **chī** eat

池 **chí** pool; pond

迟 **chí** late

匙 **chí** spoon

齿 **chǐ** tooth

翅膀 **chìbǎng** wing

吃饱了 **chī bǎo le** full up

吃不消 **chībùxiāo** unbearable

吃醋 **chīcù** be jealous

尺寸 **chǐcùn** dimension; measurement

迟到 **chídào** be late

赤道 **chìdào** equator

尺度 **chǐdù** measure; standard; rule

迟钝 **chídùn** clumsy

吃饭 **chīfàn** eat; have a meal

迟缓 **chíhuǎn** slow; hesitant

赤脚 **chìjiǎo** barefoot

吃惊 **chījīng** be surprised

吃亏 **chīkuī** disadvantaged

齿轮 **chǐlún** gear

耻辱 **chǐrǔ** disgrace

池塘 **chítáng** pond

持续 **chíxù** continue

吃药 **chīyào** take medicine

迟早 **chízǎo** sooner or later

斥责 **chìzé** reprimand

尺子 **chǐzi** ruler (*to measure*)

赤子 **chìzǐ** newborn child

赤字 **chìzì** deficit

冲 **chōng** push forward; attack; flush

虫 **chóng** insect

宠爱 **chǒng'ài** dote on

崇拜 **chóngbài** worship

充当 **chōngdāng** serve as

充电 **chōngdiàn** charge; recharge

重迭 **chóngdié** overlap

充分 **chōngfèn** full; ample

重逢 **chóngféng** meet again

重复 **chóngfù** repetition; duplicate ◊ repeat

崇高 **chónggāo** lofty

虫害 **chónghài** plague of insects

崇敬 **chóngjìng** revere

冲突 **chōngtū** conflict

宠物 **chǒngwù** pet (*animal*)

冲洗 **chōngxǐ** develop *photographs*; flush

重新 **chóngxīn** again

虫牙 **chóngyá** decayed tooth

充裕 **chōngyù** abundant

虫子 **chóngzi** insect; worm

充足 **chōngzú** sufficient

抽 **chōu** pull out; draw

稠 **chóu** thick; dense

愁 **chóu** worry

仇 **chóu** enemy; hatred

丑 **chǒu** ugly

臭 **chòu** stinking

酬报 **chóubào** reward; payment

筹备 **chóubèi** arrange

仇敌 **chóudí** enemy

丑恶 **chǒu'è** revolting

仇恨 **chóuhèn** hatred; enmity

筹集 **chóují** raise *money*

抽筋 **chōujīn** cramp

丑角 **chǒujué** clown

抽空 **chōukòng** find time

丑陋 **chǒulòu** ugly, hideous

愁闷 **chóumèn** worried; down

臭名昭著 **chòumíng zhāozhù** infamous

抽泣 **chōuqì** sob

臭气 **chòuqì** stink

抽屉 **chōutì** drawer

丑闻 **chǒuwén** scandal

抽象 **chōuxiàng** abstract

抽烟 **chōuyān** smoke

抽样 **chōuyàng** sampling

出 **chū** go out; out

橱 **chú** cupboard

除 **chú** remove; except; divide MATH

锄 **chú** hoe

雏 **chú** young (*bird*)

除 …外 **chú … wài** apart from …

穿 **chuān** wear; penetrate

传 **chuán** pass on

船 **chuán** boat

喘 **chuǎn** breathe heavily

串 **chuàn** string together ◊ *measure word for strings of things*

传播 **chuánbō** spread

船舱 **chuáncāng** cabin

穿戴 **chuāndài** wear; dress

传单 **chuándān** leaflet

传递 **chuándì** pass on; convey

传动 **chuándòng** transmission

窗 **chuāng** window

床 **chuáng** bed

床单 **chuángdān** sheet

床垫 **chuángdiàn** mattress

窗户 **chuānghu** window

创建 **chuàngjiàn** found

窗口 **chuāngkǒu** hatch; window; contact

创立 **chuànglì** found

窗帘 **chuānglián** curtains

创始人 **chuàngshǐrén** founder

窗台 **chuāngtái** window sill

创造 **chuàngzào** create

创作 **chuàngzuò** create ◊ creation

传话 **chuánhuà** pass on a message

传教 **chuánjiào** do missionary work

船票 **chuánpiào** ticket (*for ship*)

传奇 **chuánqí** legend

喘气 **chuǎnqì** gasp

传染 **chuánrǎn** infect ◊ contagious

传授 **chuánshòu** teach

传说 **chuánshuō** legend; legend has it…; it is said

传统 **chuántǒng** tradition ◊ traditional ◊ traditionally

传闻 **chuánwén** hearsay ◊ it is said

船坞 **chuánwù** dock

船舷 **chuánxián** side of a ship

传讯 **chuánxùn** summons

船员 **chuányuán** sailor

传真 **chuánzhēn** fax

传真机 **chuánzhēnjī** fax machine

穿着 **chuānzhuó** clothing

出版 **chūbǎn** publish; come out

出版社 **chūbǎnshè** publisher

储备 **chǔbèi** store; reserve ◊ stock up on; stockpile

出差 **chūchāi** go on a business trip

出丑 **chūchǒu** make a spectacle of oneself

橱窗 **chúchuāng** display window

初次 **chūcì** the first time

出点子 **chū diǎnzi** give advice

出发 **chūfā** departure; leave

厨房 **chúfáng** kitchen

处方 **chǔfāng** prescribe; prescription

除非 **chúfēi** unless

出国 **chūguó** go abroad

出汗 **chūhàn** sweat

储户 **chǔhù** depositor

出乎意料 **chūhū yìliào** unexpected ◊ strangely enough

吹 **chuī** blow

锤 **chuí** hammer

吹干 **chuīgān** blow-dry

吹鼓手 **chuīgǔshǒu** musicians

吹口哨 **chuī kǒushào** whistle

垂柳 **chuíliǔ** weeping willow

吹牛 **chuīniú** boast; talk big

吹嘘 **chuīxū** show off

垂直 **chuízhí** perpendicular; vertical

雏鸡 **chújī** baby chicken

出家人 chūjiārén Buddhist monk; Buddhist nun
出借 chūjiè lend
出境 chūjìng leave the country
初级小学 chūjí xiǎoxué lower elementary school
处决 chǔjué execute
出口 chūkǒu export ◊ exit
出口处 chūkǒuchù exit
出来 chūlái come out
除了 chúle except
处理 chǔlǐ deal with
出路 chūlù way out
出卖 chūmài sell; sell out
出名 chūmíng well-known
春 chūn spring
纯 chún pure; neat *drink*; net *price*
唇 chún lip
蠢 chǔn stupid
出纳员 chūnàyuán cashier
唇膏 chúngāo lipstick
春季 chūnjì spring
春节 Chūnjié Chinese New Year
纯洁 chúnjié innocent
纯净 chúnjìng clean
春卷 chūnjuǎn spring roll
纯熟 chúnshú proficient; skillful

春天 chūntiān spring
处女 chǔnǚ virgin (*female*)
纯正 chúnzhèng pure
绰号 chuòhào nickname
出钱 chūqián chip in; fork out
出去 chūqù go out
出身 chūshēn family background
出神 chūshén fascinated
出生 chūshēng be born
畜生 chùsheng beast; brute
出生地 chūshēng dì birthplace
出生年份 chūshēng niánfèn year of birth
出示 chūshì show
出事 chūshì go wrong; have an accident
厨师 chúshī chef
出售 chūshòu put up for sale
锄头 chútou pickax; hoe
出席 chūxí attend
除夕 Chúxī Chinese New Year's Eve
出现 chūxiàn appear
储蓄 chǔxù save; deposit
出血 chūxuè bleed
处于 chǔyú be (*in a situation*)

初中 **chūzhōng** junior high school

出租 **chūzū** rent ◊ for rent

磁 **cí** magnetism ◊ magnetic

瓷 **cí** porcelain; china

词 **cí** term; word

慈 **cí** kind

雌 **cí** female

此 **cǐ** this

刺 **cì** prick (*pain*); thorn; splinter ◊ stab

次 **cì** time

辞别 **cíbié** say goodbye

磁带 **cídài** cassette; tape

词典 **cídiǎn** dictionary

刺耳 **cì'ěr** shrill

此后 **cǐhòu** henceforth

伺候 **cihou** serve

词汇 **cíhuì** vocabulary

此刻 **cǐkè** right now

此路不通 **cǐ lù bù tōng** no thoroughfare

磁盘 **cípán** disk

瓷器 **cíqì** porcelain; china

瓷器厂 **cíqìchǎng** porcelain factory

慈善 **císhàn** benevolent; charitable

次数 **cìshù** frequency

祠堂 **cítáng** ancestral temple

辞退 **cítuì** fire

此外 **cǐwài** besides; also

刺猬 **cìwei** hedgehog

慈祥 **cíxiáng** kind; loving

刺绣品 **cìxiùpǐn** embroidery

次序 **cìxù** order

次要 **cìyào** minor; peripheral

赐予 **cìyǔ** bestow

辞职 **cízhí** resign ◊ resignation

此致 **cǐzhì** yours truly; best regards

葱 **cōng** scallion

匆 **cōng** hasty

丛 **cóng** bushes

从 **cóng** from

从不 **cóng bù** never

从此 **cóngcǐ** from now on

从来 **cónglái** ever

从来不 **cónglái bù** never

匆忙 **cōngmáng** in a hurry

聪明 **cōngmíng** intelligent ◊ intelligence

从前 **cóngqián** in the past

从容 **cóngróng** calm ◊ leisurely

从事 **cóngshì** engage in; deal with

从小 **cóngxiǎo** from childhood

从中 **cóngzhōng** from

among; between

凑合 **còuhe** rough it; make the best of ◊ so-so, average

凑巧 **còuqiǎo** by chance

粗 **cū** rough

醋 **cù** vinegar

粗笨 **cūbèn** crude

粗糙 **cūcāo** coarse

催 **cuī** urge

脆 **cuì** fragile; brittle

催促 **cuīcù** hurry up; press for

摧毁 **cuīhuǐ** destroy; devastate

脆弱 **cuìruò** weak; frail

促进 **cùjìn** further; stimulate ◊ boost

粗略 **cūlüè** rough; cursory

村 **cūn** village

存 **cún** exist; store

寸 **cùn** Chinese inch

存储器 **cúnchǔqì** memory

存货 **cúnhuò** stock

存折 **cúnzhé** bank book

错 **cuò** wrong

锉 **cuò** file

错觉 **cuòjué** misconception; illusion

磋商 **cuōshāng** consult

措施 **cuòshī** step

错误 **cuòwù** mistake

挫折 **cuòzhé** setback; failure

错综复杂 **cuòzōng-fùzá** complicated

促使 **cùshǐ** impel; spur; cause to happen

粗心 **cūxīn** careless

粗壮 **cūzhuàng** stocky

# D

答 **dá** reply

打 **dǎ** hit; get; play

大 **dà** big

答案 **dá'àn** answer

大白菜 **dàbáicài** Chinese cabbage

打扮 **dǎbàn** dress up; put on make-up

打包 **dǎbāo** package; pack; bale

大便 **dàbiàn** defecate ◊ shit; feces

搭便车 **dā biànchē** hitch a ride

大不列颠 **Dà Bùlièdiān** Great Britain ◊ British

搭车 **dāchē** thumb a ride; take a cab

大葱 **dàcōng** leek

大胆 **dàdǎn** bold

搭档 **dādàng** partner

达到 **dádào** reach

打电话 **dǎ diànhuà** call, phone

打动 **dǎdòng** touch; move

大豆 **dàdòu** soybean

打断 **dǎduàn** interrupt

大多数 **dà duōshù** bulk, majority; most

大发雷霆 **dà fā léitíng** fly off the handle

答复 **dáfù** answer; respond ◊ response

打嗝 **dǎgé** burp

大哥 **dàgē** eldest brother; *a term of address for a man of similar age to oneself*

大公无私 **dàgōng-wúsī** selfless

打鼓 **dǎgǔ** beat a drum

打鼾 **dǎ hān** snore

打哈欠 **dǎ hāqian** yawn

打火机 **dǎhuǒjī** (cigarette) lighter

带 **dài** bring ◊ belt; area

戴 **dài** wear

贷 **dài** loan ◊ borrow; lend

代表团 **dàibiǎotuán** delegation

逮捕 **dàibǔ** arrest

大夫 **dàifu** doctor

贷款 **dàikuǎn** loan

代理 **dàilǐ** represent

带领 **dàilǐng** lead; guide

袋泡茶 **dàipàochá** teabag

代替 **dàitì** substitute

呆一会儿 **dāi yíhuìr** stick around

带子 **dàizi** belt; tape; strip

袋子 **dàizi** bag

打架 **dǎjià** fight

大家 **dàjiā** everyone

打搅 **dǎjiǎo** disturb

打交道 **dǎ jiāodào** have dealings with

大姐 **dàjiě** eldest sister

搭救 **dājiù** rescue

打击 **dǎjī** blow ◊ hit; deal a blow to

打开 **dǎkāi** open; turn on

打量 **dǎliàng** size up

打猎 **dǎliè** hunt

大理石 **dàlǐshí** marble

大陆 **dàlù** mainland

大麻 **dàmá** hemp; marijuana

大麦 **dàmài** barley

大门 **dàmén** door; gate

单 **dān** simple; only; single;

**dānrén shāfā**

odd *number*
胆 **dǎn** gall bladder
蛋 **dàn** egg
淡 **dàn** faint; light; pale
弹 **dàn** bullet; bomb
蛋白 **dànbái** white (*of egg*)
担保 **dānbǎo** guarantee;
sponsor
担保人 **dānbǎorén**
guarantor; sponsor
蛋炒饭 **dànchǎofàn** egg
fried rice
诞辰 **dànchén** birthday
单程 **dānchéng** one-way
单纯 **dānchún** simple; pure
◊ alone
单词 **dāncí** word
单调 **dāndiào** monotonous
单独 **dāndú** alone;
independently
单方面 **dān fāngmiàn**
unilateral
当 **dāng** work as ◊ when
党 **dǎng** political party
挡 **dǎng** block ◊ gear
(*engine*)
荡 **dàng** shake; swing
胆敢 **dǎn'gǎn** dare
档案 **dàng'àn** file; records
档案室 **dàng'ànshì** archives
蛋糕 **dàngāo** cake

当场 **dāngchǎng**
immediately
当代 **dāngdài** contemporary
◊ the present era
党代会 **dǎngdàihuì** party
conference
当地 **dāngdì** local
当今 **dāngjīn** nowadays
当局 **dāngjú** the authorities
当前 **dāngqián** present
荡秋千 **dàng qiūqiān** swing;
rock
当然 **dāngrán** of course
当天 **dàngtiān** on the
same day
党委 **dǎngwěi** party
committee
当心 **dāngxīn** be careful
当中 **dāngzhōng** in the
middle
党中央 **dǎng-zhōngyāng**
Party Central Committee
蛋黄 **dànhuáng** yolk
担架 **dānjià** stretcher
胆量 **dǎnliàng** guts; nerve
胆怯 **dǎnqiè** cowardly
单人床 **dānrénchuáng**
single bed
单人房间 **dānrén fángjiān**
single room
单人沙发 **dānrén shāfā**

armchair

单色 **dānsè** plain, all one color

单身 **dānshēn** single

诞生 **dànshēng** be born ◊ birth

单身汉 **dānshēn hàn** bachelor

但是 **dànshì** but

淡水 **dànshuǐ** fresh water

耽误 **dānwù** delay

担心 **dānxīn** worry ◊ worried

单行道 **dānxíng dào** one-way street

弹药 **dànyào** ammunition

但愿 **dànyuàn** hopefully

胆汁 **dǎnzhī** bile

刀 **dāo** knife

岛 **dǎo** island

道 **dào** way; road; path; Tao

倒 **dào** fall; pour ◊ upside down

到 **dào** arrive; reach ◊ to; up to

盗 **dào** steal ◊ thief

盗版 **dàobǎn** pirate copy

倒闭 **dǎobì** go bankrupt

倒彩 **dàocǎi** catcall; boo

到处 **dàochù** everywhere

到达 **dàodá** arrive ◊ arrival

捣蛋 **dǎodàn** get up to mischief

倒档 **dàodǎng** reverse gear

道德 **dàodé** morals, ethics

稻谷 **dàogǔ** rice paddy

道教 **Dàojiào** Taoism

道理 **dàolǐ** sense; reason; principle; truth

道路 **dàolù** road

捣乱 **dǎoluàn** create unrest

倒霉 **dǎoméi** have bad luck

悼念 **dàoniàn** mourn

到期 **dàoqī** become due; mature; expire

道歉 **dàoqiàn** apologize ◊ apology

盗窃 **dàoqiè** steal

倒数第二 **dàoshù dì'er** penultimate

倒塌 **dǎotā** collapse

倒下 **dǎoxià** fall down

导线 **dǎoxiàn** (electrical) wire; cable

倒叙 **dàoxù** flashback

导演 **dǎoyǎn** director (*film*) ◊ direct

岛屿 **dǎoyǔ** island

打喷嚏 **dǎ pēntì** sneeze

打扫 **dǎsǎo** sweep

大厦 **dàshà** high-rise building

打闪 dǎshǎn flash (of lightning)

大赦 dàshè amnesty

大使 dàshǐ ambassador

大使馆 dàshǐguǎn embassy

打手势 dǎ shǒushì gesticulate

打算 dǎsuàn intend; plan

大蒜 dàsuàn garlic

打听 dǎtīng inquire about

大厅 dàtīng hall

打通 dǎtōng TEL get through

大腿 dàtuǐ thigh

大象 dàxiàng elephant

大西洋 dàxīyáng Atlantic

大学 dàxué university

大衣 dàyī overcoat

答应 dāyìng reply; agree

打印机 dǎyìnjī printer

大约 dàyuē around ◊ thereabouts

打招呼 dǎ zhāohu greet

大众 dàzhòng masses

打字 dǎzì type

打字机 dǎzìjī typewriter

德 dé virtue

得到 dédào get

德国 Déguó German ◊ Germany

德国人 Déguórén German

灯 dēng lamp

登 dēng climb

等 děng wait; grade

凳 dèng stool

等待 děngdài wait for

等等 děngděng and so on ◊ hang on

登广告 dēng guǎnggào advertise

等候 děnghòu wait

登记 dēngjì check in; register ◊ registration

等级 děngjí class; classification; grade

等价 děngjià of equivalent value

灯笼 dēnglong lantern

灯泡 dēngpào light bulb

登山 dēngshān mountaineering

灯芯绒 dēngxīnróng corduroy

等于 děngyú equal

凳子 dèngzi stool

得体 détǐ proper; tactful

得罪 dézuì insult; offend

滴 dī drop ◊ drip

堤 dī dike

低 dī low

敌 dí enemy

底 dǐ bottom

地 dì earth; land; ground

点 **diǎn** measure word for time

点 **diǎn** dot; (decimal) point

碘 **diǎn** iodine

电 **diàn** electric ◊ electricity

垫 **diàn** cushion; mat

店 **diàn** shop

电报 **diànbào** telegram

颠簸 **diānbǒ** jolt ◊ bumpy

点菜 **diǎncài** order (in restaurant)

电车 **diànchē** streetcar; trolleybus

电池 **diànchí** battery

颠倒 **diāndǎo** reverse

电灯 **diàndēng** electric light

电饭锅 **diànfànguō** rice cooker

淀粉 **diànfěn** starch; cornstarch

垫付 **diànfù** pay for someone else

电工 **diàngōng** electrician

电话 **diànhuà** telephone

电话磁卡 **diànhuà cíkǎ** phonecard

电缆 **diànlǎn** electricity cable

典礼 **diǎnlǐ** ceremony ◊ ceremonial

电流 **diànliú** electric current

电气 **diànqì** electricity

电器 **diànqì** electrical appliance

电扇 **diànshàn** electric fan

电视 **diànshì** television

电视机 **diànshìjī** television set

电梯 **diàntī** elevator

电筒 **diàntǒng** flashlight

点心 **diǎnxin** dim sum

典型 **diǎnxíng** characteristic; classic; representative; typical ◊ typically

电压 **diànyā** voltage

电影 **diànyǐng** movie

电影院 **diànyǐng yuàn** movie theater

店员 **diànyuán** sales clerk

垫子 **diànzi** cushion; padding

电子 **diànzǐ** electronic

电子表 **diànzǐbiǎo** quartz watch

电子邮件 **diànzǐ yóujiàn** e-mail

刁 **diāo** wily

掉 **diào** fall; drop; lose

吊 **diào** hang; suspend

碉堡 **diāobǎo** fortress

调查 **diàochá** investigate; survey ◊ investigation

调动 **diàodòng** transfer

钓竿 **diàogān** fishing rod

调换 **diàohuàn** exchange

刁难 **diāonàn** create difficulties

吊桥 **diàoqiáo** suspension bridge

掉色 **diàoshǎi** fade

调头 **diàotóu** turn around

吊唁 **diàoyàn** offer one's condolences

钓鱼 **diàoyú** go fishing

底层 **dǐcéng** first floor, *Br* ground floor

低沉 **dīchén** low and heavy

抵挡 **dǐdǎng** resist; repel

弟弟 **dìdi** younger brother

地点 **dìdiǎn** place

蝶 **dié** butterfly

跌倒 **diēdǎo** fall over

跌价 **diējià** price drop

第二点 **dì'èrdiǎn** secondly

蝶泳 **diéyǒng** butterfly stroke

地方 **dìfang** place

低估 **dīgū** underestimate

低级 **dījí** low; crude

地基 **dìjī** foundations

递交 **dìjiāo** hand over

地窖 **dìjiào** vaults

缔结 **dìjié** conclude *contract*

抵抗 **dǐkàng** resist ◊ resistance

地理 **dìlǐ** geography

叮 **dīng** sting; stab

钉 **dīng** nail; staple

丁 **dīng** cube

盯 **dīng** stare

顶 **dǐng** *measure word for hats, umbrellas*

顶 **dǐng** top

定 **dìng** set

订 **dìng** order; subscribe

钉 **dìng** nail

顶点 **dǐngdiǎn** summit

定额 **dìng'é** quota; target

顶风 **dǐngfēng** against the wind

订户 **dìnghù** customer; subscriber

订婚 **dìnghūn** engaged ◊ get engaged ◊ engagement

订货 **dìnghuò** order goods

定金 **dìngjīn** deposit

订机票 **dìng jīpiào** book a flight

定居 **dìngjū** settle down

定期 **dìngqī** regular ◊ periodically

盯梢 **dīngshāo** tail

订书机 **dìngshūjī** stapler

丁香 **dīngxiāng** lilac

定义 **dìngyì** definition

订阅 **dìngyuè** subscribe to

顶住 **dǐngzhù** resist

订桌 **dìngzhuō** book a table

钉子 **dīngzi** nail

地皮 **dìpí** plot of land to build on

底片 **dǐpiàn** negative PHOT

地平线 **dìpíngxiàn** horizon

地区 **dìqū** region ◊ regional

敌人 **dírén** enemy

第三 **dìsān** third

第三世界 **Dìsān Shìjiè** Third World

递送 **dìsòng** deliver

地毯 **dìtǎn** carpet

地铁 **dìtiě** subway

迪厅 **dítíng** disco

地图 **dìtú** map

地图册 **dìtúcè** atlas

丢掉 **diūdiào** throw away

丢失 **diūshī** lose

地下 **dìxià** underground

抵押 **dǐyā** mortgage

第一 **dìyī** first

第一流 **dìyīliú** first-class

地狱 **dìyù** hell

地震 **dìzhèn** earthquake

地址 **dìzhǐ** address

笛子 **dízi** flute

东 **dōng** east

冬 **dōng** winter

懂 **dǒng** understand

洞 **dòng** hole; cave

动 **dòng** move

冻 **dòng** freeze

栋 **dòng** *measure word for houses*

东北 **dōngběi** northeast

动产 **dòngchǎn** moveable assets

冻疮 **dòngchuāng** chilblain

动词 **dòngcí** verb

东道主 **dōngdàozhǔ** host

东方人 **dōngfāng rén** Oriental

东方 **dōngfāng** east; the East; the Orient ◊ eastern

冬菇 **dōnggū** winter mushroom

懂行 **dǒngháng** expert

恫吓 **dònghè** threaten; intimidate

动画片 **dònghuà piān** animated cartoon

动力 **dònglì** driving force; motivation

动乱 **dòngluàn** unrest; upheaval

动脉 **dòngmài** artery

冬眠 **dōngmián** hibernation

◊ hibernate

东南 **dōngnán** southeast

东南亚 **Dōngnán Yà** Southeast Asia ◊ Southeast Asian

动人 **dòngrén** moving

动身 **dòngshēn** set off

董事 **dǒngshì** director

懂事 **dǒngshì** sensible

董事会 **dǒngshì huì** board of directors

动手 **dòngshǒu** get to work

动手术 **dòng shǒushù** operate MED

冬天 **dōngtiān** winter

动物 **dòngwù** animal

动物园 **dòngwù yuán** zoo

东西 **dōngxi** thing

洞穴 **dòngxué** cave

动摇 **dòngyáo** waver

动作 **dòngzuò** movement

陡 **dǒu** steep

豆 **dòu** bean

逗 **dòu** cheer up

抖动 **dǒudòng** schütteln shake

兜风 **dōufēng** drive

豆腐 **dòufu** tofu

逗号 **dòuhào** comma

逗留 **dòuliú** stay; stop over; linger

抖落 **dǒuluò** shake off

斗篷 **dǒupeng** cape

豆芽 **dòuyá** beansprouts

斗争 **dòuzhēng** battle; struggle; fight for

都 **dū** city; capital

督 **dū** supervise

读 **dú** read

毒 **dú** poison; narcotics

独 **dú** only; alone

堵 **dǔ** block

赌 **dǔ** gamble

度 **dù** degree

妒 **dù** envy

渡 **dù** cross *water*; ferry

妒 **dù** envy

端 **duān** end; extremity ◊ carry

短 **duǎn** short

缎 **duàn** satin

断 **duàn** break

短处 **duǎnchù** shortcoming

断定 **duàndìng** conclude; decide

断绝 **duànjué** break off

短裤 **duǎnkù** shorts

锻炼 **duànliàn** exercise ◊ gymnastics; workout

短路 **duǎnlù** short circuit

段落 **duànluò** paragraph

短篇小说 **duǎnpiān xiǎoshuō** short story

短缺 **duǎnquē** shortage

短袜 **duǎnwà** sock

端午节 **Duānwǔjié** Dragon Boat Festival

锻造 **duànzào** forge

赌博 **dǔbó** bet; gamble ◊ gambling

赌场 **dǔchǎng** casino

堵车 **dǔchē** traffic jam

都城 **dūchéng** capital city

渡船 **dùchuán** ferry

督促 **dūcù** urge; press

度过 **dùguò** pass; spend *time*

堆 **duī** heap

对 **duì** right ◊ against

队 **duì** team

兑 **duì** exchange

对比 **duìbǐ** compare

对不起 **duìbùqǐ** I'm sorry

对称 **duìchèn** symmetric ◊ symmetry

对待 **duìdài** treat ◊ treatment

对方 **duìfāng** opposite side

对付 **duìfu** handle; 对付 X **duìfu X** have X to reckon with

对话 **duìhuà** dialog

兑换 **duìhuàn** exchange

堆积 **duījī** pile up

对面 **duìmiàn** opposite

对手 **duìshǒu** opponent

对外贸易 **duìwài màoyì** foreign trade

队伍 **duìwǔ** troops; ranks

兑现 **duìxiàn** cash *check*

对象 **duìxiàng** target; boyfriend; girlfriend

对照 **duìzhào** contrast

妒忌 **dùjì** envy

度假 **dùjià** spend vacation

独立 **dúlì** independence ◊ independent ◊ independently

蹲 **dūn** squat

吨 **dūn** ton

钝 **dùn** blunt

炖 **dùn** stew

顿 **dùn** *measure word for meals*

多 **duō** many; much; more

夺 **duó** take by force

朵 **duǒ** *measure word for flowers*

躲 **duǒ** hide

舵 **duò** helm; rudder

跺 **duò** stamp *foot*

躲避 **duǒbì** dodge; elude

躲藏 **duǒcáng** hide

多次 **duōcì** time and again

多亏 **duōkuī** fortunately

堕落 **duòluò** degenerate

多么 **duōme** how (*for emphasis*)

夺取 **duóqǔ** conquer

堕入 **duòrù** sink into

多少 **duōshao** how much

多数 **duōshù** majority; most

堕胎 **duòtāi** abortion

多谢 **duōxiè** thanks very much

多余 **duōyú** spare; superfluous

多雨 **duōyǔ** rainy

多云 **duōyún** overcast

毒品 **dúpǐn** drugs

肚脐 **dùqí** navel

堵塞 **dǔsè** block; jam

都市 **dūshì** metropolis

毒死 **dúsǐ** kill with poison

独特 **dútè** unique

读物 **dúwù** reading material

毒药 **dúyào** poison

独有 **dúyǒu** exclusive

读者 **dúzhě** reader

赌咒 **dǔzhòu** swear; take an oath

杜撰 **dùzhuàn** make up; invent

肚子 **dùzi** stomach

独自 **dúzì** alone; by itself; by myself etc

度 **dù** degree ◊ spend, pass time

# E

额 **é** volume (*of business*)

鹅 **é** goose

蛾 **é** moth

恶 **è** evil

饿 **è** hunger ◊ hungry

恶毒 **èdú** malevolent

恶化 **èhuà** deteriorate

恶劣 **èliè** vile

俄罗斯 **Éluósī** Russia ◊ Russian

恶梦 **èmèng** nightmare

恶魔 **èmó** devil; demon

恩 **ēn** favor; kindness

而 **ér** and; but

儿 **ér** child; son

耳 **ěr** ear

二 **èr** two

耳背 **ěrbèi** hard of hearing

儿歌 **érgē** nursery rhyme

耳光 **ěrguāng** clip round the ear

耳环 **ěrhuán** earring

二流 **èrliú** second-rate
二十 **èrshí** twenty
二手 **èrshǒu** secondhand
儿童 **értóng** children
儿媳妇 **érxífu** daughter-
　in-law
二月 **èryuè** February
儿子 **érzi** son

扼杀 **èshā** strangle
额外 **éwài** extra
恶习 **èxí** vice
恶心 **ěxin** nausea ◊ revolting
恶性 **èxìng** malignant;
　virulent
鳄鱼 **èyú** crocodile
蛾子 **ézi** moth

# F

阀 **fá** valve
罚 **fá** punish
乏 **fá** lack ◊ exhausted
筏 **fá** raft
法 **fǎ** law; method
发 **fà** hair
发表 **fābiǎo** publish; issue
发愁 **fāchóu** worry
发达 **fādá** developed
发达国家 **fādá guójiā**
　developed country
发呆 **fādāi** be in a daze
法典 **fǎdiǎn** code; statutes
法定 **fǎdìng** legal; statutory
发动机 **fādòngjī** motor
发抖 **fādǒu** shake
发奋 **fāfèn** make an effort
发疯 **fāfēng** go crazy
法官 **fǎguān** judge

发光 **fāguāng** shine
法国 **Fǎguó** France ◊ French
发慌 **fāhuāng** feel nervous
发火 **fāhuǒ** erupt; get angry
发货 **fāhuò** send goods
发奖 **fājiǎng** award prizes
发酵 **fājiào** ferment ◊
　fermentation
发掘 **fājué** find
罚款 **fákuǎn** fine
乏力 **fálì** weak
法律 **fǎlǜ** law ◊ legal
发霉 **fāméi** go moldy
发明 **fāmíng** invent ◊
　invention
帆 **fān** sail
烦 **fán** annoyed
返 **fǎn** back
饭 **fàn** cooked rice

翻版 fānbǎn reprint

反驳 fǎnbó contradict

帆布 fānbù canvas

帆布篷 fānbùpéng tarpaulin

饭菜 fàncài food

帆船 fānchuán sailboat

饭店 fàndiàn hotel

反对 fǎnduì oppose ◊ opposition

反复 fǎnfù repeated

方 fāng square; direction

防 fáng prevent

纺 fǎng spin

访 fǎng visit

放 fàng put; release

妨碍 fáng'ài hinder; obstruct

方案 fāng'àn plan; program

反感 fǎngǎn aversion; dislike

方便 fāngbiàn convenience ◊ convenient

放大 fàngdà amplify; enlarge; magnify

房东 fángdōng landlord

方法 fāngfǎ method

方格 fānggé check (pattern); box (on form)

防护 fánghù protect

防火 fánghuǒ fire prevention

放假 fàngjià be on leave; have a day off

房间 fángjiān room

房客 fángkè roomer; tenant

方面 fāngmiàn aspect; side

放弃 fàngqì give up

放晴 fàngqíng clear up (of weather)

放射 fàngshè radiate

方式 fāngshì way; manner

防水 fángshuǐ waterproof

放肆 fàngsì impertinent

放松 fàngsōng relax ◊ relaxed

方糖 fāngtáng sugar cubes

反光 fǎnguāng reflect

翻滚 fāngǔn roll

防卫 fángwèi defend; protect

访问 fǎngwèn pay a visit

方向 fāngxiàng direction

放心 fàngxīn put one's mind at rest

方言 fāngyán dialect

防御 fángyù defend ◊ defensive ◊ defense

仿造 fǎngzào copy ◊ imitation

仿照 fǎngzhào copy

方针 fāngzhēn policy; guideline

防止 **fángzhǐ** guard against

纺织品 **fǎngzhīpǐn** textiles

房子 **fángzi** house

房租 **fángzū** rent

返回 **fǎnhuí** return; turn back

反抗 **fǎnkàng** revolt

泛滥 **fànlàn** overflow; flood

烦劳 … **fánláo** …would you mind …?

繁忙 **fánmáng** busy

反面 **fǎnmiàn** reverse (side)

烦恼 **fánnǎo** annoyance ◊ annoyed

蕃茄 **fānqié** tomato

繁荣 **fánróng** thriving

反响 **fǎnxiǎng** echo; repercussion

翻译 **fānyì** translate ◊ translation; translator

反应 **fǎnyìng** react ◊ reaction

翻阅 **fānyuè** leaf through

反正 **fǎnzhèng** in any case; anyway

繁殖 **fánzhí** reproduce ◊ reproduction reproductive

犯罪 **fànzuì** commit a crime

反作用 **fǎnzuòyòng** reaction

发胖 **fāpàng** put on weight

发票 **fāpiào** invoice

发卡 **fàqiǎ** hairpin

法人 **fǎrén** legal person; legal entity

发烧 **fāshāo** have a fever

发射 **fāshè** launch; blast off

发生 **fāshēng** happen

发誓 **fāshì** swear

法庭 **fǎtíng** (law) court

乏味 **fáwèi** tasteless

发现 **fāxiàn** discover ◊ discovery

发信 **fāxìn** send off a letter

发型 **fāxíng** hairstyle

法学 **fǎxué** law

发炎 **fāyán** inflammation

发音 **fāyīn** pronounce ◊ pronunciation

发育 **fāyù** grow ◊ growth

发源 **fāyuán** spring

法院 **fǎyuàn** court; courthouse

发展 **fāzhǎn** develop; grow ◊ development; growth

飞 **fēi** fly

非 **fēi** not

非…非… **fēi … fēi …** neither …nor …

非…即… **fēi … jí …** either… or …

**fēngfù**

肥 **féi** fat; fertile ◊ fertilizer

费 **fèi** cost; fee

肺 **fèi** lung

吠 **fèi** bark (*of dog*)

废 **fèi** useless

诽谤 **fěibàng** defamation ◊ defamatory

非常 **fēicháng** extraordinary ◊ very

废除 **fèichú** abolish; repeal

非典 **fēidiǎn** SARS

非法 **fēifǎ** illegal

飞机 **fēijī** airplane

飞机场 **fēijīchǎng** airport

费劲 **fèijìn** strenuous

飞快 **fēikuài** quick as a flash

费力 **fèilì** effort ◊ laborious

肥料 **féiliào** fertilizer; manure

菲律宾 **Fēilǜbīn** the Philippines

废品 **fèipǐn** trash

废气 **fèiqì** exhaust fumes

废弃 **fèiqì** abandon ◊ disused; waste

沸腾 **fèiténg** boil

肥沃 **féiwò** fertile ◊ fertility

飞行 **fēixíng** flight; flying ◊ fly

肺炎 **fèiyán** pneumonia

费用 **fèiyòng** fee; costs

肥皂 **féizào** soap

非正式 **fēi zhèngshì** informal; unofficial

废纸 **fèizhǐ** wastepaper

非洲 **Fēizhōu** Africa ◊ African

分 **fēn** divide; split ◊ cent

坟 **fén** grave

粉 **fěn** powder

粪 **fèn** excrement

份 **fèn** measure word for portions, newspapers

粉笔 **fěnbǐ** chalk

分别 **fēnbié** separate ◊ respectively; separately

奋斗 **fèndòu** struggle

份额 **fèn'é** share

粪肥 **fènféi** manure

疯 **fēng** mad

风 **fēng** wind

峰 **fēng** summit

封 **fēng** measure word for letters

缝 **féng** sew

风暴 **fēngbào** storm

封闭 **fēngbì** seal

奉承 **fèngchéng** flatter; suck up to ◊ flattery

讽刺 **fěngcì** mock; deride

丰富 **fēngfù** abundance ◊ abundant ◊ enrich

风格 fēnggé method; style

风寒 fēnghán cold

缝合 fénghé sew up

凤凰 fènghuáng phoenix

风景 fēngjǐng view; landscape

锋利 fēnglì sharp

丰满 fēngmǎn busty; plump; rounded

蜂蜜 fēngmì honey

封面 fēngmiàn (front) cover

奉陪 fèngpéi accompany

奉劝 fèngquàn advise

缝纫 féngrèn sew ◊ sewing

丰盛 fēngshèng rich

风湿 fēngshī rheumatism

丰收 fēngshōu good harvest

封锁 fēngsuǒ blockade ◊ seal off

缝隙 fèngxì crack

风险 fēngxiǎn risk

风筝 fēngzheng kite

分号 fēnhào semicolon

粉红 fěnhóng pink

分居 fēnjū separate

分开 fēnkai break; part; separate; detach

分裂 fēnliè division ◊ divide

分泌 fēnmì secrete ◊ secretion

分娩 fēnmiǎn childbirth

坟墓 fénmù tomb

愤怒 fènnù anger ◊ angry

分配 fēnpèi assign; distribute ◊ distribution

分批 fēnpī in groups

分歧 fēnqí difference; gulf

分期付款 fēnqī fùkuǎn pay in installments

焚烧 fénshāo burn

粉饰 fěnshì gloss over

分手 fēnshǒu split up; break up ◊ breakup; separation ◊ separated

分数 fēnshù fraction; mark

粉丝 fěnsī Chinese vermicelli

分析 fēnxī analysis ◊ analyze

分子 fēnzǐ numerator MATH; molecule ◊ molecular

佛 Fó Buddha

佛教 Fójiào Buddhism ◊ Buddhist

否 fǒu no; not

否定 fǒudìng negate

否决 fǒujué overrule; throw out; veto

否认 fǒurèn denial ◊ deny; disclaim

否则 fǒuzé or else

佛爷 Fóye Buddha

夫 fū husband

敷 fū apply

孵 fū hatch

肤 fū skin

扶 fú hold up; support

福 fú happiness

服 fú take *medicine*

斧 fǔ ax

腐 fǔ rotten; stale

付 fù pay

父 fù father

富 fù rich

腹 fù abdomen

负 fù negative; minus

妇 fù wife

副本 fùběn copy

浮标 fúbiāo buoy

副标题 fùbiāotí subheading

服从 fúcóng obey; comply ◊ obedience

附带 fùdài incidental; supplementary ◊ incidentally

负担 fùdān load; burden

辅导 fǔdǎo tuition

复发 fùfā relapse

夫妇 fūfù married couple

覆盖 fùgài cover

讣告 fùgào obituary

符号 fúhào symbol

符合 fúhé tally with; conform to ◊ compatible

复活节 Fùhuójié Easter

附加 fùjiā add ◊ additional

附件 fùjiàn accessory; enclosure; attachment

附近 fùjìn close by

付款 fùkuǎn pay ◊ payment

腐烂 fǔlàn decay; rot ◊ rotten

福利 fúlì welfare

俘虏 fúlǔ capture ◊ prisoner; captive

附录 fùlù appendix

覆灭 fùmiè demise

抚摩 fǔmó caress

父母 fùmǔ parents

妇女 fùnǚ woman

福气 fúqì happiness

肤浅 fūqiǎn superficial; sketchy

父亲 fùqīn father

夫人 fūrén wife

富人 fùrén the rich; rich person

附入 fùrù enclose; add

肤色 fūsè skin color

负伤 fùshāng injured

敷设 fūshè lay *cable etc*

辐射 fúshè radiate ◊ radiation

服饰 fúshì clothes and accessories

复数 fùshù plural

复述 fùshù relate

伏特 fútè volt

伏特加 fútèjiā vodka

伏天 fútiān dog days

服贴 fútiē obedient; manageable

斧头 fǔtou ax

富翁 fùwēng rich man

服务 fúwù serve ◊ service

服务台 fúwùtái reception

服务员 fúwùyuán waiter

腹泻 fùxiè diarrhea

复写纸 fùxiězhǐ carbon paper

抚养 fǔyǎng raise

副业 fùyè sideline

复印 fùyìn copy

富裕 fùyù affluent; well-off

复杂 fùzá complicated

负载 fùzài load ELEC

负责 fùzé be responsible for ◊ responsible

付账 fùzhàng pay the bill

负重 fùzhòng burden

服装 fúzhuāng dress; clothes

副作用 fùzuòyòng side effect

# G

该 gāi should

改 gǎi change; correct

盖 gài cover ◊ lid

钙 gài calcium

改变 gǎibiàn change

改革 gǎigé reform

改建 gǎijiàn convert

改进 gǎijìn improve ◊ improvement

概况 gàikuàng survey; overview

概括 gàikuò summarize

概念 gàiniàn concept

改期 gǎiqī postpone

改善 gǎishàn improve

概述 gàishù sum up ◊ summary

改写 gǎixiě rewrite

概要 gàiyào outline

盖章 gàizhāng stamp

改正 gǎizhèng amend

盖住 gàizhù cover up

盖子 gàizi lid; cap

咖喱 gālí curry

干 gān dry ◊ dried

肝 gān liver

杆 **gān** pole

甘 **gān** sweet

敢 **gǎn** dare

赶 **gǎn** drive out; rush; 赶时髦 *gǎn shímáo* keep up with the latest fashions

秆 **gǎn** stalk

擀 **gǎn** roll out

感 **gǎn** feel ◊ sense

干 **gàn** do

干杯 **gānbēi** cheers!

干部 **gànbù** cadre

干草 **gāncǎo** hay

感到 **gǎndào** feel

感到无聊 **gǎndào wúliáo** feel bored

感动 **gǎndòng** move

钢 **gāng** steel

缸 **gāng** earthenware vessel

刚 **gāng** just

港 **gǎng** harbor

尴尬 **gāngà** embarrassed

钢笔 **gāngbǐ** fountain pen

港币 **gǎngbì** Hong Kong dollar

刚才 **gāngcái** just now

杠杆 **gànggǎn** lever

刚好 **gānghǎo** just right

港口 **gǎngkǒu** port; harbor

肛门 **gāngmén** anus

钢琴 **gāngqín** piano

岗哨 **gǎngshào** guard

岗位 **gǎngwèi** guard

港务局 **gǎngwùjú** port authorities

缸子 **gāngzi** beaker; cup

干旱 **gānhàn** drought

干涸 **gānhé** dry out; dry up

感激 **gǎnjī** appreciation ◊ appreciate; feel grateful

赶集 **gǎnjí** go to market

赶紧 **gǎnjǐn** hurry

干净 **gānjìng** clean

感觉 **gǎnjué** feeling; sensation; sense ◊ feel

赶快 **gǎnkuài** hurry ◊ quickly

橄榄 **gǎnlǎn** olive

干酪 **gānlào** cheese

感冒 **gǎnmào** cold ◊ catch a cold

擀面杖 **gǎnmiànzhàng** rolling pin

感情 **gǎnqíng** feeling; emotion

感染 **gǎnrǎn** contract, pick up; infect; influence; affect; become infected ◊ infected; infectious; septic

干扰 **gānrǎo** interference ◊ interfere with

感人 **gǎnrén** moving,

touching

赶上 **gǎnshàng** catch up

干涉 **gānshè** interfere; meddle ◊ interference

干洗 **gānxǐ** drycleaning

感谢 **gǎnxiè** thanks ◊ say thanks

甘心 **gānxīn** willingly ◊ resign oneself to

感性 **gǎnxìng** sensory

感兴趣 **gǎn xìngqù** be interested

肝炎 **gānyán** hepatitis

敢于 **gǎnyú** dare

肝脏 **gānzàng** liver

干燥 **gānzào** dry

甘蔗 **gānzhe** sugar cane

赶走 **gǎnzǒu** chase away; banish

高 **gāo** big; tall; high ◊ top (gear)

膏 **gāo** ointment; cream

糕 **gāo** cake

告别 **gàobié** say goodbye

高超 **gāochāo** masterly

高潮 **gāocháo** climax; high tide

高大 **gāodà** enormous

高等 **gāoděng** higher; advanced; elite

高等教育 **gāoděng jiàoyù** higher education

糕点 **gāodiǎn** cakes and pastries

高度 **gāodù** height

高尔夫球 **gāo'ěrfūqiú** golf

告发 **gàofā** inform; inform on

高贵 **gāoguì** noble

高级 **gāojí** high-quality

稿件 **gāojiàn** manuscript; article

高楼大厦 **gāolóu dàshà** high-rise buildings

告密 **gàomì** sneak; inform on

高尚 **gāoshàng** noble

高烧 **gāoshāo** high fever

告诉 **gàosu** tell

高速公路 **gāosù gōnglù** expressway

睾丸 **gāowán** testicles

高兴 **gāoxìng** happy ◊ happily

高压 **gāoyā** high pressure

羔羊 **gāoyáng** lamb

膏药 **gāoyao** plaster; Bandaid®

高原 **gāoyuán** plateau

高涨 **gāozhǎng** upturn

告知 **gàozhī** inform

个 **ge** general measure word

哥 gē elder brother

歌 gē song

鸽 gē dove; pigeon

格 gé grid; grating; square

革 gé leather

嗝 gé hiccups

个 gè *general measure word*

隔壁 gébì next door

个别 gèbié individual

戈壁滩 Gēbìtān Gobi Desert

胳膊 gēbo arm

胳膊肘儿 gēbozhǒur elbow

歌词 gēcí lyrics

疙瘩 gēda boil

隔断 géduàn separate

哥哥 gēge elder brother

给 gěi give

歌剧 gējù opera

隔绝 géjué cut off; isolate

阁楼 gélóu attic; loft

革命 gémìng revolution ◊ revolutionary

根 gēn root

跟 gēn follow ◊ with ◊ and

根本 gēnběn ultimate; underlying ◊ at all; fundamentally ◊ base; foundation

耕 gēng plow

耕地 gēngdì plow ◊ arable land

更多 gèngduō more

更改 gēnggǎi alter

耕牛 gēngniú draft ox

更新 gēngxīn renew; replace

更衣室 gēngyī shì cubicle

根据 gēnjù basis ◊ according to

跟随 gēnsuí follow

根源 gēnyuán origin; source ◊ originate

跟踪 gēnzōng stalk; rail

歌曲 gēqǔ song

个人 gèrén individual ◊ personal

格式 géshì layout

格式设定 géshì shèdìng format

歌手 gēshǒu singer

个体 gètǐ freelance; self-employed

格外 géwài particularly

个性 gèxìng personality; character

隔音 géyīn soundproof

革制品 gézhìpǐn leather goods

各种各样 gèzhǒnggèyàng mixed; miscellaneous

鸽子 gēzi dove; pigeon

弓 **gōng** bow

工 **gōng** worker ◊ work

攻 **gōng** attack

功 **gōng** merit; service

供 **gōng** supply; provide

恭 **gōng** respectful

公 **gōng** public; male

宫 **gōng** palace

共 **gòng** common; joint; mutual

公安局 **Gōng'ān jú** Public Security Bureau

公布 **gōngbù** announce; declare

共产党 **Gòngchǎndǎng** Communist Party

工厂 **gōngchǎng** factory

共产主义 **Gòngchǎn zhǔyì** communism ◊ communist

工程 **gōngchéng** construction

工程师 **gōngchéngshī** engineer

供词 **gòngcí** confession

公道 **gōngdào** justice

工地 **gōngdì** building site

宫殿 **gōngdiàn** palace

公共 **gōnggòng** public

公共汽车 **gōnggòng qìchē** bus

公关 **gōngguān** public relations

公害 **gōnghài** environmental damage

公函 **gōnghán** official letter

恭贺 **gōnghè** congratulate

共和国 **gònghé guó** republic

工会 **gōnghuì** labor union

公鸡 **gōngjī** rooster

攻击 **gōngjī** attack

供给 **gōngjǐ** supply

公斤 **gōngjīn** kilogram

恭敬 **gōngjìng** respect

工具 **gōngjù** tool

公开 **gōngkāi** public; open

功劳 **gōngláo** merit; service

公里 **gōnglǐ** kilometer

公路 **gōnglù** highway; road

公民 **gōngmín** citizen ◊ civic; civil

公墓 **gōngmù** cemetery

功能 **gōngnéng** function

公牛 **gōngniú** bull

供暖 **gōngnuǎn** heating

贡品 **gòngpǐn** tribute

公婆 **gōngpó** in-laws (*husband's parents*)

公顷 **gōngqīng** hectare

工人 **gōngrén** worker

供认 **gòngrèn** confess

工伤 **gōngshāng** industrial accident

公社 **gōngshè** commune

公式 **gōngshì** formula

供水 **gōngshuǐ** water supply

公司 **gōngsī** company ◊ incorporated

共同 **gòngtóng** collective; common; joint

共同体 **gòngtóngtǐ** community

恭维 **gōngwéi** compliment; flatter

公物 **gōngwù** public property

恭喜 **gōngxǐ** congratulations

贡献 **gòngxiàn** contribute; devote ◊ contribution

工业 **gōngyè** industry ◊ industrial

工艺 **gōngyì** craft; technology

工艺美术 **gōngyì měishù** arts and crafts

供应 **gōngyìng** provide ◊ provision

公寓 **gōngyù** apartment

公园 **gōngyuán** park

公约 **gōngyuē** pact; convention

公正 **gōngzhèng** fair; impartial

公证 **gōngzhèng** authenticate; witness

公证人 **gōngzhèngrén** notary

公职人员 **gōngzhí rényuán** official

公众 **gōngzhòng** public

公主 **gōngzhǔ** princess

工资 **gōngzī** wage

工作 **gōngzuò** work; job

沟 **gōu** trench; ditch

钩 **gōu** hook

狗 **gǒu** dog

购 **gòu** buy

够 **gòu** enough

构成 **gòuchéng** comprise

购买 **gòumǎi** purchase

沟通 **gōutōng** communicate ◊ communication

购物 **gòuwù** shopping ◊ do one's shopping

勾引 **gōuyǐn** pick up; seduce

构造 **gòuzào** construction; design

钩针 **gōuzhēn** crochet hook

钩子 **gōuzi** hook

姑 **gū** aunt

估 **gū** estimate

孤 **gū** orphaned; lonely

鼓 **gǔ** drum

古 **gǔ** ancient

骨 **gǔ** bone

谷 **gǔ** valley; grain

雇 **gù** employ

顾 **gù** look around

瓜 **guā** melon

刮 **guā** scrape; shave

挂 **guà** hang; drape

寡妇 **guǎfù** widow

呱呱叫 **guāguājiào** great

挂号信 **guàhào xìn** registered letter

乖 **guāi** good; well-behaved

拐 **guǎi** turn

怪 **guài** strange

拐棍 **guǎigùn** walking stick

拐角 **guǎijiǎo** turning

拐骗 **guǎipiàn** kidnap

怪人 **guàirén** freak; weirdo; crank; nerd

拐弯 **guǎiwān** turn corner

怪物 **guàiwu** monster

怪相 **guàixiàng** grimace

关 **guān** close; turn off

官 **guān** official

鳏 **guān** widowed

观 **guān** look at; observe

罐 **guàn** jar; can

灌 **guàn** pour into

鹳 **guàn** stork

惯 **guàn** used to; accustomed

关闭 **guānbì** close (down)

贯彻 **guànchè** implement;

carry out

管道 **guǎndào** pipeline; tube

观点 **guāndiǎn** point of view

官方 **guānfāng** formal; official ◊ officially

鳏夫 **guānfū** widower

光 **guāng** light

广 **guǎng** wide

逛 **guàng** wander; stroll

灌溉 **guàngài** irrigate ◊ irrigation

广播 **guǎngbō** broadcast

光彩 **guāngcǎi** brilliance

广场 **guǎngchǎng** square (in city)

广度 **guǎngdù** scope; range

广而言之 **guǎng ér yán zhī** in general

广泛 **guǎngfàn** wide ◊ widely

广告 **guǎnggào** advertisement

光滑 **guānghuá** smooth; glossy

广阔 **guǎngkuò** wide

光明 **guāngmíng** bright

光盘 **guāngpán** CD-ROM; CD

光荣 **guāngróng** honor; glory

逛商店 **guàng shāngdiàn**

walk around the shops

光秃秃 **guāng tūtū** bare; bald

观光 **guānguāng** look around; go sightseeing

光线 **guāngxiàn** light; ray

光学 **guāngxué** optics

关怀 **guānhuái** show concern for

关节 **guānjié** joint

冠军 **guànjūn** champion; championship

观看 **guānkàn** watch

管理 **guǎnlǐ** manage; operate; run ◊ administration; management

惯例 **guànlì** custom; habit

官僚制度 **guānliáo zhìdù** bureaucracy

灌木 **guànmù** bush

关税 **guānshuì** customs duty

罐头 **guàntou** can

关系 **guānxi** connection; relationship

管弦乐 **guǎnxiányuè** orchestral music

管弦乐队 **guǎnxián yuèduì** orchestra

关心 **guānxīn** care about

盥洗室 **guànxǐshì** washroom

关押 **guānyā** lock up

关于 **guānyú** with reference to

观众 **guānzhòng** audience

管子 **guǎnzi** pipe; tube

馆子 **guǎnzi** restaurant

挂毯 **guàtǎn** tapestry; wall hanging

挂衣钩 **guàyīgōu** coat hook

瓜子 **guāzi** melon seed

古巴 **Gǔbā** Cuba ◊ Cuban

古代 **gǔdài** antiquity

孤单 **gūdān** alone; solitary

古典 **gǔdiǎn** classical

固定 **gùdìng** fasten; fix ◊ fixed

股东 **gǔdōng** stockholder

古董 **gǔdǒng** antique

孤独 **gūdú** lonely; solitary

孤儿 **gū'ér** orphan

孤儿院 **gū'ér yuàn** orphanage

股份公司 **gǔfèn gōngsī** joint-stock company

辜负 **gūfù** disappoint

故宫 **gùgōng** the former imperial palace in Beijing

古怪 **gǔguài** odd; eccentric

骨灰 **gǔhuī** ashes (*after cremation*)

骨灰盒 **gǔhuīhé** urn (*for*

*ashes*)

归 **guī** return

龟 **guī** turtle

鬼 **guī** ghost

贵 **guì** expensive; noble

跪 **guì** kneel

贵宾 **guìbīn** guest of honor

轨道 **guǐdào** track; orbit

规定 **guīdìng** stipulation ◊
stipulate

规格 **guīgé** specifications

归功 **guīgōng** owing to

鬼鬼祟祟 **guǐguǐ suìsuì**
shifty-looking; sneaky

规划 **guīhuà** plan ◊ planning

归还 **guīhuán** give back;
return

规模 **guīmó** scale

桂皮 **guìpí** cinnamon

归属 **guīshǔ** belong to

归途 **guītú** way back

贵重 **guìzhòng** valuable

柜子 **guìzi** cabinet

刽子手 **guìzishǒu**
executioner

估计 **gūjì** calculate; estimate;
assess

古迹 **gǔjì** antiquities

顾及 **gùjí** take into account

故居 **gùjū** former residence

顾客 **gùkè** client; customer

古老 **gǔlǎo** ancient

鼓励 **gǔlì** encourage ◊
encouragement

谷粒 **gǔlì** grain

估量 **gūliáng** weigh up

顾虑 **gùlǜ** misgivings

滚 **gǔn** roll ◊ get lost!

滚动 **gǔndòng** roll

姑娘 **gūniang** girl

牯牛 **gǔniú** bull

棍子 **gùnzi** stick; rod

锅 **guō** pan; wok

国句 **guó** state; country

果 **guǒ** fruit; result

裹 **guǒ** wrap

过 **guò** pass

锅铲 **guōchǎn** spatula

过程 **guòchéng** process

过错 **guòcuò** mistake

过道 **guòdào** corridor

过度 **guòdù** excess ◊
excessive

果断 **guǒduàn** decisive

过分 **guòfèn** excessive;
unreasonable

果脯 **guǒfǔ** candied fruit

过高 **guògāo** exorbitant;
too high

国歌 **guógē** national anthem

过火 **guòhuǒ** exaggerated ◊
exaggerate

国籍 **guójí** citizenship; nationality

国际 **guójì** international ◊ internationally

国家 **guójiā** country; nation; state ◊ national

国家队 **guójiāduì** national team

果酱 **guǒjiàng** jam

过节 **guòjié** celebrate (a festival)

过境 **guòjìng** be in transit (between countries)

过境签证 **guòjìng qiānzhèng** transit visa

锅炉 **guōlú** boiler

过滤 **guòlǜ** filter; strain

过滤器 **guòlǜqì** filter; strainer

过滤嘴香烟 **guòlǜzuǐ xiāngyān** filter-tipped cigarette

国民 **guómín** national

过敏 **guòmǐn** allergy ◊ hypersensitive

国内 **guónèi** domestic; internal

过年 **guònián** celebrate Chinese New Year

国旗 **guóqí** national flag

国庆节 **Guóqìngjié** National Day

过剩 **guòshèng** surplus

果实 **guǒshí** fruit

过时 **guòshí** old-fashioned; out-of-date

果树 **guǒshù** fruit tree

国外 **guówài** abroad; foreign

国王 **guówáng** king

国务院 **guówùyuàn** State Council

过夜 **guòyè** stay the night

国营 **guóyíng** state-run

果汁 **guǒzhī** fruit juice

股票 **gǔpiào** stocks and shares

故事 **gùshì** story; narrative; joke

骨髓 **gǔsuǐ** bone marrow

固体 **gùtǐ** solid

骨头 **gǔtou** bone

顾问 **gùwèn** adviser; consultant

股息 **gǔxī** dividend

故乡 **gùxiāng** home town; native place

故意 **gùyì** deliberate; willful ◊ deliberately

雇佣 **gùyōng** employ

固有 **gùyǒu** inherent

雇员 **gùyuán** employee; staff

鼓掌 **gǔzhǎng** applaud ◊

applause

故障 **gùzhàng** breakdown;
defect

骨折 **gǔzhé** break a bone;

fracture ◊ broken

固执 **gùzhí** inflexible;
stubborn

雇主 **gùzhǔ** employer

# H

哈 **hā** exhale ◊ ha (ha)

还 **hái** still; as well as

海 **hǎi** sea

害 **hài** harm

海岸 **hǎi'àn** coast

海报 **hǎibào** poster

害虫 **hàichóng** pest; vermin

害处 **hàichu** damage

海带 **hǎidài** seaweed

海关 **hǎiguān** customs

海军 **hǎijūn** navy ◊ naval

海绵 **hǎimián** sponge; foam
rubber

海鸥 **hǎi'ōu** seagull

害怕 **hàipà** fear ◊ be afraid

海平面 **hǎipíngmiàn** sea
level

海滩 **hǎitān** beach

海外 **hǎiwài** overseas

害羞 **hàixiū** shy

海洋 **hǎiyáng** ocean ◊
marine

海员 **hǎiyuán** sailor

海蜇 **hǎizhé** jellyfish

孩子 **háizi** child

蛤蟆 **háma** toad

寒 **hán** cold

函 **hán** letter

喊 **hǎn** shout

汗 **hàn** sweat

旱 **hàn** dryness

焊 **hàn** weld

汉堡包 **hànbǎobāo**
hamburger

汉朝 **Hàncháo** Han Dynasty

行 **háng** line; row; trade;
profession

航班 **hángbān** flight

行家 **hángjiā** expert

航空 **hángkōng** aviation

航空邮件 **hángkōng
yóujiàn** airmail

航天 **hángtiān** space flight

航线 **hángxiàn** flight route

航向 **hángxiàng** course

行业 **hángyè** trade;

profession

旱季 hànjì dry season

罕见 hǎnjiàn rare ◊ seldom seen

喊叫声 hǎnjiàoshēng yell; scream

含酒精 hán jiǔjīng alcoholic

寒冷 hánlěng icy cold

含量 hánliàng content

汗淋淋 hànlínlín sweaty

寒流 hánliú stream of cold air

汗衫 hànshān T-shirt

函授 hánshòu correspondence course

寒暑表 hánshǔbiǎo thermometer

寒酸 hánsuān shabby

汉学 Hànxué Sinology

汉语 Hànyǔ Chinese

旱灾 hànzāi drought

汉族 Hànzú the Han people

蚝 háo oyster

毫 háo milli-; in the least

好 hǎo good; well; very

耗 hào use; consume

号 hào number

好 hào like

好吃 hǎochī delicious

好处 hǎochù advantage

耗费 hàofèi spend; use

好感 hǎogǎn fondness; affection

豪华 háohuá luxury ◊ luxurious; de luxe; plush

好看 hǎokàn good-looking

好客 hàokè hospitable

号码 hàomǎ number

毫米 háomǐ millimeter

好奇 hàoqí curious ◊ curiously

好强 hàoqiáng ambitious

好听 hǎotīng melodious; nice-sounding

毫无 háowú not in the least

好象 hǎoxiàng seem; resemble ◊ apparently ◊ as if

好笑 hǎoxiào amusing

好心 hǎoxīn kind-hearted

号召 hàozhào call; call up

好转 hǎozhuǎn improve ◊ improvement

哈腰 hāyāo stoop; bow

喝 hē drink

和 hé and

盒 hé box

颌 hé jaw

核 hé core

河 hé river

褐 hè brown

贺 hè congratulate

荷包蛋 **hébao dàn** fried egg

合并 **hébìng** merge ◊ merger

喝采 **hècǎi** applaud; cheer

合成 **héchéng** synthesis

喝倒彩 **hè dàocǎi** boo

合得来 **hédelái** get on well

核对 **héduì** check

荷尔蒙 **hé'ěrméng** hormone

合法 **héfǎ** legal; legitimate

荷花 **héhuā** lotus (flower)

黑 **hēi** black; dark

黑暗 **hēi'àn** darkness

黑白片 **hēibáipiàn** black and white movie

黑板 **hēibǎn** blackboard

黑客 **hēikè** hacker

黑啤酒 **hēipíjiǔ** dark beer

黑市 **hēishì** black market

黑手党 **hēishǒudǎng** Mafia

核计 **héjì** calculate

合计 **héjì** add up

和解 **héjiě** make up

河马 **hémǎ** hippopotamus

褐煤 **hèméi** brown coal

和睦 **hémù** harmony

很 **hěn** very; quite

狠 **hěn** hard-hearted

恨 **hèn** hate ◊ hatred

狠毒 **hěndú** malicious; venomous

横 **héng** horizontal

横贯 **héngguàn** cross

衡量 **héngliáng** consider; weigh up

恒心 **héngxīn** stamina; persistence

痕迹 **hénjì** evidence; trail; traces

很快 **hěnkuài** soon

和气 **héqi** polite; friendly

和尚 **héshàng** Buddhist monk

合身 **héshēn** fit

核实 **héshí** verification ◊ verify

合适 **héshì** suitable; appropriate

合算 **hésuàn** profitable

喝汤 **hētāng** drink soup

核桃 **hétáo** walnut

合同 **hétóng** contract ◊ contractual

贺喜 **hèxǐ** congratulate

和谐 **héxié** harmonious

核心 **héxīn** core; kernel

贺信 **hèxìn** letter of congratulation

合意 **héyì** please; appeal to

合影 **héyǐng** group photo

和约 **héyuē** peace treaty

喝醉了 **hēzuìle** drunken

红 **hóng** red

虹 **hóng** rainbow

哄 **hōng** coax

红宝石 **hóng bǎoshí** ruby

红茶 **hóngchá** black tea

宏大 **hóngdà** great

轰动 **hōngdòng** cause a sensation

轰击 **hōngjī** shoot at; bombard

烘烤 **hōngkǎo** toast

洪亮 **hóngliàng** sonorous

红绿灯 **hónglǜdēng** traffic light

轰鸣 **hōngmíng** roar

哄骗 **hōngpiàn** deceive; swindle

红薯 **hóngshǔ** sweet potato

洪水 **hóngshuǐ** flood

红外线 **hóngwàixiàn** infra-red rays

宏伟 **hóngwěi** grandiose

轰炸 **hōngzhà** bomb

猴 **hóu** monkey

喉 **hóu** throat

吼 **hǒu** roar

后 **hòu** back; behind

厚 **hòu** thick

候车室 **hòuchēshì** waiting room

后代 **hòudài** offspring

后跟 **hòugēn** heel

后果 **hòuguǒ** consequence; effect

喉结 **hóujié** Adam's apple

候机室 **hòujī shì** departure lounge

侯爵 **hóujué** marquis

后来 **hòulái** after; later

喉咙 **hóulóng** throat

后面 **hòumian** behind

候鸟 **hòuniǎo** migratory bird; migrant

后天 **hòutiān** the day after tomorrow

候选人 **hòuxuǎnrén** candidate

厚颜无耻 **hòuyán-wúchǐ** outrageous; impertinent

猴子 **hóuzi** monkey

壶 **hú** jug; kettle; pot

湖 **hú** lake

糊 **hú** stick

煳 **hú** burnt

虎 **hǔ** tiger

糊 **hù** mush

花 **huā** flower; blossom ◊ spend; cost

划 **huá** row

滑 **huá** slide; slip ◊ slippery

画 **huà** draw; paint ◊ drawing; painting

话 **huà** talk; speech

划 **huà** stroke

画报 **huàbào** magazine

哗变 **huábiàn** mutiny

滑冰 **huábīng** skate ◊ skating

滑冰场 **huábīngchǎng** ice rink

划船 **huáchuán** row; paddle

华尔兹 **huá'ěrzī** waltz

花费 **huāfèi** spend

化肥 **huàféi** artificial fertilizer

划分 **huàfēn** divide

花粉热 **huāfěn rè** hay fever

花岗岩 **huāgāngyán** granite

化工 **huàgōng** chemical industry

踝 **huái** ankle

坏 **huài** bad

坏处 **huàichù** disadvantage

怀旧 **huáijiù** nostalgia ◊ nostalgic ◊ reminisce

怀念 **huáiniàn** long for

坏人 **huàirén** rogue

坏事 **huàishì** evil (thing)

怀疑 **huáiyí** doubt; suspect; question

怀孕 **huáiyùn** pregnant

滑稽 **huájī** comical ◊ funnily

画家 **huàjiā** artist; painter

花椒 **huājiāo** Sichuan pepper

花轿 **huājiào** bridal palanquin

画廊 **huàláng** art gallery

还 **huán** return

环 **huán** ring

缓 **huǎn** leisurely

换 **huàn** change; swap

换班 **huànbān** change shifts

环保 **huánbǎo** environmental protrection

患病 **huànbìng** suffer from an illness

欢畅 **huānchàng** cheerful

幻灯 **huàndēng** slide show

幻灯片 **huàndēngpiàn** slide

荒 **huāng** desolate

慌 **huāng** nervous

黄 **huáng** yellow

谎 **huǎng** lie

晃 **huàng** swing; wave

蝗虫 **huángchóng** locust

荒诞 **huāngdàn** absurd; grotesque

黄道带 **huángdào dài** zodiac

皇帝 **huángdì** emperor ◊ imperial

晃动 **huàngdòng** shake; waggle

黄豆 **huángdòu** soybean

荒废 **huāngfèi** lie fallow

皇宫 **huánggōng** imperial palace

黄瓜 **huángguā** cucumber

黄河 **Huánghé** Yellow River

皇后 **huánghòu** empress; queen

谎话 **huǎnghuà** lie

黄昏 **huánghūn** dusk

黄金 **huángjīn** gold

荒凉 **huāngliáng** bleak; deserted

慌忙 **huāngmáng** hurried

黄色 **huángsè** yellow; pornographic

黄色人种 **huángsè rénzhǒng** the yellow race

荒疏 **huāngshū** lose the knack

黄铜 **huángtóng** brass

环顾 **huángù** look around

黄油 **huángyóu** butter

慌张 **huāngzhāng** nervous; lacking composure

缓和 **huǎnhé** détente; respite ◊ lighten

还击 **huánjī** hit back

环境 **huánjìng** environment; surroundings; setting

环境污染 **huánjìng wūrǎn** environmental pollution

欢聚 **huānjù** convivial get-together

欢乐 **huānlè** happy; cheerful

缓慢 **huǎnmàn** leisurely

化脓 **huànóng** fester

唤起 **huànqǐ** evoke; arouse

换钱 **huànqián** change money

还清 **huánqīng** pay off

环绕 **huánrào** surround

涣散 **huànsàn** loose; limp

换算 **huànsuàn** convert

幻想 **huànxiǎng** illusion; fantasy

唤醒 **huànxǐng** wake; rouse

欢迎 **huānyíng** welcome ◊ reception

花盆 **huāpén** flowerpot

花瓶 **huāpíng** vase

华侨 **Huáqiáo** overseas Chinese

花哨 **huāshao** flashy, gaudy

花生 **huāshēng** peanut

华氏 **huáshì** Fahrenheit

花束 **huāshù** bouquet

划算 **huásuàn** be worthwhile

滑梯 **huátī** slide

话题 **huàtí** topic of conversation

话务员 **huàwùyuán**

switchboard operator

化纤 huàxiān synthetic fiber

滑翔 huáxiáng glide

滑翔机 huáxiángjī glider

滑雪 huáxuě ski ◊ skiing

化学 huàxué chemistry ◊ chemical

化验室 huàyànshì laboratory

花园 huāyuán garden

画展 huàzhǎn exhibition of paintings

花招 huāzhāo trick

化妆 huàzhuāng put on make-up

化妆品 huàzhuāng pǐn make-up; cosmetics

划子 huázi rowboat

湖滨 húbīn lakeside

蝴蝶 húdié butterfly

蝴蝶结 húdié jié bow (knot)

煳饭 húfàn burnt rice

胡蜂 húfēng wasp

呼喊 hūhǎn call

呼唤 hūhuàn call

灰 huī ash; dust

回 huí return; go back

喙 huì beak; snout

会 huì be able to; meet ◊ meeting

回避 huíbì evade; duck

回车健 huíchē jiàn return key COMPUT

灰尘 huīchén dust

回答 huídá answer

挥动 huīdòng swing; wield

汇兑 huìduì transfer *money*

挥发 huīfā evaporate

恢复 huīfù recover; restore

回顾 huígù look back ◊ retrospective

汇合 huìhé join

会合 huìhé meet

悔恨 huǐhèn regret

绘画 huìhuà paint ◊ painting; picture

辉煌 huīhuáng brilliant; glorious

挥霍 huīhuò wasteful ◊ squander

回家 huíjiā go home

会见 huìjiàn meeting

灰浆 huījiāng mortar

回教 huíjiào Islam

灰烬 huījìn ash

汇款 huìkuǎn transfer *money*

汇率 huìlǜ exchange rate

会面 huìmiàn meet

毁灭 huǐmiè wreck; obliterate

汇票 huìpiào bill of

exchange

回去 **huíqù** go back

灰色 **huīsè** gray

会谈 **huìtán** have a conversation

诙谐 **huīxié** humorous

灰心 **huīxīn** discouraged

回形针 **huíxíngzhēn** paper clip

回信 **huíxìn** reply

会演 **huìyǎn** festival

回忆 **huíyì** recollect ◊ recollection

会议 **huìyì** conference; congress

徽章 **huīzhāng** badge

绘制 **huìzhì** draw

胡椒 **hújiāo** pepper

胡椒薄荷 **hújiāo bòhé** peppermint

呼救 **hūjiù** emergency call

狐狸 **húli** fox

护理 **hùlǐ** nurse

忽略 **hūlüè** neglect ◊ overlook

胡萝卜 **hú luóbo** carrot

荤 **hūn** meat or fish

混 **hùn** mix

昏暗 **hūn'àn** dark; dim

胡闹 **húnào** make trouble; fool around

混合 **hùnhé** mix; combine

婚礼 **hūnlǐ** wedding

混乱 **hùnluàn** chaos; muddle ◊ chaotic; turbulent

昏迷 **hūnmí** unconscious

混凝土 **hùnníngtǔ** concrete

馄饨 **húntun** won ton

混淆 **hùnxiáo** confuse ◊ confusion

混血儿 **hùnxuè'ér** half-caste

婚姻 **hūnyīn** marriage ◊ marital

婚约 **hūnyuē** engagement

浑浊 **húnzhuó** cloudy; muddy

或 **huò** or

火 **huǒ** fire

活 **huó** live ◊ alive

祸 **huò** accident

获 **huò** achieve

货 **huò** goods

伙伴 **huǒbàn** buddy; partner

货币 **huòbì** currency ◊ monetary

火柴 **huǒchái** match

火车 **huǒchē** train; van

火车头 **huǒchētóu** locomotive

火车站 **huǒchēzhàn** train station

货船 **huòchuán** freighter

获得 **huòdé** get; achieve; capture

活动 **huódòng** activity ◊ move

火锅 **huǒguō** hot pot

火花 **huǒhuā** spark

火化 **huǒhuà** cremate ◊ cremation

火鸡 **huǒjī** turkey

火箭 **huǒjiàn** rocket

火警 **huǒjǐng** fire alarm

火炬 **huǒjù** torch

霍乱 **huòluàn** cholera

活泼 **huópo** lively

活塞 **huósāi** piston

火山 **huǒshān** volcano

获胜 **huòshèng** win ◊ winning ◊ winner

祸首 **huòshǒu** instigator

火腿 **huǒtuǐ** ham

货物 **huòwù** goods

获悉 **huòxī** discover

或许 **huòxǔ** perhaps

火焰 **huǒyàn** flame

活跃 **huóyuè** active; vivid

货运站 **huòyùnzhàn** freight depot

或者 **huòzhě** or

糊墙纸 **húqiángzhǐ** wallpaper

忽然 **hūrán** suddenly

忽视 **hūshì** neglect

护士 **hùshì** nurse

胡同 **hútòng** alley

户头 **hùtóu** account

糊涂 **hútu** confused

呼吸 **hūxī** breath; breathing ◊ breathe

互相 **hùxiāng** reciprocal; mutual; one another

弧形 **húxíng** arched

护照 **hùzhào** passport

胡子 **húzi** beard; mustache

# J

鸡 **jī** chicken

机 **jī** machine

奇 **jī** odd *number*

集 **jí** collect

极 **jí** extreme ◊ extremely

急 **jí** impatient; in a hurry; urgent

及 **jí** and

几 **jǐ** some; a few; several ◊ how many?

寄 jì send

季 jì season

记 jì remember

系 jì button up; tie up

既 ... 又 ... jì ... yòu ... both ... and ...

加 jiā add ◊ plus

家 jiā home; family

痂 jiā scab

颊 jiá cheek

假 jiǎ false; bogus

价 jià price

假 jià vacation

加班 jiābān work overtime

甲板 jiǎbǎn deck

加倍 jiābèi double

甲虫 jiǎchóng beetle

家畜 jiāchù domestic animal

假定 jiǎdìng assume

假发 jiǎfà wig

价格 jiàgé price; cost

加工 jiāgōng process; embellish

加固 jiāgù fasten; secure

家伙 jiāhuo guy

嘉奖 jiājiǎng praise

佳节 jiājié happy celebration

家具 jiājù furniture

加剧 jiājù intensify

茄克 jiākè jacket; coat

肩 jiān shoulder

尖 jiān point

奸 jiān traitor

简 jiǎn straightforward

剪 jiǎn cut

减 jiǎn minus ◊ reduce

捡 jiǎn collect; pick up

件 jiàn *measure word for baggage, clothes etc*

键 jiàn key

见 jiàn see; meet

溅 jiàn splash; splatter

剑 jiàn sword

腱 jiàn tendon

舰 jiàn warship

箭 jiàn arrow

件 jiàn *measure word for items, clothing, furniture*

建 jiàn build; put up

加拿大 Jiānádà Canada ◊ Canadian

肩膀 jiānbǎng shoulder

鉴别 jiànbié differentiate

剪裁 jiǎncái cut to size; cut out

检查 jiǎnchá check; examine ◊ examination; inspection

检察 jiǎnchá prosecute

检察官 jiǎncháguān prosecuting attorney

简称 jiǎnchēng abbreviation

坚持 jiānchí maintain; carry

on; stand by

简单 **jiǎndān** simple ◊ simply

剪刀 **jiǎndāo** scissors

间谍 **jiàndié** spy

坚定 **jiāndìng** firm; determined

鉴定 **jiàndìng** survey; assess

监督 **jiāndū** supervise; monitor

简短 **jiǎnduǎn** brief

尖端产品 **jiānduān chǎnpǐn** top-quality product

减肥 **jiǎnféi** diet; lose weight

姜 **jiāng** ginger

缰 **jiāng** rein

桨 **jiǎng** paddle; oar

讲 **jiǎng** speak; tell

奖 **jiǎng** award; prize

降 **jiàng** lower; sink

酱 **jiàng** paste; sauce

奖杯 **jiǎngbēi** trophy

降低 **jiàngdī** decline; lower; reduce

间隔 **jiàngé** interval; distance

讲话 **jiǎnghuà** speak

讲价 **jiǎngjià** haggle

讲解 **jiǎngjiě** explain

将近 **jiāngjìn** almost

奖金 **jiǎngjīn** bonus

僵局 **jiāngjú** deadlock; stalemate

将军 **jiāngjūn** general

讲课 **jiǎngkè** teach

将来 **jiānglái** in the future

奖励 **jiǎnglì** award; reward

降落 **jiàngluò** land

降落伞 **jiàngluòsǎn** parachute

奖品 **jiǎngpǐn** prize

缰绳 **jiāngshéng** lead; reins

讲师 **jiǎngshī** lecturer

讲述 **jiǎngshù** relate; tell

坚固 **jiāngù** strong; resistant

见怪 **jiànguài** take offense

降温 **jiàngwēn** drop in temperature

奖学金 **jiǎngxuéjīn** scholarship

讲演 **jiǎngyǎn** lecture

将要 **jiāngyào** about to

僵硬 **jiāngyìng** stiff

酱油 **jiàngyóu** soy sauce

疆域 **jiāngyù** territory

奖章 **jiǎngzhāng** medal

讲座 **jiǎngzuò** lecture

简化 **jiǎnhuà** simplify

监护人 **jiānhùrén** guardian

减价 **jiǎnjià** reduce the price

渐渐 **jiànjiàn** gradually

建交 **jiànjiāo** establish

diplomatic relations

间接 **jiànjiē** indirect ◊ indirectly

坚决 **jiānjué** determined; decided; strong

健康 **jiànkāng** fit; healthy ◊ fitness; health

尖刻 **jiānkè** cutting; bitter

艰苦 **jiānkǔ** difficult; strenuous

尖利 **jiānlì** sharp; piercing

建立 **jiànlì** establish; set up; found

健美锻炼 **jiànměi duànliàn** aerobics; bodybuilding

见面 **jiànmiàn** meet

简明 **jiǎnmíng** concise

键盘 **jiànpán** keyboard

剪票 **jiǎnpiào** punch a ticket

柬埔寨 **Jiǎnpǔzhài** Cambodia ◊ Cambodian

坚强 **jiānqiáng** strong; tough

减轻 **jiǎnqīng** relieve; lighten; ease

尖锐 **jiānruì** sharp; shrill

减少 **jiǎnshǎo** reduce

建设 **jiànshè** build

健身中心 **jiànshēn zhōngxīn** fitness center

坚实 **jiānshí** solid

监视 **jiānshì** oversee; watch

见识 **jiànshí** experience; common sense

减速 **jiǎnsù** decelerate; slow down

健谈 **jiàntán** talkative

监听 **jiāntīng** listen in on; tap; bug

健忘 **jiànwàng** forgetful

奸污 **jiānwū** rape

见习 **jiànxí** become familiar with one's work; train

间隙 **jiànxì** gap

见效 **jiànxiào** effective

艰辛 **jiānxīn** suffering; hardship

饯行 **jiànxíng** have a farewell meal

检验 **jiǎnyàn** test

简要 **jiǎnyào** succinct

检疫 **jiǎnyì** quarantine

建议 **jiànyì** suggest ◊ suggestion

坚硬 **jiānyìng** rigid; hard

监狱 **jiānyù** prison

鉴于 **jiànyú** in view of

建造 **jiànzào** build ◊ building (*activity*)

见证人 **jiànzhèngrén** witness

简直 **jiǎnzhí** simply; utterly

剪纸 **jiǎnzhǐ** paper cut

建筑 **jiànzhù** building

健壮 **jiànzhuàng** robust

建筑学 **jiànzhù xué** architecture

剪子 **jiǎnzi** scissors

胶 **jiāo** glue

教 **jiāo** teach

浇 **jiāo** pour

交 **jiāo** hand over; cross

焦 **jiāo** burnt

嚼 **jiáo** chew

脚 **jiǎo** foot; bottom

角 **jiǎo** corner; jiao (Chinese money)

搅 **jiǎo** stir

叫 **jiào** call; ask

较 **jiào** relatively

教 **jiào** teach

骄傲 **jiāo'ào** proud

搅拌 **jiǎobàn** stir; whisk

脚步 **jiǎobù** footstep

交叉 **jiāochā** intersect

轿车 **jiàochē** car

搅动 **jiǎodòng** stir; move

角度 **jiǎodù** angle

娇惯 **jiāoguàn** spoil; indulge

狡猾 **jiǎohuá** crafty

交换 **jiāohuàn** exchange; barter; trade

教诲 **jiàohuì** explain; instruct ◊ explanation; instruction

交货 **jiāohuò** deliver goods

交互式 **jiāohùshì** interactive

焦急 **jiāojí** anxious ◊ anxiety

交际 **jiāojì** communication; contact

脚尖 **jiǎojiān** tip of the toe; tiptoe

交界 **jiāojiè** border (on)

胶卷 **jiāojuǎn** film

教科书 **jiàokēshū** textbook

教练 **jiàoliàn** coach

较量 **jiàoliàng** compete; compare

教练员 **jiàoliànyuán** trainer

交流 **jiāoliú** exchange; flow

交流电 **jiāoliúdiàn** alternating current

角落 **jiǎoluò** corner

角膜 **jiǎomó** cornea

酵母 **jiàomǔ** yeast

娇嫩 **jiāonèn** tender; sensitive

娇气 **jiāoqì** squeamish; fragile

郊区 **jiāoqū** suburbs; outskirts ◊ suburban

绞肉机 **jiǎoròujī** meat grinder

矫揉造作 **jiǎoróu zàozuò**

affected

礁石 jiāoshí reef

教师 jiàoshī teacher

教室 jiàoshì classroom

教授 jiàoshòu professor

教书 jiāoshū teach

教唆 jiàosuō instigate

交谈 jiāotán talk

焦炭 jiāotàn coke

教堂 jiàotáng church

交通 jiāotōng traffic

交通工具 jiāotōng gōngjù means of transportation

脚腕 jiǎowàn ankle

交往 jiāowǎng mingle; mix with; contact ◊ dealings

交响乐 jiāoxiǎngyuè symphony

胶鞋 jiāoxié sneakers

矫形 jiǎoxíng orthopedic

叫醒 jiàoxǐng wake

教训 jiàoxùn lesson

教养 jiàoyǎng manners; breeding

交易 jiāoyì deal; transaction ◊ transact

交易会 jiāoyìhuì trade fair

交易所 jiāoyìsuǒ exchange

郊游 jiāoyóu excursion

教育 jiàoyù education ◊ educational

校正 jiàozhèng correct; correction

脚趾 jiǎozhǐ toe

脚注 jiǎozhù footer; footnote

饺子 jiǎozi Chinese dumpling

叫做 jiàozuò be called

家谱 jiāpǔ family tree

假期 jiàqī vacation; leave

加强 jiāqiáng reinforce; strengthen

家人 jiārén family members

假日 jiàrì public holiday

加入 jiārù add; join

假设 jiǎshè suppose ◊ assuming

加深 jiāshēn deepen

夹生 jiāshēng half-done

驾驶 jiàshǐ drive; fly; sail ◊ driving

驾驶员 jiàshǐyuán driver

驾驶执照 jiàshǐ zhízhào driver's license

家属 jiāshǔ family members

加速 jiāsù accelerate; speed up ◊ acceleration

家庭 jiātíng family ◊ domestic

家庭妇女 **jiātíng fùnǚ**

housewife

家庭作业 **jiātíng zuòyè** homework

家兔 **jiātù** rabbit

家务 **jiāwù** housework; chores

家乡 **jiāxiāng** home; home town

假想 **jiǎxiāng** imaginary

假牙 **jiǎyá** dentures

加油 **jiāyóu** fill up; refuel ◊ come on!

加油站 **jiāyóuzhàn** gas station

家长 **jiāzhǎng** head of household; parent

假肢 **jiǎzhī** artificial limb

价值 **jiàzhí** value; worth

假装 **jiǎzhuāng** pretend; put on ◊ masquerade

架子 **jiàzi** stand; frame; shelf; airs

几百美元 **jǐbǎi měiyuán** a few hundred dollars

基本 **jīběn** basic, fundamental

级别 **jíbié** rank; level

疾病 **jíbìng** disease; illness; sickness

机场 **jīchǎng** airport; airfield

继承 **jìchéng** inherit

计程表 **jìchéngbiǎo** meter

继承人 **jìchéngrén** heir

基础 **jīchǔ** basis; foundation

挤出 **jǐchū** squeeze out

鸡蛋 **jīdàn** (hen's) egg

记得 **jìde** remember

激动 **jīdòng** excite; inflame ◊ feverish; impassioned

嫉妒 **jídù** jealousy ◊ be jealous

极度 **jídù** extreme ◊ extremely

忌妒 **jídù** envy ◊ envious

季度 **jìdù** quarter ◊ quarterly

基督教 **Jīdūjiào** Christianity ◊ Christian

饥饿 **jī'è** starvation; hunger ◊ hungry

街 **jiē** street

结 **jiē** bear *fruit*

揭 **jiē** take off *lid*

接 **jiē** contact; call for; collect

结 **jié** knot

节 **jié** festival; knot; verse

解 **jiě** untie

姐 **jiě** elder sister

借 **jiè** borrow; lend ◊ loan

界 **jiè** border; limit

结巴 **jiēba** stammer

接班人 **jiēbānrén** successor

戒备 jièbèi vigilance ◊ vigilant

结冰 jiébīng freeze

阶层 jiēcéng (social) class

劫持 jiéchí hijack; abduct

杰出 jiéchū brilliant; eminent

戒除 jièchú remove; get rid off; kick *habit*

接触 jiēchù encounter

接待 jiēdài greet; receive

街道 jiēdào street

解冻 jiědòng thaw

阶段 jiēduàn stage

揭发 jiēfā uncover; discover

解放 jiěfàng liberate ◊ liberation; the 1949 Communist victory in China

借方 jièfāng debit ◊ debtor

姐夫 jiěfū brother-in-law

结构 jiégòu structure

解雇 jiěgù dismiss; lay off ◊ dismissal

结果 jiéguǒ result ◊ end up; put away *animal*

结核病 jiéhé bìng tuberculosis

结婚 jiéhūn marry; get married

结婚证书 jiéhūn zhèngshū marriage certificate

节俭 jiéjiǎn economical

接近 jiējìn near ◊ access ◊ verge on

洁净 jiéjìng clean

劫机者 jiéjīzhě hijacker

结局 jiéjú outcome; ending

解决 jiějué solve; settle; sort out

借口 jièkǒu excuse

揭露 jiēlù expose; reveal

结论 jiélùn conclusion

睫毛 jiémáo eyelash

姐妹 jiěmèi sisters

芥末 jièmò mustard

节目 jiémù program; show

节能 jiénéng save energy

节拍 jiépāi rhythm; beat

接壤 jiērǎng border (on)

节日 jiérì festival; (public) holiday

介绍 jièshào introduce ◊ introduction; profile

节省 jiéshěng economize on; save ◊ economical

结实 jiēshi sturdy; firm

解释 jiěshì explain ◊ explanation

接收 jiēshōu receive

接受 jiēshòu accept; take; receive; admit ◊ acceptance

结束 jiéshù end

阶梯 jiētī steps; stairs

接替 jiētì replace; relieve

接吻 jiēwěn kiss

界限 jièxiàn border

介意 jièyì mind; object to

节育 jiéyù birth control

节约 jiéyuē save

解约 jiéyuē cancel a contract

戒指 jièzhi ring (on finger)

接种 jiēzhòng vaccinate

节奏 jiézòu rhythm; beat

杰作 jiézuò masterpiece

挤干 jǐgān squeeze dry

及格 jígé pass (in exam)

机构 jīgòu organization; institution; structure; mechanism

籍贯 jíguàn home; birthplace

激光唱片 jīguāng chàngpiàn compact disc

记号 jìhao mark

集合 jíhé meet; assemble

激化 jīhuà intensify; increase

计划 jìhuà plan; project; planning; figure on; structure ◊ program; project

极坏 jíhuài rotten

饥荒 jīhuang famine

计划生育 jìhuà shēngyù family planning

击毁 jīhuǐ destroy

机会 jīhuì chance

集会 jíhuì meeting; assembly

击剑 jījiàn fencing

即将 jíjiāng about to; soon

寄件人 jìjiànrén sender

季节 jìjié season

激进 jījìn radical

寂静 jìjìng quiet

基金会 jījīnhuì foundation

急救 jíjiù first aid

积极性 jījíxìng initiative; dynamism; activity

急剧 jíjù rapid; abrupt

疾苦 jíkǔ suffering

积累 jīlěi accumulate; pile up

激励 jīlì boost; spur; stimulation

吉利 jílì favorable; lucky

剂量 jìliàng dose

激烈 jīliè intense; fierce

机灵 jīling smart; sharp

记录 jìlù record; note ◊ minutes; log

纪律 jìlǜ discipline

急忙 jímáng hurried

寂寞 jìmò lonely

继母 jìmǔ stepmother

金 jīn gold

巾 jīn cloth

今 jīn now; today; the present

筋 jīn tendon

斤 jīn one jin (*500 grams*)

紧 jǐn tight; tense; taut

锦 jǐn brocade

仅 jǐn only

近 jìn close

进 jìn go in; enter

浸 jìn soak

禁 jìn prohibit

挤奶 jǐnǎi milk

锦标赛 jǐnbiāo sài championship; tournament

进步 jìnbù advance; progress ◊ progressive

禁地 jìndì restricted area

筋斗 jīndǒu somersault

技能 jìnéng technique; skills

茎 jīng stem

京 jīng capital city

井 jǐng well

景 jǐng landscape; scenery

颈 jǐng neck; throat

净 jìng clean ◊ net

镜 jìng mirror

静 jìng quiet

敬 jìng respect ◊ respectful

金刚石 jīngāngshí diamond

警报 jǐngbào alarm

精彩 jīngcǎi wonderful

警察 jǐngchá police; police officer

经常 jīngcháng often ◊ frequent; habitual

境地 jìngdì situation; position

经度 jīngdù longitude

惊愕 jīng'è dismay

胫骨 jìnggǔ shin; shinbone

经过 jīngguò pass ◊ through

惊慌 jīnghuāng alarmed

经济 jīngjì economy ◊ economic; economical

竞技 jìngjì athletics; sports

警戒 jǐngjiè warn

经纪人 jīngjìrén broker; middleman

京剧 Jīngjù Peking Opera

警觉 jǐngjué alert

镜框 jìngkuàng frame

境况 jìngkuàng circumstances

经理 jīnglǐ manager

经历 jīnglì career; experience; background ◊ go through

痉挛 jìngluán cramp

静脉 jìngmài vein

精明 **jīngmíng** clever

敬佩 **jìngpèi** respect

精辟 **jīngpì** profound

惊奇 **jīngqí** be amazed

精确 **jīngquè** precise

井然 **jǐngrán** neat; proper

惊人 **jīngrén** amazing

径赛 **jìngsài** track event

景色 **jǐngsè** scenery

精神 **jīngshén** soul; spirit ◊ mental

精神病 **jīngshénbìng** mental illness

经受 **jīngshòu** undergo; suffer

景泰蓝 **jǐngtàilán** cloisonné

惊叹 **jīngtàn** admire

晶体 **jīngtǐ** crystal

警惕 **jǐngtì** watchful ◊ warily

晶体管收音机 **jīngtǐguǎn shōuyīnjī** transistor radio

精通 **jīngtōng** be expert at; master ◊ proficient ◊ mastery

镜头 **jìngtóu** shot; photograph; lens

尽管 **jǐnguǎn** although; despite

惊吓 **jīngxià** startle

竞选活动 **jìngxuǎn huódòng** election campaign

惊讶 **jīngyà** astonishment ◊ be astonished

经验 **jīngyàn** experience

敬仰 **jìngyǎng** admire; worship

敬意 **jìngyì** respect; deference

经营 **jīngyíng** manage; run ◊ running ◊ managerial

鲸鱼 **jīngyú** whale

竞争 **jìngzhēng** compete; contend for ◊ competition

竞争者 **jìngzhēngzhě** rival

精致 **jīngzhì** exquisite

净重 **jìngzhòng** net weight

镜子 **jìngzi** mirror

今后 **jīnhòu** in future

纪念 **jìniàn** commemorate ◊ memorial

纪念碑 **jìniànbēi** memorial; monument

纪念品 **jìniàn pǐn** souvenir

紧急 **jǐnjí** urgent; imperative ◊ urgency

进口 **jìnkǒu** import

尽快 **jǐnkuài** as soon as possible

近来 **jìnlái** recent ◊ recently

进来 **jìnlai** come in

尽量 **jǐnliàng** as well as

one can

禁令 **jìnlìng** ban

今年 **jīnnián** this year

金牌 **jīnpái** gold medal

浸泡 **jìnpào** soak

筋疲力尽 **jīnpí lìjìn** exhausted

紧迫 **jǐnpò** extremely urgent

进去 **jìnqu** go in

禁区 **jìnqū** no-go area

进入 **jìnrù** enter ◊ entrance; entry

谨慎 **jǐnshèn** cautious; discreet ◊ caution; tact

近视 **jìnshì** shortsighted

金属 **jīnshǔ** metal

金属丝 **jīnshǔsī** wire

近似 **jìnsì** almost; roughly

今天 **jīntiān** today

津贴 **jīntiē** subsidy; allowance

劲头 **jìntóu** enthusiasm

浸透 **jìntòu** soak

激怒 **jīnù** infuriate; provoke ◊ enraged

妓女 **jìnǚ** prostitute

继女 **jìnǚ** stepdaughter

进行 **jìnxíng** carry out; execute; move on

进修 **jìnxiū** continue one's education

金鱼 **jīnyú** goldfish

尽早 **jǐnzǎo** as early as possible

进展 **jìnzhǎn** proceed

紧张 **jǐnzhāng** nervous; tense ◊ nervousness; tension

禁止 **jìnzhǐ** ban

鸡皮疙瘩 **jīpí gēda** gooseflesh

祭品 **jìpǐn** sacrifice

击破 **jīpò** strike down; fell

急迫 **jípò** urgent

激起 **jīqǐ** excite; work up

机器 **jīqì** machine; machinery

极其 **jíqí** extremely

技巧 **jìqiǎo** skill; knack

急切 **jíqiè** eager

激情 **jīqíng** passion

机器人 **jīqìrén** robot

既然 **jìrán** since

鸡肉 **jīròu** chicken (*meat*)

肌肉 **jīròu** muscle

及时 **jíshí** prompt; timely ◊ promptly; in time

即时 **jíshí** immediately

即使 **jíshǐ** even if

几时 **jǐshí** when; what time

集市广场 **jíshì guǎngchǎng** market place

棘手 jíshǒu tricky

奇数 jīshù odd number

技术 jìshù skill; technology ◊ technological

技术员 jìshùyuán technician

祭祀 jìsì sacrifice

计算 jìsuàn calculate; count

计算机 jìsuànjī computer; calculator

吉他 jítā guitar

祭坛 jìtán altar

集体 jítǐ collective

集团 jítuán group; clique

阄 jiū lot; ticket in a draw

酒 jiǔ alcoholic drink

九 jiǔ nine

久 jiǔ a long time

旧 jiù old

救 jiù save

就 jiù right; directly; then

酒吧 jiǔbā bar

臼齿 jiùchǐ molar

纠纷 jiūfēn dispute; quarrel

纠葛 jiūgé dispute; involvement

酒鬼 jiǔguǐ drunk; alcoholic

救护车 jiùhùchē ambulance

酒会 jiǔhuì cocktail party

旧货 jiùhuò second-hand goods

究竟 jiūjìng actually

酒精 jiǔjīng alcohol

舅舅 jiùjiù uncle

旧历 jiùlì Chinese lunar calendar

救命! jiùmìng! help!

就寝 jiùqǐn go to bed

救生衣 jiùshēng yī life jacket

九十 jiǔshí ninety

就是说 jiùshìshuō that is to say

酒席 jiǔxí banquet

就医 jiùyī go to the doctor

九月 jiǔyuè September

纠正 jiūzhèng correct

酒钻 jiǔzuàn corkscrew

就座 jiùzuò take a seat

鸡尾酒 jīwěijiǔ cocktail

挤向 jǐxiàng crowd

迹象 jìxiàng mark; sign

讥笑 jīxiào scoff; laugh at

机械 jīxiè machinery; mechanism

急性 jíxìng acute

记性 jìxìng memory

积蓄 jīxù save up; keep

继续 jìxù continue

鸡眼 jīyǎn corn; bunion

给养 jǐyǎng provisions

记忆 jìyì remember ◊

memory

集邮 **jíyóu** stamp-collecting

基于 **jīyú** because of; on the basis of

机遇 **jīyù** chance; stroke of luck

纪元 **jìyuán** era

妓院 **jìyuàn** brothel

记载 **jìzǎi** record

及早 **jízǎo** early; premature

机长 **jīzhǎng** captain (of aircraft)

记者 **jìzhě** reporter

急诊医生 **jízhěn yīshēng** emergency doctor

机智 **jīzhì** tact; wit ◊ witty; resourceful

集中 **jízhōng** concentrate ◊ cluster; focus (of attention)

脊柱 **jǐzhù** spine ◊ spinal

记住 **jìzhù** remember; memorize

脊椎 **jǐzhuī** vertebra

机组 **jīzǔ** air crew

驹 **jū** foal

局 **jú** office; bureau

举 **jǔ** raise; hold up

锯 **jù** saw

聚 **jù** assemble

剧 **jù** drama; play; theater

捐 **juān** donate; contribute

卷 **juǎn** roll; coil ◊ frizzy

卷 **juàn** volume

圈 **juàn** pen; enclosure

卷尺 **juǎnchǐ** tape measure

卷发 **juǎnfà** curly hair

绢纺 **juànfǎng** silk spinning

捐款 **juānkuǎn** donation; contribution

卷心菜 **juǎnxīn cài** cabbage

捐赠 **juānzèng** donate; contribute

举办 **jǔbàn** organize; hold

具备 **jùbèi** own; have

剧本 **jùběn** (stage) play

局部 **júbù** partial ◊ partially

巨大 **jùdà** enormous

掘 **jué** dig

觉察 **juéchá** perceive

觉得 **juéde** feel; think

决定 **juédìng** decide ◊ decision

绝对 **juéduì** absolute; total ◊ definitely; absolutely

绝妙 **juémiào** sensational; magic

诀窍 **juéqiào** knack

决赛 **juésài** final SPORT

角色 **juésè** part

绝食 **juéshí** hunger strike

爵士音乐 **juéshì yīnyuè** jazz

爵士乐队 **juéshì yuèduì**

jazz band

决算 **juésuàn** balance (sheet)

掘土机 **juétǔjī** excavator

绝望 **juéwàng** despair

决心 **juéxīn** determination

决议 **juéyì** decision; resolution

鞠躬 **jūgōng** bow

句号 **jùhào** period

聚会 **jùhuì** gathering; get-together

聚集 **jùjí** assemble; gather

拘谨 **jūjǐn** reserved

拒绝 **jùjué** refuse; reject ◊ refusal; rejection

俱乐部 **jùlèbù** club

距离 **jùlí** distance ◊ apart

拘留 **jūliú** detain; intern ◊ detention

居留 **jūliú** stay; reside

居留证 **jūliúzhèng** residence permit

局面 **júmiàn** situation

居民 **jūmín** inhabitant; resident

军 **jūn** army

均 **jūn** same; equal

军备 **jūnbèi** armament

均等 **jūnděng** equal ◊ equality

军队 **jūnduì** army; the military; troops

军官 **jūnguān** officer MIL

军舰 **jūnjiàn** warship

峻岭 **jùnlǐng** high mountains

军人 **jūnrén** serviceman

军事 **jūnshì** military

军匀 **jūnyún** even ◊ evenly

君子 **jūnzǐ** gentleman

巨人 **jùrén** giant

沮丧 **jǔsàng** depressed

拘束 **jūshù** awkward; constrained; unnatural

据说… **jùshuō…** it is said (that)…; they say (that) …

具体 **jùtǐ** concrete; definite

举行 **jǔxíng** organize; hold

具有 **jùyǒu** own; have

剧院 **jùyuàn** theater; opera house

举止 **jǔzhǐ** conduct; behavior

居住 **jūzhù** live

橘子 **júzi** mandarin orange

句子 **jùzi** sentence GRAM

锯子 **jùzi** saw

# K

卡 **kǎ** card

卡车 **kǎchē** truck

咖啡 **kāfēi** coffee

咖啡馆 **kāfēiguǎn** café

开 **kāi** open; turn on; start; drive; boil

揩 **kāi** wipe

开车 **kāichē** drive (a car)

开端 **kāiduān** start

开发 **kāifā** develop

开关 **kāiguān** switch

揩汗 **kāihàn** wipe away perspiration

开花 **kāihuā** bloom; blossom

开会 **kāihuì** hold a meeting

开阔 **kāikuò** extensive

开朗 **kāilǎng** outgoing; cheerful

开幕 **kāimù** open

开头 **kāitóu** start

开拓 **kāituò** pioneering

开玩笑 **kāi wánxiào** make a joke

凯旋 **kǎixuán** triumph

开业 **kāiyè** open a business

开支 **kāizhī** expenditure; expenses

砍 **kǎn** fell; chop

看 **kàn** see

看病 **kànbìng** see a doctor

看穿 **kànchuān** see through

砍伐 **kǎnfá** fell *trees*

看法 **kànfǎ** view; idea

康采恩 **kāngcǎi'ēn** group; concern

康复 **kāngfù** recuperate

抗菌素 **kàngjūnsù** antibiotic

慷慨 **kāngkǎi** generous

抗体 **kàngtǐ** antibody

看管 **kānguǎn** guard; look after

抗议 **kàngyì** protest

看护 **kānhù** look after; nurse

看见 **kànjiàn** see

看望 **kànwàng** visit

刊物 **kānwù** publication; periodical

烤 **kǎo** barbecue; broil; roast; bake ◊ barbecued; broiled; roasted; baked

考 **kǎo** test *student*; take *exam*

靠 **kào** lean against; be near;

rely on

靠岸 kào'àn dock

靠背 kàobèi back

考查 kǎochá examine

靠窗座位 kàochuāng zuòwèi window seat

考古学 kǎogǔ xué archeology

靠拢 kàolǒng move closer; close up

烤炉 kǎolú oven

考虑 kǎolǜ consider; think over

考试 kǎoshì exam

卡片 kǎpiàn card

棵 kē *measure word for trees*

颗 kē *measure word for small round things*

科 kē department

壳 ké shell

渴 kě thirst ◊ thirsty

可 kě can; may ◊ -able

课 kè class; lesson; subject

克 kè gram

客 kè guest

可爱 kě'ài delightful; lovable; cute

课本 kèběn textbook

可变 kěbiàn changeable

客车 kèchē passenger train

课程 kèchéng course; curriculum

客店 kèdiàn guest house; inn

刻度 kèdù scale

克服 kèfú overcome

可观 kěguān substantial

客观 kèguān objective

可贵 kěguì valuable; praiseworthy

科技 kējì science and technology

可敬 kějìng worthy; venerable

可靠 kěkào reliable

可可 kěkě cocoa

可口 kěkǒu tasty

刻苦 kèkǔ hard-working

可怜 kělián pitiful; pitiable

科目 kēmù subject

啃 kěn chew; gnaw; nibble

肯定 kěndìng certain; positive GRAM ◊ certainly ◊ it's a certainty (that)...

可能 kěnéng possibility ◊ possible ◊ possibly; maybe

可能性 kěnéngxìng possibility; probability

坑 kēng ditch; pit

坑道 kēngdào gallery; tunnel

恳求 kěnqiú implore; plead for ◊ plea

可怕 **kěpà** terrible; formidable

客气 **kèqi** polite; friendly

客人 **kèrén** visitor; guest

瞌睡 **kēshuì** sleepy

咳嗽 **késou** cough

课堂 **kètáng** classroom; lecture theater

客厅 **kètīng** living room

磕头 **kētóu** kowtow

渴望 **kěwàng** crave; long for ◊ craving; longing ◊ eager; wistful

可恶 **kěwù** horrible

可惜 **kěxī** what a shame; unfortunately

可笑 **kěxiào** ridiculous; comical

可信 **kěxìn** credible; reliable

科学 **kēxué** science ◊ scientific

科学家 **kēxuéjiā** scientist

可疑 **kěyí** suspicious

可以 **kěyǐ** can; may ◊ not bad ◊ OK

克制 **kèzhì** control oneself

空 **kōng** empty; bare; vacant

恐 **kǒng** be afraid; fear

空 **kòng** spare time

空白 **kòngbái** gap; hole; empty space

恐怖 **kǒngbù** terror

空洞 **kōngdòng** empty

空腹 **kōngfù** empty stomach

控告 **kònggào** charge; sue

恐慌 **kǒnghuāng** panic

空间 **kōngjiān** space; room

恐惧 **kǒngjù** fear

空军 **kōngjūn** air force

恐龙 **kǒnglóng** dinosaur

恐怕 **kǒngpà** I'm afraid ◊ perhaps

孔雀 **kǒngquè** peacock

控诉 **kòngsù** bring charges

空调 **kōngtiáo** air-conditioning

空闲 **kòngxián** leisure; leisure time ◊ unoccupied; at a loose end

空想 **kōngxiǎng** daydream

空心 **kōngxīn** hollow

空虚 **kōngxū** empty

控制 **kòngzhì** control

空中小姐 **kōngzhōng xiǎojie** air hostess

孔子 **Kǒngzǐ** Confucius

口 **kǒu** mouth

扣 **kòu** button up

口吃 **kǒuchī** stutter

扣除 **kòuchú** subtract; deduct

口袋 **kǒudài** pocket

口号 **kǒuhào** slogan

口渴 **kǒukě** thirsty

口令 **kǒulìng** password

扣人心弦 **kòu rén xīnxián** gripping

口水 **kǒushuǐ** saliva

口头 **kǒutóu** oral

口香糖 **kǒuxiāng táng** chewing gum

口译 **kǒuyì** interpret ◊ interpretation

口音 **kǒuyīn** accent

口语 **kǒuyǔ** colloquial language

扣子 **kòuzi** button

哭 **kū** cry

枯 **kū** dried up; parched

苦 **kǔ** bitter ◊ bitterness

库 **kù** storehouse; warehouse

裤 **kù** pants

夸 **kuā** praise; exaggerate

胯 **kuà** hip

酷爱 **kù'ài** love passionately

块 **kuài** piece; *measure word for money*

快 **kuài** quick; sharp ◊ quickly; soon

快餐 **kuàicān** fast food; quick snack

快车 **kuàichē** fast train

快感 **kuàigǎn** pleasurable feeling; thrill

会计 **kuàijì** accounting ◊ accountant

快乐 **kuàilè** joy ◊ happy

筷子 **kuàizi** chopsticks

夸奖 **kuājiǎng** praise

宽 **kuān** broad

款 **kuǎn** sum of money; article

宽敞 **kuānchang** spacious

宽度 **kuāndù** width

筐 **kuāng** basket

框 **kuàng** frame

矿藏 **kuàngcáng** mineral resources

矿工 **kuànggōng** miner

旷工 **kuànggōng** skip work

狂欢节 **kuánghuānjié** carnival

旷课 **kuàngkè** play truant

况且 **kuàngqiě** furthermore

矿泉水 **kuàngquánshuǐ** mineral water

狂热 **kuángrè** feverish

矿山 **kuàngshān** mine

矿石 **kuàngshí** ore

狂妄 **kuángwàng** arrogant; presumptuous

矿物 **kuàngwù** mineral

宽阔 **kuānkuò** wide

宽容 **kuānróng** lenient

宽恕 kuānshù forgive

跨越 kuàyuè pass; exceed

夸张 kuāzhāng exaggerate ◊ exaggerated

裤衩 kùchǎ underpants

库存 kùcún inventory

裤兜 kùdōu pants pocket

亏 kuī sustain losses

盔 kuī helmet

葵花 kuíhuā sunflower

傀儡 kuǐlěi puppet

亏损 kuīsǔn deficit; loss ◊ make a loss

溃疡 kuìyáng ulcer

馈赠 kuìzèng give a present

捆 kǔn bundle

困 kùn tired

苦恼 kǔnǎo worry

哭闹纠缠 kūnào jiūchán

whine

昆虫 kūnchóng insect

困惑 kùnhuò confused; perplexed ◊ perplexity

困倦 kùnjuàn sleepy

困难 kùnnan difficult ◊ difficulty

阔 kuò wide; rich

扩大 kuòdà expand; enlarge ◊ expansion; enlargement

括号 kuòhào parenthesis

扩建 kuòjiàn extend *house*

扩军 kuòjūn arm; build up the army

阔气 kuòqi wealthy

哭诉 kūsù moan

枯萎 kūwěi wilting

枯燥 kūzào boring

裤子 kùzi pants

## L

拉 lā pull; draw; drag

辣 là spicy

蜡 là wax

喇叭 lǎba loudspeaker; horn

拉肚子 lādùzi diarrhea

来 lái come

来回 láihuí back and forth

来历 láilì origin

来临 láilín approach; come

来往 láiwǎng contact; dealings

来由 láiyóu reason

来源 láiyuán source

垃圾 lājī garbage

辣椒 làjiāo chili pepper

拉链 lāliàn zipper

喇嘛 **lǎma** lama

栏 **lán** railing; hurdle

拦 **lán** block

蓝 **lán** blue

篮 **lán** basket

懒 **lǎn** lazy

缆 **lǎn** cable; rope

滥 **làn** excessive

烂 **làn** decayed

蓝宝石 **lánbǎoshí** sapphire

缆车 **lǎnchē** cable car

懒惰 **lǎnduò** lazy

狼 **láng** wolf

浪 **làng** wave

栏杆 **lángān** railings

朗读 **lǎngdú** read aloud

浪费 **làngfèi** waste

浪漫 **làngmàn** romantic ◊ romance

朗诵 **lǎngsòng** read out

榔头 **lángtou** hammer

懒汉 **lǎnhàn** bum

拦河坝 **lánhébà** dam

烂泥 **lànní** mud

篮球 **lánqiú** basketball

阑尾炎 **lánwěiyán** appendicitis

懒洋洋 **lǎnyángyáng** unenthusiastic; listless

蓝眼睛 **lányǎnjing** blue eyes ◊ blue-eyed

滥用 **lànyòng** misuse; abuse

篮子 **lánzi** basket

牢 **láo** prison ◊ solid; sturdy

老 **lǎo** old

老板 **lǎobǎn** boss

劳动 **láodòng** work; labor

劳动日 **láodòngrì** working day

牢固 **láogù** solid; durable

老虎 **lǎohǔ** tiger

老虎机 **lǎohǔjī** slot machine

老虎钳 **lǎohǔqián** pliers; pincers

老家 **lǎojiā** home town

老年 **lǎonián** geriatric ◊ old age

老前辈 **lǎoqiánbèi** senior citizen; senior partner

老人 **lǎorén** old person

老实 **lǎoshi** honest

老师 **lǎoshī** teacher

老是 **lǎoshì** always

老鼠 **lǎoshǔ** rat; mouse

劳损 **láosǔn** strain

邋遢 **lāta** messy *person*; scruffy

蜡烛 **làzhú** candle

勒 **lè** rein in; check

乐 **lè** joy; happiness

乐观 **lèguān** optimistic; positive ◊ optimism

雷 **léi** thunder

累 **léi** accumulate

泪 **lèi** tear

累 **lèi** tired

类 **lèi** sort

肋骨 **lèigǔ** rib

雷鸣 **léimíng** thunder

类似 **lèisì** similar

类型 **lèixíng** type

雷雨 **léiyǔ** thunderstorm

雷阵雨 **léizhènyǔ** thundery shower

累赘 **léizhuì** cumbersome

棱 **léng** edge

冷 **lěng** cold

冷淡 **lěngdàn** chilly; indifferent

冷冻 **lěngdòng** freeze ◊ frozen

冷静 **lěngjìng** calm

冷酷 **lěngkù** cold-blooded

冷却 **lěngquè** cool ◊ cooling

冷烫 **lěngtàng** cold wave

冷饮 **lěngyǐn** cold drinks

棱锥体 **léngzhuītǐ** pyramid

乐趣 **lèqù** enjoyment; fun

勒索 **lèsuǒ** extort; blackmail

乐意 **lèyì** willingly

乐园 **lèyuán** paradise; amusement park

乐于助人 **lèyú zhùrén**

obliging

梨 **lí** pear

犁 **lí** plow

离 **lí** leave

礼 **lǐ** rite; ritual; etiquette

里 **lǐ** in; inside ◊ li *(measure of distance = 500m)*

力 **lì** strength; power

立 **lì** stand

俩 **liǎ** both; two

连 **lián** link

脸 **liǎn** face

炼 **liàn** refine

练 **liàn** practice; train

链 **liàn** chain

恋爱 **liàn'ài** love

联邦 **liánbāng** federation; union

凉 **liáng** cool; cold

良 **liáng** good

量 **liáng** measure

两 **liǎng** two

量 **liàng** capacity; quantity; volume

亮 **liàng** bright; light; clear

辆 **liàng** *measure word for vehicles*

量 **liàng** capacity

炼钢厂 **liàngāngchǎng** steelworks

亮度 **liàngdù** brightness

谅解 **liàngjiě** understand; forgive

量具 **liángjù** measuring instrument

凉快 **liángkuai** pleasantly cool

两栖 **liǎngqī** amphibious

踉跄 **liàngqiàng** stagger; sway

粮食 **liángshi** grain; cereal

凉台 **liángtái** balcony

凉鞋 **liángxié** sandal

良心 **liángxīn** conscience

两种 **liǎngzhǒng** two kinds

联合 **liánhé** unite; form an alliance ◊ alliance; union ◊ united

脸红 **liǎnhóng** blush

连接 **liánjiē** connect

联结 **liánjiē** connect

连裤袜 **liánkùwà** pantyhose

连累 **liánlèi** cause difficulty for

联盟 **liánméng** coalition; alliance

怜悯 **liánmǐn** sympathize with

脸盆 **liǎnpén** washbasin

莲蓬头 **liánpéngtóu** shower head

连日 **liánrì** lasting for days

炼乳 **liànrǔ** condensed milk

联系 **liánxì** contact; connect ◊ connection

练习 **liànxí** practice

连续 **liánxù** continuous; uninterrupted

连衣裙 **liányīqún** dress

帘子 **liánzi** curtain

料 **liào** material

了不起 **liǎobùqǐ** terrific

疗法 **liáofǎ** therapy

了结 **liǎojié** deal with; settle

了解 **liǎojiě** understand; know

料理 **liàolǐ** take care of ◊ Japanese cooking

聊天 **liáotiān** chat

疗养 **liáoyǎng** convalesce

疗养院 **liáoyǎngyuàn** sanitarium

篱笆 **líba** fence

离别 **líbié** separate; part from

立场 **lìchǎng** standpoint

列 **liè** list ◊ column; row ◊ *measure word for trains*

裂 **liè** crack; split

烈 **liè** intense

劣 **liè** inferior; poor

列车 **lièchē** train

裂缝 **lièfèng** crack

裂痕 lièhén crack

烈酒 lièjiǔ spirits

列举 lièjǔ enumerate

猎枪 lièqiāng shotgun

猎区 lièqū hunting ground

猎人 lièrén hunter

烈士 lièshì martyr

理发 lǐfà haircut; hairdressing; style hair

立法 lìfǎ legislate ◊ legislation ◊ legislative

立方米 lìfāngmǐ cubic meter

理发师 lǐfàshī hairdresser

理发厅 lǐfàtīng hairdressing salon; barber shop

利害 lìhai severe; tough

离合器 líhéqì clutch

离婚 líhūn divorce; get divorced ◊ divorced

痢疾 lìji dysentery

立即 lìjí immediate ◊ immediately

理解 lǐjiě understand; perceive ◊ understanding

离开 líkāi leave; quit

利率 lìlǜ interest rate

理论 lǐlùn theory ◊ theoretical

厘米 límǐ centimeter

黎明 límíng daybreak

林 lín forest

临 lín overlook ◊ be about to

铃 líng bell

零 líng zero

另 lìng other ◊ in addition

令 lìng order

灵车 língchē hearse

凌晨 língchén early morning

领带 lǐngdài necktie

领导 lǐngdǎo leader; head ◊ lead

领导人 lǐngdǎorén leader

领海 lǐnghǎi territorial waters

领会 lǐnghuì grasp; comprehend

灵魂 línghún soul; spirit

灵活 línghuó flexible

领结 lǐngjié bow tie

伶俐 línglì nimble

陵墓 língmù mausoleum

零钱 língqián change (coins)

灵巧 língqiǎo deft; quick

令人恶心 lìngrén ěxīn disgusting

零食 língshí snacks; candy

领事 lǐngshì consul

领事馆 lǐngshì guǎn consulate

零售 língshòu retail

另外 lìngwài other ◊ in addition; apart from that

零星 língxīng scattered

领袖 lǐngxiù leader

零用钱 língyòng qián allowance

领域 lǐngyù territory; field

林火 línhuǒ forest fire

邻居 línjū neighbor

林区 línqū forestry district

吝啬 lìnsè miserly

吝啬鬼 lìnsèguǐ miser

临时 línshí provisional; temporary; casual

临时工 línshígōng temp

林荫道 línyīndào avenue

淋浴 línyù shower

礼炮 lǐpào salute

礼品 lǐpǐn gift

离奇 líqí strange; uncanny

离奇 líqí strange

沥青 lìqīng asphalt

例如 lìrú for example

利润 lìrùn profit

历史 lìshǐ history

历史性 lìshǐxìng historic; historical

理所当然 lǐsuǒdāngrán naturally; of course

礼堂 lǐtáng (ceremonial) hall; church

立体声装置 lìtǐshēng zhuāngzhì stereo system

流 liú flow; run

硫 liú sulfur

留 liú stay

柳 liǔ willow

六 liù six

流产 liúchǎn miscarriage

流畅 liúchàng smooth; fluent

流传 liúchuán spread

留话 liúhuà leave a message

留念 liúniàn keep as a memento

流逝 liúshì slip away; pass

六十 liùshí sixty

流亡 liúwáng exile

流行 liúxíng fashionable; popular

流行病 liúxíngbìng epidemic

流行歌曲 liúxíng gēqǔ pop song

留学 liúxué study abroad

留言 liúyán leave a message

流言蜚语 liúyán fēiyǔ gossip; scandal

六月 liùyuè June

流走 liúzǒu drain; flow away

例外 lìwài exception

利息 lìxī interest

理性 lǐxìng reason; sense

力学 lìxué mechanics

利益 **lìyì** interest; advantage; benefit

利用 **lìyòng** use, take advantage of

鲤鱼 **lǐyú** carp

理智 **lǐzhì** reason (*faculty*)

荔枝 **lìzhī** lychee

李子 **lǐzi** plum

里子 **lǐzi** lining

例子 **lìzi** example; case

聋 **lóng** deaf ◊ deafness

垄断 **lǒngduàn** monopolize ◊ monopoly

龙卷风 **lóngjuǎn fēng** tornado

龙虾 **lóngxiā** lobster

隆重 **lóngzhòng** festive

笼子 **lóngzi** cage

楼 **lóu** building; floor, story

搂 **lōu** hug

漏 **lòu** leak

楼层 **lóucéng** floor, story

漏洞 **lòudòng** leak; loophole

楼房 **lóufáng** building

楼梯 **lóutī** stairs

炉 **lú** oven

路 **lù** measure word for bus routes

鹿 **lù** deer

路 **lù** road; way; possibility

驴 **lǘ** donkey

铝 **lǚ** aluminum

氯 **lǜ** chlorine

绿 **lǜ** green

率 **lǜ** level; amount; rate (*of pay*)

卵 **luǎn** (human) egg

乱 **luàn** in a mess ◊ chaos

路标 **lùbiāo** landmark; roadsign

铝箔 **lǚbó** aluminum foil

绿茶 **lǜchá** green tea

旅程 **lǚchéng** itinerary

露出 **lùchū** expose, reveal

陆地 **lùdì** land; mainland ◊ terrestrial

旅店 **lǚdiàn** inn

路过 **lùguò** pass by

绿化 **lǜhuà** plant up

鹿角 **lùjiǎo** antlers

旅客 **lǚkè** passenger

履历 **lǚlì** résumé

陆路 **lùlù** track; overland route

轮 **lún** wheel; round (*of drinks*)

轮船 **lúnchuán** ship

论点 **lùndiǎn** thesis

轮换 **lúnhuàn** alternate

论据 **lùnjù** argument (*reasoning*)

轮廓 **lúnkuò** contour,

outline; silhouette

轮流 **lúnliú** alternate

轮胎 **lúntāi** tire

论文 **lùnwén** treatise

轮椅 **lúnyǐ** wheelchair

锣 **luó** gong

裸 **luǒ** naked

落 **luò** fall; sink; land (*of ball etc*); set (*of sun*)

萝卜 **luóbo** turnip; radish

落后 **luòhòu** backward; behind, trailing ◊ be behind

逻辑 **luóji** logic ◊ logical

罗马数字 **luómǎ shùzì** Roman numerals

螺母 **luómǔ** nut (*for bolt*)

络腮胡子 **luòsāi húzi** full beard

螺丝 **luósī** screw

螺丝刀 **luósīdāo** screwdriver

裸体 **luǒtǐ** naked

裸体像 **luǒtǐxiàng** nude (*painting*)

骆驼 **luòtuo** camel

螺纹 **luówén** thread (*of screw*)

螺旋 **luóxuán** spiral

录取 **lùqǔ** admit

律师 **lǜshī** attorney

露水 **lùshuǐ** dew

芦笋 **lúsǔn** asparagus

露天 **lùtiān** open-air

芦苇 **lúwěi** reed

录像 **lùxiàng** video; video recording

录像带 **lùxiàng dài** video cassette

录像机 **lùxiàngjī** video recorder, VCR

履行 **lǚxíng** fulfill ◊ fulfillment

旅行 **lǚxíng** travel

旅行社 **lǚxíng shè** travel agency

旅行支票 **lǚxíng zhīpiào** traveler's check

陆续 **lùxù** one after the other

录音 **lùyīn** recording ◊ record ◊ audio

录音机 **lùyīnjī** cassette player; cassette recorder; tape recorder

旅游业 **lǚyóu yè** tourism

旅游者 **lǚyóuzhě** tourist

旅游指南 **lǚyóu zhǐnán** guidebook

炉子 **lúzi** stove; furnace

# M

妈 **mā** mom

抹 **mā** wipe

麻 **má** hemp

马 **mǎ** horse

骂 **mà** curse

马表 **mǎbiǎo** stopwatch

抹布 **mābù** cloth; dish cloth

马达 **mǎdá** motor; engine

麻烦 **máfan** bother

吗啡 **mǎfēi** morphine

埋 **mái** bury

买 **mǎi** buy

卖 **mài** sell

脉管 **màiguǎn** blood vessel

脉搏 **màibó** pulse

迈步 **màibù** stride

埋藏 **máicáng** bury

卖方 **màifāng** seller

麦克风 **màikèfēng** microphone

麦片 **màipiàn** rolled oats

卖俏 **màiqiào** flirt

麦乳精 **màirǔjīng** malted milk

卖艺 **màiyì** work as a performer

卖淫 **màiyín** prostitute

onself

埋葬 **máizàng** bury

买主 **mǎizhǔ** purchaser; customer

麦子 **màizi** wheat

麻将 **májiàng** mah-jong

马克思主义 **Mǎkèsīzhǔyì** Marxism ◊ Marxist

马来西亚 **Mǎláixīyà** Malaysia ◊ Malaysian

马拉松 **mǎlāsōng** marathon

马力 **mǎlì** horsepower

马路 **mǎlù** street

妈妈 **māma** mom

马马虎虎 **mǎmǎhūhū** average

瞒 **mán** conceal

满 **mǎn** full

慢 **màn** slow

满不在乎 **mǎn bú zàihu** not care at all

盲 **máng** blind

忙 **máng** busy ◊ be in a rush

芒果 **mángguǒ** mango

忙碌 **mánglù** be busy

盲目 **mángmù** blind

盲人 **mángrén** blind person

盲文 **mángwén** braille

漫画 **mànhuà** comic

蔓生植物 **mànshēng zhíwù** climbing plant

馒头 **mántou** steamed bun

慢性 **mànxìng** chronic

蔓延 **mànyán** spread; sprawl (*of city*); be overrrun with ◊ contagious; sprawling

满意 **mǎnyì** satisfied

满月 **mǎnyuè** full moon

慢走 **mànzǒu** goodbye

满足 **mǎnzú** satisfied ◊ satisfy

猫 **māo** cat

锚 **máo** anchor

毛 **máo** hair; bristles; wool; mao (*Chinese money*)

矛 **máo** spear

铆 **máo** rivet

冒 **mào** give off

毛笔 **máobǐ** writing brush

毛虫 **máochóng** caterpillar

冒充 **màochōng** impersonate

冒号 **màohào** colon GRAM

毛巾 **máojīn** towel; washcloth

冒浓烟 **mào nóngyān** give off smoke

毛皮 **máopí** coat

茂盛 **màoshèng** flourishing

毛毯 **máotǎn** blanket

猫头鹰 **māotóuyīng** owl

毛线 **máoxiàn** knitting wool

冒险 **màoxiǎn** take a risk ◊ risky

冒险家 **màoxiǎnjiā** adventurer

毛衣 **máoyī** sweater

贸易 **màoyì** trade

贸易关系 **màoyì guānxi** trade relations

毛毡 **máozhān** felt

麻雀 **máquè** sparrow

骂人话 **màrénhuà** swearword

马上 **mǎshàng** immediately, right now

马蹄 **mǎtí** hoof

码头 **mǎtóu** dock; wharf; pier

马尾辫 **mǎwěibiàn** pigtail

马戏团 **mǎxìtuán** circus

蚂蚁 **mǎyǐ** ant

麻油 **máyóu** sesame oil

马掌 **mǎzhǎng** horseshoe

麻醉 **mázuì** anesthetize ◊ anesthesia

麻醉剂 **mázuìjì** anesthetic; narcotic

煤 **méi** coal

霉 **méi** mold

没 **méi** not ◊ have not

眉 **méi** eyebrow

每 **měi** every; each; per

美 **měi** lovely

妹 **mèi** younger sister

每次 **měicì** each time

梅毒 **méidú** syphilis

每个人 **měigèrén** everyone

没关系 **méi guānxi** it doesn't matter

玫瑰 **méigui** rose

美国 **Měiguó** America, USA ◊ American

美国人 **Měiguórén** American

美好 **měihǎo** wonderful; good

美化 **měihuà** beautify; brighten up

美丽 **měilì** beautiful

魅力 **mèilì** attraction; charm; glamor

眉毛 **méimao** eyebrow

美貌 **měimào** looks

妹妹 **mèimei** younger sister

美妙 **měimiào** wonderful

煤气 **méiqì** coal gas

煤气灶 **méiqìzào** gas stove

美容 **měiróng** cosmetic

美术片 **měishùpiàn**

animation

每天 **měitiān** daily ◊ every day

每晚 **měiwǎn** every evening

美味 **měiwèi** tidbit

美学 **měixué** esthetics

煤油 **méiyóu** paraffin; kerosene

没有 **méiyǒu** not have ◊ without

美元 **měiyuán** US dollar

每月 **měiyuè** monthly

闷 **mēn** stuffy

门 **mén** door

梦 **mèng** dream

蒙蔽 **méngbì** deceive ◊ deception

蒙古 **Měnggǔ** Mongolia ◊ Mongolian

梦见 **mèngjiàn** dream about

猛烈 **měngliè** fierce; violent; passionate

蒙蒙细雨 **méngméng xìyǔ** drizzle

蒙骗 **mēngpiàn** deceive

梦想 **mèngxiǎng** dream

门槛 **ménkǎn** threshold

门牌号 **ménpáihào** house number

门票 **ménpiào** entrance ticket

闷热 **mēnrè** clammy; sultry

门闩 **ménshuān** bolt; latch

闷 **mèn stickig** bored

门诊部 **ménzhěnbù** outpatients

门诊治疗 **ménzhěn zhìliáo** outpatient treatment

门柱 **ménzhù** goalpost

迷 **mí** fan

谜 **mí** mystery; riddle

米 **mǐ** rice; meter

密 **mì** thick; close

蜜 **mì** honey

棉 **mián** cotton

免 **miǎn** avoid; prohibit

面 **miàn** face; side; flour; noodle

面包 **miànbāo** bread

面包店 **miànbāo diàn** bakery

免费 **miǎnfèi** free (*no charge*)

棉花 **miánhua** cotton

面积 **miànjī** area; proportions

面具 **miànjù** mask

面孔 **miànkǒng** face

勉励 **miǎnlì** encourage

面貌 **miànmào** face; appearance

面前 **miànqián** in front of

勉强 **miǎnqiáng** reluctant ◊ reluctance ◊ reluctantly

面纱 **miànshā** veil

面食 **miànshí** pasta; pastry

面试 **miànshì** (job) interview

面熟 **miànshú** seem familiar

免税 **miǎnshuì** tax free; dutyfree

面条 **miàntiáo** noodle

面团 **miàntuán** dough

绵羊 **miányáng** sheep

免疫 **miǎnyì** immune ◊ immunity

苗 **miáo** young plant

秒 **miǎo** second

庙 **miào** temple; temple market

妙 **miào** wonderful

描绘 **miáohuì** portray; describe

妙极了 **miàojíle** fantastic

苗圃 **miáopǔ** nursery (*for plants*)

苗条 **miáotiao** slim

描写 **miáoxiě** describe

瞄准 **miáozhǔn** aim ◊ be aimed at

弥补 **míbǔ** make up for; recoup; rectify ◊ compensation

灭 **miè** put out

灭火 **mièhuǒ** put out a fire

灭火器 **mièhuǒqì** fire extinguisher

灭绝 **mièjué** wipe out

灭亡 **mièwáng** go under; be ruined

蜜蜂 **mìfēng** bee

密封 **mìfēng** close; seal

猕猴桃 **míhóutáo** kiwi fruit

迷惑 **míhuo** mislead; confuse

米酒 **mǐjiǔ** rice wine

迷路 **mílù** lose one's way

秘密 **mìmì** secret ◊ secretly

密谋 **mìmóu** conspire, plot

民 **mín** people; folk

名 **míng** name

明 **míng** bright; light

命 **mìng** life

敏感 **mǐngǎn** sensitive ◊ sensitivity

明白 **míngbai** understand ◊ clear

名称 **míngchēng** name; designation

民歌 **míngē** folk song

明亮 **míngliàng** bright ◊ brightly ◊ brightness

命令 **mìnglìng** command

命名 **mìngmíng** name

明年 **míngnián** next year

名牌 **míngpái** well-known brand

名片 **míngpiàn** card

名人 **míngrén** prominent figure; celebrity

名声 **míngshēng** reputation

名胜 **míngshèng** scenic spot

明天 **míngtiān** tomorrow

明显 **míngxiǎn** clear ◊ clearly

明星 **míngxīng** star (*movie etc*)

明信片 **míngxìnpiàn** postcard

名誉 **míngyù** fame; reputation

命运 **mìngyùn** fate

名字 **míngzi** name

民航 **mínháng** civil aviation

民间 **mínjiān** civil; folk

敏捷 **mǐnjié** quick

民意调查 **mínyì diàochá** poll

民乐 **mínyuè** folk music

民众 **mínzhòng** the people

民主 **mínzhǔ** democracy ◊ democratic

民族 **mínzú** people; ethnic group; nation; nationality

密切 **mìqiè** intimate, close

秘书 **mìshū** secretary ◊ secretarial

迷信 **míxìn** superstitious

谜语 **míyǔ** riddle

蜜月 **mìyuè** honeymoon

摸 **mō** feel

磨 **mó** grind

末 **mò** end

没 **mò** sink

墨 **mò** ink

末班车 **mòbānchē** last bus

漠不关心 **mò bù guānxīn** indifference ◊ indifferent; nonchalant

摩擦 **mócā** friction ◊ rub

模范 **mófàn** example ◊ exemplary

模仿 **mófǎng** imitate; forge ◊ imitation; forgery

磨坊 **mòfáng** mill

蘑菇 **mógū** mushroom

魔鬼 **móguǐ** devil

模糊 **móhú** vague; indistinct; fuzzy; misty ◊ blur ◊ mist over

魔力 **mólì** magic

茉莉 **mòlì** jasmine

莫名其妙 **mò míng qí miào** mysterious

陌生 **mòshēng** strange

没收 **mòshōu** confiscate

摸索 **mōsuǒ** grope

模特儿 **mótèr** model (*fashion*)

摩天大楼 **mótiān dàlóu** skyscraper

摩托 **mótuō** motor; engine

摩托车 **mótuōchē** motorcycle

某 **mǒu** certain; some

某人 **mǒurén** someone

谋杀 **móushā** murder

末尾 **mòwěi** end

模型 **móxíng** model; prototype; cast

墨鱼 **mòyú** cuttlefish

母 **mǔ** mother ◊ female

木 **mù** wood

墓 **mù** grave

目 **mù** eye

牧 **mù** tend *livestock*

暮 **mù** evening

母爱 **mǔ'ài** motherly love

墓碑 **mùbēi** gravestone

目标 **mùbiāo** target

木柴 **mùchái** firewood

牧场 **mùchǎng** pasture

目的 **mùdì** purpose

木耳 **mù'ěr** wood-ear mushroom

木筏 **mùfá** raft

木工 **mùgōng** carpenter

目光 **mùguāng** look

母鸡 **mǔjī** hen

募捐 **mùjuān** collect donations

木刻 **mùkè** wood engraving

目录 **mùlù** catalog; directory; list; table of contents

牧民 **mùmín** herdsman

母牛 **mǔniú** cow

木偶 **mù'ǒu** puppet

目前 **mùqián** at present

母亲 **mǔqīn** mother

暮色降临 **mùsè jiànglín** get dark

穆斯林 **Mùsīlín** Muslim

木炭 **mùtàn** charcoal

母语 **mǔyǔ** mother tongue

拇指 **mǔzhǐ** thumb

母猪 **mǔzhū** sow (*pig*)

# N

拿 **ná** carry (*in hand*); hold

哪个 **nǎge** which; which one

那个 **nàge** that ◊ that one

奶 **nǎi** milk

耐久 **nàijiǔ** durable

耐力 **nàilì** stamina

奶奶 **nǎinai** grandma

耐心 **nàixīn** patience ◊ patiently

耐用 **nàiyòng** hard-wearing ◊ wear well

奶油 **nǎiyóu** cream

奶嘴 **nǎizuǐ** pacifier; nipple

哪里 **nǎli** where

那里 **nàli** there

南 **nán** south ◊ southern; southerly

难 **nán** difficult

男 **nán** man ◊ male

南边 **nánbiān** south; the south side

南部 **nánbù** south

南方 **nánfāng** south

南风 **nánfēng** southerly wind

难过 **nánguò** sad

男孩 **nánhái** boy

南极 **nánjí** South Pole

难堪 **nánkān** embarrassed

难看 **nánkàn** ugly

难免 **nánmiǎn** hard to avoid

男朋友 **nánpéngyou** boyfriend

男人 **nánrén** man, male

难受 **nánshòu** feel ill-at-ease

难为情 **nánwéiqíng** ashamed; embarrassed

男性 **nánxìng** male

南亚 **Nán Yà** South Asia

脑 **nǎo** brain

闹 **nào** noisy

恼怒 **nǎonù** annoyed

闹事 **nàoshì** make a scene; riot

脑髓 **nǎosuǐ** brain

脑震荡 **nǎozhèndàng** concussion

闹钟 **nàozhōng** alarm clock

纳税人 **nàshuìrén** taxpayer

哪些 **nǎxiē** which; which ones

那些 **nàxiē** those

拿走 **názǒu** remove

内 **nèi** inside ◊ inner; internal

内部 **nèibù** inside ◊ internal; inner ◊ internally

内地 **nèidì** interior; inland

内阁 **nèigé** cabinet POL

内疚 **nèijiù** guilt; guilty conscience ◊ guilty

内科医生 **nèikē yīshēng** internist

内容 **nèiróng** content

内衣 **nèiyī** underwear

内政 **nèizhèng** domestic policy; domestic affairs

嫩 **nèn** tender

能干 **nénggàn** capable

能力 **nénglì** ability

能手 **néngshǒu** expert

泥 **ní** mud

你 **nǐ** you (*singular*)

年 **nián** year ◊ annual

念 **niàn** think of; read (out loud); study

年初 **niánchū** start of the year

年底 **niándǐ** end of the year

酿 **niàng** ferment; brew

酿酒厂 **niàngjiǔchǎng** distillery; winery

粘合剂 **niánhéjì** adhesive

粘糊糊 **niánhūhū** sticky

年龄 **niánlíng** age

年青 **niánqīng** young

碾碎 **niǎnsuì** grind

念头 **niàntou** thought, idea

粘土 **niántǔ** clay

粘液 **niányè** mucus

鸟 **niǎo** bird

尿 **niào** urine

鸟笼 **niǎolóng** birdcage

尿片 **niàopiàn** diaper

昵称 **nìchēng** pet name

你的 **nǐde** your ◊ yours

(singular)

拟订 **nǐdìng** draft

捏造 **niēzào** invent

尼姑 **nígū** Buddhist nun

你好 **nǐ hǎo** hi

霓虹灯管 **níhóngdēngguǎn** neon strip

你们 **nǐmen** you (plural)

您 **nín** you (polite)

拧 **níng** twist; pinch

拧干 **nínggān** wring

凝固 **nínggù** freeze; congeal

宁静 **níngjìng** peace ◊ peaceful

柠檬 **níngméng** lemon

柠檬汽水 **níngméng qìshuǐ** lemonade

凝视 **níngshì** gaze; peer; gaze at ◊ stare; gaze

宁愿 **nìngyuàn** would rather

牛 **niú** cattle; cow

牛犊 **niúdú** calf

牛奶 **niúnǎi** (cow's) milk

牛奶加工 **niúnǎi jiāgōng** dairy

牛肉 **niúròu** beef

扭伤 **niǔshāng** sprain

泥瓦工 **níwǎgōng** bricklayer

脓 **nóng** pus

弄 **nòng** do; make; obtain

脓包 **nóngbāo** pimple

农村 **nóngcūn** countryside

弄错 **nòngcuò** be mistaken

浓厚 **nónghòu** thick; strong

农户 **nónghù** farm

弄坏 **nònghuài** break

弄清 **nòngqīng** make clear

农田 **nóngtián** field

农业 **nóngyè** agriculture ◊ agricultural

怒 **nù** anger; rage

女 **nǚ** female; feminine

暖 **nuǎn** warm

暖房 **nuǎnfáng** hothouse

暖和 **nuǎnhuo** warm

暖气 **nuǎnqì** central heating

疟疾 **nüèjí** malaria

女儿 **nǚ'ér** daughter

女孩 **nǚhái** girl

怒号 **nùháo** howl; roar

怒吼 **nùhǒu** howl; roar; bellow

女皇 **nǚhuáng** empress

奴隶 **núlì** slave

努力 **nǔlì** attempt; endeavor ◊ laborious ◊ struggle; work hard

懦夫 **nuòfū** coward

糯米 **nuòmǐ** glutinous rice

女朋友 **nǚpéngyou** girlfriend

女人 **nǚrén** woman; female

女神 nǚshén goddess
女生 nǚshēng female student
女士 nǚshì lady ◊ ma'am

◊ Ms
女王 nǚwáng queen
女巫 nǚwū witch
女性 nǚxìng female

# O

藕 ǒu lotus root
偶尔 ǒu'ěr occasionally
欧化 ōuhuà westernize
偶然 ǒurán by chance; occasionally
呕吐 ǒutù vomit
欧洲 Ōuzhōu Europe ◊ European

# P

爬 pá climb; crawl
耙 pá rake
怕 pà fear
拍 pāi take *photograph*; shoot *movie*; clap
牌 pái plate; board; brand; card
排 pái line; tier ◊ rank (*in order*); discharge
派别 pàibié group; sect
排斥 páichì exclude; push away
排除 páichú eliminate; cut out; rule out ◊ removal
派出所 pàichūsuǒ police station
排队 páiduì stand in line
排练 páiliàn rehearse ◊ rehearsal
拍卖 pāimài auction
排尿 páiniào urinate
排球 páiqiú volleyball
拍摄 pāishè film; photograph
拍手 pāishǒu applaud
排水 páishuǐ drainage
排水工程 páishuǐ gōngchéng sewerage
排水沟 páishuǐgōu gutter
拍照 pāizhào photograph

拍子 **pāizi** bat; racket; club; stick

牌子 **páizi** sign; nameplate; brand

盘 **pán** dish; plate; set (tennis); *measure word for cassettes*

盼 **pàn** hope for; expect

盘点 **pándiǎn** check; take stock

判断 **pànduàn** judge; make a judgment; pass judgment on

旁 **páng** side

胖 **pàng** fat

旁边 **pángbiān** side

庞大 **pángdà** enormous

旁观 **pángguān** watch

胖乎乎 **pànghūhū** plump

庞然大物 **pángrán dàwù** monster

螃蟹 **pángxiè** crab

胖子 **pàngzi** fatso

判决 **pànjué** pass judgment ◊ judgment, verdict

叛逆 **pànnì** rebel

叛徒 **pàntú** traitor

盘旋 **pánxuán** twist; circle

攀缘 **pānyuán** climb

盘子 **pánzi** plate

抛 **pāo** throw

跑 **pǎo** run; run away

泡 **pào** bubble

炮 **pào** gun

炮兵 **pàobīng** artillery

跑步 **pǎobù** run; jog

泡茶 **pàochá** make tea

刨出 **páochū** dig up

跑道 **pǎodào** runway; racetrack; lane

抛锚 **pāomáo** break down

泡沫 **pàomò** foam; suds; lather

泡沫塑料 **pàomò sùliào** foam (*material*)

抛弃 **pāoqì** abandon; discard

跑腿 **pǎotuǐ** run errands

爬行 **páxíng** creep; crawl

耙子 **pázi** rake

赔 **péi** pay compensation

陪 **péi** accompany

配 **pèi** match, go together

陪伴 **péibàn** accompany

赔本 **péiběn** make a loss

赔偿 **péicháng** compensate ◊ compensation

佩服 **pèifu** admire

配合 **pèihé** cooperate

配给 **pèijǐ** ration

赔礼 **péilǐ** apologize

配偶 **pèi'ǒu** spouse

陪同 **péitóng** escort;

accompany

陪同者 **péitóngzhě** escort; companion

培训 **péixùn** train ◊ training

培养 **péiyǎng** raise; develop; cultivate

配音 **pèiyīn** dub *movie*

培植 **péizhí** cultivate *plants*

喷 **pēn** spray

盆 **pén** bowl; plant pot; *measure word for potted plants*

盆地 **péndì** basin GEOG

喷发胶 **pēnfà jiāo** hair spray

碰 **pèng** touch; knock; push; bump into; meet

碰杯 **pèngbēi** clink glasses

碰见 **pèngjiàn** meet

蓬乱 **péngluàn** unkempt; disheveled

碰碰车 **pèngpèngchē** bumper car

碰巧 **pèngqiǎo** by chance

烹调 **pēngtiáo** cook ◊ cookery ◊ culinary

碰头 **pèngtóu** meet

朋友 **péngyǒu** friend

膨胀 **péngzhàng** expand; bulge; inflate ECON ◊ expansion ◊ puffy

喷壶 **pēnhú** watering can

盆景 **pénjǐng** bonsai

喷气式飞机 **pēnqìshì fēijī** jet plane

喷泉 **pēnquán** fountain

喷嚏 **pēntì** sneeze

披 **pī** put on; drape

脾 **pí** spleen

皮 **pí** skin; hide; leather; shell

癖 **pǐ** addiction; obsession

匹 **pǐ** *measure word for horses*

屁 **pì** fart

篇 **piān** piece of writing; *measure word for paper, books etc*

骗 **piàn** cheat

片 **piàn** slice (*of bread etc*); stretch (*of land etc*); *measure word for pills, slices etc*

偏差 **piānchā** deviation

偏见 **piānjiàn** prejudice

骗局 **piànjú** deceipt; deception; fraud

片刻 **piànkè** moment

偏离 **piānlí** deviate; differ

片面 **piànmiàn** biased

偏僻 **piānpì** remote

偏偏 **piānpiān** deliberately; of all people; just

偏袒 **piāntǎn** bias (*in favor*)

◊ biased

偏头痛 **piāntóutòng** migraine

便宜 **piányi** cheap

篇章 **piānzhāng** chapter

骗子 **piànzi** cheat; fraud; crook

票 **piào** ticket

飘荡 **piāodàng** drift; float

漂亮 **piàoliang** lovely

瓢泼大雨 **piáopō dàyǔ** cloudburst

飘扬 **piāoyáng** flutter; flap; blow

皮包骨 **píbāogǔ** skinny

疲惫 **píbèi** exhausted

皮带 **pídài** leather belt

皮蛋 **pídàn** preserved egg

匹敌 **pídí** equal; evenly matched

撇号 **piěhào** apostrophe

瞥见 **piējiàn** glimpse

批发 **pīfā** wholesale

皮肤 **pífū** skin

皮革 **pígé** leather

皮革制品 **pígé zhìpǐn** leather goods

屁股 **pìgu** butt

癖好 **pǐhào** mania; passion

啤酒 **píjiǔ** beer

啤酒厂 **píjiǔchǎng** brewery

啤酒花 **píjiǔhuā** hops

疲倦 **píjuàn** tire ◊ fatigue ◊ tired; run-down

劈开 **pīkāi** split

疲劳 **píláo** exhausted

皮毛 **pímáo** fur; skin; fleece

品尝 **pǐncháng** taste; sample

频繁 **pínfán** frequently

瓶 **píng** bottle; jar; *measure word for bottles, jars etc*

平 **píng** even

平安到达 **píng'ān dàodá** arrive safe and sound

平常 **píngcháng** usually; normally ◊ common; conventional

平等 **píngděng** equal ◊ equality

平凡 **píngfán** usual; normal

平方 **píngfāng** square MATH

苹果 **píngguǒ** apple

平局 **píngjú** tie; deuce (*in tennis*)

凭据 **píngjù** evidence

平均 **píngjūn** average

凭空 **píngkōng** unfounded

评论 **pínglùn** review; commentary ◊ review; remark

平民 **píngmín** civilian

屏幕 **píngmù** screen

兵乓球 pīngpāngqiú table tennis

平时 píngshí ordinarily; usually

平坦 píngtǎn flat

平息 píngxī appease; calm down

平行 píngxíng parallel

评语 píngyǔ comment; assessment

平原 píngyuán plain

瓶子 píngzi bottle

贫瘠 pínjí barren

贫困 pínkùn poor ◊ poverty

频率 pínlǜ frequency

拼盘 pīnpán cold platter

贫穷 pínqióng poor

品位 pǐnwèi taste

品行 pǐnxíng behavior

贫血 pínxuè anemia ◊ anemic

拼音 pīnyīn pinyin

品种 pǐnzhǒng breed

批评 pīpíng criticism ◊ criticize

脾气 píqi temperament; temper

皮鞋 píxié leather shoes

皮衣 píyī leather garment

批准 pīzhǔn approve ◊ approval

坡 pō slope

破 pò break ◊ broken

破产 pòchǎn go bankrupt ◊ bankruptcy

破坏 pòhuài destroy

破裂 pòliè burst

婆婆 pópo mother-in-law

迫切 pòqiè pressing

破伤风 pòshāngfēng tetanus

迫使 pòshǐ force

剖腹产 pōufùchǎn Cesarean

剖面 pōumiàn profile; section

破晓 pòxiǎo dawn

铺 pū spread; unfold; pave

普遍 pǔbiàn general; universal

瀑布 pùbù waterfall

铺床 pūchuáng make the bed

扑粉 pūfěn powder

曝光 pùguāng expose ◊ exposure

普及 pǔjí generalize; popularize ◊ widespread; universal

扑克 pūkè poker; playing cards

谱曲 **pǔqǔ** compose

菩萨 **Púsà** Bodhisattva; Buddha

铺设 **pūshè** pave; lay

朴素 **pǔsù** simple

葡萄 **pútao** grape; vine

葡萄干 **pútáo gān** raisin

葡萄酒 **pútaojiǔ** wine

葡萄糖 **pútaotáng** glucose

普通 **pǔtōng** ordinary

普通话 **Pǔtōnghuà** Mandarin Chinese

## Q

漆 **qī** paint

七 **qī** seven

期 **qī** period

妻 **qī** wife

鳍 **qí** fin

旗 **qí** flag

骑 **qí** ride; pedal

其 **qí** his; her; its

起 **qǐ** get up

汽 **qì** vapor; steam

器 **qì** utensil; device

气 **qì** air; gas

迄 **qì** until; by

恰当 **qiàdàng** appropriate

千 **qiān** thousand

铅 **qiān** lead (*metal*)

牵 **qiān** pull

签 **qiān** sign

前 **qián** before; in front of ◊ former

钱 **qián** money

潜 **qián** dive; submerge ◊ hidden

浅 **qiǎn** shallow

欠 **qiàn** owe ◊ owed

钱包 **qiánbāo** billfold; purse

前辈 **qiánbèi** senior; elder

前臂 **qiánbì** forearm

浅薄 **qiǎnbó** shallow

虔诚 **qiánchéng** devout; ardent; pious

签订 **qiāndìng** sign; conclude *contract*

前额 **qián'é** forehead; brow

签发 **qiānfā** issue

潜伏 **qiánfú** latent; potential

枪 **qiāng** gun

强 **qiáng** strong

墙 **qiáng** wall

抢 **qiǎng** snatch

墙报 **qiángbào** wall news-sheet

枪毙 **qiāngbì** shoot

墙壁 **qiángbì** wall

强大 **qiángdà** powerful

强盗 **qiángdào** robber; bandit

强调 **qiángdiào** emphasize

强奸 **qiángjiān** rape

抢劫 **qiǎngjié** rob; hold up ◊ robbery; holdup; raid

抢救 **qiǎngjiù** rescue; recover; save

跄踉 **qiàngliàng** stumble

钳工 **qiángōng** fitter

强迫 **qiǎngpò** force; compel

牵挂 **qiānguà** worry about

墙纸 **qiángzhǐ** wallpaper

强壮 **qiángzhuàng** strong; sound; hardy

前景 **qiánjǐng** view; prospects

迁就 **qiānjiù** accommodate

迁居 **qiānjū** move house

千克 **qiānkè** kilogram

牵连 **qiānlián** involve

千米 **qiānmǐ** kilometer

前面 **qiánmian** front ◊ in front; ahead

签名 **qiānmíng** sign ◊ signature

前任 **qiánrèn** predecessor

潜入 **qiánrù** submerge

歉收 **qiànshōu** crop failure

签署 **qiānshǔ** sign

潜水 **qiánshuǐ** dive ◊ diving

潜水艇 **qiánshuǐtǐng** submarine

潜水员 **qiánshuǐyuán** diver

前提 **qiántí** prerequisite; condition

前天 **qiántiān** the day before yesterday

前途 **qiántú** future; prospects

欠妥 **qiàntuǒ** inappropriate

前夕 **qiánxī** eve

前行 **qiánxíng** proceed

谦虚 **qiānxū** modest

前言 **qiányán** foreword; preface

迁移 **qiānyí** move; migrate; transfer

潜意识 **qiányìshí** subconscious

欠债 **qiànzhài** be in debt

签证 **qiānzhèng** visa

钳子 **qiánzi** forceps; pliers; tongs

前奏 **qiánzòu** overture; prelude

敲 **qiāo** knock

桥 **qiáo** bridge

瞧 **qiáo** look

巧 **qiǎo** skillful; coincidental

瞧不起 **qiáobuqǐ** look down on

侨居 **qiáojū** live abroad

巧克力 **qiǎokèlì** chocolate

巧妙 **qiǎomiào** clever; subtle

敲诈 **qiāozhà** blackmail

恰如其分 **qià rú qí fèn** applicable; accurate

洽商 **qiàshāng** negotiate

洽谈 **qiàtán** discuss; negotiate

器材 **qìcái** equipment

汽车 **qìchē** automobile

启程 **qǐchéng** leave

气冲冲 **qìchōngchōng** furious

起初 **qǐchū** at first

气喘 **qìchuǎn** gasp ◊ asthma

起床 **qǐchuáng** get up

期待 **qīdài** expect

祈祷 **qídǎo** pray; wish for

起点 **qǐdiǎn** starting point

企鹅 **qǐ'é** penguin

切 **qiē** cut; carve *meat*

窃 **qiè** steal

怯场 **qièchǎng** stage fright

切除 **qiēchú** remove; cut out

切断 **qiēduàn** cut off

切合实际 **qièhé shíjì** realistic

窃听 **qiètīng** eavesdrop

窃听器 **qiètīngqì** bug

茄子 **qiézi** eggplant

起飞 **qǐfēi** take off ◊ takeoff

气氛 **qìfēn** atmosphere; tone

气愤 **qìfèn** outraged

乞丐 **qǐgài** beggar

汽缸 **qìgāng** cylinder (*engine*)

漆革 **qīgé** patent leather

气功 **qìgōng** qigong (*Chinese system of breath control*)

奇怪 **qíguài** odd ◊ oddly

器官 **qìguān** organ

启航 **qǐháng** sail

漆黑 **qīhēi** pitch black

起哄 **qǐhòng** jeer

气候 **qìhòu** climate

奇迹 **qíjì** miracle ◊ miraculously

迄今 **qìjīn** yet, so far

期刊 **qīkān** periodical; magazine

起立 **qǐlì** stand, rise

起码 **qǐmǎ** at least

起锚 **qǐmáo** weigh anchor

奇妙 **qímiào** wonderful

器皿 **qìmǐn** vessel; container

亲 **qīn** kiss ◊ intimate ◊

relatives

侵 **qīn** invade

禽 **qín** bird

亲爱 **qīn'ài** dear; darling

芹菜 **qíncài** celery

侵犯 **qīnfàn** encroach; breach; violate

勤奋 **qínfèn** hard-working; industrious

氢 **qīng** hydrogen

轻 **qīng** light ◊ lightness

清 **qīng** clear; pure

情 **qíng** feeling

晴 **qíng** sunny; clear

请 **qǐng** please ◊ ask

庆 **qìng** celebrate

清白 **qīngbái** pure; clear; flawless

情报 **qíngbào** intelligence; information; news

轻便 **qīngbiàn** handy

清偿 **qīngcháng** settle; pay off

清晨 **qīngchén** early morning

清楚 **qīngchu** clear ◊ clearly

青春 **qīngchūn** youth

清淡 **qīngdàn** weak; plain

倾倒 **qīngdǎo** tip over; overturn

轻浮 **qīngfú** flighty

情妇 **qíngfù** mistress (*lover*)

请假 **qǐngjià** ask for leave

请教 **qǐngjiào** ask for advice

清洁 **qīngjié** cleanse ◊ clean

情节 **qíngjié** plot

请客 **qǐngkè** invite guests; pick up the tab

情况 **qíngkuàng** situation; scenario

晴朗 **qínglǎng** sunny; clear

清凉 **qīngliáng** refreshing

情侣 **qínglǚ** couple

青年 **qīngnián** youth

青年旅社 **qīngnián lǚshè** youth hostel

青年人 **qīngniánrén** young people; young person

轻拍 **qīngpāi** pat

情人 **qíngrén** lover

青少年 **qīngshàonián** teenager ◊ teenage

轻视 **qīngshì** despise; scorn; put down

轻率 **qīngshuài** impetuous; indiscreet ◊ indiscretion

轻松 **qīngsōng** relaxed

青苔 **qīngtái** moss

请帖 **qǐngtiě** invitation

倾听 **qīngtīng** listen

蜻蜓 **qīngtíng** dragonfly

青铜 **qīngtóng** bronze

青蛙 qīngwā frog

请问 qǐngwèn excuse me; may I ask

请勿吸烟 qǐng wù xīyān no smoking

清洗 qīngxǐ rinse; flush

倾向于 qīngxiàng yú incline toward; tend toward

倾斜 qīngxié slope; tilt; lurch; dip ◊ slanting

轻信 qīngxìn credulous

情绪 qíngxù mood; spirits ◊ sentimental

轻音乐 qīngyīnyuè light music

晴雨表 qíngyǔ biǎo barometer

清真寺 qīngzhēnsì mosque

庆祝 qìngzhù celebrate

庆祝活动 qìngzhù huódòng celebration

勤快 qínkuài hardworking

勤劳 qínláo hardworking

侵略 qīnlüè invade ◊ invasion

亲密 qīnmì close; intimate ◊ intimacy

亲戚 qīnqi relatives

亲切 qīnqiè kind; familiar; genial

侵入 qīnrù intrude

亲手 qīnshǒu in person; with one's own hands

亲属关系 qīnshǔ guānxi relations ◊ related

侵吞 qīntūn embezzle

亲吻 qīnwěn kiss

亲自 qīnzì in person; personally

穷 qióng poor

穷人 qióngrén the poor; poor person

旗袍 qípáo cheongsam

欺骗 qīpiàn deceit; deception ◊ deceive; trick

气球 qìqiú balloon

齐全 qíquán complete

七十 qīshí seventy

汽水 qìshuǐ carbonated mineral water; soda

起水疱 qǐ shuǐpào blister

起诉 qǐsù sue; prosecute

其他 qítā other

乞讨 qǐtǎo beg

奇特 qítè original; unique; strange

气体 qìtǐ gas

汽艇 qìtǐng motor boat

企图 qǐtú try

秋 qiū fall

球 qiú ball

求 qiú implore

球队 qiúduì team

囚犯 qiúfàn prisoner

求婚 qiúhūn propose ◊ proposal

求救 qiújiù call for help

丘陵 qiūlíng hill

秋千 qiūqiān swing

秋天 qiūtiān fall

蚯蚓 qiūyǐn earthworm

气味 qìwèi smell

气温 qìwēn temperature

期限 qīxiàn deadline; time limit

气象 qìxiàng weather

气象学 qìxiàngxué meteorology ◊ meteorological

气压 qìyā air pressure

企业 qǐyè enterprise

企业家 qǐyèjiā entrepreneur

起义 qǐyì uprising

汽油 qìyóu gas

其余 qíyú the rest

起源 qǐyuán origin

七月 qīyuè July

其中 qízhōng among; among which; of which

起重机 qǐzhòngjī crane; hoist

妻子 qīzi wife

旗子 qízi flag

骑自行车 qí zìxíngchē cycle ◊ cycling

区 qū district; zone

蛆 qū maggot

取 qǔ take; fetch; get

曲 qǔ tune; song; music

去 qù go

圈 quān circle

拳 quán fist ◊ punch

泉 quán spring; stream

权 quán right; power; authority

全 quán whole

犬 quǎn dog

劝 quàn persuade

全部 quánbù all; entire

劝导 quàndǎo teach; advise; instruct

劝告 quàngào advise

权衡 quánhéng weigh up

拳击 quánjī box ◊ boxing; fight

拳击比赛 quánjī bǐsài boxing match

权力 quánlì power; authority

权利 quánlì right

全面 quánmiàn comprehensive

全球 quánqiú global

全权 quánquán power of

attorney; full powers

泉水 quánshuǐ spring water

劝说 quànshuō persuade

蜷缩 quánsuō writhe; double up

圈套 quāntào trap; noose

全体 quántǐ all; whole ◊ totality

拳头 quántou fist

权威 quánwēi authority

痊愈 quányù recuperate; convalesce

劝阻 quànzǔ advise against

区别 qūbié distinguish ◊ distinction

驱除 qūchú remove; drive out

渠道 qúdào drain

取得 qǔdé gain; achieve

曲调 qǔdiào tune

去掉 qùdiào remove; get rid of

驱动器 qūdòngqì disk drive

缺 quē lack; miss

瘸 qué lame

雀 què sparrow

雀斑 quèbān freckle

缺点 quēdiǎn disadvantage; weakness

确定 quèdìng confirm

◊ final

缺乏 quēfá shortage ◊ lack; be lacking

确切 quèqiè exact

确认 quèrèn confirm

确实 quèshí in fact

缺席 quēxí absent ◊ absence

缺陷 quēxiàn defect; downside

确信 quèxìn be convinced

瘸子 quézi cripple

驱赶 qūgǎn chase away; dispel

取决于 qǔjuéyú depend on

群 qún group; crowd; flock; cluster; *measure word for crowds*

去年 qùnián last year

取暖 qǔnuǎn warm up

群众 qúnzhòng the masses

裙子 qúnzi skirt

趋势 qūshì tendency, trend

去世 qùshì die ◊ demise

躯体 qūtǐ body

曲线 qūxiàn curve

取消 qǔxiāo cancel

区域 qūyù area

取之不尽 qǔ zhī bú jìn inexhaustible

驱逐 qūzhú expel; deport

# R

燃 **rán** burn; ignite
染 **rǎn** color; dye
然而 **rán'ér** but
染发 **rǎnfà** dye one's hair
让 **ràng** let; give way
让步 **ràngbù** give way ◊ concession
让路 **rànglù** give way
然后 **ránhòu** then; next; afterwards
燃料 **ránliào** fuel
燃烧 **ránshāo** burn
绕道 **ràodào** go round; detour
热 **rè** hot; warm ◊ heat ◊ warm up
热爱 **rè'ài** love passionately
热带 **rèdài** tropics
热浪 **rèlàng** heatwave
热烈 **rèliè** enthusiastic; heated *discussion*; wild *applause*
人 **rén** person; people; man
忍 **rěn** endure
认 **rèn** recognize
热闹 **rènào** exciting; lively ◊ hustle and bustle

人道 **réndào** humane ◊ humanity
扔 **rēng** throw; throw away; drop; dump
仍 **réng** still
人格 **réngé** personality
仍然 **réngrán** still
任何 **rènhé** any
认可 **rènkě** acknowledgment
人口 **rénkǒu** population
人类 **rénlèi** human race ◊ human
人力 **rénlì** labor; manpower
人们 **rénmen** people
人民 **rénmín** the people
任命 **rènmìng** appointment ◊ appoint
人民解放军 **rénmín jiěfàngjūn** People's Liberation Army
忍耐 **rěnnài** endure
人权 **rénquán** human rights
人参 **rénshēn** ginseng
认生 **rènshēng** be scared of strangers
认识 **rènshi** know; get to know

人事部 **rénshìbù** personnel (department)

人世间 **rénshìjiān** the world ◊ earthly

忍受 **rěnshòu** put up with; endure

认为 **rènwéi** consider; reckon; figure

人物 **rénwù** figure

任务 **rènwù** assignment; job

人性 **rénxìng** human ◊ humanity

任性 **rènxìng** headstrong

人行道 **rénxíngdào** sidewalk

人行横道 **rénxíng héngdào** (pedestrian) crosswalk

任意 **rènyì** arbitrary

人员 **rényuán** personnel

人造 **rénzào** synthetic

人造卫星 **rénzào wèixīng** satellite

认真 **rènzhēn** serious; earnest; conscientious

人质 **rénzhì** hostage

热情 **rèqíng** warm; enthusiastic

热水袋 **rèshuǐdài** hot-water bottle

热水瓶 **rèshuǐpíng** vacuum flask

热心 **rèxīn** enthusiastic; warm-hearted

热衷于 **rèzhōng yú** be wild about

日 **rì** sun; day

日报 **rìbào** daily paper

日本 **Rìběn** Japan ◊ Japanese

日本人 **Rìběnrén** Japanese

日常 **rìcháng** everyday; daily

日出 **rìchū** sunrise

日光灯 **rìguāngdēng** fluorescent light

日记 **rìjì** diary

日历 **rìlì** calendar

日落 **rìluò** sunset

日期 **rìqī** date

绒 **róng** down

荣 **róng** honor

熔化 **rónghuà** smelt

融化 **rónghuà** thaw

容积 **róngjī** volume

溶解 **róngjiě** dissolve

容量 **róngliàng** volume; capacity

绒毛 **róngmáo** down

容纳 **róngnà** hold

容器 **róngqì** container

融洽 **róngqià** peaceable

容忍 **róngrěn** tolerate; stand for

容许 **róngxǔ** allow

溶液 **róngyè** solution

荣誉 **róngyù** glory; honor

揉 **róu** rub

肉 **ròu** meat

柔道 **róudào** judo

肉店 **ròudiàn** butcher shop

柔和 **róuhé** soft; mild; mellow

肉末 **ròumò** ground meat

柔软 **róuruǎn** soft; supple

肉体 **ròutǐ** flesh

肉汁 **ròuzhī** gravy

如 **rú** like; similar to

乳 **rǔ** breast; milk

入 **rù** enter

乳癌 **rǔ'ái** breast cancer

软 **ruǎn** soft; tender ◊ tenderness

软骨 **ruǎngǔ** gristle

软件 **ruǎnjiàn** software

软木塞 **ruǎnmùsāi** cork (*stopper*)

软盘 **ruǎnpán** floppy disk

软卧 **ruǎnwò** soft sleeper (*on train*)

如此 **rúcǐ** thus; in this way

蠕动 **rúdòng** squirm

锐不可当 **ruì bù kě dāng** inexorable; irresistible

如今 **rújīn** nowadays; at present

入境 **rùjìng** enter *country*

入口 **rùkǒu** access; entry; way in; entrance

入迷 **rùmí** be fascinated

润肤膏 **rùnfūgāo** moisturizer

润滑 **rùnhuá** lubricate ◊ lubrication

闰年 **rùnnián** leap year

弱 **ruò** weak

弱点 **ruòdiǎn** weakness

若干 **ruògān** some; a certain number

入神 **rùshén** be engrossed

乳霜 **rǔshuāng** cream

入睡 **rùshuì** fall asleep

如同 **rútóng** just like

乳牙 **rǔyá** milk tooth

如愿 **rúyuàn** as planned; as hoped

乳制品 **rǔzhì pǐn** dairy products

# S

撒 **sǎ** scatter

洒 **sǎ** sprinkle

撒谎 **sāhuǎng** lie

塞 **sāi** stick in; stuff; plug;

赛 **sài** competition

赛马 **sàimǎ** horse race

赛跑 **sàipǎo** race (on foot)

塞子 **sāizi** plug

三 **sān** three

伞 **sǎn** umbrella

散步 **sànbù** stroll ◊ take a stroll

散布 **sànbù** spread

散步者 **sànbùzhě** stroller (person)

三等仓 **sānděngcāng** third-class cabin

散发 **sànfā** distribute

丧礼 **sānglǐ** funeral service

桑拿浴 **sāngnáyù** sauna

丧失 **sàngshī** loss ◊ lose

桑树 **sāngshù** mulberry tree

嗓子 **sǎngzi** throat

三角形 **sānjiǎo xíng** triangle ◊ triangular

三十 **sānshí** thirty

散文 **sǎnwén** prose

三心二意 **sānxīn-èryì** indecisive; half-hearted

三月 **sānyuè** March

搔 **sāo** scratch

扫 **sǎo** sweep; drag

骚乱 **sāoluàn** commotion; turmoil

扫兴 **sǎoxìng** be disappointed

搔痒 **sāoyǎng** scratch

扫帚 **sàozhou** broom

撒种 **sǎzhǒng** sow

色 **sè** color

色彩 **sècǎi** color

色盲 **sèmáng** color-blind

森林 **sēnlín** forest

色情 **sèqíng** pornographic; erotic

沙 **shā** sand

纱 **shā** thread

杀 **shā** kill

傻 **shǎ** dumb

纱布 **shābù** gauze

刹车 **shāchē** brake ◊ brakes

沙发 **shāfā** sofa

傻瓜 **shǎguā** idiot

杀害 **shāhài** kill

筛 **shāi** sift

晒 **shài** expose to the sun

晒太阳 **shài tàiyáng** sunbathe; bask

筛子 **shāizi** sieve

色子 **shǎizi** dice

沙龙 **shālóng** salon

沙漠 **shāmò** desert

山 **shān** mountain; mount

扇 **shàn** fan; *measure word for doors and windows*

善 **shàn** kind-hearted

擅长 **shàncháng** excel at

闪电 **shǎndiàn** lightning

煽动 **shāndòng** incite; rouse

山峰 **shānfēng** peak

商 **shāng** commercial

伤 **shāng** injure ◊ injury

上 **shàng** on ◊ at the top; up ◊ get on

上岸 **shàng'àn** go ashore

伤疤 **shāngbā** scar

上班 **shàngbān** go to work; be at work

上臂 **shàngbì** upper arm

商标 **shāngbiāo** brand name; trademark

上部 **shàngbù** top part

商场 **shāngchǎng** department store; bazaar

上床 **shàngchuáng** go to bed

上等货 **shàngděnghuò** top-quality goods

上帝 **shàngdì** God

商店 **shāngdiàn** store

上吊 **shàngdiào** hang oneself

商定 **shāngdìng** agree; arrange

伤风 **shāngfēng** catch a cold

伤害 **shānghài** hurt

伤寒 **shānghán** typhoid (fever)

商会 **shānghuì** chamber of commerce

伤口 **shāngkǒu** wound; injury

商量 **shāngliang** discuss

上面 **shàngmian** top ◊ at the top; up ◊ upper

商品 **shāngpǐn** commodity; goods

商人 **shāngrén** businessman

上色 **shàngshǎi** tint

上身 **shàngshēn** upper body

上升 **shàngshēng** rise; climb

赏识 **shǎngshí** have great respect for

上述 **shàngshù** above-mentioned

上司 **shàngsi** boss

上诉 **shàngsù** appeal

商讨 **shāngtǎo** discuss

山谷 **shāngǔ** valley

闪光灯 **shǎnguāngdēng** flash; flashlight

上午 **shàngwǔ** morning ◊ in the morning

伤心 **shāngxīn** heart-broken

上学 **shàngxué** go to school

上演 **shàngyǎn** perform

商业 **shāngyè** business; commerce ◊ commercial

上瘾 **shàngyǐn** be addicted to

伤员 **shāngyuán** casualty

善良 **shànliáng** generous; kind

山脉 **shānmài** mountain range

山坡 **shānpō** hill

山区 **shānqū** mountainous area

闪烁 **shǎnshuò** flash; glint; blink; gleam

山羊 **shānyáng** goat

赡养 **shànyǎng** support

闪耀 **shǎnyào** sparkle; twinkle; glare

善意 **shànyì** goodwill

善于 **shànyú** be good at

扇子 **shànzi** fan (handheld)

擅自 **shànzì** unauthorized

烧 **shāo** burn

少 **shǎo** few

少 **shào** young

少不得 **shǎobude** essential

烧毁 **shāohuǐ** burn down

烧开 **shāokāi** boil

少量 **shǎoliàng** small amount

少年 **shàonián** young person (in early teens)

烧伤 **shāoshāng** burn

少数 **shǎoshù** few; minority

少数民族 **shǎoshù mínzú** ethnic minority

稍微 **shāowēi** slightly

少许 **shǎoxǔ** a little

哨子 **shàozi** whistle

沙丘 **shāqiū** dune

杀人犯 **shārénfàn** murderer

沙滩 **shātān** sandy beach

鲨鱼 **shāyú** shark

砂质土壤 **shāzhì tǔrǎng** sandy soil

蛇 **shé** snake

舌 **shé** tongue

设备 **shèbèi** equipment

奢侈 **shēchǐ** extravagant

社会 shèhuì society ◊ social

社会学 shèhuì xué sociology

社会主义 shèhuì zhǔyì socialism ◊ socialist

谁 shéi who; whoever

射击 shèjī shoot

涉及 shèjí involve; concern ◊ reference

设计 shèjì plan

设立 shèlì set up

社论 shèlùn editorial

赦免 shèmiǎn pardon; amnesty ◊ absolve

深 shēn deep ◊ dearly (love)

身 shēn body

伸 shēn stretch

神 shén god; deity ◊ divine; spiritual

肾 shèn kidney

渗 shèn seep; leak

申辩 shēnbiàn defend oneself

身材 shēncái build; figure

审查 shēnchá check; examine

深度 shēndù depth

身分 shēnfen identity; status

生 shēng give birth to; grow; live ◊ raw; unripe

升 shēng rise; hoist ◊ liter

声 shēng sound

绳 shéng cord; rope

省 shěng province ◊ provincial

剩 shèng remain

身高 shēngāo height

生病 shēngbìng fall ill ◊ sick

生产 shēngchǎn produce ◊ production

生产线 shēngchǎnxiàn production line

生产者 shēngchǎnzhě manufacturer

声称 shēngchēng claim; profess

牲畜 shēngchù livestock

生存 shēngcún exist; live

圣诞节 Shèngdàn Jié Christmas; Christmas Day

圣诞老人 Shèngdàn Lǎorén Santa Claus

圣诞树 shèngdàn shù Christmas tree

生动 shēngdòng vivid

省会 shěnghuì provincial capital

生活 shēnghuó life

生活水平 shēnghuó shuǐpíng standard of living

牲口 shēngkou livestock

胜利 **shènglì** victory ◊
  victorious

省略 **shěnglüè** leave out

声明 **shēngmíng**
  declaration; statement ◊
  declare; state

生命 **shēngmìng** life

生气 **shēngqì** angry ◊ get
  angry ◊ anger

圣人 **shèngrén** saint; sage

生日 **shēngri** birthday

声望 **shēngwàng**
  popularity; reputation;
  standing

生物学 **shēngwù xué**
  biology

剩下 **shèngxia** remain

盛夏 **shèngxià** height of
  summer

声响 **shēngxiǎng** sound

生肖 **shēngxiào** the twelve
  animals of the Chinese
  horoscope

盛行 **shèngxíng** prevailing

生锈 **shēngxiù** get rusty

生涯 **shēngyá** career

生意 **shēngyi** business

声音 **shēngyīn** sound; noise;
  voice

生育 **shēngyù** bear *child*

声誉 **shēngyù** reputation;
  fame

剩余 **shèngyú** rest

生长 **shēngzhǎng** grow

升值 **shēngzhí** revalue

生殖器 **shēngzhíqì** genitals

绳子 **shéngzi** cord

深厚 **shēnhòu** deep

神话 **shénhuà** myth

肾结石 **shènjiéshí** kidney
  stone

神经 **shénjīng** nerve ◊
  screwed up

神经崩溃 **shénjīng bēngkuì**
  nervous breakdown

神经过敏 **shénjīng guòmǐn**
  neurotic

伸懒腰 **shēn lǎnyāo** stretch

渗漏 **shènlòu** leak; drip

什么 **shénme** what ◊
  anything

神秘 **shénmì** mysterious

申明 **shēnmíng** declare

审判 **shěnpàn** trial ◊ try

神奇 **shénqí** supernatural

申请 **shēnqǐng** apply for ◊
  application

神圣 **shénshèng** holy;
  sacred ◊ sanctity

申诉 **shēnsù** lodge
  complaint ◊ objection

审问 **shěnwèn** question

审讯 **shěnxùn** examine; hear

深夜 **shēnyè** in the dead of night

呻吟 **shēnyín** groan; moan

深渊 **shēnyuān** abyss

深远 **shēnyuǎn** far-reaching

深造 **shēnzào** continue one's education

伸展 **shēnzhǎn** stretch; extend; spread

伸展四肢 **shēnzhǎn sìzhī** stretch

甚至 **shènzhì** even

慎重 **shènzhòng** careful

舍弃 **shěqì** abandon

设施 **shèshī** facilities

摄氏 **shèshì** Celsius; centigrade

射手 **shèshǒu** marksman

舌头 **shétou** tongue

摄像机 **shèxiàngjī** video camera; camcorder

摄影 **shèyǐng** photography

诗 **shī** poem; verse; poetry

湿 **shī** wet; damp

狮 **shī** lion

师 **shī** master

失 **shī** lose

十 **shí** ten

实 **shí** real; solid

石 **shí** stone

时 **shí** time; hour

食 **shí** food ◊ eat

识 **shí** know; recognize

史 **shǐ** history

始 **shǐ** begin

使 **shǐ** send; make

事 **shì** matter

是 **shì** be ◊ yes

室 **shì** room

市 **shì** city; market

试 **shì** try

示 **shì** show; indicate

失败 **shībài** fail; lose ◊ failure; defeat

事变 **shìbiàn** incident

识别 **shíbié** recognize; distinguish

时差 **shíchā** time difference

视察 **shìchá** inspect ◊ inspection

时常 **shícháng** often

市场 **shìchǎng** market

试车 **shìchē** test drive

使吃亏 **shǐ chīkuī** put at a disadvantage

时代 **shídài** age; generation

适当 **shìdàng** suitable

食道 **shídào** gullet

是的 **shìde** yes; that's right

湿度 **shīdù** humidity

适度 **shìdù** mildly; moderately; in moderation

十二 **shí'èr** twelve

十二月 **shí'èryuè** December

释放 **shìfàng** release

施肥 **shīféi** fertilize

是否 **shìfǒu** whether or not

师傅 **shīfu** master

石膏 **shígāo** plaster

尸骨 **shīgǔ** skeleton

事故 **shìgù** accident; crash

使馆 **shǐguǎn** embassy

嗜好 **shìhào** hobby; addiction

适合 **shìhé** suit; fit; be in accordance with

事后 **shìhòu** subsequent ◊ subsequently

石灰 **shíhuī** lime

实际 **shíjì** real; practical; substantive

世纪 **shìjì** century

时间 **shíjiān** time

实践 **shíjiàn** practice

事件 **shìjiàn** event; incident; business

市郊 **shìjiāo** suburbs

世界 **shìjiè** world

世界地图 **shìjiè dìtú** map of the world

世界观 **shìjièguān** world view

世界冠军 **shìjiè guànjūn** world champion

世界记录 **shìjiè jìlù** world record

世界著名 **shìjiè zhùmíng** world-famous

什锦 **shíjǐn** mixed; miscellaneous

诗句 **shījù** verse

时刻 **shíkè** moment ◊ constantly

时刻表 **shíkèbiǎo** schedule

石窟 **shíkū** grotto

实况转播 **shíkuàng zhuǎnbō** live transmission

湿冷 **shīlěng** cold and damp

势力 **shìlì** strength and power

视力 **shìlì** sight

失恋 **shīliàn** be jilted

失灵 **shīlíng** out of order; out of action

石榴 **shíliú** pomegranate

时髦 **shímáo** fashionable

失眠 **shīmián** insomnia

市民 **shìmín** city dweller

失明 **shīmíng** go blind

使命 **shǐmìng** mission; vocation

室内 **shìnèi** indoors; inside

食品 **shípǐn** food

识破 **shípò** see through

食谱 **shípǔ** recipe;
cookbook

时期 **shíqī** term; period

拾起 **shíqǐ** pick up

事情 **shìqing** issue; matter

失去 **shīqù** lose

拾取 **shíqǔ** pick up

市区 **shìqū** city area

诗人 **shīrén** poet

施舍 **shīshě** give alms

失事 **shīshì** have an accident

时事 **shíshì** current events

事实 **shìshí** fact; truth

逝世 **shìshì** pass away

失算 **shīsuàn** miscalculate

食堂 **shítáng** cafeteria;
canteen

尸体 **shītǐ** corpse

湿透 **shītòu** soaked

石头 **shítou** stone

室外 **shìwài** outdoors;
outside ◊ outdoor

失望 **shīwàng** disap-
pointment ◊ disappointed

视网膜 **shìwǎngmó** retina

示威游行 **shìwēi yóuxíng**
demonstration

失误 **shīwù** mistake

食物 **shíwù** food; diet

事物 **shìwù** thing

实习 **shíxí** work as an intern
◊ internship

世袭 **shìxì** hereditary;
inherited

实现 **shíxiàn** fulfill; realize;
come true ◊ realization

事先 **shìxiān** beforehand
◊ prior

失信 **shīxìn** break one's
promise

时新 **shíxīn** stylish

实行 **shíxíng** carry out

失修 **shīxiū** run-down

实验 **shíyàn** experiment

誓言 **shìyán** oath; vow

试验 **shìyàn** test;
experiment; trial

试样 **shìyàng** sample

式样 **shìyàng** style; type

失业 **shīyè** unemployed ◊
unemployment

诗意 **shīyì** poetic

十一 **shíyī** eleven

十亿 **shíyì** billion

适宜 **shìyí** suitable

示意 **shìyì** give a sign

石英 **shíyīng** quartz

适应 **shìyìng** adapt;
acclimatize; readjust

石英钟 **shíyīngzhōng**
quartz clock

十一月 **shíyīyuè** November

实用 **shíyòng** practical; useful

使用 **shǐyòng** access; use

适用 **shìyòng** applicable ◊ apply

使用说明书 **shǐyòng shuōmíngshū** instructions for use

食油 **shíyóu** cooking oil

食欲 **shíyù** appetite

十月 **shíyuè** October

施展 **shīzhǎn** display; put to good use

市长 **shìzhǎng** mayor

湿疹 **shīzhěn** eczema

食指 **shízhǐ** forefinger

实质 **shízhì** essence

始终 **shǐzhōng** from start to finish

始终不渝 **shǐzhōng bù yú** consistent ◊ consistently

时装表演 **shízhuāng biǎoyǎn** fashion show

虱子 **shīzi** louse

狮子 **shīzi** lion

师资 **shīzī** teachers

柿子 **shìzi** persimmon

十字架 **shízìjià** cross

十字路口 **shízì lùkǒu** crossroads; intersection

狮子舞 **shīziwǔ** lion dance

氏族 **shìzú** family; clan

收 **shōu** receive; accept

手 **shǒu** hand

守 **shǒu** keep watch; guard; abide by

瘦 **shòu** thin; lean

兽 **shòu** beast; animal

售 **shòu** sell

受 **shòu** receive; accept

售报亭 **shòubàotíng** newsstand

手表 **shǒubiǎo** wristwatch

收成 **shōucheng** harvest

首都 **shǒudū** capital

手段 **shǒuduàn** means

守法 **shǒufǎ** comply with the law

手风琴 **shǒufēngqín** accordion

手工 **shǒugōng** manual ◊ handiwork

手工业 **shǒugōngyè** craft

手工业者 **shǒugōngyèzhě** craftsman

收购 **shōugòu** purchase ◊ purchasing

受害 **shòuhài** sustain damage; suffer an injury

守护 **shǒuhù** look after

售货员 **shòuhuòyuán** sales

clerk

收集 **shōují** collect

手机 **shōují** cell phone

售价 **shòujià** retail price

收件人 **shōujiànrén** addressee

手巾 **shōujīn** towel

收据 **shōujù** receipt

手绢 **shōujuàn** handkerchief

首领 **shōulǐng** leader

守门员 **shōuményuán** goalkeeper

售票处 **shòupiàochù** ticket office

手枪 **shōuqiāng** handgun

授权 **shòuquán** authorize ◊ authority

收入 **shōurù** income; revenue

首饰 **shōushi** jewelry

手势 **shōushì** gesture

手术 **shōushù** surgery; operation

收缩 **shōusuō** shrink

手套 **shōutào** glove

手提包 **shōutí bāo** bag; handbag

手提行李 **shōutí xíngli** hand baggage

手推车 **shōutuīchē** wheelbarrow

手腕 **shōuwàn** wrist

守卫 **shōuwèi** guard

首先 **shōuxiān** in the first place

首相 **shōuxiàng** prime minister

手写 **shōuxiě** handwritten ◊ write by hand

手续 **shōuxù** procedure

收养 **shōuyǎng** adopt

收益 **shōuyì** return

兽医 **shòuyī** veterinary surgeon

收音机 **shōuyīnjī** radio

授予 **shòuyǔ** grant; present; confer

守则 **shōuzé** rules

手掌 **shōuzhǎng** palm

手指 **shōuzhǐ** finger

手镯 **shōuzhuó** bracelet

书记 **shū** book

梳 **shū** comb

熟 **shú** cooked; ripe; familiar

赎 **shú** redeem

数 **shǔ** count

鼠 **shǔ** mouse; rat

束 **shù** *measure word for flowers*

树 **shù** tree

竖 **shù** vertical

数 **shù** number

束 shù bundle

刷 shuā clean ◊ brush

摔 shuāi fall; drop; throw down

摔倒 shuāidǎo fall; throw

摔跤 shuāijiāo wrestle

摔跤比赛 shuāijiāo bǐsài wrestling match

衰落 shuāiluò go downhill

拴 shuān tie up

双 shuāng both; even; double; dual; twin ◊ *measure word for pairs*

霜 shuāng frost

双胞胎 shuāng bāo tāi twins

双边 shuāngbiān bilateral

双重 shuāngchóng double

霜冻 shuāngdòng frost

双方 shuāngfāng both sides

孀妇 shuāngfù widow

双击 shuāngjī double click

双人床 shuāngrén chuáng double bed

双数 shuāngshù even number

栓剂 shuānjì suppository

刷牙 shuāyá brush one's teeth

刷子 shuāzi brush

书包 shūbāo schoolbag;

satchel

鼠标 shǔbiāo mouse

数不清 shǔbuqīng countless

蔬菜 shūcài vegetable

输出 shūchū output; export

书店 shūdiàn bookstore

数额 shù'é amount

书法 shūfǎ calligraphy

舒服 shūfu comfortable ◊ well

束缚 shùfù tie; bind

疏忽 shūhū oversight

谁 shuí who

水 shuǐ water

睡 shuì sleep

税 shuì tax; duty; tariff

水彩 shuǐcǎi watercolor

水彩画 shuǐcǎihuà watercolor (*painting*)

水池 shuǐchí basin

水电站 shuǐdiànzhàn hydroelectric power plant

水管 shuǐguǎn water pipe

水果 shuǐguǒ fruit

睡过头 shuì guòtóu oversleep

睡觉 shuìjiào sleep; go to bed

水坑 shuǐkēng puddle

水冷却 shuǐlěngquè water-cooling

水龙头 shuǐlóngtóu faucet

睡眠 shuìmián sleep

水墨画 shuǐmòhuà ink wash painting

水泥 shuǐní cement

水牛 shuǐniú water buffalo

水平 shuǐpíng level ◊ horizontal

水平面 shuǐpíngmiàn water level; level surface

水上运动 shuǐshàng yùndòng watersports

税收 shuìshōu tax revenue

水桶 shuǐtǒng bucket

税务局 shuìwùjú tax office

睡醒 shuìxǐng wake up

睡衣 shuìyī nightdress; pajamas; pajama jacket

水银 shuǐyín mercury

水域 shuǐyù waters; area of water

睡着 shuìzháo fall asleep

水族馆 shuǐzú guǎn aquarium

书籍 shūjí books

暑假 shǔjià summer vacation

赎金 shújīn ransom

数据 shùjù data

数据保护 shùjù bǎohù data

protection

数据库 shùjù kù database

数据载体 shùjù zàitǐ data carrier

熟客 shúkè regular visitor

漱口 shùkǒu gargle

熟练 shúliàn proficient; practised

数量 shùliàng amount

树林 shùlín wood

数码照相机 shùmǎ zhàoxiàngjī digital camera

书面 shūmiàn written ◊ in writing

数目 shùmù number; sum

吮 shǔn suck

顺便 shùnbiàn passing ◊ in passing

顺从 shùncóng obedient

顺风 shùnfēng tail wind

枢纽 shūniǔ hub; center

瞬间 shùnjiān moment

顺利 shùnlì smooth ◊ smoothly

顺心 shùnxīn satisfactory

顺序 shùnxù sequence

说 shuō talk; speak; say

说定 shuōdìng agree on; arrange

说服 shuōfú persuade

说明 shuōmíng explain ◊

explanation

说明书 shuōmíngshū instruction manual

树皮 shùpí bark

述评 shùpíng comment ◊ commentary

竖起 shùqǐ erect ◊ erection

书签 shūqiān bookmark

熟人 shúrén acquaintance

树梢 shùshāo treetop

舒适 shūshì cozy

熟食 shúshí cooked meal

叔叔 shūshu uncle

输送 shūsòng transport

熟悉 shúxī know; be familiar with

书信往来 shūxìn wǎnglái correspondence

输血 shūxuè blood transfusion

数学 shùxué mathematics ◊ mathematical

输血者 shūxuèzhě blood donor

输液 shūyè infusion

鼠疫 shǔyì plague

属于 shǔyú belong; belong to

术语 shùyǔ terminology; term

疏远 shūyuǎn drift

apart; distance oneself ◊ estranged

树枝 shùzhī branch

树脂 shùzhī resin

书桌 shūzhuō desk

梳子 shūzi hairbrush; comb

数字 shùzì digit ◊ digital

撕 sī tear (up)

思 sī think; consider

私 sī private

丝 sī silk

死 sǐ die ◊ death ◊ dead

寺 sì Buddhist temple

四 sì four

似 sì resemble, be like; seem

丝绸 sīchóu silk

丝绸之路 Sīchóu zhī lù Silk Road

司法 sīfǎ justice ◊ judicial

四方形 sìfāng xíng square

丝瓜 sīguā loofah

似乎 sìhū look like; seem

死胡同 sǐ hútòng dead end

司机 sījī driver; chauffeur

四季豆 sìjìdòu green bean

撕开 sīkāi slit; rip open

思考 sīkǎo think about

饲料 sìliào fodder

司炉 sīlú stoker

思念 sīniàn miss

私人 sīrén private; intimate

私人财产 **sīrén cáichǎn** private property

私生活 **sīshēnghuó** private life

私生子 **sīshēngzǐ** illegitimate child

四十 **sìshí** forty

撕碎 **sīsuì** tear to pieces

死亡 **sīwáng** death; fatality

私下 **sīxià** privately

撕下 **sīxià** tear out; tear off

思想 **sīxiǎng** thought; idea

死刑 **sǐxíng** death penalty; execution

嘶哑 **sīyǎ** hoarse

饲养 **sìyǎng** breed ◊ breeding

私语 **sīyǔ** whisper

寺院 **sìyuàn** temple

四月 **sìyuè** April

死者 **sǐzhě** the deceased

四肢 **sìzhī** limbs

丝织品 **sīzhīpǐn** silk products

四周 **sìzhōu** all around

松 **sōng** pine ◊ loose ◊ loosely

送 **sòng** deliver; give; escort

松弛 **sōngchí** slack; flabby ◊ slacken

松动 **sōngdong** loose ◊

work loose; loosen up

耸肩 **sǒngjiān** shrug

耸立 **sǒnglì** tower; rise

送礼 **sònglǐ** give a present

松手 **sōngshǒu** let go

松鼠 **sōngshǔ** squirrel

松树 **sōngshù** pine (tree)

搜捕 **sōubǔ** search

搜索 **sōusuǒ** search; scan

宿 **sù** stay overnight

酸 **suān** acid ◊ acidic

算 **suàn** count

蒜 **suàn** garlic

算出 **suànchū** calculate; charge

算命 **suànmìng** fortune-telling

酸奶 **suānnǎi** yogurt

算盘 **suànpan** abacus

算术 **suànshù** arithmetic; sum

酸味 **suānwèi** acidity; sourness

素菜 **sùcài** vegetarian dish

酥脆 **sūcuì** crisp

苏打 **sūdá** soda

速冻 **sùdòng** quick-freeze ◊ quick-frozen

速度 **sùdù** pace; tempo

穗 **suì** ear (of corn)

碎 **suì** shatter ◊ shattered

岁 **suì** year; years old

随便什么 **suíbiàn shénme** anything; something

隧道 **suìdào** tunnel

随后 **suíhòu** afterward

碎块 **suìkuài** fragment

碎裂 **suìliè** break up; crumble

碎片 **suìpiàn** broken pieces; fragment

虽然 **suīrán** although

随时 **suíshí** at any time

碎石 **suìshí** gravel

随意 **suíyì** as one likes

诉苦 **sùkǔ** complain

塑料 **sùliào** plastic

塑料袋 **sùliàodài** plastic bag

笋 **sǔn** bamboo shoot

损害 **sǔnhài** harm, damage

损耗 **sǔnhào** wear (and tear)

孙女 **sūnnǚ** granddaughter

损失 **sǔnshī** damage; loss; toll

孙子 **sūnzi** grandson

锁 **suǒ** lock

索道 **suǒdào** cable railway

缩短 **suōduǎn** shorten

锁骨 **suǒgǔ** collarbone

缩水 **suōshuǐ** shrink

所谓 **suǒwèi** alleged; so-called

缩小 **suōxiǎo** reduce

缩写 **suōxiě** abbreviate ◊ abbreviation

所以 **suǒyǐ** therefore

所在地 **suǒzàidì** seat; site

俗气 **súqì** tasteless, tacky

速溶咖啡 **sùróng kāfēi** instant coffee

素食 **sùshí** vegetarian

诉讼 **sùsòng** lawsuit

塑像 **sùxiàng** statue

苏醒 **sūxǐng** come to ◊ revival

宿营地 **sùyíngdì** quarters

酥油 **sūyóu** butter; cream

塑造 **sùzào** shape

素质 **sùzhì** quality

# T

他 **tā** he; him

她 **tā** she; her

它 **tā** it

塔 **tǎ** tower

踏 tà step

踏板 tàbǎn pedal

塌方 tāfāng landslide

太 tài too; very

台布 táibù tablecloth

态度 tàidu attitude

胎儿 tāi'ér embryo; fetus

泰国 Tàiguó Thailand ◊ Thai

胎记 tāijì birthmark

太空 tàikōng (outer) space

太平洋 Tàipíngyáng the Pacific Ocean

台球 táiqiú snooker; billiards

台湾 Táiwān Taiwan ◊ Taiwanese

太阳 tàiyáng sun

太阳镜 tàiyángjìng sunglasses

他们 tāmen they; them

谈 tán talk

痰 tán phlegm; sputum

坦白 tǎnbái confess ◊ frankly ◊ open

探测 tàncè probe

摊贩 tānfàn street trader

汤 tāng broth

糖 táng sugar; candy

躺 tǎng lie

淌 tǎng run (of nose etc)

烫 tàng hot

汤匙 tāngchí spoon

搪瓷 tángcí enamel

糖醋 tángcù sweet and sour

烫发 tàngfà have a perm

糖果 tángguǒ candy

糖浆 tángjiāng molasses

糖尿病 tángniào bìng diabetes ◊ diabetic

唐三彩 tángsāncǎi Tang ceramics glazed in three colors

趟水 tāngshuǐ wade

躺下 tǎngxia lie down

躺椅 tǎngyǐ deck chair; lounge chair

谈话 tánhuà talk

瘫痪 tānhuàn paralysis ◊ paralyze

弹簧 tánhuáng spring

坦克 tǎnkè tank MIL

贪婪 tānlán greedy; acquisitive

谈判 tánpàn negotiate ◊ negotiations

叹气 tànqì sigh

贪食 tānshí gluttony ◊ gluttonous

坦率 tǎnshuài open ◊ openly ◊ candor

碳酸 tànsuān carbonic acid

贪污 tānwū embezzle ◊

embezzlement

弹性 tánxìng elasticity

探照灯 tànzhàodēng searchlight

摊子 tānzi stall, booth

逃避 táobì escape; shirk; evasion

讨价还价 tǎojià huánjià bargain ◊ haggle

讨论 tǎolùn discuss ◊ discussion

逃跑 táopǎo run away; flight; getaway

陶器 táoqì ceramics; pottery; earthenware

淘气 táoqì naughty

淘汰 táotài eliminate

逃脱 táotuō escape

讨厌 tǎoyàn disgusting; tiresome ◊ detest; loathe ◊ what a nuisance!

桃子 táozi peach

套子 tàozi housing; case

逃走 táozǒu run away

太阳穴 tàiyángxué temple

特别 tèbié particular ◊ particularly

特产 tèchǎn specialty

特点 tèdiǎn characteristic

特技 tèjì trick; stunt

疼痛 téngtòng pain ◊

painful

特殊 tèshū special; exceptional

特务 tèwu secret agent

特性 tèxìng quality; trait

特征 tèzhēng characteristic

踢 tī kick

蹄 tí hoof

题 tí subject

剃 tì shave

替 tì replace; substitute

天 tiān sky; heaven; day

甜 tián sweet

田 tián field

舔 tiǎn lick; lap up

填表 tiánbiǎo fill in a form

甜菜 tiáncài sugar beet

田地 tiándì field; farmland

天鹅 tiān'é swan

天鹅绒 tiān'éróng velvet

天份 tiānfèn gift; flair

天赋 tiānfù gift

天花 tiānhuā smallpox

天花板 tiānhuābǎn ceiling

添加 tiānjiā add

田径 tiánjìng track and field; athletics

天空 tiānkōng sky

填满 tiánmǎn fill

天气 tiānqì weather

天气预报 tiānqì yùbào

weather forecast

天然 tiānrán natural ◊ naturally

天然气 tiānrán qì natural gas

天生 tiānshēng naturally ◊ innate

天使 tiānshǐ angel

甜食 tiánshí confectionery

田鼠 tiánshǔ vole

天坛 Tiāntán Temple of Heaven

天文 tiānwén astronomy

天线 tiānxiàn antenna; aerial

天性 tiānxìng disposition

天衣无缝 tiān yī wú fèng perfect

天真 tiānzhēn naïve

天主教 Tiānzhǔjiào (Roman) Catholic

条 tiáo strip; item; *measure word for long thin things*

跳 tiào jump; hop; skip

跳板 tiàobǎn springboard; gangway

挑拨 tiǎobō provoke

挑动 tiǎodòng stir up

跳动 tiàodòng beat

跳高 tiàogāo high jump

调羹 tiáogēng spoon

条件 tiáojiàn condition ◊ conditional

调节 tiáojié adjust

调解 tiáojiě mediate; reconcile ◊ mediation; reconciliation

条款 tiáokuǎn clause; provision

调料 tiáoliào spice; herb; condiment; ingredient

调皮 tiáopí naughty; rude

调情 tiáoqíng flirt

挑三拣四 tiāosān-jiǎnsì choosy

跳水 tiàoshuǐ dive; diving

调味 tiáowèi season

跳舞 tiàowǔ dance

挑衅 tiǎoxìn provoke ◊ provocation ◊ provocative

挑选 tiāoxuǎn choose

跳远 tiàoyuǎn long jump

条约 tiáoyuē treaty, pact

挑战 tiǎozhàn challenge

体操 tǐcāo gymnastics

提倡 tíchàng advocate

提出 tíchū bring up; advance

题词 tící dedication ◊ dedicate

提到 tídào mention

铁 tiě iron

贴边 tiēbiān hem; seam; edge

铁路 **tiělù** railroad

铁锹 **tiěqiāo** shovel; spade

提高 **tígāo** raise; increase; improve ◊ rise

提供 **tígōng** supply

替换 **tìhuàn** substitute; replace

剃胡子 **tì húzi** shave

体积 **tǐjī** volume

题目 **tímù** topic

听 **tīng** listen (to)

停 **tíng** stop

亭 **tíng** pavilion

挺 **tǐng** very; quite

听从 **tīngcóng** obey; respond

停电 **tíngdiàn** power cut

停放车 **tíngfàng** park

听话 **tīnghuà** listen; obey ◊ obedient

听筒 **tīngtǒng** receiver TEL

停业 **tíngyè** shut down

停止 **tíngzhǐ** stop; let up

听众 **tīngzhòng** audience; listeners

停住 **tíngzhù** stop

亭子 **tíngzi** kiosk

提前 **tíqián** early

提神 **tíshén** freshen up; refresh oneself

提升 **tíshēng** promote

提示 **tíshì** point out

体现 **tǐxiàn** embody

提醒 **tíxǐng** remind

剃须刀 **tìxū dāo** razor

提议 **tíyì** suggest

体育场 **tǐyùchǎng** stadium

体育运动 **tǐyù yùndòng** sport ◊ sporting

体质 **tǐzhì** physique; constitution

体制 **tǐzhì** system

体重 **tǐzhòng** (body) weight

梯子 **tīzi** ladder

铜 **tóng** copper

同 **tóng** same ◊ with ◊ and

童 **tóng** child

桶 **tǒng** barrel; tub; pail

痛 **tòng** pain; sore

同伴 **tóngbàn** partner

铜版画 **tóngbǎnhuà** copperplate

同胞 **tóngbāo** fellow citizen; fellow countryman

统舱 **tǒngcāng** lower deck

通常 **tōngcháng** normal ◊ normally

同等价值 **tóngděng jiàzhí** of equal value

通风 **tōngfēng** air; ventilate ◊ airy; drafty ◊ ventilation

同感 **tónggǎn** sympathy

通过 **tōngguò** pass ◊ via

童话 **tónghuà** fairy tale

通货膨胀 **tōnghuò péngzhàng** inflation

统计 **tǒngjì** statistics ◊ statistical

同居 **tóngjū** cohabit

瞳孔 **tóngkǒng** pupil

痛哭 **tòngkū** bawl

痛苦 **tòngkǔ** suffering; distress

同盟 **tóngméng** alliance

童年 **tóngnián** childhood

同年 **tóngnián** same year ◊ of the same age

通气 **tōngqì** air

同情 **tóngqíng** pity; sympathize with ◊ compassion

同时 **tóngshí** simultaneously; in the meantime ◊ simultaneous

同事 **tóngshì** colleague

通宵 **tōngxiāo** throughout the night

同性恋 **tóngxìngliàn** homosexual; lesbian

通行证 **tōngxíngzhèng** pass

同学 **tóngxué** classmate

通讯员 **tōngxùnyuán** correspondent

同样 **tóngyàng** same

同意 **tóngyì** agree; sanction

统一 **tǒngyī** unite ◊ unification

通知 **tōngzhī** inform; report ◊ circular; notice

同志 **tóngzhì** comrade

统治 **tǒngzhì** reign; rule

偷 **tōu** steal

头 **tóu** head

投 **tóu** hurl; throw in

投递 **tóudì** deliver ◊ delivery

头顶 **tóudǐng** top of the head

头发 **tóufa** hair

头巾 **tóujīn** (head)scarf

透镜 **tòujìng** lens

偷懒 **tōulǎn** laze about; goof off

投篮 **tóulán** shoot (at the basket)

头颅 **tóulú** skull

头路 **tóulù** part (in hair)

透露 **tòulù** leak out; disclose

透明 **tòumíng** transparent

头皮屑 **tóupíxiè** dandruff

偷窃 **tōuqiè** steal

投入 **tóurù** plunge into

透入 **tòurù** penetrate

偷税 **tōushuì** evade taxes

头痛 **tóutòng** headache

偷偷 tōutōu furtive

头衔 tóuxián title

投降 tóuxiáng yield; surrender ◊ submission

投影仪 tóuyǐngyí projector

头晕 tóuyūn dizzy

投资 tóuzī invest ◊ investment

涂 tú apply

图 tú picture

途 tú path; road; way

土 tǔ earth; land

吐 tù vomit

兔 tù rabbit; hare

图案 tú'àn pattern; design

团结 tuánjié unite ◊ united

团体 tuántǐ group

团圆 tuányuán reunion; get-together

团子 tuánzi dumpling

突变 tūbiàn sudden change

涂层 túcéng coat

突出 tūchū stick out ◊ prominent

吐出 tùchū spit (out)

秃顶 tūdǐng bald

图钉 túdīng thumbtack

土豆 tǔdòu potato

图画 túhuà picture

推 tuī push; jolt

腿 tuǐ leg

退 tuì move backward; retreat; retire

退步 tuìbù go backward; fall behind

推测 tuīcè suspect; assume; guess

退潮 tuìcháo ebb tide

推迟 tuīchí postpone

退出 tuìchū withdraw; exit

推辞 tuīcí decline

推动 tuīdòng push forward; promote; boost; budge

推断 tuīduàn conclude ◊ conclusion

推荐 tuījiàn recommendation; reference ◊ recommend

蜕皮 tuìpí peel; shed its skin

退让 tuìràng retreat

退烧 tuìshāo subside (of fever)

推行 tuīxíng implement; pursue

退休 tuìxiū retire ◊ retired ◊ retirement

退休金 tuìxiūjīn pension

退休者 tuìxiūzhě pensioner

途经 tújīng via

途径 tújìng way

徒劳 túláo in vain

吞 tūn swallow

吞并 **tūnbìng** annex

臀部 **túnbù** buttocks; rump; hip

囤积 **túnjī** hoard

吞食 **tūnshí** devour

吞咽 **tūnyàn** gulp

拖 **tuō** drag; pull

拖把 **tuōbǎ** mop

驼背 **tuóbèi** hunchback; hump

拖车 **tuōchē** trailer

托儿所 **tuō'érsuǒ** day-nursery, crèche

脱轨 **tuōguǐ** be derailed

脱臼 **tuōjiù** dislocation

拖拉机 **tuōlājī** tractor

脱离 **tuōlí** break away

脱落 **tuōluò** come off; fall out

陀螺 **tuóluó** (spinning) top

唾沫 **tuòmò** spittle

鸵鸟 **tuóniǎo** ostrich

拖盘 **tuōpán** tray

拖鞋 **tuōxié** slippers

妥协 **tuǒxié** compromise

脱衣服 **tuō yīfu** undress

托运 **tuōyùn** send, ship

突破 **tūpò** breakthrough; penetration

突然 **tūrán** suddenly ◊ sudden

土壤 **tǔrǎng** soil

屠杀 **túshā** massacre; slaughter

图书馆 **túshūguǎn** library

吐痰 **tǔtán** spit

徒刑 **túxíng** prison sentence

图形学 **túxíngxué** graphics

涂油漆 **tú yóuqī** paint

屠宰 **túzǎi** slaughter

屠宰场 **túzǎichǎng** slaughterhouse

图章 **túzhāng** seal

途中 **túzhōng** en route

土著 **tǔzhù** native

兔子 **tùzi** rabbit; hare

# W

挖 **wā** dig; extract

蛙 **wā** frog

瓦 **wǎ** roof tile

袜 **wà** socks; stockings

歪 **wāi** leaning; crooked

外 **wài** outside ◊ external; foreign; outward ◊ externally; outwardly

外表 **wàibiǎo** exterior; facade; veneer ◊ outward

外部 **wàibù** exterior ◊ outer; external

外出 **wàichū** go out

外公 **wàigōng** (maternal) grandfather

外观 **wàiguān** exterior; appearance; look

外国 **wàiguó** foreign country ◊ abroad ◊ foreign

外国人 **wàiguórén** foreigner

外行 **wàiháng** layman

外号 **wàihào** nickname

外汇 **wàihuì** foreign currency, foreign exchange

外交部 **wàijiāobù** Ministry of Foreign Affairs

外科医师 **wàikē yīshī** surgeon

外来语 **wàiláiyǔ** foreign loan word

外贸 **wàimào** foreign trade

外面 **wàimiàn** outside ◊ external

外婆 **wàipó** (maternal) grandmother

歪曲 **wāiqū** misrepresent

外甥 **wàisheng** nephew

外甥女 **wàishengnǚ** niece

外衣 **wàiyī** coat

外语 **wàiyǔ** foreign language

挖掘 **wājué** excavate ◊ excavation

挖空 **wākōng** excavate

瓦砾 **wǎlì** rubble

弯 **wān** bend ◊ bent

完 **wán** finish ◊ finished; complete

玩 **wán** play

碗 **wǎn** bowl

晚 **wǎn** late ◊ evening; night

万 **wàn** ten thousand

晚安 **wǎn'ān** good night

完毕 **wánbì** finished

晚餐 **wǎncān** dinner

完成 **wánchéng** complete; accomplish ◊ completion

晚点 **wǎndiǎn** delayed

豌豆 **wāndòu** pea

晚饭 **wǎnfàn** supper

王 **wáng** king

网 **wǎng** net; web; network

往 **wǎng** to; toward ◊ past

忘 **wàng** forget

望 **wàng** look ahead; expect

往返 **wǎngfǎn** there and back

王国 **wángguó** kingdom

王后 **wánghòu** queen

忘记 **wàngjì** forget

旺季 **wàngjì** high season

往来 **wǎnglái** contact; dealings; relations

网络 **wǎngluò** network; Internet

王牌 **wángpái** trump card

网球 **wǎngqiú** tennis; tennis ball

往事 **wǎngshì** the past

顽固 **wángù** obstinate; set ◇ obstinacy

王位 **wángwèi** throne

望远镜 **wàngyuǎn jìng** telescope; binoculars

网址 **wǎngzhǐ** web site; web page

王子 **wángzǐ** prince

晚会 **wǎnhuì** party; (evening) function

万金油 **wànjīnyóu** balm

玩具 **wánjù** toy

完美 **wánměi** perfect; beautiful ◇ impeccably ◇ perfection

顽强 **wánqiáng** stubborn; tenacious

完全 **wánquán** complete; total ◇ completely

完全一样 **wánquán yīyàng** exactly the same

完善 **wánshàn** perfect

晚上 **wǎnshang** evening

晚上好 **wǎnshang hǎo** good evening

弯身 **wānshēn** bend; double up

玩世不恭 **wán shì bù gōng** cynically

玩耍 **wánshuǎ** enjoy oneself

顽童 **wántóng** urchin

玩笑 **wánxiào** joke

万幸 **wànxìng** fortunate

弯腰 **wānyāo** bend down

完整 **wánzhěng** complete ◇ completely

瓦特 **wǎtè** watt

蛙泳 **wāyǒng** breaststroke

袜子 **wàzi** socks; stockings

微 **wēi** small; micro-

围 **wéi** surround; besiege

唯 **wéi** only

喂 **wèi** hello TEL; hey! ◇ feed

为 **wèi** for

味 **wèi** taste

胃 **wèi** stomach

位 **wèi** position

未 **wèi** not yet; not

尾巴 **wěiba** tail

违背 **wéibèi** violate

微薄 **wēibó** sparse; scanty ◇ sparsely; scantily

微波炉 **wēibōlú** microwave oven

未曾 **wèicéng** never

维持 **wéichí** maintain; get by; hold out

为此 **wèicǐ** for this reason

伟大 **wěidà** great ◊ greatness

味道 **wèidao** taste; flavor

尾灯 **wěidēng** tail light

纬度 **wěidù** latitude

违法 **wéifǎ** illicit; illegal ◊ illegally

违反 **wéifǎn** break

桅杆 **wéigān** mast

危害 **wēihài** damage

威吓 **wēihè** intimidate

维护 **wéihù** protect, look after

未婚 **wèihūn** unmarried

未婚夫 **wèihūnfū** fiancé

未婚妻 **wèihūnqī** fiancée

危机 **wēijī** crisis

危急 **wēijí** critical; desperate ◊ critically

围巾 **wéijīn** scarf

味精 **wèijīng** monosodium glutamate

胃口 **wèikǒu** appetite

围困 **wéikùn** besiege ◊ siege

未来 **wèilái** future

为了 **wèile** for; in order to; because of

喂奶 **wèinǎi** breast-feed

围棋 **Wéiqí** Go

围裙 **wéiqún** apron

围绕 **wéirǎo** surround ◊ around

围绕着 **wéiràozhe** revolve around

委任 **wěirèn** appoint

伪善 **wěishàn** hypocrisy

卫生 **wèishēng** hygienic ◊ hygiene

卫生带 **wèishēngdài** sanitary napkin

卫生间 **wèishēngjiān** rest room

维生素 **wéishēngsù** vitamin

卫生纸 **wèishēngzhǐ** toilet paper

为什么 **wèishénme** why

威士忌 **wēishìjì** whiskey

畏缩 **wèisuō** recoil; shy away

胃痛 **wèitòng** stomach ache

威望 **wēiwàng** prestige

微温 **wēiwēn** lukewarm

危险 **wēixiǎn** danger ◊ dangerous

微小 **wēixiǎo** tiny

微笑 **wēixiào** smile

威胁 **wēixié** threat; intimidation ◊ threaten; intimidate

猥亵 **wěixiè** obscene

卫星 **wèixīng** satellite

卫星电视 **wèixīng diànshì** satellite TV

维修 **wéixiū** repair

喂养 **wèiyǎng** feed

偎依 **wēiyī** snuggle; cling

唯一 **wéiyī** sole ◊ solely

位于 **wèiyú** be (situated)

伪造 **wěizào** forge; falsify

位置 **wèizhi** location, position

胃灼痛 **wèizhuótòng** heartburn

位子 **wèizi** seat

闻 **wén** smell

吻 **wěn** kiss

稳 **wěn** stable

稳定 **wěndìng** stability ◊ stabilize ◊ stable

温度 **wēndù** temperature

温度表 **wēndùbiǎo** thermometer

嗡嗡作响 **wēngwēng zuòxiǎng** hum; buzz

问好 **wènhǎo** ask after; send greetings

问号 **wènhào** question mark

温和 **wēnhé** mild; moderate; mellow

问候 **wènhòu** send regards; ask after

文化 **wénhuà** culture ◊ cultural

文件 **wénjiàn** document; papers; file

闻名 **wénmíng** famous

文明 **wénmíng** civilization; culture

温暖 **wēnnuǎn** warm

温柔 **wēnróu** gentle

温室 **wēnshì** greenhouse

问题 **wèntí** problem; question; matter

温习 **wēnxí** brush up; revise

文学 **wénxué** literary ◊ literature

问讯 **wènxùn** ask; inquire

问讯处 **wènxùnchù** information office

瘟疫 **wēnyì** epidemic; plague

文艺 **wényì** literature and art

文章 **wénzhāng** article

蚊帐 **wénzhàng** mosquito net

稳重 **wěnzhòng** sedate; sober

蚊子 **wénzi** mosquito

文字 **wénzì** writing; text

窝 **wō** nest

我 **wǒ** I; me

握 **wò** grasp

卧 **wò** lie down

卧车 **wòchē** sleeping car

卧倒 **wòdǎo** lie flat; drop to the ground

涡轮机 **wōlúnjī** turbine

我们 **wǒmen** we; us

蜗牛 **wōniú** snail

窝棚 **wōpeng** shed; hangar; hovel

卧铺 **wòpù** place to sleep; bed

卧室 **wòshì** bedroom

握手 **wòshǒu** handshake ◊ shake hands

乌 **wū** black ◊ crow

屋 **wū** house

无 **wú** nothing ◊ not ◊ no

五 **wǔ** five

午 **wǔ** midday

舞 **wǔ** dance

雾 **wù** fog; mist

勿 **wù** do not

物 **wù** thing

五百 **wǔbǎi** five hundred

舞伴 **wǔbàn** (dance) partner

无比 **wúbǐ** incomparable

五彩 **wǔcǎi** colorful

舞场 **wǔchǎng** dance floor

无产阶级 **wúchǎn jiējí** proletariat

无耻 **wúchǐ** outrageous, shameless

无处 **wúchù** nowhere

舞蹈家 **wǔdǎojiā** dancer

屋顶 **wūdǐng** roof

午饭 **wǔfàn** lunch

无根据 **wúgénjù** unfounded

污垢 **wūgòu** dirt

无辜 **wúgū** innocent ◊ innocently

乌龟 **wūguī** tortoise; turtle

舞会 **wǔhuì** dance; prom

误会 **wùhuì** misunderstanding

误解 **wùjiě** misunderstanding; misread ◊ misunderstanding

无可奈何 **wúkě nàihé** helpless

无可指摘 **wúkě zhǐzhāi** irreproachable

无愧 **wúkuì** worthy

无力 **wúlì** feeble

物理 **wùlǐ** physics

无聊 **wúliáo** boredom ◊ boring; bored

诬蔑 **wūmiè** smear

无名指 **wúmíngzhǐ** ring finger

无能 **wúnéng** incompetent; incapable; unable ◊ inability

物品 **wùpǐn** object; item

武器 **wǔqì** weapon

雾气 **wùqì** mist, haze

无情 **wúqíng** ruthless; callous

舞曲 **wǔqǔ** dance music

无权 **wúquán** unauthorized

污染 **wūrǎn** pollution ◊ pollute

侮辱 **wǔrǔ** insult

无声 **wúshēng** silent; mute ◊ silently

五十 **wǔshí** fifty

无数 **wúshù** countless

武术 **wǔshù** martial arts

污水 **wūshuǐ** sewage

午睡 **wǔshuì** afternoon nap

无所谓 **wúsuǒwèi** indifferent ◊ all the same

舞台 **wǔtái** stage; platform

物体 **wùtǐ** object

舞厅 **wǔtīng** ballroom; dancehall

无痛 **wútòng** painless

乌托邦 **wūtuōbāng** utopia

无味 **wúwèi** insipid; dull

无限 **wúxiàn** infinite

无线 **wúxiàn** cordless, wireless

无线电 **wúxiàndiàn** radio

无限制 **wúxiànzhì** unlimited

无效 **wúxiào** invalid; futile

无心 **wúxīn** unintentionally

五星红旗 **wǔxīng hóngqí** Chinese flag

五星级饭店 **wǔxīngjí fàndiàn** five-star hotel

午休 **wǔxiū** lunch break

乌鸦 **wūyā** crow; raven

屋檐 **wūyán** eaves

无疑 **wúyí** doubtless; easily

无意 **wúyì** unintentional ◊ unintentionally

无意识 **wúyìshí** unconscious ◊ unconsciously

无用 **wúyòng** useless

无忧无虑 **wúyōu wúlǜ** carefree

五月 **wǔyuè** May

无与伦比 **wú yǔ lúnbǐ** unique

乌云 **wūyún** dark clouds

无知 **wúzhī** ignorance ◊ ignorant

物质 **wùzhì** matter

无止境 **wúzhǐjìng** endless ◊ endlessly

武装 **wǔzhuāng** arms ◊ arm ◊ armed

# X

膝 xī knee

吸 xī inhale; smoke; suck

稀 xī rare; sparse; thin

锡 xī tin

西 xī west ◊ western

溪 xī stream

熄 xī extinguish

席 xí mat; seat; place; feast

洗 xǐ wash; shuffle *cards*; develop *photographs*

喜 xǐ pleasure; joy

铣 xǐ mill

系 xì system; department ◊ tie

细 xì thin; fine

瞎 xiā blind

虾 xiā prawn; shrimp

下 xià down, downward ◊ below; under ◊ next ◊ get off; come down; lay; finish

吓 xià scare

夏 xià summer

下巴 xiàba chin

下班 xiàbān finish work; go off duty

下车 xiàchē alight

下沉 xiàchén sink; settle

下次 xiàcì next time

峡谷 xiágǔ canyon; gorge; glen

喜爱 xǐ'ài like; love ◊ beloved; fond ◊ favor; fondness

夏季 xiàjì summer

下降 xiàjiàng decrease; decline; drop

下来 xiàlái come down; descend ◊ descent

夏令时 xiàlìngshí summer time; daylight saving time

下流 xiàliú indecent; sleazy

下面 xiàmian underneath; below

先 xiān first

鲜 xiān fresh

弦 xián chord; string

咸 xián salty; savory

闲 xián idle ◊ leisure

线 xiàn line; thread; cord

县 xiàn county

馅 xiàn filling

腺 xiàn gland

现场 xiànchǎng on the spot ◊ scene of the crime

县城 **xiànchéng** county town

现存 **xiàncún** existing; in existence; in stock

现代 **xiàndài** modern; contemporary ◊ modern times

现代化 **xiàndàihuà** modernize ◊ modernization

限定 **xiàndìng** limit

限度 **xiàndù** limit

宪法 **xiànfǎ** constitution ◊ constitutional

箱 **xiāng** box; crate; case

香 **xiāng** incense; perfume ◊ fragrant; tasty

乡 **xiāng** countryside; hometown

详 **xiáng** details

响 **xiǎng** sound ◊ loud

想 **xiǎng** think; want

向 **xiàng** to; toward

象 **xiàng** elephant

像 **xiàng** look like

香槟酒 **xiāngbīng jiǔ** champagne

相册 **xiàngcè** photo album

香肠 **xiāngcháng** sausage

相当 **xiāngdāng** quite ◊ parallel; match

想到 **xiǎngdào** think of

想法 **xiǎngfa** thought, idea

相反 **xiāngfǎn** opposite

相反方向 **xiāngfǎn fāngxiàng** opposite direction

相符 **xiāngfú** correspond, match

香港 **xiānggǎng** Hong Kong

香蕉 **xiāngjiāo** banana

橡胶 **xiàngjiāo** rubber

项链 **xiàngliàn** necklace

相连接 **xiāngliánjiē** be connected; hang together

相貌 **xiàngmào** features (*facial*)

项目 **xiàngmù** item; project

想念 **xiǎngniàn** miss

相配 **xiāngpèi** match; complement

橡皮 **xiàngpí** rubber; eraser

相片 **xiàngpiàn** photo

橡皮筋 **xiàngpíjīn** elastic band

香气 **xiāngqì** scent

想起 **xiǎngqǐ** remember; think of

象棋 **xiàngqí** Chinese chess

向前 **xiàngqián** forward; onward

向日葵 **xiàngrìkuí** sunflower

向上 **xiàngshàng** up

响声 **xiǎngshēng** sound

相识 **xiāngshí** know each other

享受 **xiǎngshòu** enjoy

橡树 **xiàngshù** oak tree

香水 **xiāngshuǐ** perfume

乡思 **xiāngsī** homesickness

相似 **xiāngsì** similar ◊ be alike ◊ similarity

相同 **xiāngtóng** equal; equivalent ◊ equally

闲逛 **xiánguàng** wander; stroll; hang about

向外 **xiàngwài** outward

详细 **xiángxì** full ◊ fully; minutely

向下 **xiàngxià** down; downward ◊ underneath

想象 **xiǎngxiàng** imagine; envisage ◊ imagination

相信 **xiāngxìn** believe; believe in; trust

香烟 **xiāngyān** cigarette

享有 **xiǎngyǒu** enjoy

香皂 **xiāngzào** toilet soap

象征 **xiàngzhēng** emblem ◊ symbolize

相撞 **xiāngzhuàng** collide; knock together

箱子 **xiāngzi** box; chest; crate

显赫 **xiǎnhè** influential

鲜花 **xiānhuā** fresh flowers

先进 **xiānjìn** advance ◊ advanced; progressive

现金 **xiànjīn** cash

现今 **xiànjīn** nowadays

陷阱 **xiànjǐng** pitfall; trap

闲聊 **xiánliáo** chatter; gossip

线路 **xiànlù** circuit; line

鲜美 **xiānměi** delicious

羡慕 **xiànmù** envy

仙女 **xiānnǚ** fairy

先驱 **xiānqū** pioneer; forerunner

线圈 **xiànquān** coil

显然 **xiǎnrán** obvious ◊ apparently

仙人掌 **xiānrénzhǎng** cactus

献身于 **xiànshēn yú** dedicate oneself to

显示 **xiǎnshì** display; show

现实 **xiànshí** realistic ◊ reality

显示器 **xiǎnshìqì** indicator; monitor

咸水 **xiánshuǐ** salt water

线索 **xiànsuǒ** clue; thread

纤维素 **xiānwéisù** cellulose

现象 **xiànxiàng** phenomenon

献血 **xiànxuè** donate blood

显眼 **xiǎnyǎn** conspicuous ◊ stand out ◊ conspicuously

嫌疑 **xiányí** suspicion

现有 **xiànyǒu** available; in existence

陷于 **xiànyú** get into

弦乐器 **xiányuèqì** stringed instrument

现在 **xiànzài** now; at the moment

限制 **xiànzhì** restriction ◊ restrict; qualify *remark*

显著 **xiǎnzhù** prominent

削 **xiāo** peel

小 **xiǎo** small; young

笑 **xiào** laugh

校 **xiào** school

小便 **xiǎobiàn** urine ◊ urinate

小吃店 **xiǎochīdiàn** snack bar

消除 **xiāochú** eliminate

哮喘 **xiāochuǎn** asthma

小刀 **xiǎodāo** pocket knife

消毒 **xiāodú** sterilize ◊ sterile

小儿麻痹症 **xiǎo'ér mábìzhèng** polio

消防队 **xiāofángduì** fire department

消费 **xiāofèi** expense; consumption ◊ consume

小费 **xiǎofèi** tip

消费者 **xiāofèizhě** consumer

效果 **xiàoguǒ** effect

小孩 **xiǎohái** child

消耗 **xiāohào** use; consume; fritter away ◊ consumption

消化 **xiāohuà** digest ◊ digestion

笑话 **xiàohua** joke

小伙子 **xiǎohuǒzi** young man

消极 **xiāojí** negative

小姐 **xiǎojie** Miss ◊ young woman

销路 **xiāolù** sales; circulation

效率 **xiàolǜ** efficiency

小马 **xiǎomǎ** pony

小米 **xiǎomǐ** millet

消灭 **xiāomiè** destroy; exterminate

消磨时间 **xiāomó shíjiān** pass the time

小朋友 **xiǎo péngyǒu** children

小气 **xiǎoqì** mean; mean-spirited

消遣 **xiāoqiǎn** amuse oneself ◊ pastime

小人书 xiǎorénshū picture-book

消失 xiāoshī disappear; go away

小时 xiǎoshí hour

小事 xiǎoshì trivial matter

消瘦 xiāoshòu emaciated

销售 xiāoshòu market ◊ marketing

小说 xiǎoshuō novel; fiction

萧条 xiāotiáo (economic) depression ◊ depressed

小提琴 xiǎotíqín violin

小偷 xiǎotōu thief; burglar

小屋 xiǎowū hut

消息 xiāoxi news

肖像 xiàoxiàng portrait

小心 xiǎoxīn be careful ◊ carefully

小学 xiǎoxué elementary school

小学生 xiǎoxuéshēng schoolchild

校长 xiàozhǎng principal (of school)

下水 xiàshuǐ launch ◊ downstream

下水道 xiàshuǐ dào drains

下榻 xiàtà stay

下午 xiàwǔ afternoon

下陷 xiàxiàn drop; subside

下雪 xiàxuě snow

下意识 xiàyìshí subconscious

下雨 xiàyǔ rain

狭窄 xiázhǎi confined

瞎子 xiāzi blind person

稀薄 xībó thin

西餐 xīcān Western cuisine

细长 xìcháng narrow; slim

吸尘器 xīchénqì vacuum cleaner

洗涤 xǐdí wash; erase *tape*

吸毒者 xīdúzhě drug addict

斜 xié oblique; diagonal

鞋 xié shoe; footwear

携带 xié carry; hold

写 xiě write

谢 xiè thank

卸 xiè unload

蟹 xiè crab

鞋带 xiédài shoelace; strap

携带 xiédài take (along)

鞋底 xiédǐ sole

鞋店 xiédiàn shoestore

协定 xiédìng agreement

邪恶 xié'è evil; spiteful

鞋跟 xiégēn heel

协会 xiéhuì association

卸货 xièhuò unload

鞋匠 xiéjiang shoemaker

泄密 xièmì reveal a secret

斜坡 **xiépō** slope; gradient

斜视 **xiéshì** squint; look sideways

鞋刷 **xiéshuā** shoe brush

斜体 **xiétǐ** italic

卸下 **xièxià** unload

谢谢 **xièxie** thanks

泻药 **xièyào** laxative

鞋油 **xiéyóu** shoe polish

楔子 **xiēzi** wedge

写作 **xiězuò** write ◊ writing

洗发剂 **xǐfàjì** shampoo

稀饭 **xīfàn** congee

西方 **xīfāng** western ◊ West

西风 **xīfēng** westerly wind

西服 **xīfú** suit

媳妇 **xífù** daughter-in-law

膝盖骨 **xīgàigǔ** kneecap

西瓜 **xīguā** watermelon

吸管 **xīguǎn** drinking straw

习惯 **xíguàn** custom; habit ◊ be accustomed to

希罕 **xīhan** rare ◊ rarity

西红柿 **xīhóngshì** tomato

喜欢 **xǐhuan** like, be fond of

袭击 **xíjī** attack; strike

细节 **xìjié** detail

喜剧 **xǐjù** comedy

戏剧 **xìjù** drama ◊ dramatic

细菌 **xìjūn** germ

戏剧性 **xìjùxìng** drama ◊

dramatic

系列 **xìliè** series; range; installment

喜马拉雅山 **Xǐmǎlāyàshān** Himalayas

熄灭 **xīmiè** put out; quench; go out

心 **xīn** heart; mind; center

新 **xīn** new; unused

信 **xìn** faith; letter ◊ believe; trust

信封 **xìnfēng** envelope

星 **xīng** star

行 **xíng** go ◊ expedition ◊ OK; you're on!

醒 **xǐng** awake ◊ rouse

擤 **xǐng** blow one's nose

杏 **xìng** apricot

性 **xìng** nature; character; gender; sex

姓 **xìng** surname

性别 **xìngbié** gender

形成 **xíngchéng** form; come into existence ◊ formation

行动 **xíngdòng** act ◊ action

刑法 **xíngfǎ** criminal law

兴奋 **xīngfèn** excited ◊ excitement ◊ get excited

幸福 **xìngfú** happy ◊ happiness

性格 **xìnggé** nature

型号 xínghào model

猩红热 xīnghóngrè scarlet fever

性急 xìngjí impatient

性交 xìngjiāo sexual intercourse ◊ have sex

幸亏 xìngkuī fortunately

行李 xíngli baggage

星期 xīngqī week

星期二 xīngqī'èr Tuesday

星期六 xīngqīliù Saturday

性情 xìngqíng temperament

星期日 xīngqīrì Sunday

星期三 xīngqīsān Wednesday

星期四 xīngqīsì Thursday

星期五 xīngqīwǔ Friday

星期一 xīngqīyī Monday

兴趣 xìngqù interest

行人 xíngrén pedestrian

行人区 xíngrén qū pedestrian precinct

形容 xíngróng describe

行善者 xíngshànzhě benefactor

行使 xíngshǐ exercise *right*

行驶 xíngshǐ drive; go; travel

刑事 xíngshì criminal

形势 xíngshì situation

形式上 xíngshì shàng

formal ◊ formally

兴旺 xīngwàng flourish ◊ flourishing

行为 xíngwéi behavior; deed

醒悟 xǐngwù awaken; realize

星象 xīngxiàng horoscope

形象 xíngxiàng image

行星 xíngxīng planet

形形色色 xíngxíng-sèsè varied

性欲 xìngyù sexual desire; lust

幸运 xìngyùn fortunate ◊ fortunately ◊ good fortune

幸灾乐祸 xìngzāi-lèhuò malicious delight

行政 xíngzhèng administration ◊ administrative

性质 xìngzhì quality; character

形状 xíngzhuàng form

信号 xìnhào signal

信笺 xìnjiān writing paper

信教 xìnjiào devout

新加坡 Xīnjiāpō Singapore

心肌梗塞 xīnjī gěngsè heart attack

辛苦 xīnkǔ arduous

信赖 xìnlài trust; rely on

新郎 xīnláng bridegroom

心理学 xīnlǐxué psychology

◊ psychological

心满意足 **xīnmǎn yìzú** happy

新年 **Xīnnián** New Year

信念 **xìnniàn** belief

新娘 **xīnniáng** bride

心情 **xīnqíng** mood

信任 **xìnrèn** trust ◊ trusting

欣赏 **xīnshǎng** appreciate ◊ appreciation

新式 **xīnshì** up-to-date

信使 **xìnshǐ** courier

新手 **xīnshǒu** beginner; rookie

薪水 **xīnshuǐ** salary

新闻广播 **xīnwén guǎngbō** newscast

欣喜 **xīnxǐ** jubilant

信息 **xìnxī** information

新鲜 **xīnxiān** fresh ◊ freshness

信箱 **xìnxiāng** mailbox

新西兰 **Xīnxīlán** New Zealand

信心 **xìnxīn** confidence

信息学 **xìnxī xué** information science

信仰 **xìnyǎng** belief, faith

信用卡 **xìnyòngkǎ** credit card

心脏病 **xīnzàng bìng** heart disease

胸 **xiōng** chest; bust

凶 **xiōng** fierce; terrible; evil

熊 **xióng** bear

雄 **xióng** male

兄弟 **xiōngdì** brothers

兄弟般 **xiōngdìbān** fraternal ◊ like brothers

熊猫 **xióngmāo** panda

胸腔 **xiōngqiāng** thorax

凶杀 **xiōngshā** murder

凶手 **xiōngshǒu** murderer

雄伟 **xióngwěi** imposing; majestic ◊ majestically

胸罩 **xiōngzhào** bra

喜鹊 **xǐque** magpie

牺牲品 **xīshēng pǐn** victim

稀释 **xīshì** water down

吸收 **xīshōu** absorb

稀疏 **xīshū** sparse

蟋蟀 **xīshuài** cricket

习俗 **xísú** custom

系统 **xìtǒng** system

羞 **xiū** shame; embarrass

修 **xiū** repair

锈 **xiù** rust

嗅 **xiù** sniff

修补 **xiūbǔ** mend; darn

羞耻 **xiūchǐ** shame

修道院 **xiūdàoyuàn** abbey; convent; monastery

修改 xiūgǎi correct; amend ◊ correction; amendment

休假 xiūjià vacation ◊ take a vacation

休克 xiūkè shock

羞愧 xiūkuì ashamed

修理 xiūlǐ repair

秀丽 xiùlì beautiful; dainty

修理车间 xiūlǐ chējiān workshop; garage

修女 xiūnǚ nun

羞怯 xiūqiè shy; sheepish

修缮 xiūshàn renovate

休息 xiūxi take a break ◊ recess

休养 xiūyǎng recover

袖珍本 xiùzhēnběn paperback

袖子 xiùzi sleeve

希望 xīwàng hope; wish

细心 xìxīn careful; considerate

吸烟车厢 xīyān chēxiāng smoking car

吸烟者 xīyānzhě smoker

洗衣店 xǐyī diàn laundry (place)

洗衣粉 xǐyīfěn detergent

洗衣机 xǐyījī washing machine

吸引 xīyǐn attract; fascinate

习以为常 xí yǐ wéi cháng usual ◊ used to

稀有 xīyǒu rare

西藏 Xīzàng Tibet ◊ Tibetan

洗澡 xǐzǎo bathe; shower

西装上衣 xīzhuāng shàngyī suit jacket

席子 xízi mat

选 xuǎn choose

选拔赛 xuǎnbásài qualifier

宣布 xuānbù declare ◊ declaration

宣传 xuānchuán promotion; propaganda ◊ promote; publicize

旋风 xuànfēng whirlwind

宣告 xuāngào announce ◊ announcement

选举 xuǎnjǔ election ◊ elect

选举权 xuǎnjǔ quán right to vote

选民 xuǎnmín voter

喧闹 xuānnào racket ◊ noisy; tumultuous ◊ blare out

悬念 xuánniàn suspense

悬赏 xuánshǎng offer a reward

宣誓 xuānshì swear an oath

选手 xuǎnshǒu competitor

旋涡 xuánwō whirlpool

选择 **xuǎnzé** choice ◊ choose

旋转 **xuánzhuǎn** revolve ◊ revolution

许多 **xǔduō** many

学 **xué** study; learn

雪 **xuě** snow

血 **xuè** blood

雪白 **xuěbái** snow-white

雪崩 **xuěbēng** avalanche

血管 **xuèguǎn** blood vessel

学会 **xuéhuì** learn ◊ academy

雪茄 **xuějiā** cigar

血淋淋 **xuè línlín** bloody

学期 **xuéqī** semester

雪橇 **xuěqiāo** sled

雪球 **xuěqiú** snowball

雪人 **xuěrén** snowman

削弱 **xuēruò** impaired ◊ weaken

学生 **xuésheng** student

学说 **xuéshuō** doctrine

学徒 **xuétú** apprentice

学位 **xuéwèi** (university) degree

穴位 **xuéwèi** acupuncture point

学问 **xuéwen** knowledge

学习 **xuéxí** study; learn ◊ studying; learning

学校 **xuéxiào** school

学校假期 **xuéxiào jiàqī** school vacation

血型 **xuèxíng** blood group

血压 **xuèyā** blood pressure

血液循环 **xuèyè xúnhuán** circulation

学院 **xuéyuàn** college

学者 **xuézhě** scholar

血肿 **xuèzhǒng** hematoma

靴子 **xuēzi** boot

续集 **xùjí** sequel

许久 **xǔjiǔ** a long time

酗酒 **xùjiǔ** drink

许可 **xǔkě** permission ◊ permit

畜牧 **xùmù** raise livestock

序幕 **xùmù** prologue

熏 **xūn** smoke

训斥 **xùnchì** reprimand

驯服 **xùnfú** tame, docile

训练 **xùnliàn** train ◊ training

训练班 **xùnliàn bān** training course

许诺 **xǔnuò** promise

询问 **xúnwèn** inquire; interrogate ◊ inquiry; interrogation

勋章 **xūnzhāng** medal; decoration

寻找 **xúnzhǎo** look for

需求 **xūqiú** demand

序曲 **xùqǔ** overture

虚弱 **xūruò** weak ◊ weakness

叙述 **xùshù** tell ◊ account

序言 **xùyán** introduction

需要 **xūyào** need; cost; take; entail ◊ need

# Y

压 **yā** press; crush ◊ pressure

鸭 **yā** duck

牙 **yá** tooth

哑 **yǎ** mute

牙齿 **yáchǐ** tooth ◊ dental

牙膏 **yágāo** toothpaste

押金 **yājīn** deposit, security

哑口无言 **yǎkǒu wúyán** speechless

压力 **yālì** pressure; stress

哑铃 **yǎlíng** dumbbell

亚麻布 **yàmá bù** linen

烟 **yān** smoke

腌 **yān** salt; pickle; cure

盐 **yán** salt

沿 **yán** along

眼 **yǎn** eye

咽 **yàn** swallow

砚 **yàn** inkstone

烟草 **yāncǎo** tobacco

延长 **yáncháng** lengthen; prolong ◊ lengthy

烟囱 **yāncōng** chimney;

ship's funnel

烟斗 **yāndǒu** pipe (*for smoking*)

厌烦 **yànfán** be fed up

羊 **yáng** sheep

洋 **yáng** ocean

阳 **yáng** yang (*opposite of yin*)

痒 **yǎng** itch

仰 **yǎng** look up

养 **yǎng** rear

样本 **yàngběn** sample

养蚕业 **yǎngcányè** silkworm breeding

洋葱 **yángcōng** onion

严格 **yángé** strict ◊ strictness ◊ strictly

羊倌 **yángguān** shepherd

阳光 **yángguāng** sunshine

养老院 **yǎnglǎo yuàn** old people's home

样品 **yàngpǐn** specimen

氧气 **yǎngqì** oxygen

阳伞 **yángsǎn** parasol

养神 **yǎngshén** relax

扬声器 **yángshēngqì** loudspeaker

样式 **yàngshì** pattern

杨树 **yángshù** poplar tree

阳台 **yángtái** balcony

验光 **yànguāng** eye test

仰望 **yǎngwàng** look up

仰卧 **yǎngwò** lie on one's back

阳性 **yángxìng** positive *result*

仰泳 **yǎngyǒng** backstroke

烟盒 **yānhé** cigarette case

咽喉 **yānhóu** gullet; larynx

延缓 **yánhuǎn** postpone

宴会 **yànhuì** dinner party; banquet

烟灰缸 **yānhuī gāng** ashtray

眼睛 **yǎnjīng** eye

眼镜 **yǎnjìng** glasses

研究 **yánjiū** study; research

厌倦 **yànjuàn** be tired of

眼泪 **yǎnlèi** teardrop

淹没 **yānmò** flood; submerge

颜色 **yánsè** color; coloring

延伸 **yánshēn** stretch

岩石 **yánshí** rock

掩饰 **yǎnshì** cover up

淹死 **yānsǐ** drown

严肃 **yánsù** serious ◊ seriously ◊ severity

燕尾服 **yànwěifú** tail coat

厌恶 **yànwù** hate

演戏 **yǎnxì** put on a play; perform

眼下 **yǎnxià** at present

延续 **yánxù** last

验血 **yànxuè** blood test

眼药水 **yǎnyàoshuǐ** eyedrops

谚语 **yànyǔ** saying

演员 **yǎnyuán** actor; actress

严重 **yánzhòng** severe, serious ◊ seriousness

燕子 **yànzi** swallow (*bird*)

演奏 **yǎnzòu** perform ◊ performance

腰 **yāo** waist

摇 **yáo** shake

咬 **yǎo** bite

舀 **yǎo** scoop

药 **yào** drug; medication

要 **yào** want; need; must ◊ if

摇摆 **yáobǎi** roll, sway

腰带 **yāodài** belt; girdle

要道 **yàodào** main street

药店 **yàodiàn** pharmacy

摇动 **yáodòng** wave; shake; flap

妖怪 **yāoguài** monster; ghost

摇晃 **yáohuang** rock; tremble

药剂师 **yàojì shī** pharmacist

遥控 **yáokòng** remote control

药片 **yàopiàn** tablet

药品 **yàopǐn** medicine

邀请 **yāoqǐng** invite ◊ invitation

要求 **yāoqiú** ask for; demand

钥匙 **yàoshi** key

腰痛 **yāotòng** lumbago

药丸 **yàowán** pill

药物 **yàowù** drug

谣言 **yáoyán** rumor

耀眼 **yàoyǎn** dazzle ◊ dazzling

遥远 **yáoyuǎn** far away

鸦片 **yāpiàn** opium

牙签 **yáqiān** toothpick

牙刷 **yáshuā** toothbrush

压缩空气 **yāsuō kōngqì** compressed air

牙痛 **yátòng** toothache

牙医 **yáyī** dentist

牙龈 **yáyín** gum

压韵 **yāyùn** rhyme

压制 **yāzhì** suppress

亚洲 **Yàzhōu** Asia ◊ Asian

亚洲人 **Yàzhōurén** Asian

也 **yě** too

野 **yě** wild

夜 **yè** night

页 **yè** page

夜班 **yèbān** night shift

野餐 **yěcān** picnic

野地 **yědì** wilderness

夜间 **yèjiān** at night

冶炼厂 **yěliàn chǎng** iron and steel works

野兽 **yěshòu** wild beast

液体 **yètǐ** liquid

夜晚 **yèwǎn** night

腋窝 **yèwō** armpit

夜校 **yèxiào** night school

也许 **yěxǔ** perhaps

野丫头 **yěyātou** tomboy

爷爷 **yéye** (paternal) grandfather

夜莺 **yèyīng** nightingale

业余时间 **yèyú shíjiān** spare time

野猪 **yězhū** wild boar

椰子 **yēzi** coconut

叶子 **yèzi** leaf

夜总会 **yèzǒnghuì** nightclub; nightspot

一 **yī** one

姨 **yí** (maternal) aunt

疑 **yí** doubt; suspect

倚 yǐ lean on; depend on

已 yǐ already

易 yì easy ◊ change; exchange

亿 yì hundred million

译 yì translate

一般 yìbān usual; mediocre ◊ usually, generally

一半 yíbàn half

遗产 yíchǎn estate; legacy

异常 yìcháng exceptional; unusual ◊ exceptionally; unusually

溢出 yìchū overflow; slop

遗传 yíchuán genetic; hereditary ◊ heredity ◊ pass on

一次 yícì once

依次 yīcì in turn

以此 yǐcǐ for this reason; consequently; hence

依从 yīcóng obey

意大利 Yìdàlì Italy ◊ Italian

一点儿 yìdiǎnr a little

一定 yídìng definitely

移动 yídòng move; shift; remove ◊ removal; cell phone

移动电话 yídòng diànhuà cellular phone

衣服 yīfu clothes

衣钩 yīgōu coat hook

衣柜 yīguì closet

异国 yìguó foreign country

遗憾 yíhàn sad ◊ regret

颐和园 Yíhéyuán Summer Palace

以后 yǐhòu later, afterward

议会 yìhuì parliament

以及 yǐjí and

衣架 yījià coathanger

意见 yìjiàn opinion; suggestion; complaint

已经 yǐjīng already

依据 yījù basis; grounds

一开始 yìkāishǐ from the start

依靠 yīkào rely on ◊ support

倚靠 yǐkào lean against

一刻钟 yíkèzhōng quarter of an hour

依赖 yīlài depend on ◊ dependent ◊ dependence

医疗保险 yīliáo bǎoxiǎn health insurance

一流 yīliú first-class, first-rate

遗留 yíliú leave behind; bequeath

一律 yílǜ without exception

一路平安 yílù píng'ān have a good trip

衣帽间 yīmào jiān checkroom (*for coats*)

移民 yímín immigrate; emigrate ◊ immigrant; emigrant; immigration; emigration

因 yīn because ◊ reason

阴 yīn yin (*opposite of yang*) ◊ overcast

银 yín silver

阴暗 yīn'àn gloomy

疑难 yínán problematic

引爆装置 yǐnbào zhuāngzhì detonator

音标 yīnbiāo phonetics

隐藏 yǐncáng hide

阴沉 yīnchén overcast

因此 yīncǐ so; therefore; thus

阴道 yīndào vagina ◊ vaginal

引导 yǐndǎo lead

引渡 yǐndù extradite ◊ extradition

印度 Yìndù India ◊ Indian

印度洋 yìndùyáng Indian Ocean

音符 yīnfú note

鹰 yīng eagle

赢 yíng win; beat

硬 yìng hard

硬币 yìngbì coin

应承 yìngchéng promise

赢得 yíngdé gain; win

硬度 yìngdù hardness

婴儿 yīng'ér baby

应该 yīnggāi should; ought to

英格兰 Yīnggélán England ◊ English

英国 Yīngguó Britain ◊ British

硬件 yìngjiàn hardware COMPUT

迎接 yíngjiē greet, welcome

盈利 yínglì profit; surplus

英明 yīngmíng brilliant; wise

影射 yǐngshè allude to

樱桃 yīngtáo cherry (*fruit*)

鹦鹉 yīngwǔ parrot

影响 yǐngxiǎng influence; impact ◊ influence; affect

英雄 yīngxióng hero

营养 yíngyǎng nourishment; nutrition

硬要 yìngyào impose (oneself)

营业时间 yíngyè shíjiān business hours

应用 yìngyòng use; apply ◊ applied

英语 Yīngyǔ English

影子 yǐngzi shadow

银行 yínháng bank FIN

引号 yínhào quotation mark

银婚 yínhūn silver wedding (anniversary)

音节 yīnjié syllable

引进 yǐnjìn introduce ◊ introduction

阴茎 yīnjīng penis

音量 yīnliàng volume (of radio etc)

饮料 yǐnliào drink

淫乱 yínluàn indecent

隐瞒 yǐnmán conceal; disguise

阴谋 yīnmóu plot

银幕 yínmù screen

引起 yǐnqǐ cause; produce; inspire; arouse

引人注目 yǐn rén zhùmù stand out; attract attention ◊ spectacular; striking

印刷厂 yìnshuā chǎng printing works

饮水 yǐnshuǐ water animals

因素 yīnsù ingredient; factor

因特网 yīntèwǎng Internet

因特网接口 yīntèwǎng jiēkǒu Internet connection

引退 yǐntuì resign

因为 yīnwèi because ◊ on account of

引文 yǐnwén quote

阴险 yīnxiǎn devious; insidious ◊ deviously; insidiously

印象 yìnxiàng impression

印象深刻 yìnxiàng shēnkè impressive

阴性 yīnxìng feminine GRAM; negative results

隐形眼镜 yǐnxíng yǎnjìng contact lens

引用 yǐnyòng quote

饮用水 yǐnyòng shuǐ drinking water

引诱 yǐnyòu seduce ◊ seduction

音乐 yīnyuè music ◊ musical

音乐会 yīnyuèhuì concert

音乐家 yīnyuèjiā musician

引证 yǐnzhèng cite

银质 yínzhì silver

印子 yìnzi imprint

一起 yìqǐ together ◊ along

仪器 yíqì apparatus; instrument

以前 yǐqián before; formerly; previously ◊ former; past

一切 yíqiè everything; all

易燃 yìrán combustible

医生 yīshēng doctor

遗失 yíshī lose

仪式 yíshì ceremony; ritual

意识 yìshí awareness

意识到 yìshí dào realize

艺术 yìshù art ◊ artistic

艺术家 yìshùjiā artist

艺术品 yìshù pǐn work of art

意思 yìsi meaning; interest

伊斯兰教 Yīsīlán jiào Islam ◊ Islamic

一条裤子 yītiáo kùzi a pair of pants

意图 yìtú intention

意外 yìwài accidental ◊ unexpectedly

疑问 yíwèn doubt; query

译文 yìwén translation

义务 yìwù obligation; duty ◊ voluntary *work*

以下 yǐxià under; following

一下子 yīxiàzi all at once; in one go

一些 yìxiē some, a few

疑心 yíxīn suspicion

医学 yīxué medicine ◊ medical

一样 yīyàng just as; just the same

一言为定 yī yán wéi dìng it's a deal

意义 yìyì meaning; point

异议 yìyì objection

医院 yīyuàn hospital, infirmary

议员 yìyuán representative; congressman

译员 yìyuán interpreter

一月 yīyuè January

依仗 yīzhàng count on

译者 yìzhě translator

一直 yìzhí all the time, all along

抑制 yìzhì restrain; refrain

移植 yízhí transplant; graft

遗址 yízhǐ ruin

一致 yízhì uniform; unanimous ◊ uniformly; unanimously

意志 yìzhì will, willpower

以至于 yǐzhìyú so that

遗嘱 yízhǔ legacy; will

椅子 yǐzi chair

用 yòng use; apply ◊ with

拥抱 yōngbào cuddle; embrace; hug

涌出 yǒngchū pour

勇敢 yǒnggǎn brave; bravely ◊ bravery

用户 yònghù user; consumer

拥挤 yōngjǐ crowd; jostle ◊ crowded

佣金 yòngjīn commission

用量 yòngliàng dose

勇气 yǒngqì courage; spirit

佣人 yōngrén servant

用途 yòngtú use

永远 yǒngyuǎn for ever

用早餐 yòng zǎocān have breakfast

油 yóu oil; fat; grease

有 yǒu have; there is; there are

右 yòu right ◊ on the right

又 yòu again

幽暗 yōu'àn dark

油菜 yóucài rape

幼虫 yòuchóng larva

邮戳 yóuchuō postmark

由此 yóucǐ from this

优待 yōudài favor; special treatment

邮递 yóudì mail delivery

优点 yōudiǎn merit

邮递员 yóudìyuán mailman

幼儿 yòu'ér infant

诱饵 yòu'ěr bait, decoy

幼儿园 yòu'éryuán kindergarten

有轨电车 yǒuguǐ diànchē streetcar

有规律 yǒu guīlǜ regular ◊ regularly

有害元素 yǒuhài yuánsù harmful substance

友好 yǒuhǎo friendly; kind ◊ goodwill

油画 yóuhuà oil painting

邮汇 yóuhuì money order

有机 yǒujī organic ◊ organically

邮件 yóujiàn mail

有价证券 yóujià zhèngquàn bond, security

邮局 yóujú post office

由来 yóulái origin

游览 yóulǎn visit; tour; go sightseeing

游乐场 yóulèchǎng amusement park

有理 yǒulǐ reasonable; rational; in the right

有利 yǒulì advantageous; favorable

忧虑 yōulǜ worry ◊ worried; distracted

优美 yōuměi graceful; dainty ◊ grace

幽默 yōumò humor

有耐心 yǒu nàixīn patient

油腻 yóunì greasy; rich

右派 yòupài right; right

winger

邮票 **yóupiào** stamp

尤其 **yóuqí** especially

有趣 **yǒuqù** fun, amusing, entertaining; interesting

优势 **yōushì** superiority

有时 **yǒushí** sometimes

有失体统 **yǒu shī tǐtǒng** offensive

幼兽 **yòushòu** cub

犹太人 **Yóutàirén** Jew

有弹性 **yǒu tánxìng** springy, elastic; supple

油田 **yóutián** oil field

游戏 **yóuxì** play; game

优先 **yōuxiān** preferential, priority ◊ take priority

有线电视 **yǒuxiàn diànshì** cable TV

邮箱 **yóuxiāng** mailbox

优先权 **yōuxiān quán** priority

有些 **yǒuxiē** some

游行 **yóuxíng** march, parade

优秀 **yōuxiù** excellent ◊ excellence

有益 **yǒuyì** beneficial; useful

友谊 **yǒuyì** friendship

有意 **yǒuyì** deliberate ◊ deliberately

游泳 **yóuyǒng** swim ◊ swimming

有用 **yǒuyòng** useful

游泳池 **yóuyǒngchí** swimming pool

游泳裤 **yóuyǒngkù** swimming shorts

游泳衣 **yóuyǒng yī** swimsuit

忧郁 **yōuyù** gloom ◊ gloomy

由于 **yóuyú** with; through ◊ because of; due to

犹豫 **yóuyù** hesitate ◊ hesitation ◊ tentative

犹豫不定 **yóuyù búdìng** indecisive

优越 **yōuyuè** superior

邮政编码 **yóuzhèng biānmǎ** zip code

幼稚 **yòuzhì** childish; naive ◊ childishness; child

邮资 **yóuzī** postage

柚子 **yòuzi** pomelo

鱼 **yú** fish

与 **yǔ** and ◊ with

雨 **yǔ** rain

玉 **yù** jade

欲 **yù** desire

圆 **yuán** round ◊ circle

元 **yuán** yuan (*Chinese currency*)

园 **yuán** garden

远 **yuǎn** far; distant

愿 **yuàn** wish

远处 **yuǎnchù** distant place

元旦 **Yuándàn** New Year's Day

园丁 **yuándīng** gardener

远东 **Yuǎndōng** Far East

原告 **yuángào** claimant; plaintiff

园规 **yuánguī** compass

远见 **yuǎnjiàn** vision

原来 **yuánlái** original ◊ originally

原谅 **yuánliàng** forgive ◊ forgiveness

原料 **yuánliào** raw material; ingredient

圆盘 **yuánpán** disk

原始 **yuánshǐ** primitive

远视 **yuǎnshì** long-sighted

元素 **yuánsù** element CHEM

愿望 **yuànwàng** wish

圆形 **yuánxíng** round

园艺 **yuányì** gardening; horticulture

愿意 **yuànyì** willing ◊ willingness ◊ want

原因 **yuányīn** cause

元音 **yuányīn** vowel

原则 **yuánzé** principle

援助 **yuánzhù** support, help

圆珠笔 **yuánzhūbǐ** ballpoint pen

院子 **yuànzi** yard; courtyard

原子弹 **yuánzǐ dàn** atom bomb

原子能 **yuánzǐ néng** atomic energy

远足 **yuǎnzú** excursion; hike

预报 **yùbào** forecast

预备 **yùbèi** prepare

愚蠢 **yúchǔn** stupid ◊ stupidity

鱼刺 **yúcì** fishbone

遇到 **yùdào** meet, run into

预定 **yùdìng** book ◊ booking

约 **yuē** arrange

月 **yuè** month

乐 **yuè** music

越…越… **yuè…yuè…** the more…the more…

约定 **yuēdìng** agree; arrange to meet

阅读 **yuèdú** read ◊ reading

乐队 **yuèduì** band; orchestra

岳父 **yuèfù** father-in-law

月光 **yuèguāng** moonlight

越过 **yuèguò** exceed, pass; get over

月经 **yuèjīng** period; menstruation

月经带 **yuèjīngdài** sanitary napkin

越来越 **yuèláiyuè** increasingly

阅览室 **yuèlǎnshì** reading room

月亮 **yuèliàng** moon ◊ lunar

岳母 **yuèmǔ** mother-in-law

越南 **Yuènán** Vietnam ◊ Vietnamese

月票 **yuèpiào** monthly ticket

乐器 **yuèqì** musical instrument

约束 **yuēshù** restrain; curb; bind; restrict ◊ restriction

越野 **yuèyě** cross-country

乐音 **yuèyīn** tone

语法 **yǔfǎ** grammar

预防 **yùfáng** prevent ◊ prevention

预防措施 **yùfáng cuòshī** precaution; preventive measure

预付 **yùfù** advance ◊ pay in advance

鱼竿 **yúgān** fishing pole

鱼肝油 **yúgānyóu** cod-liver oil

预告 **yùgào** forecast

宇航 **yǔháng** space travel

宇航员 **yǔhángyuán** astronaut

愈合 **yùhé** heal

预计 **yùjì** estimate; plan

预见 **yùjiàn** foresee

遇见 **yùjiàn** meet

浴巾 **yùjīn** bath towel

郁金香 **yùjīnxiāng** tulip

愉快 **yúkuài** happy

娱乐 **yúlè** entertainment; pleasure; recreation

预料 **yùliào** expect; foretell ◊ anticipation

羽毛 **yǔmáo** feather; plume

羽毛球 **yǔmáoqiú** badminton; shuttlecock

玉米 **yùmǐ** corn

玉米花 **yùmǐhuā** popcorn

渔民 **yúmín** fisherman

云 **yún** cloud

熨 **yùn** iron

晕 **yùn** dizzy

运 **yùn** transport

晕船 **yùnchuán** seasick ◊ get seasick

运动 **yùndòng** move; movement; campaign; sport; exercise

运动场 **yùndòng chǎng** playing field

运动员 **yùndòngyuán** sportsman; sportswoman; athlete; player

熨斗 **yùndǒu** iron

孕妇 **yùnfù** pregnant woman

运河 **yùnhé** canal

晕机 **yùnjī** airsickness

愚弄 **yúnòng** tease

云雀 **yúnquè** lark

运输 **yùnshū** transportation

运输公司 **yùnshū gōngsī** shipping company

允许 **yǔnxǔ** allow

浴盆 **yùpén** bathtub

语气 **yǔqì** tone

雨伞 **yǔsǎn** umbrella

于是 **yúshì** then; consequently

浴室 **yùshì** bathroom

预算 **yùsuàn** calculate ◊ budget

欲望 **yùwàng** desire; longing

雨靴 **yǔxuē** rain boot

语言 **yǔyán** language ◊ linguistic

预言 **yùyán** prophecy; prediction ◊ predict

渔业 **yúyè** fishing industry

雨衣 **yǔyī** raincoat

浴衣 **yùyī** bathrobe

预约 **yùyuē** arrange; reserve ◊ advance booking

预兆 **yùzhào** sign

宇宙 **yǔzhòu** universe

# Z

杂草 **zácǎo** weed

杂货店 **záhuò diàn** grocery store

栽 **zāi** plant

在 **zài** at; in; on

再 **zài** again; further

在…里 **zài…lǐ** inside…

在…旁 **zài…páng** beside…

在…上面 **zài…shàngmian** on…; above…

在…同时 **zài…tóngshí** during…

在…下面 **zài…xiàmiàn** under…

在…之间 **zài…zhījiān** between…

在…之前 **zài…zhīqián** before…

在场 **zàichǎng** presence ◊ be present

灾害 **zāihài** disaster

在乎 **zàihu** mind; care

灾祸 **zāihuò** disaster

再见 **zàijiàn** goodbye

灾难 **zāinàn** disaster

栽培 **zāipéi** cultivation

再说 **zàishuō** besides; moreover

再一次 **zàiyícì** once more

杂技 **zájì** acrobatics

杂乱无章 **záluàn-wúzhāng** disorder; mess ◊ messy

暂 **zàn** temporary

赞成 **zànchéng** approve; agree with ◊ favorable, agreeable ◊ approval

脏 **zāng** dirty

葬礼 **zànglǐ** funeral; burial

脏物 **zāngwù** dirt

赞美 **zànměi** praise; compliment ◊ complimentary

咱们 **zánmen** us; we

赞赏 **zànshǎng** appreciate

暂时 **zànshí** temporarily ◊ temporary

赞同 **zàntóng** agree with; approve

暂行 **zànxíng** temporary ◊ temporarily

赞助 **zànzhù** support; patronage; sponsorship

凿 **záo** chisel

早 **zǎo** morning ◊ early ◊ beforehand

灶 **zào** stove; hearth

早餐 **zǎocān** breakfast

早产 **zǎochǎn** premature birth

早晨 **zǎochén** morning ◊ in the morning

遭到 **zāodào** meet with

造反 **zàofǎn** revolt

糟糕 **zāogāo** bad ◊ badly

早就 **zǎojiù** for a long time; a long time ago

早上好 **zǎoshang hǎo** good morning

遭受 **zāoshòu** suffer

噪音 **zàoyīn** noise

凿子 **záozi** chisel

枣子 **zǎozi** Chinese date

杂志 **zázhì** magazine

责备 **zébèi** blame; reproach; reprimand

责骂 **zémà** scold

憎恨 **zēnghèn** hate

增加 **zēngjiā** increase ◊ raise ◊ increasing

增刊 **zēngkān** supplement

增强 **zēngqiáng** strengthen

赠送 **zèngsòng** give ◊ complimentary

曾孙 **zēngsūn** great-grandchild

增长 **zēngzhǎng** grow ◊

growth

增值 zēngzhí increase in value

增值税 zēngzhí shuì value-added tax

曾祖父 zēngzǔfù great-grandfather

曾祖母 zēngzǔmǔ great-grandmother

怎么 zěnme how

责任 zérèn responsibility, duty; blame

闸 zhá lock; sluice

炸 zhà blow up; explode

榨出 zhàchū extract; squeeze out ◊ extraction

炸弹 zhàdàn bomb

轧辊 zhágǔn roller

摘 zhāi pick

窄 zhǎi narrow

债 zhài debt

摘录 zhāilù extract

债券 zhàiquàn promissory note; bond

债权人 zhàiquánrén creditor

债务 zhàiwù debt

栅栏 zhàlán fence; railings; bars

蚱蜢 zhàměng grasshopper

粘 zhān stick

毡 zhān felt

占 zhàn occupy; take; constitute; make up

站 zhàn stand ◊ stop; station

展出 zhǎnchū exhibit; display

战斗 zhàndòu combat; fight

战俘 zhànfú prisoner of war

章 zhāng chapter

长 zhǎng grow ◊ head

障碍 zhàng'ài obstacle; barrier

障碍物 zhàng'àiwù barrier

涨潮 zhǎngcháo incoming tide ◊ come in (of tide)

章程 zhāngchéng rules; statutes

长大 zhǎngdà grow up; develop

账单 zhàngdān check; invoice

丈夫 zhàngfu husband

涨价 zhǎngjià price rise

张开 zhāngkāi open, unfold

樟脑 zhāngnǎo camphor

帐篷 zhàngpeng tent

掌声 zhǎngshēng applause

掌握 zhǎngwò grasp; master; control

展览 zhǎnlǎn display, exhibit

展览会 **zhǎnlǎnhuì** exhibition

占领 **zhànlǐng** capture; occupy ◊ occupation

战胜 **zhànshèng** conquer ◊ victorious

战士 **zhànshì** soldier; warrior; fighter

站台 **zhàntái** platform

粘贴 **zhāntiē** stick

站位 **zhànwèi** standing room

占线 **zhànxiàn** busy ◊ the line is busy

战线 **zhànxiàn** front; battle line

战役 **zhànyì** battle

占有 **zhànyǒu** own; take

占有者 **zhànyǒuzhě** owner

战争 **zhànzhēng** war; conflict; hostilities

站住 **zhànzhù** stop

辗转 **zhǎnzhuǎn** toss and turn

找 **zhǎo** look for; ask for

招待 **zhāodài** entertain; serve *customer*

招待会 **zhāodài huì** reception

照顾 **zhàogù** look after; tend ◊ care

照管 **zhàoguǎn** look after

着急 **zháojí** worry

召集 **zhàojí** call

召开 **zhàokāi** convene, hold

照看 **zhàokàn** watch, keep an eye on

照明 **zhàomíng** illuminate, light ◊ lighting

照片 **zhàopiàn** photograph

招聘 **zhāopìn** recruit ◊ recruitment

招认 **zhāorèn** confess

招手 **zhāoshǒu** wave; beckon

朝霞 **zhāoxiá** dawn

照相 **zhàoxiàng** take a photo

照像机 **zhàoxiàngjī** camera

照耀 **zhàoyào** shine

罩衣 **zhàoyī** coverall

沼泽 **zhǎozé** swamp

眨眼 **zhǎyǎn** blink; wink

炸药 **zhàyào** dynamite; gunpowder; explosive

这 **zhè** this; the

这次 **zhècì** this time

折叠 **zhédié** fold ◊ folding

折断 **zhéduàn** break; break off; fracture

这个 **zhège** this ◊ this one

折扣 **zhékòu** discount; rebate

这里 **zhèlǐ** here

折磨 **zhémo** torture

针 **zhēn** needle

真 **zhēn** real

珍宝 **zhēnbǎo** treasure; gem

侦察 **zhēnchá** reconnoiter ◊ reconnaissance

震颤 **zhènchàn** throb; tremble; twitch

真诚 **zhēnchéng** sincere ◊ sincerely ◊ sincerity

针刺 **zhēncì** acupuncture

镇定 **zhèndìng** calm

震动 **zhèndòng** shudder; vibrate ◊ vibration; tremor

振动 **zhèndòng** vibrate ◊ vibration

蒸 **zhēng** steam

正 **zhèng** positive; plus; upright; just

挣 **zhēng** earn; struggle

政策 **zhèngcè** policy

正常 **zhèngcháng** normal ◊ normally ◊ normality

正常运转 **zhèngcháng yùnzhuǎn** normal operation

争吵 **zhēngchǎo** quarrel

证词 **zhèngcí** testimony

正当 **zhèngdàng** proper; legitimate; right

挣得 **zhèngde** earn

正点 **zhèngdiǎn** on schedule

争斗 **zhēngdòu** fight

整顿 **zhèngdùn** regulation; arrangement

蒸发 **zhēngfā** evaporate; steam

正方形 **zhèngfāng xíng** square

征服 **zhēngfú** conquer ◊ conquest

政府 **zhèngfǔ** government

正好 **zhènghǎo** just right

证件 **zhèngjiàn** ID

整洁 **zhěngjié** neat, tidy

拯救 **zhěngjiù** save ◊ salvation

证据 **zhèngjù** evidence; proof

整理 **zhěnglǐ** arrange; sort out; clear up

争论 **zhēnglùn** argue; dispute ◊ argument; controversy

正面 **zhèngmiàn** front; façade

证明 **zhèngmíng** certify; prove

正派 **zhèngpài** decent; law-abiding; straight ◊ decency

蒸汽 **zhēngqì** steam

整齐 zhěngqí neat, tidy

挣钱 zhèngqián earn money

蒸汽机车 zhēngqì jīchē steam locomotive

政权 zhèngquán regime

正确 zhèngquè correct ◊ correctly

证人 zhèngrén witness

证实 zhèngshí confirm

正式 zhèngshì formal; official ◊ formally; officially

征收 zhēngshōu impose; collect

证书 zhèngshū certificate; qualification

整体 zhěngtǐ whole

正义 zhèngyì just ◊ justice

证章 zhèngzhāng badge

正直 zhèngzhí be right ◊ decent

政治 zhèngzhì politics ◊ political

政治家 zhèngzhìjiā politician

症状 zhèngzhuàng symptom

正字法 zhèngzìfǎ spelling

震撼 zhènhàn shake

赈济 zhènjì charity

贞洁 zhēnjié chaste ◊ virginity

震惊 zhènjīng shock

镇静 zhènjìng composed ◊ composure

真理 zhēnlǐ truth

珍品 zhēnpǐn gem

真实 zhēnshí real; true ◊ really

诊所 zhěnsuǒ clinic

侦探 zhēntàn detective

侦探片 zhēntànpiàn detective movie

枕套 zhěntào pillowcase

镇痛 zhèntòng analgesic

枕头 zhěntou pillow

真相 zhēnxiàng fact; truth

阵雨 zhènyǔ shower (of rain)

真正 zhēnzhèng authentic; real ◊ really

针织品 zhēnzhīpǐn knitwear

珍珠 zhēnzhū pearl

榛子 zhēnzi hazelnut

这些 zhèxiē these

哲学 zhéxué philosophy

这样 zhèyàng like this; so ◊ such

遮阴 zhēyīn shade ◊ shady

汁 zhī juice

织 zhī weave

直 zhí straight

只 zhǐ only

纸 zhǐ paper

指 **zhǐ** finger ◊ point to

至 **zhì** to; up to ◊ reach

纸板 **zhǐbǎn** cardboard

纸板盒 **zhǐbǎn hé** cardboard box

纸币 **zhǐbì** bill

织布机 **zhībùjī** loom

支撑 **zhīchēng** support; sustain

支持 **zhīchí** support

支出 **zhīchū** pay ◊ expenditure

直达 **zhídá** direct

知道 **zhīdao** know

直到 **zhídào** until

指导 **zhǐdǎo** guide; instruct; coach ◊ instructions; guidance; directory

值得 **zhídé** deserve; be worthwhile ◊ desirable; recommended

制动 **zhìdòng** brake

制度 **zhìdù** system

至多 **zhìduō** at most

脂肪 **zhīfáng** fat

支付 **zhīfù** pay

制服 **zhìfú** uniform

支付手段 **zhīfù shǒuduàn** means of payment

制革 **zhìgé** tan *leather*

职工 **zhígōng** workforce

智慧 **zhìhuì** wisdom; intelligence

支架 **zhījià** upright; support

指甲 **zhǐjia** fingernail

指甲油 **zhǐjia yóu** nail polish

直接 **zhíjiē** direct ◊ directly

至今 **zhìjīn** until now

直径 **zhíjìng** diameter

指控 **zhǐkòng** accuse; charge ◊ allegation

智力 **zhìlì** intellect; intelligence ◊ intellectual

质量 **zhìliàng** quality

治疗 **zhìliáo** treatment; therapy ◊ treat

支流 **zhīliú** tributary

直流电 **zhíliúdiàn** direct current

支路 **zhīlù** side road

芝麻 **zhīma** sesame

芝麻油 **zhīmayóu** sesame oil

殖民地 **zhímíndì** colony ◊ colonial

知名 **zhīmíng** famous; prominent

指明 **zhǐmíng** point out

致命 **zhìmìng** fatal ◊ fatally

指南针 **zhǐnánzhēn** compass

执拗 **zhíniù** stubborn

侄女 **zhínǚ** niece

支票 **zhīpiào** check FIN

志气 **zhìqi** ambition

支气管炎 **zhīqìguǎnyán** bronchitis

支取 **zhīqǔ** withdraw

掷骰子 **zhì shǎizi** throw dice

至少 **zhìshǎo** at least

直升飞机 **zhíshēng fēijī** helicopter

知识 **zhīshi** knowledge; learning

指示 **zhǐshì** indicate; instruct ◊ indication; directions

肢体语言 **zhītǐ yǔyán** body language

制图 **zhìtú** make maps

职位 **zhíwèi** position

质问 **zhìwèn** question, challenge

植物 **zhíwù** plant ◊ botanical

职务 **zhíwù** duties; job

植物学 **zhíwùxué** botany

窒息 **zhìxī** suffocate ◊ suffocation

支线 **zhīxiàn** branch line

直线 **zhíxiàn** straight line

志向 **zhìxiàng** ambition

致谢 **zhìxiè** extend one's thanks

执行 **zhíxíng** carry out

秩序 **zhìxù** order

止血 **zhǐxuè** stop bleeding ◊ styptic

只要 **zhǐyào** provided that; so long as

职业 **zhíyè** business; profession; occupation ◊ vocational; occupational; professional

致意 **zhìyì** greeting

指引 **zhǐyǐn** guide, show

只有 **zhǐyǒu** only if; nothing but

治愈 **zhìyù** cure

职员 **zhíyuán** employee

志愿者 **zhìyuànzhě** volunteer

制造 **zhìzào** manufacture ◊ manufacturing

指责 **zhǐzé** rebuke; reproach ◊ disapproval ◊ reproachful

执照 **zhízhào** license

指针 **zhǐzhēn** needle (on dial); hand (on clock)

制止 **zhìzhǐ** prevent; deter; stem; block

蜘蛛 **zhīzhū** spider

侄子 **zhízǐ** nephew

知足 **zhīzú** undemanding

制作 **zhìzuò** produce ◊ production

钟 **zhōng** clock; bell

中 **zhōng** middle; medium; China

肿 **zhŏng** swell ◊ swollen

种 **zhòng** plant

仲裁 **zhòngcái** arbitrate ◊ arbitration

中餐 **zhōngcān** Chinese food

忠诚 **zhōngchéng** faithful

重大 **zhòngdà** serious

终点 **zhōngdiǎn** finish, end

重点 **zhòngdiǎn** stress; key point; emphasis

终点站 **zhōngdiǎnzhàn** terminus

中东 **Zhōngdōng** Middle East

中毒 **zhòngdú** poisoning

中断 **zhōngduàn** interrupt; break off ◊ interruption

中耳炎 **zhōng'ěryán** middle ear infection

中饭 **zhōngfàn** lunch

中风 **zhòngfēng** stroke MED

重工业 **zhònggōngyè** heavy industry

中国 **Zhōngguó** China ◊ Chinese

中国人 **Zhōngguórén** Chinese (person)

中华人民共和国 **Zhōng-huá Rénmín Gònghéguó** People's Republic of China, PRC

中间 **zhōngjiān** middle ◊ halfway

终究 **zhōngjiū** finally

中肯 **zhòngkěn** apt ◊ aptly

肿块 **zhŏngkuài** lump

种类 **zhŏnglèi** kind; species

中立 **zhōnglì** disinterested; neutral

重力 **zhònglì** gravity PHYS

重量 **zhòngliàng** weight

肿瘤 **zhŏngliú** tumor

中年 **zhōngnián** middle age ◊ middle-aged

中篇小说 **zhōngpiān xiǎoshuō** novella

中秋节 **Zhōngqiūjié** Mid-Autumn Festival, Moon Festival

终身 **zhōngshēn** lifelong; for life

终身伴侣 **zhōngshēn bànlǚ** life partner

忠实 **zhōngshí** devoted

重视 **zhòngshì** value

中世纪 **Zhōngshìjì** Middle Ages ◊ medieval

众所周知 **zhòngsuǒ zhōuzhī** well-known

中文 **Zhōngwén** Chinese

中午 **zhōngwǔ** midday

中心 **zhōngxīn** center; heart

衷心 **zhōngxīn** sincere; warm

中学 **zhōngxué** middle school; junior high school

中央 **zhōngyāng** central ◊ middle

重要 **zhòngyào** important

重要性 **zhòngyàoxìng** importance

终于 **zhōngyú** in the end

肿胀 **zhǒngzhàng** swell up ◊ swollen ◊ swelling

中止 **zhōngzhǐ** cease

中指 **zhōngzhǐ** middle finger

终止 **zhōngzhǐ** end

种植 **zhòngzhí** plant; cultivate

种植园 **zhòngzhíyuán** plantation

种子 **zhǒngzi** seed

洲 **zhōu** continent

周 **zhōu** week

粥 **zhōu** rice porridge

轴 **zhóu** shaft; axle

皱 **zhòu** crease

周到 **zhōudao** considerate; tactful

周末 **zhōumò** weekend ◊ on the weekend

周期 **zhōuqī** cycle; period

周围 **zhōuwéi** around ◊ surrounding ◊ surroundings

皱纹 **zhòuwén** crease

绉纹纸 **zhòuwénzhǐ** crepe paper

猪 **zhū** pig

竹 **zhú** bamboo

煮 **zhǔ** boil (*cook*)

住 **zhù** live; stop

柱 **zhù** pillar

祝 **zhù** wish

爪 **zhuǎ** claw

砖 **zhuān** brick; tile

转 **zhuǎn** turn; transfer ◊ turning

转变 **zhuǎnbiàn** shift ◊ swing; changeover

转播 **zhuǎnbō** relay *signal*

转车 **zhuǎnchē** change (trains/buses)

转达 **zhuǎndá** pass on

转达问候 **zhuǎndá wènhòu** send one's regards

转动 **zhuàndòng** turn

桩 **zhuāng** stake; peg

装 **zhuāng** pack

撞 **zhuàng** hit

壮 **zhuàng** strong

装扮 **zhuāngbàn** disguise

oneself; dress up

装备 zhuāngbèi equipment ◊ equip; furnish

撞翻 zhuàngfān knock over

庄稼 zhuāngjia crops

状况 zhuàngkuàng state

装饰 zhuāngshì decorate ◊ decoration ◊ decorative

装载 zhuāngzài load

装作 zhuāngzuò pretend; pose as

传记 zhuànjì biography

专家 zhuānjiā expert, specialist

专利 zhuānlì patent

专门 zhuānmén special

转让 zhuǎnràng entrust; transfer

转身 zhuǎnshēn turn around

转弯处 zhuǎnwānchù curve; corner

转向 zhuǎnxiàng change direction; turn around; move on ◊ change of direction; U-turn

专心 zhuānxīn concentrate ◊ concentration ◊ devotion

专有知识 zhuānyǒu zhīshi know-how

专业 zhuānyè professional ◊ professionally ◊ field

专业知识 zhuānyè zhīshi specialized knowledge

抓住 zhuāzhù grab, grasp

爪子 zhuǎzi claw; paw

珠宝 zhūbǎo jewel; jewelry

珠宝商 zhūbǎoshāng jeweler

逐步 zhúbù progressively; step by step

住处 zhùchù residence; lodging

贮存 zhùcún store

住房 zhùfáng housing

逐个 zhúgè one by one

主观 zhǔguān subjective

主管 zhǔguǎn be in charge of ◊ supervisor

祝贺 zhùhè congratulate

追求 zhuīqiú seek; pursue

追溯 zhuīsù date back to; backdate ◊ retroactive

逐渐 zhújiàn gradual ◊ gradually

主角 zhǔjué leading role

著名 zhùmíng famous

准 zhǔn allow ◊ accurate

准备 zhǔnbèi plan; prepare; fix ◊ preparation

准确 zhǔnquè accurate; precise

准确性 zhǔnquèxìng accuracy

准时 zhǔnshí punctual ◊ punctually

准许 zhǔnxǔ approve

准予 zhǔnyǔ grant

桌布 zhuōbù tablecloth

着陆 zhuólù land ◊ landing

啄木鸟 zhuómùniǎo woodpecker

捉弄 zhuōnòng take in

啄食 zhuóshí peck at one's food

着想 zhuóxiǎng consider

卓有成效 zhuó yǒu chéngxiào effective; successful

卓越 zhuōyuè outstanding; remarkable; notable ◊ remarkably

桌子 zhuōzi table

捉住 zhuōzhù catch, capture

主人 zhǔrén host; owner

猪肉 zhūròu pork

侏儒 zhūrú dwarf

注射 zhùshè inject ◊ injection

注视 zhùshì gaze ◊ gaze at

注释 zhùshì note; gloss

助手 zhùshǒu assistant

竹笋 zhúsǔn bamboo shoots

主题 zhǔtí subject, topic ◊ topical

铸铁 zhùtiě cast iron

助听器 zhùtīngqì hearing aid

主席 zhǔxí chair

助学金 zhùxuéjīn grant (for studies)

主要 zhǔyào main ◊ mainly

主意 zhǔyì idea

注意 zhùyì notice; pay attention to

铸造 zhùzào cast

主张 zhǔzhāng cause; position ◊ advocate; stand up for; represent

柱子 zhùzi pillar

字 zì word; character; handwriting

自 zì self ◊ from

资本 zīběn capital

资本主义 zīběn zhǔyì capitalism ◊ capitalist

滋补 zībǔ nutritious

资产 zīchǎn asset FIN

资产阶级 zīchǎn jiējí bourgeoisie

自从 zìcóng since

子弹 zǐdàn bullet; cartridge;

pellet

字典 **zìdiǎn** dictionary

自动 **zìdòng** automatic ◊ automatically; by itself

自发 **zìfā** spontaneous

自负 **zìfù** pompous; arrogant; conceited ◊ arrogance; conceit

资格 **zīgé** qualification

子宫 **zǐgōng** womb

自豪 **zìháo** pride ◊ proud ◊ proudly

自己 **zìjǐ** self; oneself ◊ own ◊ by oneself

紫禁城 **Zǐjìnchéng** Forbidden City

自来水 **zìláishuǐ** running water

自来水笔 **zìláishuǐbǐ** fountain pen

字面 **zìmiàn** literal ◊ literally

字母 **zìmǔ** letter (*of alphabet*)

字幕 **zìmù** subtitle

字母表 **zìmǔbiǎo** alphabet

自然 **zìrán** nature ◊ natural ◊ naturally, of course

自然保护 **zìrán bǎohù** conservation

自然灾害 **zìrán zāihài** natural disaster

紫色 **zǐsè** purple

自杀 **zìshā** suicide ◊ commit suicide

姿势 **zīshì** position; posture

自私自利 **zìsī-zìlì** selfish

字体 **zìtǐ** font; typeface

滋味 **zīwèi** flavor; taste

自卫 **zìwèi** self-defense

自我控制 **zìwǒ kòngzhì** self-control

仔细 **zǐxì** careful ◊ closely

自信 **zìxìn** confident; self-confident; assertive ◊ self-confidence

自行车 **zìxíngchē** bicycle

自信心 **zìxìnxīn** self-confidence

自选 **zìxuǎn** self-service ◊ optional

咨询 **zīxún** advice; consultancy

自由 **zìyóu** freedom, liberty ◊ free; liberal

自愿 **zìyuàn** voluntary ◊ of one's own accord

自助餐 **zìzhùcān** buffet, self-service meal

自尊心 **zìzūnxīn** self-respect

总 **zǒng** total; general; main; gross FIN ◊ always

总部 **zǒngbù** head office

总裁 **zǒngcái** president

总共 **zǒnggòng** altogether

纵横交错 **zònghéng jiāocuò** checkered

总机 **zǒngjī** telephone exchange

踪迹 **zōngjì** trace

总计 **zǒngjì** total

宗教 **zōngjiào** religion ◊ religious

总结 **zǒngjié** summary

总理 **zǒnglǐ** premier; prime minister

棕榈树 **zōnglǘshù** palm tree

棕色 **zōngsè** brown

总是 **zǒngshì** always

总数 **zǒngshù** total; sum

总统 **zǒngtǒng** president ◊ presidential

走 **zǒu** walk; go; move; leave; run; navigate COMPUT

奏 **zòu** play *instrument*

揍 **zòu** beat up; punch

走过来 **zǒu guòlai** approach

走进 **zǒujìn** enter

走开 **zǒukāi** buzz off; walk away

走廊 **zǒuláng** corridor; passageway

走私 **zǒusī** smuggle ◊ smuggling

走运 **zǒuyùn** be lucky

租 **zū** rent; hire; lease

足 **zú** foot ◊ enough

组 **zǔ** group; team, crew

阻碍 **zǔ'ài** hinder; frustrate ◊ setback

钻孔 **zuānkǒng** bore a hole

钻头 **zuàntóu** drill

组成 **zǔchéng** comprise

阻挡 **zǔdǎng** obstruct; keep, detain ◊ tackle

祖父母 **zǔfùmǔ** grand-parents

足够 **zúgòu** ample ◊ amply

祖国 **zǔguó** native country, homeland

嘴 **zuǐ** mouth; spout

罪 **zuì** crime

醉 **zuì** drunk

最 **zuì** most, *used to form superlatives*

最初 **zuìchū** first; original

嘴唇 **zuǐchún** lip

最多 **zuìduō** maximum ◊ at most

罪犯 **zuìfàn** criminal; culprit; offender

最高 **zuìgāo** highest; topmost; tallest

最好 **zuìhǎo** best

最后 **zuìhòu** last; ultimate ◊ lastly; in the end

最近 **zuìjìn** recent; closest ◊ recently; soon

罪人 **zuìrén** sinner; offender

最小 **zuìxiǎo** least

罪行 **zuìxíng** crime; offense

最终 **zuìzhōng** eventual; final ◊ eventually; finally

租金 **zūjīn** rental

遵从 **zūncóng** comply with ◊ compliance

尊敬 **zūnjìng** respect; esteemed

遵守 **zūnshǒu** abide by ◊ observance

遵循 **zūnxún** follow

尊严 **zūnyán** dignity

尊重 **zūnzhòng** respect; honor

左 **zuǒ** left

坐 **zuò** sit; sit down; catch

作 **zuò** make; do

做 **zuò** make; do; perform, carry out

作伴 **zuòbàn** keep company

左边 **zuǒbian** left, the left-hand side ◊ left-hand

做出反应 **zuòchū fǎnyìng** respond

作坊 **zuōfang** workshop

作废 **zuòfèi** expire

作家 **zuòjiā** writer

作料 **zuóliào** seasoning

坐落在 **zuòluòzài** be situated

做梦 **zuòmèng** dream

琢磨 **zuómo** ponder

左派 **zuǒpài** the left

作品 **zuòpǐn** work; production

作曲家 **zuòqǔ jiā** composer

左手 **zuǒshǒu** left hand

昨天 **zuótiān** yesterday

昨天晚上 **zuótiān wǎnshang** last night

作为 **zuòwéi** as; by way of

座位 **zuòwèi** place, seat

坐下 **zuòxia** sit down

作业 **zuòyè** job, task; homework; assignment

作用 **zuòyòng** function

作者 **zuòzhě** author, writer

作证 **zuòzhèng** testify

足球 **zúqiú** soccer

阻塞 **zǔsè** block ◊ traffic jam

祖先 **zǔxiān** ancestor; ancestry

租用 **zūyòng** lease

阻止 **zǔzhǐ** stop, prevent; block

诅咒 **zǔzhòu** curse

# A

**a, an** *no translation*

**abandon** pāoqì 抛弃; *car* líqì 离弃; *plan* fàngqì 放弃

**abbreviation** suōxiě 缩写

**ability** nénglì 能力

**able: be ~ to** néng 能

**abolish** fèichú 废除

**abortion** rénggōng liúchǎn 人工流产

**about 1** *prep (concerning)* guānyú ...关于...; *what's it ~?* jiǎng shénmede? 讲什么的？**2** *adv (roughly)* dàyuē 大约; *be ~ to ...* zhèng zhǔnbèi ... 正准备... 

**above 1** *prep* bǐ ...gāo 比...高; *(more than)* bǐ ...duō 比...多; *~ all* zuì zhòngyào 最重要**2** *adv* zài shàngtou 在上头

**abroad** *live* guówài 国外; *go ~* chūguó 出国

**abrupt** *departure* tūrán 突然; *manner* shēngyìng 生硬

**absent** *adj* quēxí 缺席

**absent-minded** xīnbú zàiyān 心不在焉

**absolutely** *(completely)* wánquán 完全

**absorb** xīshōu 吸收

**abstain** *(in vote)* qìquán 弃权

**abstract** *adj* chōuxiàng 抽象

**absurd** huāngtáng 荒唐

**abuse** *n (insults)* rǔmà 辱骂

**academic** *n* xuézhě 学者

**accelerate 1** *v/i* jiāsù 加速**2** *v/t output* jiākuài 加快

**accent** kǒuyīn 口音; *(emphasis)* zhòngyīn 重音

**accept** *v/t offer* jiēshòu 接受

**acceptance** jiēshòu 接受

**access** *n (to building)* rùkǒu 入口

**accident** shìgù 事故; *(not done on purpose)* bùxiǎoxīn 不小心

**accommodations** zhùsuǒ 住所

**accompany** péitóng 陪同;

MUS bànzòu 伴奏

**accomplice** bāngxiōng 帮凶

**according:** ~ **to** gēnjù 根据

**account** n FIN zhàngmù 帐目; (*description*) xùshù 叙述

**accountant** kuàijì 会计

**accounts** zhàngmù 帐目

**accumulate** v/t & v/i lěijī 累积

**accuracy** zhǔnquèxìng 准确性

**accurate** zhǔnquè 准确

**accusation** zéguài 责怪; (*public*) qiǎnzé 谴责

**accuse** zhǐkòng 指控; (*publicly*) qiǎnzé 谴责

**accused:** the ~ LAW bèigào 被告

**ache** n & v/i tòng 痛

**achieve** huòdé 获得

**achievement** (*of ambition*) huòdé 获得; (*thing achieved*) chéngjiù 成就

**acid** n suān 酸

**acknowledge** chéngrèn 承认

**acknowledg(e)ment** rènkě 认可

**acquaintance** (*person*) shúrén 熟人

**acquire** skill huòdé 获得;

property qǔdé 取得

**acquit** LAW xuānpàn wúzuì 宣判无罪

**acrobat** zájì yǎnyuán 杂技演员

**across 1** prep (*on other side of*) zài ...de língyíbiān 在 ...的另一边 ◊ (*to other side of*) héngguò 横过; (*of street etc*) guò 过 **2** adv (*to other side*) guòlái 过来

**act 1** v/i THEA biǎoyǎn 表演; ~ as línshí dānrèn 临时担任 **2** n (*deed*) xíngdòng 行动; (*of play*) mù 幕; (*in vaudeville*) jiémù 节目; (*pretense*) jiǎzhuāng 假装

**acting 1** n (*profession*) biǎoyǎn yè 表演业; (*performance*) biǎoyǎn 表演 **2** adj (*temporary*) dàilǐ 代理

**action** xíngdòng 行动

**active** huóyuè 活跃

**activity** huódòng 活动

**actor** yǎnyuán 演员

**actress** nǚyǎnyuán 女演员

**actual** shíjì 实际

**acupuncture** zhēnjiǔ 针灸

**acute** pain jùliè 剧烈

**adapt 1** v/t (*for TV etc*)

gǎibiān 改编; *machine* gǎiyòng 改用 2 v/i (of *person*) shìyìng 适应

**adapter** ELEC shìpèiqì 适配器

**add** v/t jiā 加

**addict** n chéngyǐnzhě 成瘾者

**addiction** yǐn 瘾

**addition** MATH jiāfǎ 加法; (*to list etc*) bǔchōng 补充

**additional** fùjiā 附加

**additive** tiānjiājì 添加剂

**address** n dìzhǐ 地址

**address book** tōngxùn lù 通讯录

**adequate** chōngfèn 充分; (*satisfactory*) jǐn gòu mǎnyì 仅够满意

**adhesive** yǒu niánxìng 有粘性

**adjourn** v/i (of *meeting*) xiūhuì 休会

**adjust** v/t tiáozhěng 调整

**administration** xíngzhèng 行政; (of *country*) zhìlǐ 治理; (*government*) zhèngfǔ 政府

**administrative** xíngzhèng 行政

**admiration** qīnpèi 钦佩

**admire** qīnpèi 钦佩

**admission** (*confession*) chéngrèn 承认; ~ *free* miǎnfèi rùchǎng 免费入场

**admit** (*to hospital etc*) jiēnà 接纳; (*confess*) chéngrèn 承认

**adolescent** n qīngshàonián 青少年

**adopt** *child* lǐngyǎng 领养; *plan* cǎinà 采纳

**adult** chéngrén 成人

**adultery** sītōng 私通

**advance** n (*money*) tòuzhī 透支; (*in science etc*) xiānjìn 先进; MIL jìngōng 进攻; *in* ~ yùxiān 预先

**advanced** *country* xiānjìn 先进; *level* gāoděng 高等; *learner* gāojí 高级

**advantage** hǎochù 好处

**adventure** màoxiǎn 冒险

**advertise** v/t & v/i dēng guǎnggào 登广告

**advertisement** guǎnggào 广告

**advice** zīxún 咨询

**advisable** kěqǔ 可取

**advise** *person* quàngào 劝告; *caution etc* zhōnggào 忠告; ~ *X to* ... jiànyì X zuò ... 建议X做...

adviser gùwèn 顾问

aerobics jiànměicāo 健美操

affair (matter) shì 事; (business) shìwù 事务; (love) liàn'ài 恋爱

affect yǐngxiǎng 影响; MED qīnxí 侵袭

affection àimù 爱慕

affectionate shì'ài示爱

afford (financially) fùdān de qǐ 负担得起

afraid: be ~ (of) hàipà 害怕

Africa Fēizhōu 非洲

African 1 adj Fēizhōu 非洲 2 n Fēizhōurén 非洲人

after 1 prep zhīhòu 之后; ~ all bìjìng 毕竟; it's ten ~ two liǎngdiǎn shífēn 两点十分 2 adv (afterward) hòulái 后来; the day ~ dì'èrtiān 第二天

afternoon xiàwǔ 下午

aftershave xūhòushuǐ 须后水

afterward hòulái 后来

again zài 再

against lean kào 靠; X ~ Y SP X duì Y X 对 Y; I'm ~ the idea wǒ fǎnduì zhège zhǔyì 我反对这个主意

age n (of person, object)

niánjì 年纪; (era) shídài 时代

agency dàilǐchù 代理处

agenda yìchéng 议程

agent dàilǐrén 代理人

aggressive hào xúnxìn 好 寻衅

agitated jiāolù bù'ān 焦虑不安

ago: 2 days ~ liǎngtiān qián 两天前; long ~ hěnjiǔ yǐqián 很久以前

agree v/i/t tóngyì 同意

agreement (consent) tóngyì 同意; (contract) xiéyì 协议

agriculture nóngyè 农业

ahead: be ~ lǐngxiān 领先

Aids àizībìng 艾滋病

aim 1 n (in shooting) miáozhǔn 瞄准; (objective) mùbiāo 目标 2 v/i: ~ to do X lìqiú zuò X 力求做X

air n kōngqì 空气; by ~ travel zuò fēijī 坐飞机; send mail hángkōng 航空

air-conditioned yǒu kōngtiáo 有空调

airport jīchǎng 机场

alarm n jǐngbào 警报

alarm clock nàozhōng 闹钟

album (for photos) yǐngjí 影

集; (record) chàngpiān 唱片

**alcohol** jiǔ 酒

**alcoholic 1** n xùjiǔzhě 酗酒者 **2** adj hán jiǔjīng 含酒精

**alert** adj jǐjìng 机警

**alien** n (foreigner) wàiguórén 外国人

**alike** adj: be ~ xiāngsì 相似

**alimony** shànyǎng fèi 赡养费

**alive:** be ~ huózhe 活着

**all 1** adj dōu 都; ~ *Chinese cities* Zhōngguó suǒyǒude chéngshì 中国所有的城市 **2** pron: ~ of them tāmen dōu 他们都; that's ~, thanks jiù zhèixie, xièxie 就这些, 谢谢; not at ~ alike gēnběn búxiàng 根本不像; not at ~! yìdiǎnr yě bù! 一点儿也不 ! ; two ~ (in score) èrpíng 二平

**allergic:** be ~ to ... duì ... guòmǐn 对...过敏

**allergy** guòmǐn 过敏

**alliance** tóngméng 同盟

**allow** (permit) yǔnxǔ 允许; (calculate for) jìsuàn 计算

**allowance** (money) jīntiē 津贴

**ally** n tóngméngzhě 同盟者

**almost** jīhū 几乎

**alone** dāndú 单独

**along 1** prep: ~ this path yánzhe zhètiáo xiǎolù 沿着这条小路 **2** adv: ~ with hé 和

**aloud** chūshēngdì 出声地

**alphabet** zìmǔ biǎo 字母表

**already** yǐjīng 已经

**alright:** that's ~ (doesn't matter) méi guānxi 没关系; (when s.o. says thank you) búxiè 不谢; (it quite good) búcuò 不错; I'm ~ (not hurt) wǒ méi shìr 我没事儿; can I? – ~ kěyǐ ma? – kěyǐ 可以吗 ? – 可以

**also** yě 也

**alter** v/t gǎibiàn 改变

**alteration** gēnggǎi 更改

**alternate 1** v/i jiāotì 交替 **2** adj měigé 每隔

**alternative 1** n xuǎnzé 选择 **2** adj lìngyī kě xuǎnzé 另一可选择; lifestyle, music etc bùtóng zhǒng 不同种

**alternatively** huòzhě 或者

**although** jǐnguǎn 尽管

**altitude** hǎibá 海拔; (of plane) gāodù 高度)

**altogether** (completely)

wánquán 完全; (*in all*) yīgòng 一共

aluminum lǚ 铝

always zǒngshì 总是

amateur *n* yèyú àihàozhě 业余爱好者

amaze shǐ dàwéi chījīng 使大为吃惊

amazement jīngqí 惊奇

amazing jīngrén 惊人; (*very good*) méizhìle 没治了

ambassador dàshǐ 大使

ambiguous hánhú 含糊

ambition zhìxiàng 志向; *pej* yěxīn 野心

ambitious *plan* xióngxīn bóbó 雄心勃勃

ambulance jiùhùchē 救护车

amendment xiūgǎi 修改

amends: **make ~** bǔguò 补过

America Měiguó 美国

American 1 *adj* Měiguó 美国 2 *n* Měiguórén 美国人

ammunition jūnhuǒ 军火

amnesty *n* shèmiǎn 赦免

among(st) zài …zhīzhōng 在…之中

amount shùliàng 数量; (*sum of money*) jīn'é 金额

♦ amount to děngyú 等于

amplifier fàngdàqì 放大器

amputate jiézhī 节肢

amuse (*make laugh*) dòuxiào 逗笑; (*entertain*) yúlè 娱乐

amusement lèqù 乐趣; (*entertainment*) yúlè 娱乐

amusing yǒuqù 有趣

analysis fēnxī 分析

analyze fēnxī 分析

anatomy jiěpōu 解剖

ancestor zǔxiān 祖先

ancient *adj* gǔlǎo 古老

and ◊ (*joining nouns*) hé 和 ◊ (*joining adjectives*) yòu …yòu… 又…又… ◊ (*~ then*) ránhòu 然后 ◊ (*when listing, not translated*): **two beers ~ a coffee** liǎnggè píjiǔ yígè kāfēi 两个啤酒一个咖啡

anemic: **be ~** pínxuè 贫血

anesthetic *n* mázuì 麻醉

anger *n* fènnù 愤怒

angle *n* jiǎodù 角度

angry fènnù 愤怒; **be ~ with X** duì X shēngqì 对X生气

animal dòngwù 动物

animated cartoon dònghuà piān 动画片

animosity díyì 敌意

ankle jiǎowàn 脚腕

**annex** 1 *n* (*building*) kuòjiàn bùfèn 扩建部分 2 *v/t state* tūnbìng 吞并

**anniversary** (*wedding ~*) zhōunián 周年

**announce** xuānbù 宣布

**announcement** xuāngào 宣告

**announcer** TV, RAD bōyīnyuán 播音员

**annoy** shǐ fánnǎo 使烦恼

**annual** *adj* (*once a year*) nián nián; (*of a year*) niándù 年度

**anonymous** nìmíng 匿名

**another** *adj & pron* (*different*) lìng yígè 另一个; (*additional*) yòu yígè 又一个; *can I have ~ ... ?* wǒ kěyǐ zài lái yígè ... ma? 我可以再来一个...吗?; *one ~* hùxiāng 互相

**answer** 1 *n* dáfù 答复; (*to problem, question*) dá'àn 答案 2 *v/t* dáfù 答复; *question* huídá 回答

**answerphone** lùyīn diànhuà 录音电话

**antenna** (*of insect*) chùjiǎo 触角; (*for TV*) tiānxiàn 天线

**antibiotic** *n* kàngjūnsù 抗

**antiseptic** *n* kàngjūnjì 抗菌剂

**anticipate** yùliào 预料

**antiseptic** *n* kàngjūnjì 抗菌剂

**anxiety** jiāojí 焦急

**anxious** (*worried*) jiāojí 焦急

**any** 1 *adj*: *are there ~ glasses?* yǒuméiyǒu bēizi? 有没有杯子? 2 *pron*: *do you have ~?* nǐ yǒu méiyǒu? 你有没有?

**anybody** ◊ (*emphatic*) rènhérén 任何人 ◊ (*with negatives*): *there wasn't ~ there* méirén zài nàr 没人在那儿 ◊ (*in questions, conditionals*) shéi 谁

**anyhow** (*summarizing*) zǒngzhī 总之; (*at least*) zhìshǎo 至少

**anyone** → *anybody*

**anything** shénme 什么

**anyway** → *anyhow*

**anywhere** wúlùn nǎlǐ 无论哪里; *I can't find it ~* wǒ nǎr dōu zhǎobùzháo 我哪儿都找不着

**apart** (*in distance*) jùlí 距离; *live ~* fēnjū 分居

**apartment** gōngyù 公寓

**apartment block** gōngyù dàshà 公寓大厦

**apologize** dàoqiàn 道歉

**apology** dàoqiàn 道歉

**apparently** hǎoxiàng 好象

**appeal** n (charm) xīyǐn lì 吸引力; (for funds etc) hūyù 呼吁; LAW shàngsù 上诉

**appear** chūxiàn 出现; (look, seem) xiǎndé 显得

**appearance** (arrival) dàolái 到来; (look) wàibiǎo 外表

**appendicitis** lánwěiyán 阑尾炎

**appetite** wèikǒu 胃口; fig yùwàng 欲望

**applaud** v/i gǔzhǎng 鼓掌

**applause** gǔzhǎng 鼓掌

**apple** píngguǒ 苹果

**appliance** qìxiè 器械

**applicant** shēnqǐngzhě 申请者

**application** (for job, visa etc) shēnqǐng 申请

**apply** (of rule) shìyòng 适用
♦ **apply for** shēnqǐng 申请

**appoint** rènmìng 任命

**appointment** (to position) rènmìng 任命; (meeting) yuēhuì 约会

**appreciate 1** v/t (value) xīnshǎng 欣赏; (be grateful for) gǎnjī 感激 **2** v/i FIN tígāo jiàzhí 提高价值

**apprehensive** dānxīn 担心

**approach 1** n línjìn 临近; (offer, proposal) tíyì 提议; (to problem) fāngshì 方式 **2** v/t (get near to) línjìn 临近; (contact) liánxì 联系; problem chǔlǐ 处理

**appropriate** adj qiàdàng 恰当

**approve 1** v/i zànchéng 赞成 **2** v/t pīzhǔn 批准

**approximate** adj dàyuē 大约

**April** sìyuè 四月

**Arab 1** adj Ālābó 阿拉伯 **2** n Ālābórén 阿拉伯人

**archeologist** kǎogǔ xué jiā 考古学家

**archeology** kǎogǔ xué 考古学

**architect** jiànzhù shī 建筑师

**architecture** jiànzhù xué 建筑学

**archives** dǎng'àn 档案

**area** (region) dìqū 地区; (of activity, study) fànwéi 范围; (square feet etc) miànjī 面积

**area code** TELEC qūhào 区号

**argue 1** v/i (*fight*) chǎojià 吵架 **2** v/t: ~ *that* jiānchí 坚持

**argument** chǎojià 吵架; (*reasoning*) zhēnglùn 争论

**arise** (*of situation, problem*) chéngxiàn 呈现

**arithmetic** suànshù 算术

**arm** n shǒubì 手臂; (*of chair*) fúshǒu 扶手

**armchair** fúshǒu yǐ 扶手椅

**armed** wǔzhuāng 武装

**armed robbery** chíxiè qiǎngjié 持械抢劫

**arms** (*weapons*) wǔqì 武器

**army** jūnduì 军队

**around 1** prep (*in circle*) wéirǎo 围绕; (*roughly*) dàyuē 大约 **2** adv (*in the area*) zài zhèr 在这儿; (*encircling*) zhōuwéi 周围; (*near*) zài fùjìn 在附近

**arouse** suspicion etc yǐnqǐ 引起; (*sexually*) jīfā 激发

**arrange** (*put in order*) zhěng-lǐ 整理; *furniture* bùzhì 布置; *flowers* chā 插; *music* gǎibiān 改编; *meeting, time etc* ānpái 安排

**arrangement** (*plan*) ānpái 安排; (*agreement*) xiéyì 协议;

(*of furniture etc*) bùzhì 布置; (*of flowers*) chāhuā 插花; (*of music*) gǎibiān 改编

**arrest** n & v/t dàibǔ 逮捕

**arrive** dàodá 到达

**arrogance** àomàn 傲慢

**arrogant** jiāo'ào zìdà 骄傲自大

**art** yìshù 艺术

**artery** MED dòngmài 动脉

**article** wùjiàn 物件; (*in newspaper*) wénzhāng 文章

**artificial** rénzào 人造

**artist** (*painter*) huàjiā 画家

**artistic** yǒu yìshùxìng 有艺术性; *skills* yìshù 艺术

**as 1** conj ◊ (*while, when*) dāng ...de shíhou 当...的时候 ◊ (*like*) xiàng 像; ~ *if* hǎoxiàng 好像; ~ *usual* rútóng wǎngcháng 如同往常 **2** adv: ~ *high* ... hé ...yíyàng gāo 和...一样高 **3** prep zuòwéi 作为; ~ *a child* zuòwéi háizi 作为孩子

**ashamed** xiūkuì 羞愧; *be ~ of* wèi ...diūliǎn 为...丢脸

**ashore** zài ànshàng 在岸上

**ashtray** yānhuī gāng 烟灰缸

**Asia** Yàzhōu 亚洲

**Asian 1** *adj* Yàzhōu 亚洲
**2** *n* Yàzhōurén 亚洲人
**aside** yībiān 一边；**~ from**
(*excepting*) chúle 除了；(*in addition to*) cǐwài 此外
**ask** *v/t person* wèn 问；
(*invite*) jiào 叫；*question* tíwèn 提问；*favor* qǐngqiú 请求；**~ X for ...** gēn X shuō ... 跟 X 要 ...；**~ X to ...** yào X ... 要 X ...
♦**ask for** yāoqiú 要求；
*person* zhǎo 找
♦**ask out** yuēhuì 约会
**asleep**: **be ~** shúshuì 熟睡；
**fall ~** shuìzháo le 睡着了
**aspect** fāngmiàn 方面
**aspirin** āsīpǐlín 阿司匹林
**assassinate** ànshā 暗杀
**assault** *n* gōngjī 攻击；
(*physical*) ōudǎ 殴打；
(*verbal*) wēixié 威胁
**assemble 1** *v/t parts* zǔ-zhuāng 组装 **2** *v/i* (*of people*) jízhōng 集中
**assembly** zǔzhuāng 组装；
POL yìhuì 议会
**assertive** *person* zìxìn 自信
**assess** pínggū 评估
**asset** FIN zīchǎn 资产；*fig* bǎobèi 宝贝

**assignment** rènwù 任务
**assist** bāngzhù 帮助
**assistant** zhùshǒu 助手
**associate 1** *v/i*: **~ with** jiéjiāo 结交 **2** *n* tóngshì 同事
**association** xiéhuì 协会；
**in ~ with** yǔ ...hézuò 与 ... 合作
**assume** (*suppose*) jiǎshè 假设
**assumption** shèxiǎng 设想
**assurance** bǎozhèng 保证；
(*confidence*) xìnxīn 信心
**assure** (*reassure*) shǐ quèxìn 使确信
**asthma** xiàochuǎn 哮喘
**astonish** shǐ jīngyà 使惊讶
**astonishing** lìngrén jīngyà 令人惊讶
**astonishment** jīngyà 惊讶
**astronomical** *price etc* jùdà 巨大
**asylum** (*political*) bìhù 庇护
**at** (*with places*) zài 在；**~ Joe's** zài Qiáo jiālǐ 在乔家里；**~ 10 dollars** biāojià shí měiyuán 标价十美元；**~ 5 o'clock** wǔ diǎnzhōng 五点钟；**be good ~ X** shàncháng yú X 擅长于 X
**atheist** wú shén lùnzhě 无

神论者
athlete yùndòngyuán 运动员
athletics tiánjìng yùndòng 田径运动
Atlantic Dàxīyáng 大西洋
ATM (= *automated teller machine*) qǔkuǎnjī 取款机
atmosphere (*of earth*) dàqì 大气; (*ambiance*) qìfēn 气氛
atomic yuánzǐ 原子
atrocity bàoxíng 暴行
attach shuānláo 栓牢
attack n & v/t (*physical*) ōudǎ 殴打; MIL xíjī 袭击; (*verbal*) pēngjī 抨击
attempt 1 n chángshì 尝试 2 v/t shìtú 试图
attend cānjiā 参加
attendance chūqín 出勤
attention zhùyì 注意力; *pay* ~ zhùyì 注意
attitude tàidu 态度
attorney lǜshī 律师
attract *person, attention* xīyǐn 吸引
attraction xīyǐn lì 吸引力; (*romantic*) mèilì 魅力
attractive yǒu xīyǐn lì 有

audible tīngdejiàn 听得见
audience (*at concert*) tīngzhòng 听众; THEA, TV guānzhòng 观众
audiovisual shìtīng 视听
audition n & v/i shìyàn 试演
auditor shěnjì shī 审计师
August bāyuè 八月
aunt (*own, paternal*) gū 姑; (*own, maternal*) yí 姨; (*somebody else's*) āyí 阿姨
Australia Àodàlìyà 澳大利亚
Australian 1 adj Àodàlìyà 澳大利亚 2 n Àodàlìyà rén 澳大利亚人
authentic *antique* zhēnzhèng 真正; *accent* dìdao 地道
author zuòzhě 作者
authority quánwēi 权威; (*permission*) xǔkě 许可
authorize shòuquán 授权; *be ~d to* shòuquán … 授权…
auto n MOT qìchē 汽车
autobiography zìzhuàn 自传
automate shǐ zìdònghuà 使自动化
automatic adj & n zìdòng 自动

**automatically** zìdòng 自动

**automobile** qìchē 汽车

**available** *product* kě dédào 可得到; *person* yǒukòng 有空

**avenue** dàdào 大道

**average 1** *adj* píngjūn 平均; (*ordinary*) pǔtōng 普通 **2** *n* píngjūn shuǐzhǔn 平均水准; **on ~** píngjūn láishuō 平均来说

**avoid** bìmiǎn 避免

**awake** *adj* xǐng 醒

**award 1** *n* (*prize*) jiǎnglì 奖励 **2** *v/t* jiǎnglì 奖励; *damages* pàngěi 判给

**aware: be ~ of X** zhīdào X 知

道X; **become ~ of X** dézhī X 得知X

**awareness** yìshí 意识

**away: be ~** (*traveling, sick etc*) búzài 不在; **walk / run ~** zǒu /pǎo kāi 走/跑开; **it's 2 miles ~** liǎng yīnglǐ yuǎn 两英里远

**awesome** F (*terrific*) gàilemòle 盖了帽了

**awful** zāogāo 糟糕

**awkward** (*clumsy*) bènzhuō 笨拙; (*difficult*) nányí duìfù 难以对付;(*embarrassing*) gāngà 尴尬

**ax 1** *n* fǔ 斧 **2** *v/t project, jobs* xiāojiǎn 削减

# B

**baby** *n* yīng'ér 婴儿

**baby-sitter** línshí bǎomǔ 临时保姆

**bachelor** dānshēn hàn 单身汉

**back 1** *n* (*of person*) hòubèi 后背;(*of car, bus*) hòubù 后部;(*of paper, jacket, house, book*) bèimiàn 背面;(*of chair*) kàobèi 靠

背; SP hòuwèi 后卫; **in ~** zài hòumian 在后面;**~ to front** qiánhòu diāndǎo 前后颠倒 **2** *adj* hòu 后;**~ road** xiǎolù 小路 **3** *adv*: **please stand ~** qǐng hòutuì 请后退;**give X ~ to Y** jiāng X huángeǐ Y 将X还给Y;**she'll be ~ tomorrow** tā míngtiān huílái 她明天

回来 4 *v/t* (support) zhīchí 支持; car dǎochē 倒车

♦ **back down** fàngqì 放弃

♦ **back up 1** *v/t* (support) zhīchí 支持; argument zhèngshí 证实; file bèifèn 备份

**backdate** zhuīsù 追溯

**backer** zànzhùrén 赞助人

**background** bèijǐng 背景; (of person) jīnglì 经历

**backing** (support) zhīchí 支持; (musicians) bànzòu 伴奏; (singers) bànchàng 伴唱

**backpacker** bēibāo lǚxíngzhě 背包旅行者

**backward** *adj* child chídùn 迟钝; society luòhòu 落后; glance xiànghòu 向后

**bacon** xūn xiánròu 熏咸肉

**bacteria** xìjūn 细菌

**bad** bùhǎo 不好; weather èliè 恶劣; headache jùliè 剧烈; mistake, accident yánzhòng 严重; (rotten) huài 坏; **it's not ~** hái kě yǐ 还可以

**badge** zhèngzhāng 证章

**badly** behave bùhǎo 不好; injured, damaged yánzhòng

严重; perform chà 差

**bad-tempered** bàozào 暴躁

**baffle** shǐ kùnhuò 使困惑

**bag** (plastic, paper) dàizi 袋子; (for school, traveling) bāo 包; (purse) shǒutí bāo 手提包

**baggage** xíngli 行李

**bake** *v/t* kǎo 烤

**balance 1** *n* pínghéng 平衡; (remainder) chā'é 差额; (of bank account) jiécún 结存 **2** *v/t & v/i* pínghéng 平衡

**balance sheet** juésuàn biǎo 决算表

**balcony** yángtái 阳台; (in theater) lóutīng 楼厅

**bald** man tūdǐng 秃顶

**ball** qiú 球

**ballet** bālěiwǔ 芭蕾舞

**balloon** (child's) qìqiú 气球; (for flight) rè qìqiú 热气球

**ballot** *n* tóupiào 投票

**ballpoint (pen)** yuánzhū bǐ 圆珠笔

**bamboo** zhúzi 竹子

**bamboo shoots** zhúsǔn 竹笋

**ban 1** *n* jìnlìng 禁令 **2** *v/t* jìnzhǐ 禁止

**banana** xiāngjiāo 香蕉

band (*musical*) yuèduì 乐队

bandage n bēngdài 绷带

Band-Aid® chuàngkětiē 创可贴

bang 1 n (*noise*) hōngde yīshēng 轰的一声; (*blow*) měngjī 猛击 2 v/t *door* shuāi 摔; (*hit*) zhuàng 撞

bank¹ (*of river*) hé'àn 河岸

bank² n FIN yínháng 银行

bank account yínháng zhànghù 银行账户

bankrupt adj pòchǎn 破产; *go* ~ pòchǎn 破产

baptize xǐlǐ 洗礼

bar¹ (*iron, chocolate*) tiáo条; (*for drinks*) jiǔbā 酒吧; (*counter*) guìtái 柜台

bar² v/t jìnzhǐ 禁止

barbecue 1 n shāokǎo huì 烧烤会; (*equipment*) kǎojià 烤架 2 v/t kǎo 烤

barbed wire yǒucì tiěsī 有刺铁丝

barber tìtóu jiàng 剃头匠

bare adj (*naked*) guāng 光; *room* kōng 空; *hillside, floor* guāng tūtū 光秃秃

barefoot: *be* ~ guāngjiǎo 光脚

barefoot doctor chìjiǎo yīshēng 赤脚医生

barely jǐnjǐn 仅仅

bargain 1 n (*deal*) jiāoyì 交易; (*good buy*) piányí huò 便宜货 2 v/i tǎojià huánjià 讨价还价

bark n & v/i (*of dog*) fèi 吠

barracks MIL yíngfáng 营房

barrel (*container*) tǒng 桶

barricade n lùzhàng 路障

barrier lángān 栏杆; (*cultural*) zhàng'ài 障碍

base 1 n (*bottom end*) dǐbù 底部; (*underside*) dǐzuò 底座; (*center, MIL*) jīdì 基地 2 v/t yǐ... wéi jīchǔ 以…为基础

baseball (*ball*) bàngqiú 棒球; (*game*) bàngqiú yùndòng 棒球运动

baseball cap bàngqiú mào 棒球帽

basement dìxiàshì 地下室; (*of store*) dìcéng 底层

basic (*rudimentary*) jīběn 基本; (*fundamental*) zhǔyào 主要

basically jīběnshang 基本上

basics: *the* ~ jīběn yuánlǐ 基本原理

basin (*for washing*) shuǐchí

水池

**basis** jīchǔ 基础; (of argument) gēnjù 根据

**basket** lánzi 篮子; (in basketball) wǎng 网

**basketball** lánqiú 篮球

**bass** adj nán dīyīn 男低音

**bat¹** n (for baseball) qiúgùn 球棍; (for table tennis) qiúpāi 球拍

**bat²** (animal) biānfú 蝙蝠

**bath** zǎopén 澡盆; have a ~ xǐzǎo 洗澡

**bathrobe** yùyī 浴衣

**bathroom** xǐzǎo jiān 洗澡间; (toilet) xǐshǒu jiān 洗手间

**bathtub** yùgāng 浴缸

**battery** diànchí 电池

**be** ⋄ shì 是; there is, there are yǒu 有; ~ careful xiǎoxīn 小心; don't ~ sad bié shāngxīn 别伤心; I've never been to Beijing wǒ cóngméi qùguò Běijīng 我从没去过北京 ⋄ (passive) bèi 被; he was killed tā bèi shāsǐ le 他被杀死了

**beach** hǎitān 海滩

**beam 1** n (in roof) héngliáng 横梁 **2** v/i (smile) xiàoróng

mǎnmiàn 笑容满面

**bean curd** dòufu 豆腐

**beansprouts** dòuyá 豆芽

**bear** v/t weight chéngshòu 承受; costs chéngdān 承担; (tolerate) rěnshòu 忍受

**bearable** kě róngrěn 可容忍

**beard** húzi 胡子

**beat 1** (of heart) tiàodòng 跳动; (of music) jiézòu 节奏 **2** v/t (in game) jībài 击败; (hit) dǎ 打

**beating** (physical) dǎ 打

**beautiful** woman, house, day měilì 美丽; meal fēngshèng kěkǒu 丰盛可口; vacation wánměi 完美; story, movie dòngrén 动人

**beauty** měilì 美丽

**because** yīnwèi 因为; ~ of yóuyú 由于

**become** biànchéng 变成; what's ~ of her? tā jiūjìng zěnmeyàng? 她究竟怎么样?

**bed** chuáng 床; (of flowers) tán 坛; (of sea, river) chuáng 床; go to ~ shuìjiào 睡觉

**bedroom** wòshì 卧室

**beef** n niúròu 牛肉

**beer** píjiǔ 啤酒

**before 1** prep & conj zhīqián 之前 **2** adv yǐqián 以前; **the week / day ~** qián yīgè xīngqī / tiān 前一个星期/天

**beforehand** shìxiān 事先

**beg** v/i yàofàn 要饭

**begin** v/t & v/i kāishǐ 开始

**beginner** chūxuézhě 初学者

**beginning** kāishǐ 开始; (origin) qǐyuán 起源

**behalf: on or in ~ of** dàibiǎo 代表

**behave** v/i biǎoxiàn 表现; **~ (oneself)** shǒu guījǔ 守规矩

**behavior** xíngwéi 行为

**behind 1** prep zài … hòumian 在…后面; (in progress, order) luòhòu 落后; **be ~ …** (responsible for) zài … bèihòu 在…背后; (support) zhīchí 支持 **2** adv (at the back) zài hòumian 在后面; leave, stay liúxià 留下

**Beijing** Běijīng 北京

**being** (existence) shēngcún

生存; (creature) shēngwù 生物

**belief** (trust) xìnrèn 信任; (religion) xìnyǎng 信仰; (opinion) kànfǎ 看法

**believe** xiāngxìn 相信
♦ **believe in** xiāngxìn 相信; ghosts xìn 信; person xìnrèn 信任

**bell** (on bike, door) líng 铃; (in church, school) zhōng 钟

**bellhop** shìzhě 侍者

**belly** dùzi 肚子

**belong** v/i shǔyú 属于
♦ **belong to** shǔyú 属于; club, organization shì … chéngyuán 是…成员

**belongings** suǒyǒu wù 所有物

**below 1** prep zài … de xiàmian 在…的下面; (in amount) dīyú 低于 **2** adv zài xiàmian 在下面; **10 degrees ~** língxià shídù 零下十度

**belt** yāodài 腰带

**bend 1** n wānqū 弯曲 **2** v/t wān 弯 **3** v/i wān 弯; (of person) wānshēn 弯身
♦ **bend down** wānyāo 弯腰

beneath **1** *prep* zài … xiàmiàn 在 … 下面; (*in status, value*) dīyú 低于 **2** *adv* xiàbiān 下边

beneficial yǒuyì 有益

benefit **1** *n* hǎochù 好处 **2** *v/t* yǒuyì yú 有益于

beside zài … pángbiān 在 … 旁边

besides **1** *adv* zàishuō 再说 **2** *prep* (*apart from*) chúle 除了

best **1** *adj & adv* zuìhǎo 最好 **2** *n*: *do one's ~* jìnlì érwéi 尽力而为; *the ~* zuìhǎo 最好

best before date zàicǐ rìqī qián shǐyòng 在此日期前使用

best man (*at wedding*) nán bīnxiàng 男傧相

bet **1** *n* dǔzhù 赌注 **2** *v/i* dǔbó 赌博

betray bèipàn 背叛

better **1** *adj* gènghǎo 更好; *get* ~ gǎijìn 改进; (*in health*) hǎozhuǎn 好转; *he's ~* (*in health*) tā hǎodiǎn le 他好点儿了 **2** *adv* gènghǎo 更好; *I'd really ~ not* wǒ háishì

bùyào le 我还是不要了

better off *adj* fùyù 富裕

between *prep* zài … zhījiān 在 … 之间

beware: ~ *of* xiǎoxīn 小心

beyond **1** *prep* (*in space*) yuǎnyú 远于; (*in degree, extent*) chāochū 超出 **2** *adv* gèngyuǎn 更远

bias(s)ed (*against*) piānjiàn 偏见; (*in favor of*) piāntǎn 偏袒

Bible shèngjīng 圣经

bicycle *n* zìxíng chē 自行车

bid *n* (*at auction*) chūjià 出价

big *adj* dà 大; (*tall*) gāo 高

bike *n* zìxíng chē 自行车

bill *n* zhàngdān 账单; (*money*) chāopiào 钞票

billboard guǎnggào pái 广告牌

billfold qiánbāo 钱包

billion shíyì 十亿

bind *v/t* (*tie*) bǎng 绑; (*oblige*) yuēshù 约束

binding *adj agreement* yǒu yuēshù lì 有约束力

binoculars wàngyuǎn jìng 望远镜

biography zhuànjì 传记

biological shēngwù 生物

**biology** shēngwù xué 生
物学

**biotechnology** shēngwù
gōngyì xué 生物工艺学

**bird** niǎo 鸟

**birth** (of child) chūshēng 出
生; (labor) fēnmiǎn 分娩;
**date of ~** chūshēng rìqī 出
生日期

**birth certificate** chūshēng
zhèng 出生证

**birth control** jiéyù 节育

**birthday** shēngrì 生日;
**happy ~!** shēngrì kuàile! 生
日快乐!

**bit** n (piece) xiǎokuàir 小块
儿; (length) xiǎoduànr 小
段儿; (part) bùfen 部分;
**a ~** (a little) yǒudiǎnr 有点
儿; (of time) yīhuìr 一会
儿; **a ~ of** (a little) yīdiǎn
一点

**bitch** n (dog) mǔgǒu 母狗;
F (woman) pōfù 泼妇

**bite** n & v/t (of dog, snake)
yǎo 咬; (of mosquito)
dīng 叮

**bitter** kǔ 苦; person
chōngmǎn yuànhèn 充
满怨恨

**black 1** adj hēi 黑; coffee

etc wúnǎi 无奶**2** n (color)
hēisè 黑色; (person) hēirén
黑人

**blackboard** hēibǎn 黑板

**black box** hēi xiázi 黑匣子

**black eye** qīngzhǒng
yǎnkuàng 青肿眼眶

**blackmail** n & v/t xiépò 胁迫

**black market** hēishì 黑市

**blackout** ELEC tíngdiàn 停
电; MED hūnmí 昏迷

**blade** (of knife, sword)
rèn 刃

**blame 1** n zébèi 责备;
(responsibility) zérèn 责任
**2** v/t zéguài 责怪

**blank** adj page, tape kòngbái
空白; look mángrán 茫然

**blanket** n tǎnzi 毯子

**blast** n (explosion) bàozhà
爆炸; (gust) yīgǔ 一股

**blatant** míngxiǎn 明显

**blaze** n (fire) huǒyàn 火焰

**bleach 1** n piǎobáijì 漂白剂
**2** v/t hair shǐ tuōsè 使脱色

**bleak** countryside huāngliáng
荒凉; future àndàn 暗淡

**bleed** v/i liúxuè 流血

**blend** n & v/i hùnhé 混合

**bless** zhùfú 祝福

**blind 1** adj máng 盲**2** n: the

~ mángrén 盲人

**blind spot** mángdiǎn 盲点; fig wúzhī 无知

**blink** v/i (of person) zhǎyǎn 眨眼; (of light) shǎnshuò 闪烁

**blister** n shuǐpào 水泡

**blizzard** bàofēngxuě 暴风雪

**bloc** POL jítuán 集团

**block 1** n kuài 块; (in town) jiēqū 街区 **2** v/t dǔsè 堵塞

**blockage** dǔsè 堵塞

**blond** adj jīnfà 金发

**blonde** n (woman) jīnfà nǚláng 金发女郎

**blood** xuèyè 血液

**blood pressure** xuèyā 血压

**bloom** v/i kāihuā 开花

**blossom 1** n huā 花 **2** v/i kāihuā 开花; fig fāzhǎn 发展

**blouse** chènshān 衬衫

**blow¹** n jī击; (setback) zǔ'ài 阻碍

**blow²** 1 v/t (of wind) chuī 吹; (whistle blow) chuīshào 吹哨; ~ one's nose xǐng bítì 擤鼻涕 2 v/i (of wind) guāfēng 刮风; (of fuse) shāoduàn 烧断; (of tire) bàozhà 爆炸

♦ **blow up** v/t (with explosive) zhà 炸; (balloon) chōngqì 充气; PHOT fàngdà 放大

**blow-dry** v/t chuīgān 吹干

**blue** adj lánsè 蓝色

**blues** MUS bólǔsī yīnyuè 勃鲁斯音乐

**bluff** v/i xiàhu 吓唬

**blunt** adj dùn 钝; person zhíshuài 直率

**bluntly** speak tǎnbái 坦白

**blush** v/i liǎnhóng 脸红

**blusher** (cosmetic) yānzhī 胭脂

**BO** (body odor) tǐxiù 体臭

**board 1** n bǎn 板; (for game) qípán 棋盘; (for notices) pái pái 牌; ~ (of directors) dǒngshì huì 董事会; on ~ (plane) zài fēijī shàng 在飞机上; (train) zài huǒchē shàng 在火车上; (boat) zài chuán shàng 在船上 **2** v/t airplane etc shàng 上

**board game** qípán yóuxì 棋盘游戏

**boarding card** dēngjīkǎ 登机卡

**board meeting** dǒngshìhuì huìyì 董事会会议

**boast** n & v/i chuīniú 吹牛

**boat** chuán 船

**body** shēntǐ 身体；(*dead*) shītǐ 尸体

**bodyguard** bǎobiāo 保镳

**boil** v/t zhǔ 煮

**boiled rice** báifàn 白饭

**boiled water** kāishuǐ 开水

**boiler** guōlú 锅炉

**bold 1** *adj* dàdǎn 大胆 **2** *n* (*print*) cūtǐ 粗体

**bolt 1** *n* luóshuān 螺栓；(*on door*) chāxiāo 插销 **2** v/t (*fix with bolts*) shuānzhù zhù 栓住；(*close*) shuān 闩

**bomb 1** *n* zhàdàn 炸弹 **2** v/t hōngzhà 轰炸

**bomber** (*airplane*) hōngzhàjī 轰炸机；(*terrorist*) tóudàn shǒu 投弹手

**bond** *n* (*tie*) liánjié 联结；FIN zhàiquàn 债券

**bone** *n* gǔtou 骨头

**bonus** (*money*) jiǎngjīn 奖金；(*extra*) éwài pǐn 额外品

**boo 1** v/t speaker hè dàocǎi 喝倒彩 **2** v/i fāchū xūxu shēng 发出嘘嘘声

**book 1** *n* shū 书 **2** v/t (*reserve*) yùdìng 预定；(*of policeman*) dēngjì 登记

**bookcase** shūjià 书架

**booklet** xiǎo cèzi 小册子

**Book of Changes** Yìjīng 易经

**bookstore** shūdiàn 书店

**boom** *n & v/i* (*in business*) fánróng 繁荣

**boost 1** *n* (*to sales, confidence*) jīlì 激励；(*to economy*) cùjìn 促进 **2** v/t sales zēngjiā 增加；confidence zēngqiáng 增强

**boot** *n* xuēzi 靴子

**booth** (*at market*) huòtān 货摊；(*at exhibition*) tānzi 摊子；(*in restaurant*) cānzuò 餐座

**border** *n* (*of country*) biānjiè 边界；(*edge*) biānyuán 边缘

**bore¹** v/t hole zuānkǒng 钻孔

**bore²** *n* (*person*) wúqùderén 无趣的人 v/t shǐ yànfán 使厌烦

**bored: be ~** mèn 闷

**boredom** wúliáo 无聊

**boring** fáwèir 乏味儿

**born: be ~** chūshēng 出生

**borrow** jiè 借

**boss** shàngjí 上级

**botanical** zhíwù 植物

**box**

both 1 *adj & pron* liǎnggè 两
个; ~ *of them* (*things*) nà
liǎnggè 那两个; (*people*)
nà liǎngrén 那两人 2 *adv*:
~ ... *and* ... yòu ... yòu ...
又 ... 又 ...

bother 1 *n* máfán 麻烦; *it's
no* ~ méi wèntí 没问题
2 *v/t* (*disturb*) máfán 麻烦;
*person working* dǎjiǎo 打
搅; (*worry*) shǐdānxīn 使
担心 3 *v/i*: *don't* ~ (*you
needn't do it*) búyòng le
不用了

bottle *n* píngzi 瓶子; (*for
baby*) nǎipíng 奶瓶

bottled water píngzhuāng
shuǐ 瓶装水

bottleneck (*in road, work*)
zǔsāi diǎn 阻塞点

bottle-opener kāipíngqì
开瓶器

bottom 1 *adj* zuìdī 最低
2 *n* (*underside*) dǐmiàn 底
面; (*on the inside*) dǐbù
底部; (*of hill*) shāndǐ 山脚;
(*of pile*) zuìdǐ 最底; (*of
street*) zuìdǐchù 最底处;
(*buttocks*) pìgu 屁股

♦ **bottom out** dá zuìdī diǎn
达最低点

bottom line *fig* (*financial*)
lìrùn 利润; (*real issue*)
zhēnzhèng wèntí 真正
问题

bounce *v/i* (*of ball*) tánqǐ 弹
起; (*on sofa etc*) tántiào
弹跳; (*of check*) bèi jù fù
tuìhuí 被拒付退回

bouncer bǎménrén 把门人

bound: *be* ~ *to do* (*sure*)
kěndìng zuò 肯定做;
(*obliged*) bìxū zuò 必须做

boundary biānjiè 边界

bouquet (*flowers*) huāshù
花束; (*of wine*) fāngxiāng
芳香

bourbon bōpáng wēishìjì jiǔ
波旁威士忌酒

bout MED fāzuò 发作; (*in
boxing*) jiàoliàng 较量

bow¹ *n & v/i* (*as greeting*)
jūgōng 鞠躬

bow² (*knot*) húdié jié 蝴蝶
结; MUS gōng 弓

bowels jiécháng 结肠

bowl (*large*) pén 盆; (*small
container for rice*) wǎn 碗

bowling bǎolíng qiú 保龄球

bow tie lǐngjié 领结

box *n* hézi 盒子; (*on form*)
fānggé 方格

**boxer** quánjīshǒu 拳击手

**boxing** quánjī 拳击

**boxing match** quánjī bǐsài 拳击比赛

**box office** shòupiàochù 售票处

**boy** nánháir 男孩儿; (son) érzi 儿子

**boycott** n & v/i dǐzhì 抵制

**boyfriend** nán péngyou 男朋友

**bracelet** shǒuzhuó 手镯

**bracket** (for shelf) tuōjià 托架; (in text) kuòhào 括号

**brag** v/i chuīniú 吹牛

**braid** n (in hair) biànzi 辫子; (trimming) suìdài 穗带

**brain** nǎo 脑

**brains** (intelligence) nǎozi 脑子

**brake** n & v/i shāchē 刹车

**branch** n (of tree) shùzhī 树枝; (of bank) fēnháng 分行; (of company) fēn gōngsī 分公司; (of chain store) fēndiàn 分店

**brand** n páizi 牌子

**brand name** shāngbiāo 商标; (famous) míngpái shāngpǐn 名牌商品

**brand-new** zhǎnxīn 崭新

**brandy** báilándì 白兰地

**brassière** xiōngzhào 胸罩

**brat** pej táoqìbāo 淘气包

**brave** adj yǒnggǎn 勇敢

**bravery** yǒnggǎn 勇敢

**breach** (violation) wéifàn 违犯; (in party) fēnliè 分裂

**breach of contract** LAW wéifàn hétong 违反合同

**bread** miànbāo 面包

**breadth** kuāndù 宽度; (of knowledge) guǎngdù 广度

**break** 1 n (in bone) gǔzhé 骨折; (rest) xiūxi 休息; (in relations) fēnkāi 分开 2 v/t & v/i device, toy sǔnhuài 损坏; stick, leg zhéduàn 折断; glass, egg pòsuì 破碎; law, promise wéifàn 违反; record dǎpò 打破

♦ **break down** 1 v/i (of vehicle) chū máobìng 出毛病; (of talks) pòliè 破裂; (in tears) kòngzhì bùzhù 控制不住 2 v/t door dǎsuì 打烂; figures fēnlèi 分类

♦ **break even** COM shōuzhī pínghéng 收支平衡

♦ **break up** (of couple) fēnshǒu 分手; (of band, meeting) jiěsàn 解散

breakdown (of vehicle, machine) gùzhàng 故障; (of talks) pòliè 破裂; (nervous ~) bēngkuì 崩溃; (of figures) fēnlèi 分类

breakfast n zǎocān 早餐

break-in dàoqiè 盗窃

breakthrough tūpò 突破

breakup (of marriage etc) fēnshǒu 分手

breast (of woman) rǔfáng 乳房

breastfeed v/t bǔrǔ 哺乳

breath hūxī 呼吸

Breathalyzer® hūqì yànzuìqì 呼气验醉器

breathe v/i hūxī 呼吸

breathtaking jīngrén 惊人

breed 1 n pǐnzhǒng 品种 2 v/t & v/i (of animals) fánzhí 繁殖

breeze wēifēng 微风

brew 1 v/t beer niàngzào 酿造; tea pào 泡 2 v/i (of storm, trouble) yùnniàng 酝酿

bribe n & v/t huìlù 贿赂

bribery huìlù 贿赂

brick zhuāntóu 砖头

bride xīnniáng 新娘

bridegroom xīnláng 新郎

bridesmaid bànniáng 伴娘

bridge n qiáo 桥; (of ship) jiàshítái 驾驶台

brief adj jiǎnduǎn 简短

briefcase gōngwén bāo 公文包

briefing jiǎnbào 简报

briefly (for short period) yīhuìr 一会儿; (in a few words) jiǎndān 简单; (to sum up) zǒngzhī 总之

briefs (for women) duǎn nèikù 短内裤; (for men) sānjiǎo kù 三角裤

bright color xiānyàn 鲜艳; light qiánglìè 强烈; future guāngmíng 光明; room míngliàng 明亮; (intelligent) cōngmíng 聪明

♦ brighten up v/i (of weather) zhuǎnqíng 转晴; (of person) gāoxìng qǐlái 高兴起来

brilliant sunshine etc míngliàng 明亮; (very good) jiéchū 杰出; (very intelligent) yǒu cáihuá 有才华; idea yīngmíng 英明

bring dàilái 带来; sth close by nálái 拿来; person dài 带

♦ **bring back** (*return*) huán
hái; (*re-introduce*) huīfù 恢
复; *memories* shǐ huíyì qǐ
使回忆起

♦ **bring down** *government*
shǐ kuǎtái 使垮台;
*airplane* shèluò 射落; *price*
shǐ jiàngdī 使降低

♦ **bring out** (*produce: book*)
chūbǎn 出版; *video, CD,
new product* tuīchū 推出

♦ **bring up** *child* yǎngyù 养
育; *subject* tíchū 提出;
(*vomit*) ǒutù 呕吐

**Britain** Yīngguó 英国;
(*formal use*) Dà Bùlièdiān
大不列颠

**British 1** *adj* Yīngguó 英
国 **2** *n: the ~* Yīngguórén
英国人

**broad** *adj street, shoulders*
kuān 宽; *smile* kuānróng
宽容; (*general*) gàikuòxìng
概括性

**broadcast** *n & v/t* guǎngbō
广播

**broadcasting** bōyīn 播音

**broadminded** xīnxiōng
kuānkuò 心胸宽阔

**brochure** xiǎo cèzi 小册子

**broil** *v/t* kǎo 烤

**broiler** *n* (*on stove*) kǎopán
烤盘; (*chicken*) nènjī nènjī 嫩鸡

**broke** F (*temporarily*)
méiyǒu yīgè zǐr 没有一个
子儿; (*long term*) bùmíng
yīwén 不明一文

**broken** *adj* chū máobìng 出
毛病; *glass, window* pòsuì
破碎; *neck, arm* gǔzhé 骨
折; *home* pòliè 破裂

**broken-hearted** xīnsuì 心碎

**bronchitis** qìguǎn yán 气
管炎

**brooch** xiōngzhēn 胸针

**broth** (*soup*) tāng 汤; (*stock*)
liàotāng 料汤

**brothel** jìyuàn 妓院

**brother** (*own, elder*) gēge 哥
哥; (*own, younger*) dìdi 弟
弟; (*somebody else's, elder
or younger*) xiōngdì 兄弟;
*~s and sisters* xiōngdì jiě
mèi 兄弟姐妹

**brother-in-law** (*elder sister's
husband*) jiěfū 姐夫;
(*younger sister's husband*)
mèifū 妹夫; (*husband's
younger brother*) xiǎoshūzi
小叔子; (*husband's older
brother*) dàbózi 大伯
子; (*wife's older brother*)

nèixiōng 内兄; (*wife's younger brother*) nèidì 内弟

brown *adj* zōngsè 棕色; (*tanned*) shàihēile 晒黑了

browse (*in store*) suíbiàn kànkan 随便看看

bruise *n* cuòshāng 挫伤

brunette zōngfà nǚzǐ 棕发女子

brush *n & v/t* shuā 刷

brutal cánrěn 残忍

brutality bàoxíng 暴行

bubble *n* qìpào 气泡

buck F (*dollar*) kuài 块

bucket shuǐtǒng 水桶

buckle¹ *n* dāgōu 搭钩

buckle² *v/i* (*of wood, metal*) biànxíng 变形

Buddha Fó 佛

Buddhism Fójiào 佛教

Buddhist 1 *n* Fójiàotú 佛教徒; *he's a ~* tā xìn Fó 他信佛 2 *adj* Fójiào 佛教

Buddhist temple sì 寺

buddy F huǒbàn 伙伴; (*form of address*) gēmen 哥们儿

budget *n* yùsuàn 预算; (*of family*) kāizhī 开支

buffalo yěniú 野牛; *water ~*

shuǐniú 水牛

bug 1 *n* (*insect*) kūnchóng 昆虫; (*virus*) bìngdú 病毒; (*spying device*) qiètīngqì 窃听器; COMPUT gùzhàng 故障 2 *v/t* F (*annoy*) shǐ nǎonù 使恼怒

buggy (*for baby*) yīng'ér chē 婴儿车

build *v/t* jiànzào 建造

◆build up 1 *v/t strength* zēngqiáng 增强; *relationship* fāzhǎn 发展 2 *v/i* zhújiàn jījù 逐渐积聚

builder jiànzhù gōngrén 建筑工人; (*company*) jiànzhù gōngsī 建筑公司

building jiànzhù 建筑; (*activity*) jiànzào 建造

building site jiànzhù gōngdì 建筑工地

build-up jījù 积聚; (*publicity*) yúlùn zhǔnbèi 舆论准备

built-up area jiànzhù qū 建筑区

bulb BOT qiújīng 球茎; (*light ~*) diàndēng pào 电灯泡

bulge *v/i* (*of pocket*) gǔgu nāngnang 鼓鼓囊囊; (*of wall, eyes*) péngzhàng 膨胀

**bulk** dà duōshù 大多数; *in ~* zhěngpī 整批

**bulky** *parcel* tǐjī dà 体积大; *sweater* féidà 肥大

**bulldozer** tuītǔjī 推土机

**bullet** zǐdàn 子弹

**bulletin** bùgào 布告

**bulletin board** (*on wall*) bùgào bǎn 布告板

**bullet-proof** fángdàn 防弹

**bull's-eye** bǎxīn 靶心

**bully** *n* èbà 恶霸; (*child*) xiǎo táoqì 小淘气

**bum** *n* F (*hobo*) lǎnhàn 懒汉; (*worthless person*) méiyòng de dōngxi 没用的东西

**bump 1** *n* (*swelling*) zhǒngkuàir 肿块儿; (*in road*) tūkuàir 凸块儿 **2** *v/t* zhuàng 撞

**bunch** (*of people*) huǒ'r 伙; (*of keys*) chuàn 串; *a ~ of flowers* yīshù huā 一束花

**bundle** (*of clothes*) bāo 包

**bungle** *v/t* gǎozāo 搞糟

**bunk** *n* chuángpù 床铺

**burden** *n* fùzhòng 负重; *fig* fùdān 负担

**bureau** (*furniture*) dǒuchú 斗橱; (*office*) bànshìchù 办事处

**bureaucracy** (*red tape*) guānliáo zhǔyì 官僚主义; (*system*) xíngzhèng xìtǒng 行政系统

**bureaucrat** guānliáo 官僚

**bureaucratic** guānliáo 官僚

**burger** hànbǎobāo 汉堡包

**burglar** xiǎotōu 小偷

**burglar alarm** fángqiè jǐngbàoqì 防窃警报器

**burglarize** hànbǎobāo 汉堡包

**burglary** dàoqiè 盗窃

**burial** zànglǐ 葬礼

**burn 1** *n* shāoshāng 烧伤 **2** *v/t* shāo 烧; *toast, meat* shāojiāo 烧焦; (*of sun*) shàishāng 晒伤

♦ **burn down** *v/t & v/i* shāohuǐ 烧毁

**burp 1** *n & v/i* dǎgé 打嗝

**burst 1** *n* (*in pipe*) lièkǒu 裂口 **2** *v/i* (*of balloon, tire*) bàoliè 爆裂; *~ out laughing* túrán dàxiào 突然大笑

**bury** máizàng 埋葬

**bus** *n* gōnggòng qìchē 公共汽车; (*long distance*) chángtú qìchē 长途汽车

**bush** (*plant*) guànmù 灌木;

(*land*) huāngyě 荒野

**business** (*trade*) shēngyi 生意; (*company*) gōngsī 公司; (*work*) gōngzuò 工作; (*affair, matter*) shìjiàn 事件

**businessman** shāngrén 商人

**business studies** shāngyè xué 商业学

**business trip** chūchāi 出差

**businesswoman** nǚshāng-rén 女商人

**bus station** gōnggòng qìchē zōngzhàn 公共汽车总站

**bus stop** chēzhàn 车站

**bust** *n* (*of woman*) xiōng 胸

**busy** *adj* máng 忙; *street* yōu shēngqì 有生气; *store, restaurant: (making money)* shēngyì xīnglóng 生意兴隆; (*full of people*) xīxi rǎngrang 熙熙攘攘; TELEC zhànxiàn 占线

**but** dànshì 但是; *not me ~ ...* būshì wǒ ér shì ... 不是

我而是...

**butcher** màiròu de 卖肉的

**butter** *n* huángyóu 黄油

**butterfly** (*insect*) húdié 蝴蝶

**buttocks** túnbù 臀部

**button** *n* kòuzi 扣子; (*on machine*) ànniǔ 按钮; (*badge*) huīzhāng 徽章

**buy** *v/t* mǎi 买

**buyer** mǎijiā 买家

**buzzer** fēngmíngqì 蜂鸣器

**by** *prep* (*agency*) bèi 被; (*near, next to*) kàojìn 靠近; (*no later than*) bù chíyú 不迟于; (*past*) jīngguò 经过; (*with mode of transportation*) chéng 乘; *~ day / night* zài báitiān / wǎnshàng 在白天/晚上; *a play ...* yóu ...xiěde jùzuò 由 ...写的剧作; *~ oneself* zìjǐ 自己

**bye (-bye)** zàijiàn 再见

**by-product** fù chǎnpǐn 副产品

## C

**cab** (*taxi*) chūzū qìchē 出租汽车; (*van-type*) miàndī 面的; (*of truck*) jiàshǐ shì 驾驶室

**cabin** (*of plane*) zuòcāng 座舱; (*of ship*) chuáncāng 船舱

**cabin crew** jīzǔrényuán 机组人员

**cabinet** (*cupboard*) guìzi 柜子; (*display ~*) chénlièguì 陈列柜; POL nèigé 内阁

**cable** (*electrical*) diànxiàn 电线; ~ (*TV*) yǒuxiàn diànshì 有线电视

**cab stand** chūzūchē zhàn 出租车站

**café** xiǎo fànguǎnr 小饭馆

**cafeteria** shítáng 食堂

**caffeine** kāfēiyīn 咖啡因

**cage** lóng 笼

**cake** *n* dàngāo 蛋糕

**calculate** (*work out*) gūjì 估计; (*in math*) jìsuàn 计算

**calculation** jìsuàn jiéguǒ 计算结果

**calculator** jìsuànqì 计算器

**calendar** rìlì 日历

**calf** (*young cow*) xiǎoniú 小牛

**call 1** *n* TELEC diànhuà 电话; hǎnjiào 喊叫 **2** *v/t* TELEC dǎ diànhuà gěi 打电话给; (*summon*) jiào jiào; *meeting* zhàojí 召集;

(*describe as*) shuōchéng shì 说成是; (*shout*) dàhǎn 大喊 **3** *v/i* TELEC dǎ diànhuà 打电话; (*shout*) hūhǎn 呼喊

♦ **call back 1** *v/t* TELEC huí diànhuà 回电话 **2** *v/i* TELEC zài dǎ diànhuà 再打电话; (*visit again*) zàilái 再来

♦ **call for** *person* jiē 接; *goods* qùná 去拿; (*require*) bìxū yào 必须要

♦ **call in** *v/t expert* qǐng 请

♦ **call on** (*urge*) dūncù 敦促; (*visit*) bàifǎng 拜访

**caller** TELEC dǎ diànhuàzhě 打电话者; (*visitor*) tànfǎngzhě 探访者

**calligraphy** shūfǎ 书法

**calm** *adj weather* píngjìng 平静; *person* lěngjìng 冷静

♦ **calm down** *v/i* píngjìng xiàlai 平静下来

**calorie** kǎlùlǐ 卡路里

**Cambodia** Jiǎnpǔzhài 柬埔寨

**Cambodian 1** *adj* Jiǎnpǔzhài 柬埔寨 **2** *n* (*person*) Jiǎnpǔzhài rén 柬埔寨人

**camcorder** shèxiàngjī 摄像机

**camera** zhàoxiàngjī 照像机

**camouflage** *n* wěizhuāng 伪装

**camp 1** *n* yíng 营 **2** *v/i* lùyíng 露营

**campaign** *n* yùndòng 运动

**camper** yěyíngzhě 野营者; *(vehicle)* yěyíng chē 野营车

**campsite** yíngdì 营地

**campus** xiàoyuán 校园

**can¹** néng 能; *I~'t* wǒ bùnéng 我不能; *as fast as you ~* yuèkuài yuèhǎo 越快越好 ◊ *(with skills)* huì 会; ~ *you speak French?* nǐ huì shuō Fǎyǔ ma? 你会说法语吗？◊ *(permission)* kěyǐ 可以; ~ *I take this one?* wǒ kěyǐ ná zhège ma? 我可以拿这个吗？; ~ *I have a coffee?* qǐng lái bēi kāfēi? 请来杯咖啡？

**can²** *n* *(for drinks etc)* guàntóu 罐头

**Canada** Jiānádà 加拿大

**Canadian 1** *adj* Jiānádà 加拿大 **2** *n* Jiānádà rén 加拿大人

**canal** *(waterway)* yùnhé 运河

**cancel** qǔxiāo 取消

**cancellation** qǔxiāo 取消

**cancer** áizhèng 癌症

**candid** tǎnshuài 坦率

**candidacy** hòuxuǎn 候选

**candidate** *(for position)* hòuxuǎnrén 候选人; *(in exam)* yìngkǎorén 应考人

**candle** làzhú 蜡烛

**candor** tǎnshuài 坦率

**candy** táng 糖

**canned** *fruit etc* guànzhuāng 罐装

**cannot** → *can¹*

**can opener** kāiguànqì 开罐器

**canteen** *(in factory)* shítáng 食堂

**Canton** Guǎngdōng 广东

**Cantonese 1** *adj* Guǎngdōng 广东 **2** *n* Guǎngdōngrén 广东人; *(language)* Guǎngdōnghuà 广东话

**cap** *(hat)* màozi 帽子; *(of bottle, lens)* gàizi 盖子

**capability** nénglì 能力

**capable** nénggàn 能干; *be ~ of* yǒu nénglì 有能力

**capacity** *(of container)* róngliàng 容量; *(of*

*engine*) róngliàng 容量; (*of factory*) chǎnliàng 产量

**capital** n (*of country*) shǒudū 首都; (*letter*) dàxiě zìmǔ 大写字母; (*money*) zījīn 资金

**capitalism** zīběn zhǔyì 资本主义

**capitalist 1** *adj* zīběn zhǔyì 资本主义 **2** n (*believer*) zīběn zhǔyìzhě 资本主义者; (*businessman*) zīběn jiā 资本家

**capital punishment** sǐxíng 死刑

**capsize** v/i fānchuán 翻船

**capsule** MED jiāonáng 胶囊; (*space ∼*) tàikōng cāng 太空舱

**captain** n (*of ship*) chuánzhǎng 船长; (*of aircraft*) jīzhǎng 机长; (*of team*) duìzhǎng 队长

**caption** n shuōmíng 说明

**captivate** zháomí 着迷

**captivity** bèi guān 被关

**capture** v/t person zhuōdào 捉到; animal bǔhuò 捕获; city gōngxià 攻下; mood miáohuì 描绘

**car** chē 车; (*of train*) chē-

xiāng 车厢

**carbohydrate** tànshuǐ huàhéwù 碳水化合物

**carbon monoxide** yīyǎng huàtàn 一氧化碳

**carbureter** qìhuàqì 汽化器

**card** (*to mark special occasion*) kǎpiàn 卡片; (*post∼*) míngxìnpiàn 明信片; (*business ∼*) míngpiàn 名片; (*playing ∼*) zhǐpái 纸牌

**cardboard** yìng zhǐbǎn 硬纸板

**care 1** n (*of baby, elderly, sick*) zhàogù 照顾; (*medical*) yīliáo 医疗; (*worry*) yōulǜ 忧虑; *take ∼* (*be cautious*) xiǎoxīn 小心; *I don't ∼!* wǒbù zàihu! 我不在乎! **2** v/i guānxīn 关心

♦ **care about** guānxīn 关心

**career** (*profession*) shìyè 事业; (*path through life*) jīnglì 经历

**careful** (*cautious*) jǐnshèn 谨慎; (*thorough*) zǐxì 仔细; *person* xìxīn 细心

**careless** *person* cūxīn 粗心; *work* cǎoshuài 草率

cargo huòwù 货物

caricature n (picture) fěngcì huà 讽刺画

caring adj yǒu àixīn 有爱心

carousel (at fairground) xuánzhuǎn mùmǎ 旋转木马

carp (fish) lǐyú 鲤鱼

carpet dìtǎn 地毯

car rental qìchē chūzū gōngsī 汽车出租公司

carrier (company) yùnshū gōngsī 运输公司; (of disease) dàijùnzhě 带菌者

carrot húluóbo 胡萝卜

carry v/t (in hand) ná 拿; (on back) bēi 背; (hold in front) bàozhe 抱; (move: goods) bānyùn 搬运; (have on one's person) dàizhe 带着; (of ship, plane, bus etc) zàiyǒu 载有

♦ carry out survey etc jìnxíng 进行; orders etc zhíxíng 执行

cart (horsedrawn) mǎchē 马车; (for baggage) xíngli chē 行李车

cartel liánhé qǐyè 联合企业

carton (for milk, eggs etc) zhǐhé 纸盒; a ~ of

cigarettes yītiáo xiāngyān 一条香烟

cartoon (in newspaper) fěngcì huà 讽刺画; (on TV, film) kǎtōng piān 卡通片

cartridge (for gun) zǐdàn 子弹

carve meat qiē 切; wood kè 刻

case¹ (container) hé 盒; (of Scotch, wine) xiāng 箱

case² n (instance) lìzi 例子; (argument) gēnjù 根据; (for police, attorney) ànjiàn 案件; MED bìnglì 病例; in ~ ... wànyī ... 万一...; in any ~ zǒngzhī 总之

cash 1 n xiànjīn 现金 2 v/t check duìxiàn 兑现

cash desk fùkuǎntái 付款台

cash flow xiànjīn liú 现金流

cashier n (in store etc) chūnàyuán 出纳员

cash machine qǔkuǎnjī 取款机

cash register xiànjīn chūnàjī 现金出纳机

casino dǔchǎng 赌场

casket (coffin) guāncai 棺材

cassette cídài 磁带

cassette player lùyīnjī 录

音机

**cast** n (*of play*) yǎnyuán biǎo 演员表
**casual** suíbiàn 随便; (*not permanent*) línshí 临时
**casualty** shāngwáng rénshì 伤亡人士
**cat** māo 猫
**catalog** n mùlù 目录
**catastrophe** zāinàn 灾难
**catch** 1 n jiē 接; (*of fish*) bǔhuò wù 捕获物; (*locking device*) shuān 闩; (*problem*) wèntí 问题 2 v/t ball jiēzhù 接住; prisoner zhuōzhù 捉住; (*get on: bus, train*) zuò 坐; (*not miss: bus, train*) gǎnshàng 赶上; fish with rod diàodào 钓到; fish with net bǔdào 捕到; (*in order to speak to*) zhǎodào 找到; illness rǎnshàng 染上; ~ (*a*) cold dé gǎnmào 得感冒
♦**catch up** v/i gǎnshàng 赶上
♦**catch up on** míbǔ 弥补
**catcher** (*in baseball*) jiēshǒu 接手
**catching** disease chuánrǎnxìng 传染性

**category** fànchóu 范畴
**Catholic** 1 adj Tiānzhǔjiào 天主教 2 n Tiānzhǔjiào tú 天主教徒
**cattle** niú 牛
**cause** 1 n yuányīn 原因; (*grounds*) lǐyóu 理由; (*aim of movement, charity etc*) zhǔzhāng 主张 2 v/t yǐnqǐ 引起
**caution** n (*carefulness*) jǐnshèn 谨慎
**cautious** jǐnshèn 谨慎
**cave** dòng 洞
**cavity** (*in tooth*) zhùdòng 蛀洞
**CD** guāngpán 光盘
**cease** v/t & v/i zhōngzhǐ 中止
**cease-fire** tínghuǒ 停火
**ceiling** tiānhuābǎn 天花板; (*limit*) zuìgāo xiàngdù 最高限度
**celebrate** qìngzhù 庆祝
**celebration** qìngzhù huì 庆祝会
**celebrity** míngrén 名人
**cell** (*for prisoner*) láofáng 牢房; BIO xìbāo 细胞
**cellar** dìjiào 地窖
**cell(ular) phone** shǒujī 手机

**championship**

cemetery mùdì 墓地

censor v/t shěnchá 审查

censorship shěnchá zhìdù 审查制度

cent fēn 分

centenary, centennial yìbǎi zhōunián 一百周年

center n zhōngxīn 中心; POL zhōngjiān pài 中间派

central zhōngbù 中部; *apartment* zhōngyāng 中央; *(main)* zhǔyào 主要

central heating zhōngyāng nuǎnqì 中央暖气

centralize jízhōng 集中

century shìjì 世纪

CEO (= *Chief Executive Officer*) zǒng jīnglǐ 总经理

cereal *(grain)* gǔlèi 谷类

ceremony *(event)* diǎnlǐ 典礼; *(ritual)* yíshì 仪式

certain *(sure)* kěndìng 肯定; *(particular)* mǒuzhǒng 某种

certainly *(definitely)* yídìng 一定; *(of course)* méi wèntí 没问题

certainty *(confidence)* quèxìn 确信; *(inevitability)* bìránxìng 必然性

certificate *(qualification)* zhèngshù 证书; *(official paper)* zhèngmíng 证明

certify zhèngmíng 证明

Cesarean n pōufù 剖腹

CFC (= *chlorofluorocarbon*) fúlǜ huàtàn 氟氯化碳

chain n liàntiáo 链条; COM liánsuǒdiàn 连锁店

chair 1 n yǐzi 椅子; *(armchair)* fúshǒu yǐ 扶手椅 2 v/t *meeting* zhǔchí 主持

chairman zhǔxí 主席

Chairman Mao Máo Zhǔxí 毛主席

chairperson, chairwoman zhǔxí 主席

challenge 1 n tiǎozhàn 挑战 2 v/t *(defy)* fǎnduì 反对; *(call into question)* zhìyí 质疑; ~ *X to Y* tiǎozhàn X zuò Y 挑战X 做Y

challenging *job* yǒu tiǎozhànxìng 有挑战性

champagne xiāngbīn jiǔ 香槟酒

champion n SP guànjūn 冠军; *(of cause)* hànwèizhě 捍卫者

championship *(event)* jīnbiāosài 锦标赛; *(title)*

guànjūn 冠军

**chance** (*possibility*) kěnéng 可能; (*opportunity*) jīhuì 机会; (*risk*) fēngxiǎn 风险

**change 1** *n* gǎibiàn 改变; (*small coins*) língqián 零钱; (*from purchase*) zhǎoqián 找钱; *for a ~* huàn kǒuwèi 换口味 **2** *v/t* (*alter*) gǎibiàn 改变; *bankbill, trains, clothes,* (*replace*) huàn 换 **3** *v/i* biàn 变; (*put on different clothes*) huàn yīfu 换衣服; (*in traveling*) huàn 换

**channel** (*on TV*) píndào 频道; (*waterway*) hǎixiá 海峡

**chant** *v/i* gāohū 高呼

**chaos** hùnluàn 混乱

**chaotic** hùnluàn 混乱

**chapter** zhāng 章

**character** (*nature*) běnxìng 本性; (*person*) rén 人; (*in book, play*) rénwù 人物; (*personality*) xìnggé 性格; (*for writing Chinese etc*) zì 字

**characteristic 1** *n* tèdiǎn 特点 **2** *adj* diǎnxíng 典型

**charbroiled** kǎo 烤

**charge 1** *n* (*fee*) fèiyòng 费

用; LAW kònggào 控告; *be in* ~ fùzé 负责; *take* ~ jiēguǎn 接管 **2** *v/t sum of money* shōufèi 收费; (*put on account*) jìzhàng 记账; LAW zhǐkòng 指控; *battery* chōngdiàn 充电

**charge account** shēgòuzhì 赊购制

**charge card** jìzhàngkǎ 记账卡

**charitable** císhàn 慈善

**charity** (*organization*) císhàn jīgòu 慈善机构

**charm** *n* mèilì 魅力; (*on bracelet*) xiǎo zhuāngshì pǐn 小装饰品

**charming** mírén 迷人

**chart** túbiǎo 图表; (*for ship*) hánghǎi tú 航海图; (*for airplane*) hángkōng tú 航空图

**charter** *v/t* bāozū 包租

**chase 1** *n* zhuīzhú 追逐 **2** *v/t* zhuī 追

**chat 1** *n* liáotiān 聊天 **2** *v/i* liáo 聊

**chatter** *v/i* (*talk*) xiánliáo 闲聊; (*of teeth*) dǎzhàn 打颤

**chatterbox** ráoshézhě 饶舌者

chauffeur n sījī 司机

chauvinist (male ~) dà nánrén zhǔyìzhě 大男人主义者

cheap adj piányi 便宜; (mean) xiǎoqì 小气

cheat 1 n (person) piànzi 骗子 2 v/t piàn骗 3 v/i (in exam) zuòbì 作弊; (at cards etc) dǎoguǐ 搞鬼

check¹ n & adj (in pattern) fānggé 方格

check² FIN zhīpiào 支票; (in restaurant etc) zhàngdān 账单

check³ 1 n (to verify) jiǎnchá 检查2 v/t (verify) chá查; (with ✓mark) dǎgōu 打勾; coat, package etc cúnfàng 存放 3 v/i chá查

♦ check in (at airport) lǐng dēngjīkǎ 领登机卡; (at hotel) dēngjì 登记

♦ check out v/i (of hotel) jiézhàng 结账

checkbook zhīpiào běn 支票本

check-in (counter) lǐng dēngjīkǎ guìtái 领登机卡柜台

checking account zhīpiào zhànghù 支票帐户

check-in time lǐng dēngjī kǎ shíjiān 领登机卡时间

checklist héduìbiǎo 核对表

check mark gōuhào 勾号

checkout (in store) guìtái 柜台

checkpoint guānqiǎ 关卡

checkroom (for coats) yīmào jiān 衣帽间; (for bags) xínglǐ cúnfàngchù 行李存放处

checkup medical jiànkāng jiǎnchá 健康检查

cheek miànjiá 面颊

cheer 1 n huānhū 欢呼; ~s! (toast) gānbēi! 干杯！2 v/t shòu huānyíng 受欢迎 3 v/i hècǎi 喝采

♦ cheer up v/i gāoxìng qǐlái 高兴起来; ~! qǐ gǔ jìnr lái! 鼓起劲儿来！

cheerful kuàihuó 快活

cheerleader lālāduì yuán 啦啦队员

cheese nǎilào 奶酪

chef chúshī 厨师

chemical 1 adj huàxué 化学 2 n huàxué zhìpǐn 化学制品

chemist huàxué jiā 化学家

chemistry huàxué 化学; *fig* mòqì 默契

chemotherapy huàxué liáofǎ 化学疗法

chess xiàngqí 象棋

chessboard qípán 棋盘

chest xiōng 胸; (*box*) xiāngzi 箱子

chew v/t jiáo 嚼; (*of dog, rats*) kěn 啃

chewing gum kǒuxiāng táng 口香糖

chicken n jī 鸡; (*food*) jīròu 鸡肉

chief 1 n tóunǎo 头脑 2 adj zhǔyào 主要

chiefly zhǔyào 主要

child háizi 孩子

childhood tóngnián 童年

childish pej yòuzhì 幼稚

chill n (*in air*) lěngqì 冷气; (*illness*) gǎnmào 感冒

chilly weather hánlěng 寒冷

chimney yāncōng 烟囱

chin xiàba 下巴

China Zhōngguó 中国

Chinese 1 adj Zhōngguó 中国; (*in Chinese*) Zhōngwén 中文 2 n (*written language*) Zhōngwén 中文; (*spoken language*) Zhōngguó

huà 中国话; (*person*) Zhōngguórén 中国人

Chinese character hànzì 汉字

chip n (*fragment*) suìxiè 碎屑; (*damage*) liè kǒu 裂口; (*in gambling*) chóumǎ 筹码; COMPUT xīnpiàn 芯片; *potato ~s* shǔpiàn 薯片

chocolate qiǎokèlì 巧克力

choice n xuǎnzé 选择; (*selection*) gèsè gèyàng 各色各样; (*preference*) xuǎnzé 选择

choir héchàngtuán 合唱团

choke 1 n MOT zǔfēngmén 阻风门 2 v/i qiǎ 卡

cholesterol dǎngùchún 胆固醇

choose 1 v/t xuǎnzé 选择 2 v/i tiāoxuǎn 挑选

chop 1 n kǎn 砍; (*meat*) páigǔ 排骨; (*seal*) túzhāng 图章 2 v/t wood kǎn 砍; food duò 剁

chopsticks kuàizi 筷子

chore (*household*) jiāwù 家务

chorus héchàng 合唱; (*singers*) héchàng tuán 合唱团

christen xǐlǐ 洗礼

Christian 1 n Jīdūtú 基督徒
2 adj Jīdūjiào 基督教

Christmas Shèngdànjié 圣
诞节; *Merry ~!* Shèngdàn
kuàilè!圣诞快乐！

Christmas card Shèngdànkǎ
圣诞卡

Christmas Day Shèngdànjié
圣诞节

Christmas Eve Shèngdàn yè
圣诞夜

Christmas present
Shèngdàn lǐwù 圣诞礼物

Christmas tree Shèngdàn
shù 圣诞树

chrome, chromium gè 铬

chronic mànxìng 慢性

chronological shíjiān shùnxù
时间顺序

church jiàotáng 教堂

CIA (= **Central Intelligence
Agency**) Zhōngyāng
Qíngbào Jú 中央情报局

cigar xuějiā 雪茄

cigarette xiāngyān 香烟

cinema diànyǐng 电影; (*Br:
building*) diànyǐng yuàn
电影院

circle 1 n yuánquān 圆圈;
(*group*) quānzi 圈子 2 v/i

(*of plane, bird*) pánxuán
盘旋

circular adj yuánxíng 圆形

circulate v/t *memo etc*
chuányuè 传阅

circulation BIO xúnhuán 循
环; (*of newspaper*) xiāolù
销路

circumstances qíngkuàng
情况

circus mǎxìtuán 马戏团

citizen gōngmín 公民

citizenship guójí 国籍

city chéngshì 城市

civil (*not military*) mínjiān
民间; (*polite*) yǒu lǐmào
有礼貌

civil engineer tǔmù
gōngchéngshī 土木工程师

civilian n píngmín 平民

civilization wénmíng 文明

civil servant gōngwùyuán
公务员

civil war nèizhàn 内战

claim 1 n (*request*) suǒpéi 索
赔; (*assertion*) zhǔzhāng 主
张 2 v/t (*as a right*) suǒqǔ
索取; (*assert*) shēngchēng
声称; *lost and found*
lǐng 领

clamp n (*fastener*) jiázi 夹子

**clandestine** mìmì 秘密

**clap 1** v/i (applaud) pāishǒu
拍手 **2** v/t pāi 拍

**clarify** chéngqīng 澄清

**clarity** qīngxīdù 清晰度

**clash 1** n chōngtū 冲突;
(of personalities) bù xiétiáo 不
协调 **2** v/i fāshēng chōngtū
发生冲突

**clasp 1** n jiázi 夹子 **2** v/t (in
hand) jǐnwò 紧握

**class** n (lesson) kè 课;
(group of people) bān 班;
(category) děngjí 等级;
(social) jiēcéng 阶层

**classic 1** adj (typical)
diǎnxíng 典型; (definitive)
quánwēixìng 权威性 **2** n
jīngdiǎn zuòpǐn 经典作品

**classical** music gǔdiǎn 古典

**classified** information jīmì
机密

**classified** ad fēnlèi
guǎnggào 分类广告

**classify** fēnlèi 分类

**classroom** jiàoshì 教室

**clause** n (in contract) tiáokuǎn
条款

**claustrophobia** yōubì
kǒngbù zhèng 幽闭恐
怖症

**claw** n (of lobster, crab)
qiánzi 钳子; (of cat) zhuǎzi
爪子

**clean 1** adj gānjìng 干净
**2** v/t teeth, shoes shuā 刷;
room dǎsǎo 打扫; car,
hands, clothes xǐ 洗

**cleaning** woman qīngjié
nǚgōng 清洁女工

**cleanser** (for skin) qīngjiéjì
清洁剂

**clear 1** adj explanation,
voice qīngchu 清楚; (obvious)
míngxiǎn 明显;
weather, sky qínglǎng 晴
朗; water qīngchè 清澈;
conscience qīngbái 清白
**2** v/t roads qīngchú 清除;
(acquit) chéngqīng 澄清;
(authorize) yǔnxǔ 允许
**3** v/i (of mist) qíngle 晴了

♦**clear up** v/i (tidy up)
shōushi 收拾; (of weather)
zhuǎnqíng 转晴; (of illness,
rash) xiāoshī 消失

**clearance** (authorization)
xǔkě 许可

**clearly** (with clarity) qīngchu
清楚; (evidently) míngxiǎn
明显

**clench** teeth yǎojǐn 咬紧; fist

wòjǐn 握紧

clerk *(administrative)* zhíyuán 职员; *(in store)* fúwùyuán 服务员

clever cōngmíng 聪明; *gadget* qiǎomiào 巧妙

client gùkè 顾客

climate qìhòu 气候

climax *n* gāocháo 高潮

climb 1 *n (up hill)* pāndēng 攀登 2 *v/t & v/i* pá 爬

climber dēngshānzhě 登山者

clinic zhěnsuǒ 诊所

clip¹ *n (fastener)* jiāzi 夹子

clip² 1 *n (extract)* jiǎnjí 剪辑 2 *v/t* hair, jiǎn 剪

clipping *(from newspaper)* jiǎnbào 剪报

clock zhōng 钟

clock radio shōuyīnjī nàozhōng 收音机闹钟

clockwise shùn shízhēn 顺时针

close¹ *adj friend* qīnmì 亲密; *resemblance* xiāngjìn 相近; *it's ~ to the stores* lí shāngdiàn jìn 离商店近

close² *v/t & v/i* guān 关

closed *store* guānmén 关门; *eyes* bìshàng 闭上

closely *listen, watch* zǐxì 仔细; *cooperate* mìqiè 密切

closet yīguì 衣柜

closing time guānmén shíjiān 关门时间

closure guānbì 关闭

clot *n (of blood)* xuèkuài 血块

cloth *(fabric)* bùliào 布料; *(for cleaning)* mābù 抹布

clothes yīfu 衣服

cloud *n* yún 云

cloudy yīntiān 阴天

club *n* jùlèbù 俱乐部; *(golf iron)* qiúgǎn 球杆

clue xiànsuǒ 线索

clumsy *person* bènshǒu bènjiǎo 笨手笨脚

clutch 1 *n* MOT líhéqì 离合器 2 *v/t* jǐnwò 紧握

coach 1 *n (trainer)* jiàoliàn 教练 2 *v/t* zhǐdǎo 指导

coarse *fabric* cūcāo 粗糙; *(vulgar)* cūsú 粗俗

coast *n* hǎibiān 海边

coastal línhǎi 临海

coastguard hǎi'àn jǐngwèi duì 海岸警卫队

coat 1 *n* wàiyī 外衣; *(over~)* dàyī 大衣; *(of paint etc)* céng 层 2 *v/t (cover)* jiā shàng yīcéng 加上一层

**coating** céng 层

**coax** hǒng 哄

**cocaine** kěkǎyīn 可卡因

**cock** n (chicken) gōngjī 公鸡

**cockpit** (of plane) zuòcāng 座舱

**cockroach** zhāngláng 蟑螂

**code** n mìmǎ 密码

**co-educational** nánnǚhéxiào 男女合校

**coexistence** gòngchǔ 共处

**coffee** kāfēi 咖啡

**coffee break** xiǎoxī 小息

**coffee shop** kāfēi diàn 咖啡店

**coffin** guāncái 棺材

**cog** lúnchǐ 轮齿

**coherent** liánguàn 连贯

**coin** n yìngbì 硬币

**coincide** qiǎohé 巧合

**coincidence** qiǎohé 巧合

**Coke®** kěkǒu kèlè 可口可乐

**cold 1** adj lěng 冷; it's ~ tiān lěng 天冷 **2** n hánlěng 寒冷; I have a ~ wǒ gǎnmàole 我感冒了

**collaborate** hézuò 合作; (with enemy) gōujié 勾结

**collaboration** hézuò 合作;

(with enemy) gōujié 勾结

**collapse** dǎotā 倒塌; (of person) bēngkuì 崩溃

**collar** lǐngzi 领子; (for dog, cat) xiàngquān 项圈

**colleague** tóngshì 同事

**collect 1** v/t person jiē 接; tickets, cleaning etc ná 拿; (gather, as hobby) shōují 收集 **2** adv: **call ~** shòuhuàrén fùfèi 受话人付费

**collection** shōucángpǐn 收藏品; (fashion) shízhuāng zhǎnlǎn 时装展览

**collective** n POL jítǐ 集体

**collector** shōucáng jiā 收藏家

**college** xuéyuàn 学院

**collision** xiāngzhuàng 相撞

**colonial** adj zhímíndì 殖民地

**colony** zhímíndì 殖民地

**color** n yánsè 颜色; (in cheeks) liǎnsè 脸色

**colorful** xiānyàn 鲜艳; account jīngcǎi 精彩

**color photograph** cǎisè zhàopiàn 彩色照片

**column** liè 列; (architectural) yuánzhù 圆柱; (text) lán

栏; (in newspaper) zhuān-
lán 专栏

**columnist** zhuānlán zuòjiā
专栏作家

**coma** hūnmí 昏迷

**comb 1** n shūzi 梳子 **2** v/t
shū 梳; area sōuxún 搜寻

**combat 1** n zhàndòu 战斗
**2** v/t yǔ...zuò dòuzhēng yǔ
...做斗争

**combination** zǔhé 组合; (of
safe) mìmǎ 密码

**combine** v/t hùnhé 混合

**come** (toward speaker) lái
lái; (toward listener) qù 去;
(of train, bus) láile 来了

♦ **come back** huílái 回来

♦ **come down** xià lái 下来;
(in price etc) xiàjiàng 下降

♦ **come in** zǒu jìnlái 走进
来; (of tide) zhǎngcháo 涨
潮; ~! qǐngjìn! 请进！

♦ **come off** (of handle etc)
tuōluò 脱落

♦ **come on** (progress)
jìnzhǎn 进展; ~! kuàidiǎnr!
快点儿！; (in disbelief)
bùkěnéng 不可能

♦ **come out** (of person)
chū 出; (of sun, results,
product) chūlái 出来; (of

stain) xiāoshī 消失; (of
book, record) fāxíng 发行

**comedian** xǐjù yǎnyuán 喜
剧演员; pej chǒujiǎo 丑角

**comedy** xǐjù 喜剧

**comfort 1** n xiǎngshòu 享受;
(consolation) ānwèi 安慰
**2** v/t ānwèi 安慰

**comfortable** shūfu 舒服

**comic 1** n (to read) mànhuà
漫画 **2** adj yǒuqù 有趣

**comma** dòuhào 逗号

**command** n & v/t mìnglìng
命令

**commander** zhǐhuīguān
指挥官

**commemorate** jìniàn 纪念

**comment 1** n yìjiàn 意见
**2** v/i fābiǎo yìjiàn 发表
意见

**commentary** pínglùn 评论

**commentator** pínglùn jiā
评论家

**commercial 1** adj shāngyè
商业 **2** n (ad) guǎnggào
广告

**commission 1** n (payment)
yòngjīn 佣金; (job)
chéngbāo 承包;
(committee) wěiyuánhuì
委员会 **2** v/t (for a job)

wěituō 委托

**commit**: ~ *a crime* fànzuì 犯罪；~ *oneself* tóurù 投入

**commitment** zérèn 责任

**committee** wěiyuánhuì 委员会

**commodity** shāngpǐn 商品

**common** (*not rare*) píngcháng 平常；(*shared*) gòngtóng 共同

**common sense** chángshí 常识

**communicate** *v/i* (*make self understood*) gōutōng 沟通

**communications** tōngxùn yè 通讯业

**communicative** ài shuōhuà 爱说话

**Communism** Gòngchǎnzhǔyì 共产主义

**Communist** 1 *adj* Gòngchǎnzhǔyì 共产主义 2 *n* Gòngchǎndǎngyuán 共产党员

**Communist China** Zhōnggòng 中共

**Communist Party** Gòngchǎndǎng 共产党

**community** shèqū 社区

**commute** *v/i* (*to work*) tōngqín 通勤

**compact disc** MUS jīguāng chàngpiān 激光唱片；COMPUT guāngpán 光盘

**companion** bànlǚ 伴侣

**company** COM gōngsī 公司；(*companionship*) péibàn 陪伴；(*guests*) kèrén 客人

**comparatively** xiāngduì éryán 相对而言

**compare** *v/t* bǐjiào 比较；~ *X with Y* jiāng X yǔ Y xiāng bǐjiào 将X与Y相比较

**comparison** bǐjiào 比较

**compassion** tóngqíng 同情

**compatible** *people* hédelái 合得来；*blood, life styles* fúhé 符合；COMPUT jiānróng 兼容

**compel** (*force*) qiǎngpò 强迫

**compensate** *v/t* (*with money*) péicháng 赔偿

**compensation** (*money*) péicháng 赔偿；(*comfort*) ānwèi 安慰

**compete** jìngzhēng 竞争；(*take part*) cānjiā 参加；~ *for* zhēngduó 争夺

**competent** *person* chèngzhí 称职；*work* hégé 合格

**competition** jìngzhēng 竞争；

SP bǐsài 比赛; (*competitors*) duìshǒu 对手

competitive *price* yǒu jìngzhēng lì 有竞争力; *person* hào jìngzhēng 好竞争

competitor (*in contest*) bǐsàizhě 比赛者; COM jìngzhēng duìshǒu 竞争对手

complain *v/i* bàoyuàn 抱怨; (*to store, manager*) tóusù 投诉

complaint tóusù 投诉; MED jíbìng 疾病

complete 1 *adj* (*total*) shízú 十足; (*full*) wánzhěng 完整; (*finished*) wángōng 完工 2 *v/t course, task etc* wánchéng 完成; *form* tiánxiě 填写

completely wánquán 完全

completion wánchéng 完成

complex 1 *adj* fùzá 复杂 2 *n* PSYCH qíngjié 情节; (*of buildings*) zhōngxīn 中心

complicated fùzá 复杂

compliment *n & v/t* zànměi 赞美

complimentary zànměi 赞美; (*free*) miǎnfèi 免费; (*in restaurant, hotel*) zèngsòng 赠送

comply fúcóng 服从; ~ with ... zūnshǒu ... 遵守...

component bùfen 部分

compose *v/t* zǔchéng 组成; MUS chuàngzuò 创作

composer MUS zuòqǔjiā 作曲家

composure zhènjìng 镇静

comprise (*consist of*) bāohán 包含; (*make up*) gòuchéng 构成; be ~d of ... yóu ... zǔchéng 由...组成

compromise *n* tuǒxié 妥协

compulsory yìwù 义务; *class* bìxiū 必修

computer diànnǎo 电脑

computer game diànzǐ yóuxì 电子游戏

conceal *fact, truth* yǐnmán 隐瞒; *object* yǐncáng 隐藏

conceited zìgào zìdà 自高自大

concentrate *v/i* (*on task*) jízhōng jīnglì 集中精力

concentration zhuānxīn 专心

concept gàiniàn 概念

concern 1 *n* (*anxiety*) dānyōu 担忧; (*care*) guānxīn

关心; (*company*) gōngsī 公司 **2** *v/t* (*involve*) shèjí 涉及; (*worry*) dānyōu 担忧

**concerned** (*anxious*) gǎndào bù ān 感到不安; (*caring*) guānxīn 关心; (*involved*) yǒuguān 有关

**concert** yīnyuè huì 音乐会

**conclude 1** *v/t* (*deduce*) tuīduàn chū 推断出 **2** *v/i* jiéshù 结束

**conclusion** (*deduction*) jiélùn 结论; (*end*) jiéwěi 结尾

**concrete** *n* hùnníngtǔ 混凝土

**concussion** zhèndàng 震荡

**condition** *n* (*state, of health*) zhuàngtài 状态; (*requirement, term*) tiáojiàn 条件; **~s** (*circumstances*) tiáojiàn 条件

**conditioner** (*for hair*) hùfà sù 护发素

**condolences** diàoyàn 吊唁

**condom** bìyùn tào 避孕套

**conduct 1** *n* (*behavior*) jǔzhǐ 举止 **2** *v/t* (*carry out*) shíshī 实施; ELEC chuándǎo 传导; MUS zhǐhuī 指挥

**conductor** MUS zhǐhuī jiā 指挥家; RAIL lièchēzhǎng 列车长

**conference** tǎolùn huì 讨论会

**confess** *v/t & v/i* chéngrèn 承认; (*to police*) tǎnbái 坦白

**confession** gòngrèn 供认; (*to police*) rènzuì shū 认罪书; REL chànhuǐ 忏悔

**confidence** (*assurance*) xìnxīn 信心; (*trust, secret*) xìnrèn 信任

**confident** (*assured*) zìxìn 自信; (*convinced*) kěndìng 肯定

**confidential** jīmì 机密

**confirm** *v/t* quèdìng 确定; *theory, fears* zhèngshí 证实

**confirmation** zhèngmíng 证明; (*of theory, fears*) zhèngshí 证实

**confiscate** mòshōu 没收

**conflict 1** *n* (*disagreement*) zhēngyì 争议; (*clash*) chōngtū 冲突; (*war*) zhànzhēng 战争 **2** *v/i* (*clash*) chōngtū 冲突

**conform** zūnshǒu 遵守; (*of product*) fúhé 符合

**confront** (*face*) miànduì 面

对; (*tackle*) shǐ duìzhì 使对质

confrontation chōngtū 冲突

confuse hùnxiáo 混淆; ~ **X** with **Y** bǎ X dāngchéng Y 把X当成Y

confusing lìngrén hútú 令人糊涂

confusion hùnxiáo 混淆

congestion MOT dǔsè 堵塞; (*in chest*) chōngxuè 充血

congratulate zhùhè 祝贺

congratulations zhùhè 祝贺

congress dàibiǎo dàhuì 代表大会; **Congress** (*of US*) Guóhuì 国会

Congressional Guóhuì 国会

Congressman Guóhuì yìyuán 国会议员

conjunctivitis jiémó yán 结膜炎

connect (*join*) liánjiē 连接; TELEC jiētōng 接通; (*link*) yǒu guānxì 有关系; (*to power supply*) jiētōng diànlù 接通电路

connecting flight liányùn fēijī 联运飞机

connection (*in wiring*) liánjiē 连接; (*link, personal contact*) guānxi 关系; (*when traveling*) liányùn 联运; ~ **to the Internet** yīntèwǎng jiēkǒu 因特网接口

conquer zhēngfú 征服; *fear etc* zhànshèng 战胜

conscience liángxīn 良心

conscious *adj* (*aware*) zìjué 自觉; MED qīngxǐng 清醒

consciousness yìshí 意识; MED zhījué 知觉

consecutive liánxù 连续

consent **1** *n* zànxǔ 赞许 **2** *v/i* tóngyì 同意

consequence hòuguǒ 后果

consequently suǒyǐ 所以

conservative *adj* bǎoshǒu 保守; *clothes* lǎoqì 老气

consider (*regard*) rènwéi 认为; (*show regard for, think about*) kǎolǜ 考虑

considerable xiāngdāng dà 相当大

considerate tǐtiē 体贴

consideration (*thought*) kǎolǜ 考虑; (*thoughtfulness, concern*) guānxīn 关心; *take X into* ~ kǎolǜ X 考虑 X

consignment COM huòwù 货物

♦consist of bāokuò 包括

consistent yīguàn 一贯

consolation ānwèi 安慰

console v/t ānwèi 安慰

conspicuous xiǎnyǎn 显眼

conspiracy yīnmóu 阴谋

constant bùduàn 不断

constipation biànmì 便秘

constitution POL xiànfǎ 宪法

construction jiànzào 建造

construction industry jiànzhù yè 建筑业

construction worker jiànzhù gōngrén 建筑工人

constructive yǒu jiànshèxìng 有建设性

consul lǐngshì 领事

consulate lǐngshì guǎn 领事馆

consult (seek the advice of) hé ... shāngliàng 和... 商量

consultancy (company) zīxún gōngsī 咨询公司; (advice) zīxún 咨询

consultant gùwèn 顾问

consumer gùkè 顾客

consumption (of energy etc) xiāohào 消耗

contact 1 n (person) shóurén 熟人; (communication, physical) jiēchù 接触 2 v/t liánluò 联络

contact lens yǐnxíng yǎnjìng 隐形眼镜

contagious chuánrǎn 传染; fig mànyán 蔓延

contain tears, laughter kòngzhì 控制; it ~ed my camera wǒde zhàoxiàngjī zài lǐmiàn 我的照像机在里面

container róngqì 容器; COM jízhuāng xiāng 集装箱

contemporary 1 adj dāngdài 当代 2 n tóngdàirén 同代人; (at school) tóngjiè 同届

contempt qīngmiè 轻蔑

contender jìngzhēngzhě 竞争者; (against position) zhēngduózhě 争夺者; POL jìngxuǎnrén 竞选人

content¹ n nèiróng 内容

content² adj mǎnzú 满足

contentment mǎnzú 满足

contents nèiróng 内容

contest¹ (competition) bǐsài 比赛; (for power) zhēngduó 争夺

contest² v/t leadership etc jìngzhēng 竞争

contestant cānsàizhě 参赛者

context shàngxià wén 上下

文; **look at X in ~** gēnjù jùtǐ huánjìng lái kǎolǜ X 根据具体环境来考虑X

**continent** *n* dàlù 大陆

**continual** bùduàn 不断

**continue** *v/t & v/i* jìxù 继续

**continuous** bùtíng 不停

**contraception** bìyùn 避孕

**contraceptive** *n* bìyùnqì 避孕器; *(pill)* bìyùn yào 避孕药

**contract** *n* hétóng 合同

**contractor** chéngbāorén 承包人

**contradict** *statement* yǔ... yǒu máodùn 与...有矛盾; *person* fǎnbó 反驳

**contrary**[1] **1** *adj* duìlì 对立; **~ to** ~ yǔ...xiāngfǎn 与...相反 **2** *n*: **on the ~** zhèng xiāngfǎn 正相反

**contrast** *n & v/t* duìzhào 对照

**contribute** *v/t money* juānxiàn 捐献

**control 1** *n (of country, emotion etc)* kòngzhì 控制 **2** *v/t (govern)* kòngzhì 控制; *(restrict)* xiànzhì 限制; *(regulate)* guǎnlǐ 管理

**control panel** kòngzhì pán 控制盘

**control tower** zhǐhuī diàodùtái 指挥调度台

**controversial** yǒu zhēngyì 有争议

**convalescence** liáoyǎng qī 疗养期

**convenience** fāngbiàn 方便

**convenience store** fāngbiàn xiǎo shāngdiàn 方便小商店

**convenient** *location* fāngbiàn 方便; *time, arrangement* héshì 合适

**convention** *(tradition)* shèhuì xísú 社会习俗; *(conference)* dàhuì 大会

**conventional** píngcháng 平常

**convention center** huìyì zhōngxīn 会议中心

**conversation** jiāotán 交谈

**conversion** *(of figures, money)* zhésuàn 折算

**convert 1** *n* guīfùzhě 皈附者 **2** *v/t house, room etc* gǎijiàn 改建; *unit of measurement* zhéhé 折合; *energy* zhuǎnhuà 转化

**convertible** *n (car)* zhépéng chē 折蓬车

**convict** 1 *n* qiúfàn 囚犯
2 *v/t* LAW xuānpàn yǒuzuì
宣判有罪

**conviction** LAW dìngzuì 定
罪; (*belief*) quèxìn 确信

**convince** shuōfú 说服

**convincing** lìngrén xìnfú 令
人信服

**cook** 1 *n* chúshī 厨师 2 *v/t*
& *v/i* zuò 做; (*roast, bake*)
kǎo 烤; (*steam*) zhēng 蒸;
(*stir fry*) chǎo 炒 3 *v/i* (*of
person*) zuòfàn 做饭

**cookbook** pēngrèn shū 烹
饪书

**cookie** qūqí 曲奇

**cooking** (*food*) fàncài 饭菜

**cool** 1 *adj* *weather*
liángshuǎng 凉爽; *drink*
liáng 凉; (*calm*) lěngjìng 冷
静; (*unfriendly*) lěngmò 冷
漠; F (*great*) kù 酷 2 *v/i* (*of
food*) lěngquè 冷却; (*of
tempers*) píngxī 平息

**cooperate** hézuò 合作

**cooperative** 1 *n* COM hézuò
shè 合作社 2 *adj* COM
hézuò 合作; (*helpful*) lèyì
乐意 pèihé 乐意 配合

**coordinate** *activities* xiétiáo
协调

**coordination** xiétiáo 协调

**cop** F jǐngchá 警察

**cope** yìngfu 应付; ~ *with* ...
yìngfu ... 应付...

**copier** (*machine*) fùyìnjī
复印机

**copy** 1 *n* (*imitation*) fùzhì pǐn
复制品; (*duplicate*) fùběn
副本; (*photocopy*) fùyìn
jiàn 复印件; (*of book*) běn
本; (*of record, CD*) pán 盘
2 *v/t* (*imitate*) fǎngzào 仿
造; (*duplicate*) fùxiě 复写;
(*photocopy*) fùyìn 复印;
COMPUT: *file* fùzhì 复制; (*in
writing*) chāoxiě 抄写; (*in
order to cheat*) chāoxí 抄袭

**cord** (*string*) shéng 绳;
(*cable*) xiàn 线

**core** 1 *n* (*of fruit*) hé 核;
(*of problem*) yàodiǎn 要
点; (*of organization, party*)
héxīn 核心 2 *adj* *issue* zuì
zhòngyào 最重要

**cork** (*in bottle*) píngsāi 瓶塞;
(*material*) ruǎnmù 软木

**corkscrew** luósī qǐzi 螺丝
起子

**corner** *n* (*of room*) jiǎoluò
角落; (*of table*) zhuōjiǎo
桌角; (*bend: on road*)

zhuǎnwān 转弯; (*in soccer*) jiǎoqiú 角球

**corporate** COM jítuán 集团

**corpse** sǐshī 死尸

**correct 1** *adj* zhèngquè 正确

**2** *v/t* jiūzhèng 纠正; *proofs, homework* xiūgǎi 修改

**correspondence** (*letters*) xìnjiàn 信件; (*exchange of letters*) tōngxìn 通信

**correspondent** (*reporter*) tōngxùnyuán 通讯员

**corridor** zǒuláng 走廊

**corroborate** zhèngshí 证实

**corrosion** fǔshí 腐蚀

**corrupt** *adj* fǔbài 腐败; COMPUT pòhuài破坏

**corruption** shòuhuì 受贿

**cosmetics** huàzhuāng pǐn 化妆品

**cosmetic surgery** zhěngróng wàikē 整容外科

**cost 1** *n* (*price*) jiàgé 价格; (*in finance*) chéngběn 成本; *fig* dàijià 代价; **~s** COM fèiyòng 费用 **2** *v/t* $50 *etc* xūyào 需要

**cost of living** shēnghuó fèiyòng 生活费用

**cot** (*camp-bed*) xíngjūn chuáng 行军床

**cotton 1** *n* miánhua 棉花 **2** *adj* miánbù 棉布

**couch** *n* cháng shāfā 长沙发

**cough** *n & v/i* késou 咳嗽

**could**: ~ *I ...?* wǒ kěyǐ ...ma? 我可以...吗?; ~ *you ...?* qǐng nǐ ...? 请你...?; *you ~ be right* méizhǔn nǐshì duìde没准儿你是对的

**council** (*assembly*) yìhuì 议会; (*authority*) zhèngfǔ 政府

**councilor** yìyuán 议员

**counselor** LAW lǜshī 律师

**count 1** *v/i* (*to ten etc*) shǔ 数; (*calculate*) jìsuàn 计算; (*be important*) yǒu zhòngyào yìyì 有重要意义; (*qualify*) suàn 算 **2** *v/t* (~ *up*) shǔ 数; (*calculate*) jìsuàn 计算; (*include*) bāokuò 包括

♦**count on** yīkào 依靠

**countdown** dào shǔshù 倒数数

**counter¹** (*in store, café*) guìtái 柜台; (*in game*) chóumǎ 筹码

**counter²** *v/t* fǎnjī 反击

**counteract** zhōnghé 中和

**counterbalance** pínghéng lì

平衡力

**counterfeit** v/t & adj wěizào 伪造

**counterpart** (person) duìfāng 对方

**counterproductive** qǐ fǎn zuòyòng 起反作用

**countless** shǔbù jìn 数不尽

**country** guójiā 国家; (not town) xiāngxià 乡下

**countryside** nóngcūn 农村

**coup** POL zhèngbiàn 政变

**couple** (married) fūqī 夫妻; (man & woman) qínglǚ 情侣; *just a ~* zhǐyǒu jǐgè 只有几个; *a ~ of* jǐgè 几个

**courage** yǒngqì 勇气

**courier** xìnshǐ 信使; (with tourists) dǎoyóu 导游

**course** n (lessons) kèchéng 课程; (of meal) dào 道; (of ship, plane) hángxiàng 航向; (for horse race, golf) chǎng 场; (for cross-country running, skiing) dào 道; *of ~* (certainly) dāngrán 当然; (naturally) zìrán 自然

**court** n LAW fǎtíng 法庭; SP chǎng 场

**courthouse** fǎyuàn 法院

**courtroom** shěnpàn shì 审判室

**cousin** (older male on father's side) tángxiōng 堂兄; (younger male on father's side) tángdì 堂弟; (older female on father's side) tángjiě 堂姐; (younger female on father's side) tángmèi 堂妹; (older male on mother's side) biǎoxiōng 表兄; (younger male on mother's side) biǎodì 表弟; (older female on mother's side) biǎojiě 表姐; (younger female on mother's side) biǎomèi 表妹

**cover 1** n (protective) zhào 罩; (of book, magazine) fēngmiàn 封面; (for bed) bèizi 被子; (shelter) yǎnbì 掩蔽 **2** v/t fùgài 覆盖; (hide) yǎngài 掩盖; distance xíngshǐ 行使

♦**cover up 1** v/t gàizhù 盖住; fig yǎngài 掩盖 **2** v/i fig yǐnmán 隐瞒

**coverage** (by media) bàodào 报道

**covert** mìmì 秘密

**coverup** n yǎnshì 掩饰

**cow** n mǔniú 母牛

**coward** dǎnxiǎo guǐ 胆小鬼

**cozy** shūshì 舒适

**crack 1** n lièfèng 裂缝; (joke) xiàohua 笑话 **2** v/t cup shǐ chǎnshēng lièfèng 使产生裂缝; nut zá 砸; code pòyì 破译
♦ **crack down on** zhìcái 制裁

**cracker** (to eat) bócuì bǐnggān 薄脆饼干

**craft** (skill) gōngyì 工艺; (trade) zhíyè 职业

**craftsman** shǒuyìrén 手艺人

**cramped** room zhǎixiǎo 窄小

**cramps** chōujīn 抽筋

**crane** (machine) qǐzhòngjī 起重机

**crash 1** n (noise) huālā shēng 哗啦声; (accident), COMPUT sǐjī 死机; (plane ~) fēijī shīshì 飞机失事; COM dǎobì 倒闭 **2** v/i (of car) zhuàng 撞; (of airplane) zhuìhuǐ 坠毁; (of market) bàodiē 暴跌; COMPUT sǐjī 死机

**crash helmet** fángzhuàng tóukuī 防撞头盔

**crawl** v/i (on floor) pá 爬; (move slowly) huǎnmàn xíngjìn 缓慢行进

**crazy** adj fāfēng 发疯; **be ~ about ...** duì ...zháomí 对 ...着迷

**cream** n (for skin, coffee) rǔshuāng 乳霜

**crease** n zhòuwén 皱纹; (deliberate) kùxiàn 裤线

**create** v/t (make) chuàngzào 创造; (lead to) yǐnqǐ 引起

**creative** yǒu chuàngzào lì 有 创造力

**credible** (believable) kě xiāngxìn 可相信; candidate etc kě xìnrèn 可信任

**credit** n FIN shēqiàn 赊欠; (use of ~ cards) xìnyòng 信用; (honor) zànyáng 赞扬; (payment received) dàifāng 贷方

**credit card** xìnyòngkǎ 信用卡

**creditor** zhàizhǔ 债主

**creek** xiǎohé 小河

**creep 1** n pej tǎoyàn guǐ 讨厌鬼 **2** v/i nièshǒu nièjiǎo de zǒu 蹑手蹑脚地走

**cremation** huǒhuà 火化

**crew** n (*of ship, airplane*) quántǐ gōngzuò rényuán 全体工作人员

**crime** zuìxíng 罪行

**criminal 1** n zuìfàn 罪犯 **2** adj xíngshì 刑事; (*shameful*) lìngrén yíhàn 令人遗憾

**crisis** wēijī 危机

**crisp** adj lettuce, apple xīnxiān ér cuìshēng 新鲜而脆生; shirt, bill tǐngkuò 挺括

**criterion** biāozhǔn 标准

**critic** pínglùn jiā 评论家

**critical** (*making criticisms*) tiāocìr 挑刺儿; (*serious*) wēijī wēijí 危急; *moment etc* jǐnyào 紧要; MED yánzhòng 严重

**criticism** pīpíng 批评

**criticize** v/t pīpíng 批评

**crook** n (*dishonest*) piànzi 骗子

**crooked** (*not straight*) wānqū 弯曲; (*dishonest*) bù lǎoshí 不老实

**crop 1** n shōucheng 收成 **2** v/t hair, photo xiūjiǎn 修剪

**cross 1** adj (*angry*) shēngqì

生气 **2** n (X) chāzi 叉子; (*Christian*) shízìjià 十字架 **3** v/t (*go across*) chuānguò 穿过 **4** v/i (*go across the road*) guò mǎlù 过马路; (*of lines*) jiāochā 交叉

♦**cross out** qǔxiāo 取消

**cross-examine** LAW pánjié 盘诘

**crosswalk** rénxíng héngdào 人行横道

**crossword** (*puzzle*) zònghéng zì mí 纵横字迷

**crouch** v/i dūnxi 蹲下

**crowd** n rénqún 人群; (*at sports event*) guānzhòng 观众

**crowded** yōngjǐ 拥挤

**crucial** guānjiàn 关键

**crude** adj (*vulgar*) cūlǔ 粗鲁; (*unsophisticated*) jiǎnlòu 简陋

**cruel** cánrěn 残忍

**cruelty** cánrěn 残忍

**crumb** zhāzi 渣子

**crumble** v/i suìliè 碎裂; fig (*of opposition*) bēngkuì 崩溃

**crush** v/t yā yā压; (*crease*) nòngzhòu 弄皱

**cry** v/i (*weep*) kū 哭

cube (*shape*) lìfāngxíng
立方形

cuddle n & v/t yōngbào 拥抱

cue n (*for actor etc*) tíshì 提
示; (*for pool*) qiúgān 球杆

cuff n (*of shirt*) xiùkòu 袖口;
(*of pants*) kùjiǎo fānbiān 裤
角翻边

culinary pēngtiáo 烹调

culprit zuìfàn 罪犯

cult zōngpài 宗派

cultivate land gēngzuò 耕作

cultivated person yǒu
xiūyǎng 有修养

cultural (*of arts*) yǒu xiūyǎng
有修养; (*of a country's
identity*) wénhuà 文化

Cultural Revolution Wénhuà
Dàgémìng 文化大革命

culture n (*artistic*) wénmíng
文明; (*of a country*)
wénhuà 文化

cunning n & adj jiǎohuá
狡猾

cup n bēi 杯

cupboard guìzi 柜子

curb 1 n (*of street*) lùyuán 路
缘 2 v/t kòngzhì 控制

cure MED 1 n liáofǎ 疗法
2 v/t zhìhǎo 治好

curiosity (*inquisitiveness*)

hàoqí xīn 好奇心

curious (*inquisitive*) hàoqí
好奇; (*strange*) qítè 奇特

currency (*money*) huòbì 货
币; **foreign ~** wàihuì 外汇

current 1 n (*in sea*) jīliú 激
流; ELEC diànliú 电流2 adj
(*present*) mùqián 目前

currently mùqián 目前

curse 1 n (*spell*) zǔzhòu 诅
咒 2 v/i (*swear*) màrén 骂人

curtain chuānglián 窗帘;
THEA wéimù 帷幕

curve 1 n qūxiàn 曲线 2 v/i
(*bend*) wānqū 弯曲

cushion n kàodiàn 靠垫

custody (*of children*) fúyǎng
quán 扶养权; **in ~** LAW bèi
jūliú 被拘留

custom (*tradition*) xíguàn 习
惯; COM huìgù 惠顾

customer gùkè 顾客

customs hǎiguān 海关

customs officer hǎiguān
guānyuán 海关官员

cut 1 n (*with knife, scissors*)
qièkǒu 切口; (*injury*)
shāngkǒu 伤口2 v/t qiè 切;
(*reduce*) xiāojiǎn 削减;
COMPUT: text jiǎnqiē 剪切;
**get one's hair ~** jiǎn tóufa

剪头发
♦ **cut back** v/i (in costs)
suōjiǎn 缩减
♦ **cut down 1** v/t tree kǎndǎo
砍倒 **2** v/i (in smoking etc)
jiǎnshǎo 减少
♦ **cut off** (with scissors etc)
jiǎndiào 剪掉; (isolate)
géjué 隔绝; TELEC
duànxiàn 断线
**cute** (pretty) kě'ài 可爱;
(sexually, male) yīngjùn
英俊; (sexually, female)

piàoliang 漂亮
**cutting** adj remark shāngrén
gǎnqíng 伤人感情
**cycle 1** n (bicycle) zìxíngchē
自行车 **2** v/i qí xíngchē
骑自行车
**cyclist** qí zìxíngchē de rén 骑
自行车的人
**cylinder** MOT qìgāng 汽缸
**cynic** fènshì jísúzhě 愤世
嫉俗者
**cynical** fènshì jísú 愤世嫉
俗

# D

**DA** (= **district attorney**)
dìfāng jiǎnchá guān 地方
检查官
**dad** bà ba 爸爸
**daily 1** n (paper) rìbào 日报
**2** adj měirì 每日
**dairy products** rǔzhì pǐn
乳制品
**dam** n (for water) shuǐbà
水坝
**damage 1** n sǔnshī 损失; fig
(to reputation etc) sǔnhài 损
害 **2** v/t sǔnhuài 损坏
**damages** LAW péicháng

赔偿
**damn** interj & adj gāisǐ 该死
**damp** shī 湿
**dance 1** n tiàowǔ 跳舞;
(event) wǔhuì 舞会 **2** v/i
tiàowǔ 跳舞
**dancer** wǔdǎo jiā 舞蹈
家; (performer) wǔdǎo
yǎnyuán 舞蹈演员
**dancing** wǔdǎo 舞蹈
**danger** wēixiǎn 危险
**dangerous** wēixiǎn 危险
**dare** v/i & v/t gǎn 敢
**daring** adj dàdǎn 大胆

**dark 1** *n* hēi'àn 黑暗 **2** *adj room*, *night* hēi 黑; *hair*, *eyes* shēn yánsè 深颜色

**dash 1** *n* (*in text*) pòzhé hào 破折号 **2** *v/i* jíchōng 急冲

**data** shùjù 数据

**database** shùjù kù 数据库

**date** *n* rìqī 日期; (*meeting*) yuēhuì 约会; *what's the ~ today?* jīntiān jǐhào? 今天几号？; *out of ~ clothes* guòshí 过时; *passport* guòqī 过期

**daughter** nǔ'ér 女儿

**daughter-in-law** érxífù 儿媳妇

**dawn** *n* pòxiǎo 破晓

**day** tiān 天; *~ by ~* yī tiāntiān de 一天天地; *the other ~* (*recently*) zuìjìn 最近

**daylight** rìguāng 日光

**dazed** (*by blow*) fāhūn 发昏

**dazzle** *v/t* (*of light*) huǎng 晃

**dead 1** *adj* sǐ 死; *battery*, *phone* shīlíng 失灵; F (*place*) sǐqì chénchén 死气沉沉 **2** *n*: *the ~* sǐrén 死人

**dead end** (*street*) sǐ hútòng 死胡同

**deadline** qīxiàn 期限

**deadlock** *n* jiāngjú 僵局

**deaf** lóng 聋

**deafening** jí dàshēng 极大声

**deal** *n* jiāoyì 交易; *a good ~* (*bargain*) hǎo jiàqián 好价钱; *a great ~* (*a lot*) hěnduō 很多

**dealer** shāngrén 商人; (*drug ~*) fàndúzhě 贩毒者

**dealings** (*business*) jiāowǎng 交往

**dear** *adj* qīn'ài 亲爱; *Dear Sir* zūnjìngde xiānsheng 尊敬的先生; *Dear Wang Li* qīn'àide Wáng Lì 亲爱的王丽

**death** sǐwáng 死亡

**debate** *n* (*between opposing sides*) biànlùn 辩论; (*discussion*) tǎolùn 讨论

**debit** *n & v/t* jièfāng 借方

**debris** cánjì 残迹

**debt** zhài 债

**debtor** jièfāng 借方

**decade** shínián 十年

**decaffeinated** wú kāfēiyīn 无咖啡因

**decay** *n* fǔlàn 腐烂

**deceased**: *the ~* sǐzhě 死者

**deceitful** bù lǎoshi 不老实

deceive qīpiàn 欺骗

December shí'èryuè 十二月

decency zhèngpài 正派

decent *person* zhèngpài 正派; *salary* kě jiēshòu 可接受

deception qīpiàn 欺骗

deceptive kàobuzhù 靠不住

decide *v/t* juédìng 决定; (*settle*) pànjué 判决

decipher jiě mìmǎ 解密码

decision juédìng 决定

decision-maker dāngquánzhě 当权者

decisive guǒduàn 果断; (*crucial*) juédìngxìng 决定性

deck (*of ship*) jiǎbǎn 甲板; (*of cards*) yìfù zhǐpái 一副纸牌

declare shēngmíng 声明; *independence* xuānbù 宣布; (*at customs*) chéngbào 呈报

decline 1 *n* xiàjiàng 下降 2 *v/t invitation* xièjué 谢绝 3 *v/i* (*refuse*) xièjué 谢绝; (*decrease*) jiǎnshǎo 减少; (*of health*) shuāituì 衰退

decode yìmǎ 译码

décor zhuānghuáng 装璜

decorate zhuāngxiū 装修; *soldier* shòuxūn 授勋

decoy *n* yòu'ěr 诱饵

decrease 1 *n* xiàjiàng 下降 2 *v/t* suōjiǎn 缩减 3 *v/i* xiàjiàng 下降

dedicate *book etc* tíxiàn 题献

dedication (*to cause, work*) zhìlì 致力

deduce tuīlǐ 推理

deduct: ~ *X* from *Y* cóng Y zhōng jiǎnqù X 从 Y 中减去X

deduction (*from salary*) kòuchú 扣除; (*conclusion*) tuīlùn 推论

deed *n* (*act*) xíngwéi 行为; LAW qìyuē 契约

deep shēn 深; *voice* shēnchén 深沉; *thinker* shēnrù 深入

deep freeze *n* bīngxiāng 冰箱

deep-fry yóuzhá 油炸

deface sǔnhuài biǎomiàn 损坏表面

defamation fěibàng 诽谤

defeat 1 *n* (*conquering*) jíbài 击败; (*losing*) shībài 失败 2 *v/t* jíbài 击败

defect n quēxiàn 缺陷

defective yǒu quēxiàn 有缺陷

defend bǎowèi 保卫; (*justify*) biànhù 辩护

defendant bèigào 被告

defense n bǎowèi 保卫; SP fángshǒu 防守; LAW bèigào 被告; (*justification*) biànhù 辩护

defiance duìkàng 对抗

defiant tiǎozhàn 挑战

deficit kuīsǔn 亏损

define word xià dìngyì 下定义; objective míngquè 明确

definite date, reply míngquè 明确; (*certain*) kěndìng 肯定

definitely kěndìng 肯定

definition dìngyì 定义; (*of objective*) chǎnshù 阐述

deformity jīxíng 畸形

defraud piànqǔ 骗取

defrost v/t food jiědòng 解冻; icebox huàbīng 化冰

defuse chāichú yǐnxìn 拆除引信; situation tiáojiě 调解

defy wéikàng 违抗

degrading dījí 低级

degree dù 度; (*from university*) xuéwèi 学位

dehydrated tuōshuǐ 脱水

dejected jǔsàng 沮丧

delay 1 n yánchí 延迟 2 v/t tuīchí 推迟

delegate 1 n dàibiǎo 代表 2 v/t shòuquán 授权

delegation shòuquán 授权

delete shānchú 删除

deli shóushí diàn 熟食店

deliberate 1 adj gùyì 故意 2 v/i zǐxì kǎolǜ 仔细考虑

deliberately gùyì 故意

delicate fabric jīngzhì 精致; problem mǐngǎn 敏感; health xūruò 虚弱

delicious hǎochī 好吃

delight n xìngfèn 兴奋

delighted gāoxìng 高兴

delightful yúkuài 愉快

deliver sòng 送; baby shēng 生

delivery sònghuò 送货; (*of baby*) fēnmiǎn 分娩

delusion wàngxiǎng 妄想

demand 1 n yāoqiú 要求; COM xūqiú 需求 2 v/t yāoqiú 要求

demanding job gāo yāoqiú 高要求; person kēkè 苛刻

democracy mínzhǔ 民主

democrat mínzhǔzhǔyìzhě 民主主义者; **Democrat** POL Mínzhǔ dǎngrén 民主党人

democratic mínzhǔ 民主

demolish chāihuǐ 拆毁

demonstrate 1 v/t zhèngmíng 证明; *machine* shìfàn 示范 2 v/i *(politically)* shìwēi 示威

demonstration xiǎnshì 显示; *(protest)* shìwēi 示威; *(of machine)* shìfàn 示范

demonstrator *(protester)* shìwēizhě 示威者

demoralized qìněi 气馁

denial *(of accusation)* fǒurèn 否认; *(of request)* jùjué 拒绝

denomination FIN miàn'é 面额; REL jiàopài 教派

dense nónghòu 浓厚; *foliage* chóumì 稠密; *crowd* mìjí 密集; *(stupid)* chídùn 迟钝

dent 1 n āochù 凹处 2 v/t shǐ āoxià 使凹下

dental *treatment* yáchǐ 牙齿; *hospital* yákē 牙科

dentist yáyī 牙医

dentures jiǎyá 假牙

deny *charge, rumor* fǒurèn 否认; *right, request* jùjué 拒绝

deodorant chúxiùjì 除臭剂

department *(of company, store)* bùmén 部门; *(at university)* xì 系; POL bù 部

department store bǎihuò shāngchǎng 百货商场

departure chūfā 出发; *(of person from job)* líkāi 离开

depend: *that ~s* shì qíngxíng ér dìng 视情形而定; *it ~s on the weather* kàn tiānqì ba 看天气吧

dependence yīlài 依赖

dependent n yīkàozhě 依靠者

deplorable lìngrén yíhàn 令人遗憾

deport qūchú chūjìng 驱除出境

deposit 1 n *(in bank)* cúnchǔ 存储; *(on purchase)* dìngjīn 定金 2 v/t *cash* cúnchǔ 存储

depressed *person* yōuyù 忧郁

depressing lìngrén shāngxīn 令人伤心

depression MED yōuyù

zhèng 忧郁症；(*economic*) xiāotiáo 萧条；(*in weather*) dīyāqū 低压区

deprive: ~ X of Y cóng X nàlǐ názǒu Y 从 X 那里拿走 Y

deprived pínkùn 贫困

depth shēndù 深度

deputy dàilǐ 代理

derelict *adj* shīxiū 失修

derive *v/t* dédào 得到

derogatory biǎnyì 贬义

descend *v/i* (*of airplane*) xiàjiàng 下降；(*of road*) xiàxié 下斜

descendant hòuyì 后裔

descent (*from mountain*) xiàlái 下来；(*of airplane*) xiàjiàng 下降；(*ancestry*) zǔxiān 祖先

describe miáoshù 描述

description miáoshù 描述

desert¹ *n also fig* shāmò 沙漠

desert² *v/t* pāoqì 抛弃

deserted huāngliáng 荒凉

deserter MIL táobīng 逃兵

deserve yīngdé 应得

design *n* 1 shèjì 设计；(*pattern*) tú'àn 图案 2 *v/t* shèjì 设计

designer shèjì shī 设计师

desire *n* (*wish*) yuànwàng 愿望；(*sexual*) xìngyù 性欲

desk shūzhuō 书桌；(*in hotel*) wènxùntái 问讯台

desktop publishing zhuōmiàn páibǎn 桌面排版

despair *n & v/i* juéwàng 绝望

desperate *person* zǒutóu wúlù 走投无路；*action* gūzhù yīzhì 孤注一掷

despise kànbùqǐ 看不起

despite jǐnguǎn 尽管

dessert tiánpǐn 甜品

destination mùdìdì 目的地

destitute pínkùn 贫困

destroy cuīhuǐ 摧毁

destruction pòhuài 破坏

detach fēnkāi 分开

detached (*objective*) wú piānjiàn 无偏见

detail *n* zhījié 枝节；(*piece of information*) xìjié 细节

detailed xiángxì 详细

detain (*hold back*) dānge 耽搁；(*as prisoner*) jūliú 拘留

detainee: *political ~* zhèngzhì fàn 政治犯

detect chájué 察觉；(*of device*) jiǎncè 检测

detective zhēntàn 侦探

detention (prison) jūliú 拘留

deter (frighten) wēishè 危慑；(stop) zhìzhǐ 制止

detergent xǐdíjì 洗涤剂

deteriorate èhuà 恶化

determination juéxīn 决心

determined xià juéxīn 下决心；effort jiānjué 坚决

deterrent n wēishè yīnsù 危慑因素

detest tǎoyàn 讨厌

devaluation FIN biǎnzhí 贬值

develop 1 v/t film chōngxǐ 冲洗；site jiànshè 建设；business kuòdà 扩大；(originate) fāmíng 发明；(improve on) gǎijìn 改进；illness kāishǐ 开始 2 v/i (grow) fāzhǎn 发展

development (of film) chōngxǐ 冲洗；(of site) jiànshè 建设；(of business, country) fāzhǎn 发展；(event) shìjiàn 事件；(origination) fāmíng 发明；(improving) gǎijìn 改进

device (tool) qìjù 器具

devise fāmíng 发明

devote gòngxiàn 贡献

devotion zhuānxīn 专心

devour lángtūn hǔyàn 狼吞虎咽

diagonal adj xié 斜

diagram tú 图

dial 1 n (of meter) yíbiǎo 仪表 2 v/t TELEC: number bō 拨

dialog duìhuà 对话

diameter zhíjìng 直径

diamond zuànshí 钻石；(shape) língxíng 菱形

diaper niàobù 尿布

diarrhea lādùzi 拉肚子

diary rìjì 日记

dictator dúcáizhě 独裁者

dictionary zìdiǎn 字典

die sǐ 死

diet 1 n shíwù 食物；(for losing weight) jiǎnféi shípǐn 减肥食品 2 v/i (to lose weight) jiǎnféi 减肥

differ (be different) bùtóng 不同

difference chābié 差别

different bùtóng 不同

difficult bù róngyì 不容易

difficulty kùnnan 困难

dig v/t wā 挖

digest v/t xiāohuà 消化

digestion xiāohuà 消化

**digital** shùzì 数字

**digital camera** shùmǎ zhàoxiàngjī 数码照相机

**dignified** yǒu zūnyán 有尊严

**dignity** zūnyán 尊严

**dilapidated** tānhuǐ 坍毁

**dilemma** jìntuì liǎngnán 进退两难

**dilute** v/t xīshì 稀释

**dim** adj light hūn'àn 昏暗; outline bù xiǎnzhù 不显著

**dimension** (measurement) chǐcùn 尺寸

**diminish** v/i biànshǎo 变少

**dim sum** diǎnxin 点心

**dine** yòngcān 用餐

**diner** (person) yòngcānzhě 用餐者; (restaurant) xiǎo cānguǎn 小餐馆

**dining car** cānchē 餐车

**dining room** cānshì 餐室

**dinner** (evening) wǎncān 晚餐; (midday) wǔcān 午餐

**dinner party** yànhuì 宴会

**dip** n (for food) zhānliào 沾料; (in road) āoxiàn 凹陷

**diploma** wénpíng 文凭

**diplomat** wàijiāo guān 外交官

**diplomatic** wàijiāo 外交

(tactful) lǎoliàn 老练

**direct 1** adj zhíjiē 直接; flight, train zhídá 直达; person zhíshuǎng 直爽 **2** v/t (to a place) zhǐyǐn 指引; play, movie dǎoyǎn 导演

**direction** fāngxiàng 方向; ~**s** (instructions) zhǐshì 指示; (to a place) fāngwèi 方位; (for use) zhǐdǎo 指导; (for medicine) yòngfǎ 用法

**director** (of company) zhǔguǎn 主管; (of play, movie) dǎoyǎn 导演

**directory** zhǐdǎo 指导; TELEC diànhuà bù 电话簿

**dirt** zāng dōngxi 脏东西

**dirty** adj zāng 脏; (pornographic) huángsè 黄色

**disabled** adj cánjí 残疾

**disadvantage** n bùlì zhīchù 不利之处

**disagree** (of person) bù tóngyì 不同意

**disagreement** bùtóng yìjiàn 不同意见; (argument) zhēngzhí 争执

**disappear** xiāoshī 消失; (run away) páodiào 跑掉

**disappearance** (of item)

xiāoshī 消失; *(of person)* shīzōng 失踪

**disappoint** shǐ shīwàng 使失望

**disappointment** shīwàng 失望

**disapproval** zhǐzé 指责

**disapprove** bū zànchéng 不赞成

**disaster** zāinàn 灾难

**disastrous** sǔnshī cǎnzhòng 损失惨重

**discharge** v/t *(from hospital)* yǔnxǔ chūyuàn 允许出院; *(from army)* qiǎnsàn 遣散

**discipline** n jìlǜ 纪律

**disc jockey** DJ DJ

**disco** *(place)* dítīng 迪厅

**disconnect** *appliance* shǐ bù jiētōng 使不接通; *supply, telephone* qiēduàn 切断

**discount** n zhékòu 折扣

**discourage** *(dissuade)* quànzǔ 劝阻; *(dishearten)* shǐ jǔsàng 使沮丧

**discover** fāxiàn 发现

**discovery** fāxiàn 发现

**discreet** jǐnshèn 谨慎; *restaurant* kǎolǜ zhōudào 考虑周到

**discrepancy** chācuò 差错

**discretion** pànduàn nénglì 判断能力

**discrimination** qíshì 歧视

**discuss** tǎolùn 讨论

**discussion** tǎolùn 讨论

**disease** jíbìng 疾病

**disembark** v/i *(from plane)* xià fēijī 下飞机; *(from ship)* xià chuán 下船

**disgrace** n xiūchǐ 羞耻

**disgraceful** yǒushī tǐmiàn 有失体面

**disguise** n wěizhuāng 伪装; *(costume, make-up)* jiǎ miànjù 假面具

**disgust 1** n jíwéi fǎngǎn 极为反感 **2** v/t shǐ fǎngǎn 使反感

**disgusting** lìngrén zuò'ǒu 令人作呕

**dish** *(container)* diézi 碟子; *(part of meal)* cài 菜

**dishonest** bù chéngshí 不诚实

**dishonesty** bù chéngshí 不诚实

**dishonor** n chǐrǔ 耻辱

**disinfectant** xiāodújì 消毒剂

**disintegrate** lièkāi 裂开; *(of marriage, wall)* wǎjiě 瓦解

**disjointed** tuōjié 脱节

**disk** (*shape*) yuánpán 圆盘；COMPUT cípán 磁盘

**diskette** ruǎn cípán 软磁盘

**dislike** v/t bù xǐhuān 不喜欢

**dislocate** tuōwèi 脱位

**disloyal** bù zhōngchéng 不忠诚

**dismal** *weather* zāogāo 精糕；*news* lìngrén jǔsàng 令人沮丧；*person* (*sad*) yōuxīn chōngchōng 忧心忡忡

**dismantle** chāi 拆；*company* shǐ jiětǐ 使解体

**dismay 1** *n* (*alarm*) jīng'è 惊愕；(*disappointment*) shīwàng 失望 **2** v/t shǐ huīxīn 使灰心

**dismiss** *employee* jiěgù 解雇；*idea* bù kǎolǜ 不考虑

**disobedience** bù fúcóng 不服从

**disobedient** juéjiàng 倔强

**disobey** wéibèi 违背

**disorder** (*unrest*) bàoluàn 暴乱；MED shītiáo 失调

**disorganized** wú zǔzhī 无组织

**disoriented** míhuò 迷惑

**display 1** *n* zhǎnlǎn 展览；(*of emotion*) biǎoshì 表示；COMPUT xiǎnshì 显示 **2** v/t *emotion* xiǎnshì 显示；(*at exhibition*) zhǎnlǎn 展览；(*for sale*) chénliè 陈列；COMPUT xiǎnshì 显示

**displeasure** bùmǎn 不满

**disposable** yīcìxìng 一次性

**disposal** rēngdiào 扔掉；(*of waste*) chǔlǐ 处理；*put X at Y's ~* ràng Y zìyóu zhīpèi X 让 Y 自由支配 X

**dispose**: *~ of* rēngdiào 扔掉

**disprove** fǎnzhèng 反证

**dispute** *n* zhēnglùn 争论

**disqualify** qǔxiāo zīgé 取消资格

**disrupt** *trains* shǐ tíngdùn 使停顿；*meeting* pòhuài 破坏

**disruptive** pòhuàixìng 破坏性

**dissatisfaction** bùmǎn 不满

**dissatisfied** bù mǎnyì 不满意

**dissent** *n* chí yìyì 持异议

**dissident** *n* chí bùtóng zhèngjiànzhě 持不同政见者

**dissolve** v/t & v/i róngjiě 溶解

**dissuade** quànzhǐ 劝止

**distance** *n* jùlí 距离

**distant** yuǎn 远; *fig (aloof)*
bǎochí yídìngde jùlí 保持
一定的距离

**distinct** *(clear)* míngxiǎn 明
显; *(different)* bùtóng 不同

**distinctive** tèyǒu 特有

**distinctly** qīngchǔ 清楚;
*(decidedly)* míngxiǎn 明显

**distinguish** *(see)* biànbié
辨别; **~ between X and Y**
qūfēn X hé Y 区分 X 和 Y

**distinguished** *(famous)*
zhùmíng 著名; *(dignified)*
yǔzhòng bùtóng 与众不同

**distort** wāiqū 歪曲

**distract** *person* shǐ fēnxīn
使分心; *attention* fēnsàn
zhùyì lì 分散注意力

**distraught** xīnshén búdìng
心神不定

**distress** *n (mental)* kǔnǎo 苦
恼; *(physical)* tòngkǔ 痛苦

**distribute** fēngěi 分给;
*leaflets* sànfā 散发; *wealth*
fēnpèi 分配; COM jīngxiāo
经销

**distribution** *(handing out)*
fēnfā 分发; *(of wealth)*
fēnpèi 分配; COM jīngxiāo
经销

**distributor** COM jīngxiāo

shāng 经销商

**district** qū 区

**district attorney** dìfāng
jiǎnchá guān 地方检查官

**distrust** *n & v/t* huáiyí 怀疑

**disturb** *(interrupt)* dǎjiǎo 打
搅; *(upset)* dānyōu 担忧

**disturbance** *(interruption)*
gānrǎo 干扰; **~s** sāoluàn
骚乱

**disturbed** *(worried)* dānxīn
担心

**disturbing** lìngrén shāngxīn
令人伤心

**ditch** *n* kēng 坑

**dive** *n & v/i* tiàoshuǐ 跳水;
*(underwater)* qiánshuǐ 潜
水; *(of plane)* fǔchōng
俯冲

**diver** *(off board)* tiàoshuǐzhě
跳水者; *(underwater)*
qiánshuǐzhě 潜水者

**diverge** chàkāi 岔开

**diversify** *v/i* COM duōzhǒng
jīngyíng 多种经营

**diversion** MOT gǎixiàn 改线;
*(to distract)* qiānzhì 牵制

**divert** *traffic* gǎixiàn 改线; **~**
**attention** fēnsàn zhùyì lì 分
散注意力

**divide** fēn 分; *fig: country,*

*family* fēnliè 分裂

**dividend** FIN gǔxī 股息

**division** MATH chúfǎ 除法；
(*in party etc*) fēnliè 分裂；
(*splitting into parts*) fēngē
分割；(*of company*) bùmén
部门

**divorce** *n, v/t & v/i* líhūn
离婚

**divorced** líhūn 离婚

**dizzy:** *feel* ~ tóuyūn 头晕

**do 1** *v/t* zuò 做；*what are
you ~ing tonight?* nǐ
jīnwǎn gànshénme? 你今
晚干什么？；*I don't know
what to* ~ wǒbùzhī gāi
zěnme bàn 我不知该怎么
办 **2** *v/i:* *well done!* gōngxǐ!
恭喜！；*how* ~ *you* ~ *?* nǐ
hǎoma? 你好吗？

**dock¹ 1** *n* NAUT chuánwù 船
坞 **2** *v/i* (*of ship*) kào mǎtóu
靠码头

**dock²** LAW bèigào xí 被告席

**doctor** *n* MED yīshēng 医生

**document** *n* wénjiàn 文件

**documentary** (*program*) jìlù
piān 纪录片

**documentation** wénjiàn
文件

**dodge** *v/t blow* shǎnkāi 闪

开；*question* bìkāi 避开

**dog** *n* gǒu 狗

**dogma** jiàotiáo 教条

**do-it-yourself** zìjǐ dòngshǒu
自己动手

**doll** (*toy*) wáwa 娃娃

**dollar** měiyuán 美元

**domestic** *adj chore* jiātíng 家
庭；*news, policy* guónèi 国
内；(*in agriculture*) jiāchù
家畜

**domestic flight** guónèi
hángbān 国内航班

**dominant** zhǔyào 主要；
*member* zhǔdǎo 主导

**dominate** kòngzhì 控制；
*landscape* gāosǒng yú 高
耸于

**donate** juān 捐

**donor** juānxiànzhě 捐献者

**donut** zhá miànbǐngquān 炸
面饼圈

**door** mén 门

**doorbell** ménlíng 门铃

**doorman** shǒuménrén 守
门人

**dose** *n* yòngliàng 用量

**dot** *n* (*also in e-mail*) diǎn 点

**double 1** *n* (*amount*)
shuāngbèi 双倍；(*person*)
chóngyǐng 重影；(*of movie*

*star*) tìdài yǎnyuán 替代
演员 **2** *adj* (*twice as much*)
liǎngbèi 两倍; *whiskey* jiā
bèi 加倍 **3** *v/t* jiābèi 加倍

**double bed** shuāngrén
chuáng 双人床

**doublecheck** *v/t & v/i* fùchá
复查

**doublecross** *v/t* qīpiàn 欺骗

**double room** shuāngrén fáng
双人房

**doubt 1** *n* yíwèn 疑问;
(*uncertainty*) yóuyù 犹豫
**2** *v/t* huáiyí 怀疑

**doubtful** *remark, look* zhídé
huáiyí 值得怀疑; *be ~ (of
person*) ná bùzhǔn 拿不准

**doubtless** wúyí 无疑

**dough** shēngmiàn tuán 生
面团

**down 1** *adv* xià 下; ~ *there*
zài xiàbiān 在下边; *$200
~ (deposit*) xiànfù èrbǎi
měiyuán 现付二百美元;
*be ~ (of price, rate*) xiàjiàng
下降; (*not working*) shīlíng
失灵 **2** *prep* xiàngxià 向下;
(*along*) yánzhe 沿着

**downfall** *n* kuǎtái 垮台; (*of
politician*) xiàtái 下台

**download** COMPUT xiàzǎi

下载

**downmarket** *adj* dījí 低级

**down payment** dìngjīn 定金

**downpour** qīngpén dàyǔ 倾
盆大雨

**downstairs** *adj & adv* lóuxià
楼下

**down-town** *adj & adv* shì
zhōngxīn 市中心

**downturn** (*in economy*)
xiàjiàng qūshì 下降趋势

**doze** *n & v/i* dǎdùn 打盹

**dozen** shí'èr 十二

**draft** *n* (*of air*) guòtáng fēng
过堂风; (*of document*)
cǎogǎo 草稿; MIL
zhēngbīng 征兵; *beer on ~*
shēng píjiǔ 生啤酒

**drag 1** *v/t* (*pull*) lā拉;
COMPUT tuōdòng 拖动
**2** (*of show, movie*) méijìnr
没劲儿

**dragon** lóng 龙

**drain 1** *n* (*pipe*) xiàshuǐ
guǎndào 下水管道;
(*under street*) xiàshuǐ dào
下水道 **2** *v/t water* lǜ 滤;
*oil* páigān 排干; *land* shǐ
gānhé 使干涸; *glass, tank*
dàoguāng 倒光

**drama** xìjù 戏剧; (*play on*

TV) jiémù 节目; (*dramatic event*) xìjùxìng shìjiàn 戏剧性事件; (*excitement*) xīngfèn 兴奋

**dramatic** xìjù 戏剧; (*exciting*) xìjùxìng 戏剧性

**drapes** chuānglián 窗帘

**drastic** yánzhòng 严重; *measure* jíduàn 极端; *change* jídà 极大

**draw 1** n (*in competition*) píngjú 平局; (*in lottery*) kāijiǎng 开奖; (*attraction*) xīyǐn 吸引 **2** v/t *picture* huà 画; *cart, curtain* lā 拉; *knife* chōuchū 抽出; (*attract*) xīyǐn 吸引

**drawback** bìduān 弊端

**drawer** (*in desk*) chōuti 抽屉

**drawing** (*picture*) huà 画; (*skill*) huìtú 绘图

**dread** v/t hàipà 害怕

**dreadful** zāogāo 糟糕

**dream 1** n mèng 梦 **2** v/t & v/i zuòmèng 做梦; (*day~*) mèngxiǎng 梦想

**dreary** chénmèn 沉闷

**dress 1** n (*for woman*) liányīqún 连衣裙; (*clothing*) fúzhuāng 服装 **2** v/i chuān yīfu 穿衣

服; (*well, in black etc*) chuānzhe 穿着

**dresser** (*dressing table*) shūzhuāngtái 梳妆台; (*in kitchen*) wǎndié guì 碗碟柜

**dressing** (*for salad*) tiáowèi zhī 调味汁; MED fūliào 敷料

**dress rehearsal** cǎipái 彩排

**dried** *fruit etc* gān 干

**drier** shuǎigānjī 甩干机

**drift** v/i (*of ship*) piāofú 漂浮; (*go off course*) piāobó 漂泊; (*of person*) liúdàng 流荡

**drill 1** n (*tool*) zuàn 钻; MIL cāoliàn 操练 **2** v/t *hole* zuàn 钻 **3** v/i (*for oil*) zuàn 钻

**drink 1** n yǐnliào 饮料; (*alcohol*) jiǔ 酒 **2** v/t & v/i hē 喝

**drinking water** yǐnyòng shuǐ 饮用水

**drip** v/i dī 滴流

**drive 1** n lǚtú 旅途; (*outing*) dōufēng 兜风; (*energy*) jīnglì 精力; COMPUT qúdòngqì 驱动器 **2** v/t *vehicle* jiàshǐ 驾驶; (*take*

*in car*) yòng chē sòng 用车
送;TECH qūdòng 驱动3 *v/i*
jiàshǐ 驾驶

**driver** sījī 司机

**driver's license** jiàshǐ
zhízhào 驾驶执照

**driving** *n* jiàshǐ 驾驶

**drizzle** *n* máomao yǔ 毛毛雨

**droop** *v/i* xiàchuí 下垂;(*of
plant*) kūwěi 枯萎

**drop 1** *n* (*of rain*) dī 滴;
(*small amount*) yīdiǎn 一
点;(*in price, temperature*)
diē 跌;(*in number*) xiàjiàng
下降 **2** *v/t* rēng 扔;(*and
lose*) diūshī 丢失;*person
from car* ràng …… 下车;
*person from team* chúqù 除去;*charges,
demand* qǔxiāo 取消
**3** *v/i* (*to ground*) diēluò 跌落;(*decline*)
xiàjiàng 下降;(*of wind*)
jiǎnhuǎn 减缓

**drought** gānhàn 干旱

**drown** *v/i* yānsǐ 淹死

**drug** *n* MED yào 药;(*illegal*)
dúpǐn 毒品

**drug addict** xīdú
chéngyǐnzhě 吸毒成瘾者

**drug dealer** fàndúzhě 贩
毒者

**druggist** yàojì shī 药剂师

**drugstore** yàofáng 药房

**drug trafficking** fàndú 贩毒

**drum** *n* MUS gǔ 鼓;
(*container*) tǒng 桶

**drunk 1** *n* zuìguǐ 醉鬼 **2** *adj*
hēzuìle 喝醉了

**drunk driving** jiǔhòu kāichē
酒后开车

**dry 1** *adj* gān 干 **2** *v/t dishes*
cāgān 擦干 **3** *v/i* liànggān
晾干

**dry cleaner** gānxǐ diàn 干
洗店

**dry cleaning** (*clothes*) gānxǐ
yīwù 干洗衣物

**due** (*owed*) qiàn 欠;(*proper*)
shìdàng 适当; *is there a
train ~?* huǒchē shìbùshì
gāiláile? 火车是不是该来
了?; *~ to* yóuyú 由于

**dull** *weather* yīn chénchen
阴沉沉;*sound* bù qīngcuì
不清脆;*pain* dùn dùn 钝;
(*boring*) dāndiào 单调

**duly** (*as expected*) zhǔnshí
准时;(*properly*) shìdàng
适当

**dump 1** *n* (*for garbage*) lā
jīzhàn 垃圾站;(*unpleasant
place*) guǐdìfāng 鬼地方

**2** v/t (*deposit*) qīngdào 倾倒; (*dispose of*) rēng 扔; *waste* diūqì 丢弃

**dumpling** tuánzi 团子

**duration** qījiān 期间

**during:** ~ *X* zài *X* qījiān 在 *X* 期间

**dusk** huánghūn 黄昏

**dust** *n* chéntǔ 尘土

**duty** zérèn 责任; (*task*) rènwù 任务; (*on goods*) shuì 税; *be on* ~ zhíbān 值班; *be off* ~ xiàbān 下班

**duty-free** *adj* miǎnshuì 免税

**DVD** shùzì shìpín guāngpán 数字视频光盘

**dye** v/t rǎnsè 染色

**dying** chuísǐ 垂死; *tradition etc* jíjiāng mièjué 即将灭绝

**dynamic** *person* jīnglì chōngpèi 精力充沛

## E

**each** *adj & pron* měigè 每个; ~ *other* bǐcǐ 彼此

**eager** kěwàng 渴望

**ear** ěrduo 耳朵

**early** *adj & adv* (*not late*) zǎo 早; (*ahead of time*) tíqián 提前; (*farther back in time*) zǎoqī 早期; (*in the near future*) xùnsù 迅速

**earn** zhèng 挣; *respect* yíngdé 赢得

**earnings** zhuànde qián 赚的钱

**earphones** ěrjī 耳机

**earring** ěrhuán 耳环

**earth** tǔ 土; (*world, planet*)

**dìqiú** 地球

**earthquake** dìzhèn 地震

**east 1** *n* dōngfāng 东方 **2** *adj* dōng 东 **3** *adv travel* xiàng dōngfāng 向东方

**East China Sea** Dōnghǎi 东海

**Easter** Fùhuójié 复活节

**eastern** dōngbù 东部; (*Oriental*) Dōngfāng 东方

**eastward** xiàngdōng 向东

**easy** róngyì 容易; (*relaxed*) fàngsōng 放松

**eat** v/t & v/i chī 吃

**eccentric** *adj* gǔguài 古怪

**echo 1** *n* huíshēng 回声 **2** v/i

huídàng 回荡

**eclipse** n (of sun) rìshí 日食;
(of moon) yuèshí 月食

**ecofriendly** lǜsè 绿色

**ecological** shēngtài 生态

**ecology** shēngtàixué 生态学

**economic** jīngjì 经济

**economical** (cheap) jīngjì 经
济; (thrifty) jiéshěng 节省

**economics** jīngjìxué 经济
学; (financial aspects) jīngjì
qíngkuàng 经济情况

**economist** jīngjìxuéjiā 经
济学家

♦ **economize on** jiéshěng
节省

**economy** jīngjì 经济;
(saving) jiéshěng 节省

**economy class** jīngjìcāng
经济舱

**edge** n (of knife) fēng 锋; (of
table, road) biānyuán 边缘

**edible** kě shíyòng 可食用

**edit** text biānjí 编辑; TV
program biānjí 剪辑

**edition** bǎnběn 版本

**editor** biānjí 编辑

**educate** jiàoyù 教育

**education** jiàoyù 教育

**effect** n xiàoguǒ 效果;
(negative) hòuguǒ 后果;

**come into** ~ shíshī 实施

**effective** (efficient) yǒuxiào
有效

**efficiency** xiàolǜ 效率

**efficient** yǒu xiàolǜ 有效率

**effort** (struggle) fèilì 费力;
(attempt) nǔlì 努力

**egg** (of hen) jīdàn 鸡蛋; (of
bird) dàn 蛋

**eggcup** jīdànbēi 鸡蛋杯

**eggplant** qiézi 茄子

**ego** PSYCH zìwǒ 自我; (self-
esteem) zìzūn 自尊

**either 1** adj rèn yígè 任一
个; (both) liǎng 两 **2** pron
nǎge dōuxíng 哪个都行
**3** adv: **I won't go** ~ wǒ yě
bú qù 我也不去 **4** conj: ~
... **or** huòzhě …huòzhě 或
者…或者

**eject** v/t zhúchū 逐出

**elaborate** adj jīngxīn zhìzuò
精心制作

**elastic** n sōngjǐndài 松紧带

**elbow** n zhǒu 肘

**elder** adj niánzhǎng 年长

**elderly** shàng niánjì 上年纪

**eldest** adj: ~ **brother** dàgē 大
哥; ~ **sister** dàjiě 大姐

**elect** v/t xuǎn 选

**election** xuǎnjǔ 选举

**election campaign** jìngxuǎn huódòng 竞选活动

**electric** diàn 电

**electrician** diàngōng 电工

**electricity** diàn 电

**electrocute** diànsǐ 电死

**electronic** diànzǐ 电子

**electronics** diànzǐxué 电子学

**elegant** gāoyǎ 高雅

**elementary** (*rudimentary*) chūjí 初级

**elementary school** xiǎoxué 小学

**elevator** diàntī 电梯

**eligible** hégé 合格

**eliminate** (*get rid of*) chúdiào 除掉; (*rule out*) páichú 排除; *be ~d (from competition*) bèi táotài 被淘汰

**elite 1** *n* jīngyīng 精英 **2** *adj* gāoděng 高等

**eloquent** xióngbiàn 雄辩

**else:** *anything ~?* hái yào biéde ma? 还要别的吗? *no one ~* méiyǒu biérén 没有别人; *something ~* biéde dōngxi 别的东西; *or ~* fǒuzé 否则

**elsewhere** biéchù 别处

**e-mail** *n* diànzǐ yóujiàn 电子邮件

**e-mail address** diànzǐ xìnxiāng 电子信箱

**embargo** *n* jìnyùn 禁运

**embark** *v/i* shàngchuán 上船
♦**embark on** kāishǐ 开始

**embarrass** shǐ gāngà 使尴尬

**embarrassed** gāngà 尴尬

**embarrassing** lìngrén gāngà 令人尴尬

**embarrassment** gāngà 尴尬

**embassy** dàshǐguǎn 大使馆

**embrace** *v/i* yōngbào 拥抱

**emerge** (*appear*) chūxiàn 出现

**emergency** jǐnjí qíngkuàng 紧急情况

**emergency exit** jǐnjí chūkǒu 紧急出口

**emergency landing** jǐnjí zhuólù 紧急着陆

**emigrate** yíjū guówài 移居国外

**eminent** jiéchū 杰出

**emotion** qínggǎn 情感

**emotional** qínggǎn 情感; (*full of emotion*) fùyú qínggǎn 富于情感

**emperor** huángdì 皇帝

emphasis qiángdiào 强调

emphasize qiángdiào 强调

empire dìguó 帝国

employ gùyòng 雇佣; (*use*) shǐyòng 使用

employee gùyuán 雇员

employer gùzhǔ 雇主

employment gōngzuò 工作

empress huánghòu 皇后

empty 1 *adj* kōng 空 2 *v/t* glass, bottle dào kōng 倒空

enable shǐ nénggòu 使能够

enclose (*in letter*) fùrù 附入; *area* wéizhù 围住

enclosure (*in letter*) fùjiàn 附件

encore *n* zàilái yīgè 再来一个

encounter *v/t* problem yùdào 遇到

encourage gǔlì 鼓励

encouragement gǔlì 鼓励

end 1 *n* (*extremity*) jìntóu 尽头; (*conclusion*) jiéwěi 结尾; *in the ~* zuìhòu 最后; *at the ~ of July* qīyuèmò 七月末 2 *v/t & v/i* jiéshù 结束

endless wúzhǐjìng 无止境

endorse check bèishū 背书; *candidacy* zhīchí 支持; *product* cùxiāo 促销

end product zhōngduān chǎnpǐn 终端产品

endurance rěnnàilì 忍耐力

endure 1 *v/t* rěnnài 忍耐 2 *v/i* (*last*) chíxù 持续

end-user zhōngduān yònghù 终端用户

enemy dírén 敌人

energetic yǒu jīngshen 有精神

energy jīnglì 精力; (*gas, electricity etc*) néngyuán 能源

enforce shíshí 实施

engaged (*to be married*) dìnghūn 订婚

engagement (*appointment*) yuēhuì 约会; (*to be married*) dìnghūn 订婚

engagement ring dìnghūn jièzhǐ 订婚戒指

engine fādòng 引擎

engineer *n* gōngchéngshī 工程师; NAUT lúnjīzhǎng 轮机长

engineering gōngchéng 工程

England Yīngguó 英国

English 1 *adj* Yīngguó 英国 2 *n* (*language*) Yīngyǔ 英语

enjoy xǐhuan 喜欢; ~

*oneself* guòde kuàilè 过得快乐;**?~!** *(said to s.o. eating)* chīhǎo! 吃好!

**enjoyable** lìngrén yúkuài 令人愉快

**enjoyment** lèqù 乐趣

**enlarge** kuòdà 扩大

**enlist** *v/i* MIL bàomíng cānjūn 报名参军

**enormous** jùdà 巨大;*satisfaction etc* jídà 极大

**enough** *adj & pron* zúgòu 足够;**will $50 be ~?** wǔshí měiyuán gòu le ma? 五十美元够了吗?;**I've had ~!** wǒshòugòu le 我受够了!

**enroll** *v/i* zhùcè 注册

**ensure** bǎozhèng 保证

**enter 1** *v/t room* jìnrù 进入;*competition* cānjiā 参加;COMPUT jiànrù 键入 **2** *v/i* jìnrù 进入;*(in competition)* bàomíng 报名 **3** *n* COMPUT huíchējiàn 回车键

**enterprise** jìnqǔxīn 进取心;*(venture)* qǐyè 企业

**entertain 1** *v/t (amuse)* shǐrén kuàilè 使人快乐 **2** *v/i (have guests)* zhāodài 招待

**entertaining** *adj* yǒuqù 有趣

**entertainment** yúlè 娱乐

**enthusiasm** rèqíng 热情

**enthusiast** rèzhōngzhě 热中者

**enthusiastic** rèxīn 热心

**entire** zhěnggè 整个

**entirely** wánquán 完全

**entitle** fùyù quánlì 赋予权利

**entitled** *book* dìngmíng 定名

**entrance** *n (doorway)* rùkǒu 入口;*(entering)* jìnrù 进入

**entrance fee** rùchǎngfèi 入场费

**entrust**:**~ X with Y** bǎ Y wěituōgěi X 把 Y 委托给X

**entry** *(way in)* rùkǒu 入口;*(admission)* jìnrù 进入;*(for competition)* cānjiā zhě 参加者;*(in diary, accounts)* xiàngmù 项目

**entry form** cānsàibiǎo 参赛表

**envelope** xìnfēng 信封

**envious** jídù 嫉妒;**be ~ of X** xiànmù X 羡慕X

**environment** huánjìng 环境

**environmentalist** *n* huánjìng bǎohùlùn zhě 环境保护论者

**environmentally friendly** lǜsè 绿色

**envisage** xiǎngxiàng 想象

**envy 1** n jídù 嫉妒 **2** v/t dùxiàn 妒羡

**epidemic** liúxíngxìng 流行性

**episode** (of story) yìjí 一集; (happening) shìjiàn 事件

**equal 1** adj xiāngtóng 相同 **2** n děngtóng 等同

**equality** píngděng 平等

**equally** tóngděng 同等; ~, ... cǐwài, ...此外...

**equate:** ~ X with Y děngtóng X hé Y 等同 X 和 Y

**equator** chìdào 赤道

**equip** zhuāngbèi 装备

**equipment** zhuāngbèi 装备

**equivalent** adj xiāngtóng 相同; **be ~ to** xiāngdāngyú 相当于

**era** jìyuán 纪元

**eradicate** gēnchú 根除

**erase** (with eraser) cādiào 擦掉; tape xǐdiào 洗掉; COMPUT shānchú 删除

**erosion** qīnshí 侵蚀; fig qīnfàn 侵犯

**erotic** sèqíng 色情

**errand** chāishì 差使

**erratic** wúcháng 无常

**error** cuòwù 错误

**erupt** (of volcano) bàofā 爆发; (of violence) túrán fāshēng 突然发生

**escalate** zhúbù shēngjí 逐步升级

**escalator** zìdòngfútī 自动扶梯

**escape 1** n & v/i táotuō 逃脱; (of gas) lòuchū 漏出

**escort** n péitóng 陪同; (guard) hùwèi 护卫

**especially** yóuqí 尤其

**espionage** jiàndié huódòng 间谍活动

**essential** adj bìyào 必要

**establish** (create) chuàngzào 创造; (determine) quèdìng 确定; company chénglì 成立

**establishment** (firm, store etc) jīgòu 机构

**estimate** n & v/t gūjì 估计

**eternal** yǒnghéng 永恒

**ethical** dàodé 道德

**ethnic** zhǒngzú 种族

**ethnic minority** shǎoshù mínzú 少数民族

**Europe** Ōuzhōu 欧洲

**European 1** adj Ōuzhōu 欧

洲 **2** *n* Ōuzhōurén 欧洲人

**evacuate** (*clear people from*) chèkōng 撤空; (*leave*) chèlí 撤离

**evade** bìkāi 避开

**evasive** bùtǎnshuài 不坦率

**even 1** *adj* (*regular*) jūnyún 均匀; (*level*) píng 平; (*number*) ǒushù 偶数 **2** *adv* shènzhì 甚至; ~ **bigger / better** gèngdà / hǎo 更大/好; **not** ~ lián …yěbù 连…也不; ~ **if** jíshǐ 即使

**evening** wǎnshang 晚上; **this** ~ jīntiān wǎnshang 今天晚上; **good** ~ wǎnshang hǎo 晚上好

**evening class** yèxiào 夜校

**evenly** (*regularly*) jūnyún 均匀

**event** shìjiàn 事件; SP bǐsài xiàngmù 比赛项目

**eventually** zhōngyú 终于

**ever** *adv* (*with past or perfect tense questions*) céngjīng 曾经; (*with past or perfect tense negative*) cónglái 从来; (*with conditionals*) yídàn 一旦; **for** ~ yǒngyuǎn 永远; ~ **since** cóng nà yǐhòu 从那以后

**Everest: Mount** ~ Zhūmùlǎngmǎfēng 珠穆朗玛峰

**every** měiyī 每一

**everybody** měigèrén 每个人

**everyday** měitiān 每天

**everyone** měigèrén 每个人

**everything** yíqiè 一切

**everywhere** gèchù 各处; (*wherever*) dàochù 到处

**evidence** hénjì 痕迹; LAW zhèngjù 证据

**evidently** (*clearly*) míngxiǎn 明显; (*apparently*) xiǎnrán 显然

**evil 1** *adj* xié'è 邪恶 **2** *n* è 恶

**evolution** jìnhuà 进化

**evolve** *v/i* (*develop*) zhújiàn xíngchéng 逐渐形成

**ex** *n* F (*wife*) qiánqī 前妻; (*husband*) qiánfū 前夫

**exact** *adj* quèqiè 确切

**exactly** qiàqià 恰恰

**exaggerate 1** *v/t* kuādà 夸大 **2** *v/i* kuāzhāng 夸张

**exam** kǎoshì 考试

**examine** diàochá 调查; MED jiǎnchá 检查; EDU kǎo 考

**example** lìzi 例子; **for** ~ bǐrú 比如

**exceed** (*be more than*)

chāoguò 超过 (*go beyond*);
chāochū 超出

**exceedingly** jíduān 极端

**excellence** yōuxiù 优秀

**excellent** hěn hǎo 很好

**except** chúle 除了; **~ that ...** zhǐshì ... 只是...

**exception** lìwài 例外

**exceptional** (*very good*) jiéchū 杰出; (*special*) tèshū 特殊

**excess 1** n guòdù 过度 **2** *adj* duōyú 多余

**excess baggage** chāozhòngde xíngli 超重的行李

**exchange 1** n (*of information*) jiāohuàn 交换; (*between schools*) jiāoliú 交流; **in ~** zuòwéi jiāohuàn 作为交换; **in ~ for** yònglái huànqǔ 用来换取 **2** *v/t addresses* hùhuàn 互换; **~ X for Y** yòng X huàn Y 用 X 换 Y

**exchange rate** FIN duìhuànlǜ 兑换率

**excited** xīngfèn 兴奋

**exciting** lìngrén xīngfèn 令人兴奋

**exclude** páichú 排除

**exclusive** *hotel* dútè 独特; *rights* dúyǒu 独有

**excuse 1** n jièkǒu 借口 **2** *v/t* (*forgive*) yuánliàng 原谅; **~ me** (*to get attention*) qǐngwèn 请问; (*to get past*) láojià 劳驾; (*interrupting*) hěn bàoqiàn 很抱歉

**execute** *criminal* chǔjué 处决; *plan* shíshī 实施

**execution** (*of criminal*) sǐxíng 死刑; (*of plan*) shíshī 实施

**executive** n zhǔguǎn rényuán 主管人员

**exempt**: **be ~ from** miǎnchú 免除

**exercise 1** n (*physical*) duànliàn 锻炼; EDU liànxí 练习 **2** *v/t muscle* duànliàn 锻炼; *dog* liù 遛

**exert** *authority* xíngshǐ 行使; **~ oneself** yònglì 用力

**exertion** fèilì 费力

**exhale** hūchū 呼出

**exhaust 1** n (*fumes*) fèiqì 废气; (*pipe*) páiqìguǎn 排气管 **2** *v/t* (*use up*) yòngjìn 用尽

**exhausted** (*tired*) jīnpílìjìn 筋疲力尽

exhausting lìngrén píjuàn 令人疲倦

exhaustion láolèi guòdù 劳累过度

exhibition zhǎnlǎnhuì 展览会

exile n liúwáng 流亡; (person) liúfàngzhě 流放者

exist cúnzài 存在

existence cúnzài 存在; (life) shēngcún 生存

existing xiàncún 现存

exit n chūkǒu 出口; THEA tuìchǎng 退场 2 v/i COMPUT tuìchū 退出

exorbitant guògāo 过高

exotic fùyòu yìguó qíngdiào 富有异国情调

expand 1 v/t kuòdà 扩大 2 v/i zēngzhǎng 增长; (of metal) péngzhàng 膨胀

expansion zēngzhǎng 增长; (of metal) péngzhàng 膨胀

expect 1 v/t qīdài 期待; baby huáiyùn 怀孕; (suppose) rènwéi 认为; (demand) yāoqiú 要求 2 v/i I ~ so wǒ xiǎng huì de 我想会的

expectation qīwàng 期望;

~s (demands) zhīwàng 指望

expedition tànxiǎn 探险

expel person kāichú 开除

expenditure huāfèi 花费

expense xiāofèi 消费

expenses kāizhī 开支

expensive ángguì 昂贵

experience 1 n (event) jīnglì 经历; (in life) tǐyàn 体验; (in particular field) jīngyàn 经验 2 v/t pain, pleasure gǎnjué 感觉; difficulty yùdào 遇到

experienced yǒujīngyàn 有经验

experiment n & v/i shíyàn 实验

expert 1 adj shúliàn 熟练 2 n zhuānjiā 专家

expertise zhuānmén zhīshi 专门知识

expiration qīmǎn 期满

expiration date zhōngzhǐ rìqī 终止日期

expire dàoqī 到期

explain 1 v/t shuōmíng 说明 2 v/i jiěshì 解释

explanation jiěshì 解释

explode v/i & v/t bomb bàozhà 爆炸

**exploit** v/t person bōxuē 剥削; resources lìyòng 利用

**exploration** tànsuǒ 探索

**explore** country kǎochá 考察; possibility tàntǎo 探讨

**explosion** bàozhà 爆炸; (in population) jīzēng 激增

**export** n & v/t chūkǒu 出口

**exporter** chūkǒushāng 出口商

**expose** scandal jiēlù 揭露; person jiēchuān 揭穿

**express 1** adj (fast) xùnsù 迅速; (explicit) míngquè 明确 **2** n (train) tèkuài 特快; (bus) kuàisù 快速 **3** v/t (speak of) biǎoshì 表示; feelings biǎodá 表达

**expression** (voiced) biǎoshì 表示; (on face) biǎoqíng 表情; (phrase) biǎodá 表达

**expressway** gāosù gōnglù 高速公路

**expulsion** (from school) kāichú 开除; (of diplomat) qūzhú 驱逐

**extend** v/t kuòdà 扩大; runway yáncháng 延长; contract, visa yánqī 延期

**extension** (to house) kuòjiàn 扩建; (of contract, visa) yánqī 延期; TELEC fēnjī 分机

**extensive** guǎngfàn 广泛

**extent** chéngdù 程度

**exterior 1** adj wàibù 外部 **2** n (of building) wàiguān 外观; (of person) wàibiǎo 外表

**external** wàimiàn 外面

**extinct** species juézhǒng 绝种

**extinguish** fire pūmiè 扑灭; cigarette xīmiè 熄灭

**extortion** lèsuǒ 勒索

**extra 1** n (sth ~) éwàide 额外的 shìwù 额外的事物 **2** adj éwài 额外; be ~ (cost more) lìngwài shōufèi 另外收费

**extract 1** n xuǎnlù 选录 **2** v/t qǔchū 取出; oil, juice zhàchū 榨出; tooth báchū 拔出; information huòqǔ 获取

**extradition** yǐndù 引渡

**extraordinary** bùpíngcháng 不平常

**extravagant** (with money) huīhuò 挥霍

**extreme 1** n jíduān 极端 **2** adj jídù 极度; views

**familiar**

piānjī 偏激
**extremely** jíqí 极其
**extremist** n jíduānzhǔyì zhě 极端主义者
**eye** n yǎnjīng 眼睛
**eyebrow** méimao 眉毛

**eyelid** yǎnjiǎn 眼睑
**eyeliner** yǎnxiànyè 眼线液
**eyeshadow** yǎnyǐnggāo 眼影膏
**eyesight** shìlì 视力
**eyesore** bú shùnyǎn 不顺眼

# F

**fabric** bùliào 布料
**fabulous** jíhǎo 极好
**face** 1 n liǎn 脸 2 v/t person, the sea miànduì 面对
**facilitate** shǐ ... biànlì 使 ... 便利
**facilities** shèshī 设施
**fact** shìshí 事实; in ~ shíjì shang 实际上
**factor** yīnsù 因素
**fade** v/i (of colors) xiāotuì 消褪
**fail** v/i shībài 失败
**failure** shībài 失败
**faint** 1 adj bù míngxiǎn 不明显 2 v/i hūndǎo 昏倒
**fair**[1] n COM jiāoyìhuì 交易会
**fair**[2] hair qiǎnsè 浅色; (just) gōngzhèng 公正; (quite) xiāngdāng 相当
**fairly** treat gōngzhèng 公正; (quite) xiāngdāng 相当

**faith** xìnxīn 信心; REL xìnyǎng 信仰
**faithful** zhōngchéng 忠诚
**fake** 1 n yànpǐn 赝品 2 adj fǎngzhì 仿制
**fall**[1] (autumn) qiūtiān 秋天
**fall**[2] 1 v/i (of person) shuāidǎo 摔倒; (of government) kuǎtái 垮台; (of prices, temperature) xiàjiàng 下降; (of night) láilín 来临 2 n (of person) shuāidǎo 摔倒; (of government, minister) dǎotái 倒台; (in price, temperature) xiàjiàng 下降
♦**fall out** (of hair) diàoluò 掉落; (argue) nào bièniu 闹别扭
**false** cuòwù 错误
**fame** míngyù 名誉
**familiar** adj (intimate) qīnjìn 亲近

亲近
**family** jiātíng 家庭
**family planning** jìhuà
shēngyù 计划生育
**famine** jīhuāng 饥荒
**famous** zhùmíng 著名
**fan¹** n (supporter) mí 迷
**fan²** n (electric) diànshàn 电
扇; (handheld) shànzi 扇子
**fanatic** kuángrèzhě 狂热者
**fanatical** kuángrè 狂热
**fantastic** (very good)
bàngjíle 棒极了; (very big)
jùdà 巨大
**far** adv yuǎn 远; (much)
fēicháng 非常; **~ away**
yáoyuǎn 遥远; **how ~
is it to ...?** dào ... qù yǒu
duōyuǎn? 到 ... 去有多
远？; **as ~ as I know**
jùwǒsuǒzhī 据我所知
**fare** n (for travel) piàojià
票价
**Far East** Yuǎndōng 远东
**farm** n nóngchǎng 农场
**farmer** nóngfū 农夫
**farsighted** yǒu yuǎnjiàn 有
远见; (optically) yuǎnshì
远视
**farther** adv gèngyuǎn 更远
**farthest** zuìyuǎn 最远

**fascinate** v/t shǐ zháomí
使着迷
**fascinating** mírén 迷人
**fascination** (with subject)
chīmí 痴迷
**fashion** n shíshàng 时尚;
(manner) fāngshì 方式
**fashionable** shímáo 时髦
**fashion designer** shízhuāng
shèjìshī 时装设计师
**fast** adj & adv kuài 快; **~
asleep** shúshuì 熟睡
**fasten** v/t shǐ gùdìng 使固定
**fast food** kuàicān 快餐
**fat 1** adj pàng 胖 **2** n (on
meat) zhīfáng 脂肪
**fatal** zhìmìng 致命; error
wúkě wǎnjiù 无可挽救
**fatality** sǐwáng 死亡
**fate** mìngyùn 命运
**father** n fùqīn 父亲
**father-in-law** (woman's)
gōnggong 公公; (man's)
yuèfù 岳父
**fatigue** n píjuàn 疲倦
**faucet** lóngtóu 龙头
**fault** n (defect) máobìng 毛
病; **it's your / my ~** shì
nǐde / wǒde cuò 是你的/
我的错
**favor** n xǐ'ài 喜爱; **be in ~ of**

... zhīchí ... 支持...

**favorable** *reply etc* zànchéng 赞成

**favorite** *adj* zuì xǐhuān 最喜欢

**fax 1** *n* chuánzhēn 传真 **2** *v/t* yòng chuánzhēn chuán 用传真传

**FBI** (= *Federal Bureau of Investigation*) Liánbāng Diàochájú 联邦调查局

**fear 1** *n* kǒngjù 恐惧 **2** *v/t* hàipà 害怕

**feasible** qièshí kěxíng 切实可行

**feature** *n* tèsè 特色; (*in paper*) zhuāntí 专题; (*movie*) zhèngpiān 正片 **2** *v/t* (*of movie*) yóu ... zhǔyǎn 由 ... 主演

**February** èryuè 二月

**federal** liánbāngzhì 联邦制

**fed up** *adj* F yànfán 厌烦

**fee** fèi 费

**feed** *v/t* gōngyǎng 供养; *animal* wèi 喂

**feedback** fǎnkuì 反馈

**feel 1** *v/t* (*touch*) chùmō 触摸; (*sense*) gǎndào 感到; *pain, pleasure* gǎnzhī 感知; (*think*) rènwéi 认为 **2** *v/i:*

*I ~ tired* wǒ gǎnjué lèi le 我感觉累了

**feeling** (*of happiness*) gǎnjué 感觉; (*emotion*) gǎnqíng 感情; (*sensation*) zhījué 知觉

**felony** zhòngzuì 重罪

**female 1** *adj* cíxìng 雌性; (*referring to people*) nǚxìng 女性 **2** *n* (*of animals, plants*) cíxìng dòngzhíwù 雌性动植物; (*person*) nǚxìng 女性

**feminine** *adj* *qualities* yǒu nǚxìng qìzhì 有女性气质

**feminism** nǚquán zhǔyì 女权主义

**feminist 1** *n* nǚquán zhǔyìzhě 女权主义者 **2** *adj* nǚquán 女权

**fen** (*Chinese money*) fēn 分

**fence** *n* zhàlán 栅栏

**fender** MOT yìzǐbǎn 翼子板

**fertile** néng shēngyù 能生育; *soil* féiwò 肥沃

**fertility** fányù 繁育; (*of soil*) féiwò 肥沃

**fertilizer** (*for soil*) féiliào 肥料

**festival** jiérì 节日

**festivities** huānqìng 欢庆

**fetch** *person* jiē 接; *thing* ná 拿; *price* màidé 卖得

**fetus** tāi'ér 胎儿

**feud** *n* shìchóu 世仇

**few 1** *adj (not many)* hěnshǎo 很少; *a ~ (things)* jǐgè 几个; *quite a ~* xiāngdāngduō 相当多 **2** *pron (not many)* shǎoshù jǐgè 少数几个; *a ~ (some)* yìxiē 一些; *quite a ~* xǔduō 许多

**fewer** *adj* gèngshǎo 更少

**fiancé** wèihūnfū 未婚夫

**fiancée** wèihūnqī 未婚妻

**fiber** xiānwéi 纤维

**fiction** *(novels)* xiǎoshuō 小说

**fictitious** xūgòu 虚构

**fidget** *v/i* fánzào bù'ān 烦躁不安

**field** *n* tiándì 田地; *(for sport)* chǎng 场; *(competitors in race)* cānsàizhě 参赛者; *(of knowledge etc)* lǐngyù 领域

**fierce** *animal* xiōngměng 凶猛; *wind, storm* qiánglìè 强烈

**fifty-fifty** *adv* duìbàn 对半

**fight 1** *n* zhàndòu 战斗; *(for survival, championship)* zhēngdòu 争斗; *(in boxing)* quánjī 拳击 **2** *v/t enemy* yǔ ... dǎzhàng 与 ... 打仗; *disease, injustice* yǔ ... zuò dòuzhēng 与 ... 作斗争 **3** *v/i* dǎjià 打架

♦ **fight for** zhēngqǔ 争取

**figure** *n (digit)* shùzì 数字; *(of person)* xíngtǐ 形体; *(form, shape)* túxíng 图形

**file**[1] *n (of documents)* dàng'àn 档案; COMPUT wénjiàn 文件

**file**[2] *n (tool)* cuòdāo 锉刀

**file cabinet** dàng'ànxiāng 档案箱

**fill** *v/t* zhùmǎn 注满

♦ **fill in** *hole* tiánmǎn 填满

♦ **fill out** *form* tiánxiě 填写

**filling 1** *n (in sandwich)* xiàn 馅; *(in tooth)* bǔyá 补牙 **2** *adj food* róngyì bǎorén 容易饱人

**film** *n (for camera)* jiāojuǎn 胶卷; *(movie)* diànyǐng 电影 **2** *v/t* pāishè 拍摄

**film star** diànyǐng míngxīng 电影明星

**filter 1** *n* guòlùqì 过滤器 **2** *v/t* guòlù 过滤

**filthy** āngzāng 肮脏

**final 1** *adj* (*last*) zuìhòu 最后; *decision* quèdìng 确定 **2** *n* SP juésài 决赛

**finalist** cānjiā juésài zhě 参加决赛者

**finalize** quèdìng 确定

**finally** zuìhòu 最后; (*at last*) zhōngyú 终于

**finance 1** *n* jīnróng 金融 **2** *v/t* tígōng zījīn 提供资金

**financial** jīnróng 金融

**find** *v/t* zhǎodào 找到

♦**find out 1** *v/t* huòzhī 获知 **2** *v/i* (*inquire*) cháxún 查询; (*discover*) liǎojiědào 了解到

**fine¹** *adj weather* qínglǎng 晴朗; *wine, performance* hǎo 好; *distinction* xìwēi 细微; *that's ~* hǎo 好

**fine²** *n* (*penalty*) fájīn 罚金 **2** *v/t* fákuǎn 罚款

**finger** *n* shǒuzhǐ 手指

**fingernail** shǒuzhǐjiǎ 手指甲

**finish 1** *v/t & v/i* jiéshù 结束 **2** *n* (*of product*) zuìhòu bùfèn 最后部分; (*of race*) zhōngdiǎn 终点

**fire 1** *n* huǒ 火; (*electric, gas*) nuǎnlú 暖炉; (*blaze*) shīhuǒ 失火; *be on ~*

zháohuǒ 着火 **2** *v/i* (*shoot*) shèjī 射击 **3** *v/t* F (*dismiss*) jiěgù 解雇

**fire alarm** huǒjǐng 火警

**fire department** xiāofángduì 消防队

**fire escape** ānquán chūkǒu 安全出口

**fire extinguisher** mièhuǒqì 灭火器

**firefighter** xiāofángduìyuán 消防队员

**fireplace** bìlú 壁炉

**fireworks** yànhuǒ 焰火; (*display*) yànhuǒ biǎoyǎn 焰火表演

**firm¹** *adj grip* wěn ér yǒulì 稳而有力; *muscles* jiēshí 结实; *voice* jiāndìng 坚定

**firm²** *n* COM gōngsī 公司

**first 1** *adj* dìyī 第一 **2** *n* dìyīgè 第一个 **3** *adv arrive, finish* dìyī 第一; (*beforehand*) xiān 先; *at ~* qǐchū 起初

**first aid** jíjiù 急救

**first class** *adj* tóuděng 头等; (*very good*) yīliú 一流

**first floor** yīlóu 一楼

**firstly** shǒuxiān 首先

**first name** míngzi 名字

**fish** n yú 鱼

**fisherman** yúfū 渔夫

**fishing** bǔyú 捕鱼

**fist** quán 拳

**fit**[1] n MED hūnjué 昏厥

**fit**[2] adj (physically) jiànkāng 健康; (morally) qiàdàng 恰当

**fit**[3] v/t (of clothes) héshì 合适; (of furniture) róngdexià 容得下

**fitness** jiànkāng 健康

**fix** v/t (attach) dìngláo 钉牢; (repair) xiūlǐ 修理; meeting, lunch zhǔnbèi 准备; (dishonestly) zuòbì 作弊

**flabby** muscles sōngchí 松弛

**flag** n qí 旗

**flame** n huǒyàn 火焰

**flash 1** n (of light) shǎnshuò 闪烁; PHOT shǎnguāngdēng 闪光灯 **2** v/i (of light) shǎnliàng 闪亮

**flashlight** shǒudiàntǒng 手电筒

**flat** adj píngtǎn 平坦; battery yòngwán diàn 用完电; tire qì bùzú 气不足; shoes píngdǐ 平底

**flatter** v/t fèngcheng 奉承

**flattery** fèngcheng 奉承

**flavor** n wèidào 味道

**flee** v/i táopǎo 逃跑

**fleet** n NAUT jiànduì 舰队; (of taxis, trucks) chēduì 车队

**flesh** ròutǐ 肉体; (of fruit) guǒròu 果肉

**flexible** línghuó 灵活

**flicker** v/i shǎndòng 闪动

**flight** (in airplane) hángbān 航班; (flying) fēixíng 飞行

**flight path** fēixíng lùxiàn 飞行路线

**flimsy** furniture bù jiēshi 不结实; material qīng'érbó 轻而薄; excuse bù zúxìn 不足信

**fling** v/t rēng 扔

**flirt** v/i tiáoqíng 调情

**float** v/i piāofú 漂浮

**flood 1** n hóngshuǐ 洪水 **2** v/t (of river) yānmò 淹没

**floor** n dìbǎn 地板; (story) lóucéng 楼层

**floppy** (disk) ruǎnpán 软盘

**flour** miànfěn 面粉

**flourish** v/i fánróng 繁荣

**flow** v/i (of river, traffic) liúdòng 流动 **2** n (of information) jiāoliú 交流

**flower** *n* huā 花

**flu** liúgǎn 流感

**fluctuate** *v/i* bōdòng 波动

**fluent** *adj* liúlì 流利

**fluid** *n* liútǐ 流体

**flush** *v/t & v/i toilet* chōngxǐ 冲洗

**fly**[1] *n (insect)* cāngying 苍蝇

**fly**[2] *(on pants)* lāliàn'r 拉链儿

**fly**[3] *v/i* fēixíng 飞行; *(in airplane)* chéngjī 乘机

**flying** *n* fēixíng 飞行

**foam** *n (on liquid)* pàomò 泡沫

**focus** *n (of attention)* jízhōng 集中; PHOT jiāojù 焦距

**fog** wù 雾

**foggy** duōwù 多雾

**fold** *v/t paper etc* zhédié 折叠; ~ **one's arms** hébào shuāngbì 合抱双臂

**folder** *also* COMPUT wénjiànjiā 文件夹

**folk** *(people)* rénmen 人们

**follow 1** *v/t person* gēnsuí 跟随; *road* yánzhe …qiánjìn 沿着…前进; *instructions* zūnxún 遵循; *TV series, news* liánxù kàn 连续看 **2** *v/i (logically)* bìrán fāshēng 必然发生

♦**follow up** *v/t letter, inquiry* hòuxù 后续

**following** *adj day, night* jìzhe 接着; *points* xiàshù 下述

**fond** *(loving)* xǐ'ài 喜爱; *be ~ of* xǐhuan 喜欢

**food** shíwù 食物

**fool** *n* chǔnrén 蠢人; *make a ~ of oneself* chūchǒu 使自己出丑

**foolish** yúchǔn 愚蠢

**foot** jiǎo 脚; *(length)* yīngchǐ 英尺; *on ~* búxìng 步行

**football** měishì zúqiú 美式足球; *(ball)* gǎnlǎnqiú 橄榄球; *(soccer, ball)* zúqiú 足球

**for** ◊ *(purpose, destination etc)* wèile 为了; *a train ~ X* qù X de huǒchē 去X的火车; *this is ~ you* zhè shì gěi nǐde 这是给你的 ◊ *(time)*: *~ three days* sān tiān 三天 ◊ *(instead of, in behalf of)*: *let me do that ~ you* ràng wǒ gěi nǐ zuò ba 让我给你做吧

**forbid** jìnzhǐ 禁止

**Forbidden City** Zǐjìnchéng 紫禁城

**force 1** *n (violence)* wǔlì 武

力；(*of explosion, punch*) lìliàng 力量；***the ~s*** MIL bùduì 部队 **2** v/t:**~ X to do Y** qiǎngpò X zuò Y 强迫 X 做 Y

**forecast** n yùcè 预测；(*of weather*) yùbào 预报

**foreground** qiánjǐng 前景

**forehead** é 额

**foreign** wàiguó 外国

**foreign currency** wàibì 外币

**foreigner** wàiguórén 外国人

**foreign policy** wàijiāo zhèngcè 外交政策

**foresee** yùjiàn 预见

**forest** sēnlín 森林

**foretell** yùliào 预料

**forever** adv yǒngyuǎn 永远

**forfeit** v/t *right* sàngshī 丧失

**forge** v/t (*counterfeit*) wěizào 伪造

**forgery** wěizàopǐn 伪造品

**forget** wàngjì 忘记

**forgetful** jiànwàng 健忘

**forgive 1** v/t yuánliàng 原谅 **2** v/i liàngjiě 谅解

**forgiveness** yuánliàng 原谅

**fork** n chāzi 叉子；(*in road*) chàkǒu 岔口

**form 1** n (*shape*) xíngzhuàng 形状；(*document*) biǎogé

表格 **2** v/t xíngchéng 形成 **3** v/i (*take shape*) xíngchéng 形成

**formal** zhèngshì 正式；*recognition* guānfāng 官方

**format 1** v/t *disk* shǐ géshìhuà 使格式化；*document* ānpái ... bǎnshì 安排...版式 **2** n kāiběn 开本

**former** yǐqián 以前；***the ~*** qiánzhě 前者

**formidable** kěpà 可怕

**formula** MATH gōngshì 公式；CHEM fēnzǐshì 分子式

**forth:** *back and ~* láihuí 来回；*and so ~* děngděng 等等

**fortnight** Br liǎngzhōu 两周

**fortunate** xìngyùn 幸运

**fortune** yùnqì 运气；(*money*) dàbǐde qián 大笔的钱

**forward 1** adv xiàngqián 向前 **2** n SP qiánfēng 前锋 **3** v/t *letter* zhuǎndì 转递

**foul 1** n SP fànguī 犯规 **2** adj *smell, taste* nánwén 难闻；*weather* èliè 恶劣

**found** v/t chuàngbàn 创办

**foundation** (*of organization etc*) chénglì 成立

(*organization*) jījīnhuì 基金会

foundations dìjī 地基

founder n chuàngjiànrén 创建人

four-star sìxīngjí 四星级

fracture 1 n gǔzhé 骨折 2 v/t zhéduàn 折断

fragile yìsuì 易碎

fragment n yíbùfen 一部分

frail xūruò 虚弱

frame n kuāng 框

frank tǎnshuài 坦率

frantic fāfēng 发疯

fraud qīpiàn 欺骗; (*person*) piànzi 骗子

freak 1 n (*event*) fǎncháng xiànxiàng 反常现象; F (*strange person*) guàirén 怪人 2 adj wind, storm etc yìcháng qiángliè 异常强烈

freckle quèbān 雀斑

free 1 adj (*at liberty*) zìyóu 自由; (*no cost*) miǎnfèi 免费; room, table kòngyú 空余 2 v/t prisoners shìfàng 释放

freedom zìyóu 自由

freelance adj zìyóu zhíyè 自由职业

free speech zìyóu yánlùn 自由言论

freeway gāosù gōnglù 高速公路

freeze 1 v/t lěngdòng 冷冻; bank account dòngjié 冻结; video zàntíng 暂停 2 v/i (*of water*) nínggù 凝固

freezer lěngdòngshì 冷冻室

freight n huòwù 货物; (*costs*) yùnfèi 运费

frequency pínlǜ 频率; (*of radiowave*) bōduàn 波段

frequent adj jīngcháng 经常

frequently shícháng 时常

fresh fruit, meat xīnxiān 新鲜; (*of air*) liángshuǎng 凉爽; (*new*) xīn 新; (*impertinent*) cūlǔ 粗鲁

friction PHYS mócā 摩擦; (*in group*) chōngtú 冲突

Friday xīngqīwǔ 星期五

fridge bīngxiāng 冰箱

fried egg jiāndàn 煎蛋

friend péngyou 朋友

friendly adj yǒuhǎo 友好

friendship yǒuyì 友谊

fries shǔtiáo 薯条

fright jīngxià 惊吓

frighten v/t jīngxià 惊吓; be ~ed hàipà 害怕

**frill** (on dress etc) shìbiān 饰边; (extra) fùjiāwù 附加物

**from** ◊ (in space, time) cóng 从 ◊ (origin): **a letter ~ Jo Qiáo de láixìn** 乔的来信; **I'm ~ New Jersey** wǒ láizì Xīn Zéxī zhōu 我来自新泽西州

**front 1** n zhèngmiàn 正面; (of weather) fēng fēng 锋; **in ~** zài qiánmiàn 在前面; (in race) lǐngxiān 领先; **in ~ of X** zài X de qiánmian 在 X 的前面 **2** adj wheel, seat qiánmian 前面

**front door** qiánmén 前门

**frontier** biānjiāng 边疆; fig (of science etc) qiányán 前沿

**front page** tóubǎn 头版

**frost** n shuāng 霜

**frosting** tángshuāng 糖霜

**frown** n & v/i zhòuméi 皱眉

**frozen** feet etc bīngliáng 冰凉; food lěngdòng 冷冻

**fruit** shuǐguǒ 水果

**fruit juice** guǒzhī 果汁

**frustrated** jǔsàng 沮丧

**frustrating** shǐrén xīnfán 使人心烦

**fry** v/t (stir-~) chǎo 炒; (deep-~) yóuzhá 油炸

**fuel** n ránliào 燃料

**fulfill** v/t shíxiàn 实现

**full** mǎn 满; report xiángxì 详细

**full moon** mǎnyuè 满月

**full-time** adv quánrì 全日

**fully** wánquán 完全

**fumes** fèiqì 废气

**fun** kāixīn 开心; **have ~!** jìnqíng wánr ba! 尽情玩儿吧！; **make ~ of X** qǔxiào X 取笑 X

**function** n zuòyòng 作用; (reception etc) jíhuì 集会

**fund 1** n jījīn 基金 **2** v/t project etc bōkuǎn 拨款

**fundamental** jīběn 基本

**funeral** zànglǐ 葬礼

**funny** (comical) kěxiào 可笑; (odd) gǔguài 古怪

**fur** máopí 毛皮

**furious** (angry) fènnù 愤怒

**furnish** room zhuāngbèi 装备

**furniture** jiājù 家具

**further 1** adj (additional) jìnyíbù 进一步; (more distant) gèngyuǎn 更远 **2** adv walk, drive gèngyuǎn 更远; **2 miles ~ (on)** zài

zǒu liǎng yīnglǐ 再走两
英里

**furthest** adj & adv zuìyuǎn
最远

**fury** (anger) bàonù 暴怒

**fuse** ELEC **1** n bǎoxiǎnsī
保险丝 **2** v/i bǎoxiǎnsī

shāoduàn 保险丝烧断

**fuss** n dàjīng xiǎoguài 大
惊小怪

**fussy** person tiāotī 挑剔

**futile** wúxiào 无效

**future** n wèilái 未来; in ~
jīnhòu 今后

# G

**gadget** xiǎozhuāngzhì 小
装置

**gain** v/t (acquire) yíngdé
赢得

**gallery** (for art) huàláng
画廊

**gallon** jiālún 加仑

**gamble** dǔbó 赌博

**gambler** dǔtú 赌徒

**gambling** dǔbó 赌博

**game** n (match) bǐsài 比
赛; (sport) yùndòng 运动;
(children's) yóuxì 游戏; (in
tennis) yìjú 一局

**gang** yìbāng 一帮

**Gang of Four** Sìrénbāng
四人帮

**gangway** tiàobǎn 跳板

**gap** (in wall) lièfèng 裂缝;
(in time) jiànxì 间隙

**gape** v/i (of person) zhāng-
kǒu 张口

**garage** for parking chēkù
车库; for gas jiāyóuzhàn
加油站; for repairs qìchē
xiūlǐzhàn 汽车修理站

**garbage** lājī 垃圾; fig
(nonsense) fèihuà 废话

**garbage can** lājīxiāng 垃
圾箱

**garden** huāyuán 花园

**garlic** dàsuàn 大蒜

**gas** n qìtǐ 气体; (gasoline)
qìyóu 汽油

**gasp** v/i qìchuǎn 气喘

**gas station** jiāyóuzhàn 加
油站

**gate** dàmén 大门; (at
airport) dēngjīkǒu 登机口

**gather** v/t facts sōují 搜集

**gay** n & adj tóngxìngliàn 同性恋

♦ **gaze at** níngshì 凝视

**gear** n (equipment) yòngjù 用具; MOT chǐlún 齿轮

**gear shift** biànsùgǎn 变速杆

**gender** xìngbié 性别

**gene** jīyīn 基因

**general 1** n (in army) jiāngjūn 将军 **2** adj (overall, miscellaneous) zǒngde 总的; (widespread) pǔbiàn 普遍

**generalize** gàikuò 概括

**generally** yìbānde 一般地

**generate** chǎnshēng 产生; ~ *electricity* fādiàn 发电

**generation** dài dài 代

**generator** fādiànjī 发电机

**generosity** dàfang 大方

**generous** dàfang 大方; (not too critical) kuānhóng dàliàng 宽宏大量

**genetic** yíchuán 遗传

**genetics** yíchuánxué 遗传学

**genitals** shēngzhíqì 生殖器

**genius** tiāncái 天才

**gentle** wēnróu 温柔

**genuine** zhēnpǐn 真品; (sincere) zhēnchéng 真诚

**geographical** dìlǐ 地理

**geography** dìlǐxué 地理学

**geological** dìzhì 地质

**geology** dìzhìxué 地质学

**geometry** jǐhé 几何

**germ** bìngjūn 病菌

**gesture** n (with hand) shǒushì 手势; fig (of friendship) biǎoshì 表示

**get** (obtain) dédào 得到; (fetch) gěi ...ná 给...拿; (receive: letter) shōudào 收到; (catch: bus, train etc) zuò 坐; (understand) míngbai 明白 ◊ (become, grow): ~ *tired* / ~ *old* lèi le / lǎo le 累了 / 老了 ◊ (causative) bǎ ... le ...了; *one's hair cut* bǎ tóufa jiǎn le 把头发剪了; ~ *X to do Y* jiào X zuò Y 叫 X 做 Y ◊: *have got* yǒu 有 ◊: *have got to* bìxū 必须

♦ **get on** v/i (be friendly) chǔdelái 处得来; (make progress) jìnzhǎn 进展; ~ *the train* / *bus* / *one's bike* shàng chē 上车

♦ **get out 1** v/i (of car etc) chūlái 出来; ~! gǔnchūqù! 滚出去! **2** v/t nail etc nòngchū 弄出

♦ **get up 1** v/i (in morning)
qǐchuáng 起床; (from
chair) zhànqǐlái 站起来
**2** v/t hill pá 爬

**ghost** n guǐ 鬼

**giant** n jùrén 巨人

**gift** lǐwù 礼物

**gigantic** jùdà 巨大

**giggle** n gēge de xiào 咯
咯地笑

**gin** dùsōngzǐjiǔ 杜松子酒

**ginseng** rénshēn 人参

**girl** nǚhái 女孩

**girlfriend** (of boy) nǚ
péngyou 女朋友; (of girl)
nǚxìng péngyou 女性朋友

**gist** yàozhǐ 要旨

**give** gěi 给; ~ **a talk** zuò
jiǎngzuò 作讲座

♦ **give away** (as present)
sòng 送; (betray) xièlù
泄露

♦ **give in** v/i (surrender)
qūfú 屈服 **2** v/t (hand in)
jiāochū 交出

♦ **give up** v/t smoking etc
jiè 戒 **2** v/i (cease habit)
jiè 戒; (stop trying) fàngqì
放弃

**glad** gāoxìng 高兴

**gladly** yúkuài 愉快

**glamor** mèilì 魅力

**glamorous** yǒu mèilì 有
魅力

**glance** n yìpiē 一瞥

♦ **glance at** sǎoshì 扫视

**glare** v/i (of light) shǎnyào
闪耀

♦ **glare at** nùmù ér shì 怒
目而视

**glass** (material) bōli 玻璃;
(for drink) bōlibēi 玻璃杯

**glasses** (eye~) yǎnjìng 眼镜

**glimpse** v/t piējiàn 瞥见

**gloat** v/i zhānzhānzìxǐ 沾
沾自喜

**global** quánqiú 全球;
(without exceptions) pǔbiàn
普遍

**global warming** quánqiú
biànnuǎn 全球变暖

**globe** (earth) dìqiú 地球;
(model) dìqiúyí 地球仪

**gloomy** room yīn'àn 阴暗;
mood, person yōuchóu
忧愁

**glorious** weather qínglǎng 晴
朗; victory guāngróng 光荣

**glove** shǒutào 手套

**glow** n guānghuī 光辉

**glue 1** n jiāo 胶 **2** v/t: ~ **X to
Y** bǎ X zhānzài Y shàng 把

X 粘在 Y 上

**glutinous rice** nuòmǐ 糯米

**go** v/i 去 去; (*leave*) líkāi 离开; (*work, function*) yùnzhuǎn 运转; (*become*) biànde 变得; (*cease: of pain etc*) méile 没了; (*match: of colors etc*) pèi 配; *I must be ~ing* wǒ déi zǒule 我得走了; *let's ~* zǒuba 走吧; *hamburger to ~* hànbǎobāo, dàizǒu 汉堡包带走; *be all gone* (*finished*) yòngwánle 用完了; *be ~ing to do X* yàozuò X 要做 X

◆ **go back** (*return*) huíqù 回去; (*date back*) zhuīsù 追溯

◆ **go down** xiàqù 下去; (*of sun, ship*) luòxià 落下; (*of swelling*) xiāoqù 消去

◆ **go in** (*to room, house*) jìnqù 进去; (*fit: of part etc*) ān 安

◆ **go off** v/i (*leave*) líkāi 离开; (*of bomb*) bàozhà 爆炸; (*of gun*) zǒuhuǒ 走火; (*of alarm*) xiǎngqǐ 响起

◆ **go on** (*continue*) jìxù 继续; (*happen*) fāshēng 发生

◆ **go out** (*of person*) chūqù

出去; (*of light, fire*) xīmiè 熄灭

**goal** mùbiāo 目标; (*sport: point*) bǐfēn 比分

**goalkeeper** shǒuményuán 守门员

**go-between** zhōngjiānrén 中间人

**Gobi Desert** Gēbìtān 戈壁滩

**god** shén 神

**gold 1** n huángjīn 黄金 **2** adj jīn 金

**golf** gāo'ěrfū 高尔夫

**gong** luó 锣; (*in wrestling*) míngluó líng 鸣锣令

**good** hǎo 好; (*food* hǎochī 好吃; *be ~ at* ... shànyú ... 善于...; *be ~ for X* duì X yǒuyòng 对 X 有用

**goodbye** zàijiàn 再见

**good-looking** hǎokàn 好看

**good-natured** píqí hǎo 脾气好

**goods** COM shāngpǐn 商品

**gorgeous** day fēnghé rìlì 风和日丽; *dress, woman* piàoliang 漂亮

**gossip 1** n (*rumor*) fēiyǔ 流言蜚语; (*person*) ràoshézhě 饶舌者 **2** v/i xiánliáo 闲聊

government zhèngfǔ 政府

governor zhōuzhǎng 州长

grab v/t zhuāzhù 抓住

grade n (quality) děngjí 等级; EDU year niánjí 年级

gradual zhújiàn 逐渐

graduate n bìyèshēng 毕业生

grain lì 粒; (in wood) mùwén 木纹

grand adj zhuàngguān 壮观

granddaughter (son's daughter) sūnnǚ 孙女; (daughter's daughter) wàisūnnǚ 外孙女

grandfather (paternal) zǔfù 祖父; (maternal) wàizǔfù 外祖父

grandmother (paternal) zǔmǔ 祖母; (maternal) wàizǔmǔ 外祖母

grandparents (paternal) zǔfùmǔ 祖父母; (maternal) wàizǔfùmǔ 外祖父母

grandson (son's son) sūnzi 孙子; (daughter's son) wàisūnzi 外孙子

grant n money bōkuǎn 拨款; (for school) zhùxuéjīn 助学金

grape pútao 葡萄

grapefruit pútaoyòu 葡萄柚

graph túbiǎo 图表

graphics COMPUT túxíngxué 图形学

grasp 1 n (physical) zhuā 抓; (mental) zhǎngwò 掌握 2 v/t (physically) zhuāzhù 抓住

grass cǎo 草

grate v/i (of sounds) cāxiǎng 擦响

grateful gǎnjī 感激

gratitude gǎn'ēn 感恩

grave n fénmù 坟墓

gray adj huīsè 灰色

graze 1 v/t arm etc cāshāng 擦伤 2 n mùcǎo 牧草

greasy food yóunì 油腻; hair, plate duō yóuzhī 多油脂

great hěndà 很大; quantity dàliàng 大量; composer, writer wěidà 伟大; (very good) hěnbàng 很棒

Great Leap Forward Dàyuèjìn 大跃进

greatly fēicháng 非常

Great Wall (of China) (Wànlǐ) Chángchéng (万里)长城

greed tānxīn 贪心

**greedy** tānlán 贪婪

**green** lǜsè 绿色

**greet** yíngjiē 迎接

**greeting** wènhòu 问候

**grief** bēishāng 悲伤

**grieve** bēitòng 悲痛

**grim** kěbù 可怖

**grin 1** n liězuǐ xiào 咧嘴笑 **2** v/i lòuchǐ'érxiào 露齿而笑

**grind** v/t coffee, meat niǎnsuì 碾碎

**grip 1** n (on rope etc) jǐnwò 紧握 **2** v/t zhuāzhù 抓住

**groan** v/i shēnyín 呻吟

**gross** adj (coarse) cūsú 粗俗; FIN zǒng 总

**ground 1** n dìmiàn 地面; (reason) lǐyóu 理由; ELEC dìxiàn 地线 **2** v/t ELEC shǐjiēdì 使接地

**group** n zǔ 组

**grow 1** v/i shēngzhǎng 生长; (of number, amount) zēngzhǎng 增长; (of business) fāzhǎn 发展; ~ tired lèi le 累了 **2** v/t rice, crop zhòngzhí 种植

♦**grow up** zhǎngdà 长大; (of city etc) kuòdà 扩大

**growl** v/i páoxiào 咆哮

**grown-up** n chéngrén 成人

**growth** chéngzhǎng 成长; (of company) fāzhǎn 发展; (increase) zēngzhǎng 增长; MED liú 瘤

**grumble** n & v/i bàoyuàn 抱怨

**grunt** n hūlushēng 呼噜声

**guarantee 1** n bǎozhèng 保证 **2** v/t dānbǎo 担保

**guard 1** n (security ~) jǐngwèi 警卫; MIL wèibīng 卫兵; (in prison) kānshǒu 看守 **2** v/t shǒuwèi 守卫

**guerrilla** yóujīduì 游击队

**guess 1** n cāicè 猜测 **2** v/t answer cāixiǎng 猜想 **3** v/i cāi 猜

**guest** kèrén 客人

**guidance** zhǐdǎo 指导

**guide 1** n (person) dǎoyóu 导游; (book) zhǐnán 指南 **2** v/t xiàngdǎo 向导

**guilt** yǒukuì 有愧; (guilty feeling) nèijiù 内疚

**guilty** LAW yǒuzuì 有罪; (responsible) nèijiù 内疚

**guitar** jítā 吉他

**gulf** hǎiwān 海湾

**gum** (in mouth) chǐyín 齿龈; (glue) shùjiāo 树胶

*(to chew)* kǒuxiāngtáng 口香糖

**gun** qiāng 枪

**gutter** yáncáo 檐槽; *(on roof)* tiāngōu 天沟

**guy** F jiāhuo 家伙

**gym** tǐyùguǎn 体育馆; *(in school)* yùndòngshì 运动室

**gynecologist** fùkē yīshēng 妇科医生

# H

**habit** xíguàn 习惯

**hacker** COMPUT hēikè 黑客

**hair** tóufa 头发; *(on body, animal)* máo 毛

**hairbrush** shūzi 梳子

**haircut** lǐfà 理发

**hairdresser** lǐfàshī 理发师

**hairdrier** chuīfēngqì 吹风器

**hairstyle** fàxíng 发型

**half** n yíbàn 一半; **~ past ten** shídiǎnbàn 十点半; **~ an hour** bàngè xiǎoshí 半个小时

**half time** n SP bànchǎng 半场

**halfway 1** adj stage bàntú 半途 **2** adv zhōngjiān 中间

**hall** tīng 厅; *(hallway in house)* zǒuláng 走廊

**halt 1** v/i tíngzhǐ 停止 **2** v/t zhǐzhù 止住

**halve** v/t fēnchéng liǎngbàn 分成两半

**hamburger** hànbǎobāo 汉堡包

**hammer** n chuízi 锤子

**hamper** v/t zǔ'ài 阻碍

**hand 1** n shǒu 手; *(of clock)* zhēn 针; *(worker)* gōngrén 工人; **on the one ~ ... , on the other ~** yìfāngmiàn ...lìngyìfāngmiàn ...一方面...另一方面...

◆**hand over** yíjiāo 移交; *to authorities* shàngjiāo 上交

**hand baggage** shǒutí xínglǐ 手提行李

**handcuffs** shǒukào 手铐

**handicap** n zhàng'ài 障碍

**handicapped** *(physically)* cánjí 残疾

**handkerchief** shǒujuàn 手绢

**handle 1** n bǎshou 把手 **2** v/t goods bānyùn 搬运; *case, deal* chǔlǐ 处理

**handmade** shǒugōng zhìzuò 手工制作

**handsome** shuài 帅

**handwriting** bǐjì 笔迹

**handwritten** shǒuxiě 手写

**handy** *device* fāngbiàn 方便

**hang 1** *v/t picture* guà 挂; *person* diàosǐ 吊死 **2** *v/i* (*of dress, hair*) chuíxià 垂下

◆**hang up** TELEC guàduàn 挂断

**hanger** yīfújià 衣服架

**hangover** (*jiǔhòu*) tóutòng (酒后)头痛

**haphazard** ǒurǎnxìng 偶然性

**happen** fāshēng 发生; *what has ~ed to you?* nǐ zěnme le? 你怎么了?

**happily** gāoxìng 高兴; (*luckily*) xìngyùn 幸运

**happiness** xìngfú 幸福

**happy** kuàilè 快乐

**harass** sāorǎo 骚扰

**harassment** sāorǎo 骚扰

**harbor** *n* gǎngwān 港湾

**hard** yìng 硬; (*difficult*) nán 难; *facts, evidence* bùrónghuáiyí 不容怀疑

**hardback** yìngpíshū 硬皮书

**hard-boiled** *egg* zhǔ de lǎo 煮得老

**hard currency** yìngtōnghuò 硬通货

**hardliner** qiángyìng lùxiànzhě 强硬路线者

**hardly** jīhūbù 几乎不

**hard seat** RAIL yìngzuò 硬座

**hardship** jiānnán 艰难

**hardware** jīnshǔqìjù 金属器具; COMPUT yìngjiàn 硬件

**hard-working** qínmiǎn 勤勉

**harm** *n & v/t* sǔnhài 损害

**harmful** yǒuhài 有害

**harmless** wúhài 无害

**harsh** jiānkè 尖刻

**harvest** *n* shōuhuò 收获

**hasty** cǎoshuài 草率

**hat** màozi 帽子

**hate** *n & v/t* zēnghèn 憎恨

**have** (*possess*) yǒu 有; *do you ~...* nǐ yǒu ...ma? 你有...吗? ◊ *breakfast, lunch* chī 吃◊: *can I ~ a ...?* qǐng gěiwǒ ...请给我...◊ (*must*): *~ (got) to* bìxū 必须 ◊ (*causative*) bǎ 把; *I had my hair cut* wǒ bǎ tóufa jiǎnle 我把头发剪了

◆**have on** (*wear*) chuān

穿; (*have planned*) yǒu shì 有事

**hay fever** huāfěnrè 花粉热

**hazy** *view* wùméngméng 雾蒙蒙; *memories* móhu 模糊

**he** tā 他

**head 1** n tóu 头; (*boss, leader*) lǐngdǎo 领导; (*of line*) qiánmiàn 前面 **2** v/t (*lead*) lǐngdǎo 领导

**headache** tóutòng 头痛

**heading** (*in list*) biāotí 标题

**headlight** qiándēng 前灯

**headline** dàzì biāotí 大字标题

**head office** zǒngbù 总部

**headphones** ěrjī 耳机

**headquarters** zǒng zhǐhuībù 总指挥部

**heal** v/t & v/i tīngjiàn 听见

**health** jiànkāng 健康

**healthy** jiànkāng 健康

**heap** n duī 堆

**hear** tīngjiàn 听见

**hearing** tīnglì 听力

**hearing aid** zhùtīngqì 助听器

**heart** xīn 心; (*of city etc*) zhōngxīn 中心; *know X by ~* shóujì X 熟记X

**heart attack** xīnzàngbìng 心脏病

**heat** rè 热

**heated** *pool* jiā le rè 加了热; *discussion* rèliè 热烈

**heater** fārèqì 发热器

**heating** nuǎnqì 暖气

**heatwave** rèlàng 热浪

**heaven** tiāntáng 天堂

**heavy** zhòng 重; *rain* dà 大; *traffic* yōngjǐ 拥挤; *food* yóunì 油腻; *financial loss* chénzhòng 沉重

**hectic** fánmáng 繁忙

**heel** (*of foot*) jiǎohòugēn 脚后跟; (*of shoe*) xiégēn 鞋跟

**height** gāodù 高度; (*of season*) shèng 盛

**heir** jìchéngrén 继承人

**helicopter** zhíshēngfēijī 直升飞机

**hell** dìyù 地狱

**hello** nǐ hǎo 你好; TELEC wèi 喂

**helmet** tóukuī 头盔

**help** n & v/t bāngzhù 帮助; *~!* jiùmìng! 救命！; *can you ~ me?* jiègè shǒu, xíngma? 借个手行吗？; *~ oneself* (*to food*) suíbiàn chī suíbiàn chī; **I can't ~ it** wǒ rěnbúzhù 我忍不住

**helpful** yǒu bāngzhù 有帮助

**helpless** wúzhù 无助

**hemisphere** bànqiú 半球

**hemorrhage** n & v/i chūxuè 出血

**her 1** adj tāde 她的 **2** pron tā 她

**herb** yàocǎo 药草

**herb(al) tea** yàocǎochá 药草茶

**herbal medicine** cǎoyào 草药

**here** zhèr 这儿; **~ you are** (giving sth) gěi nǐ 给你; **~ we are!** (finding sth) zài zhèr! 在这儿!

**hereditary** yíchuán 遗传

**heritage** yíchǎn 遗产

**hero** yīngxióng 英雄

**heroin** hǎiluòyīn 海洛因

**heroine** nǚyīngxióng 女英雄

**herpes** MED pàozhěn 疱疹

**hers** tāde 她的

**herself** tāzìjǐ 她自己

**hesitate** yóuyù 犹豫

**hesitation** yóuyù 犹豫

**heterosexual** adj yìxìng'ài 异性爱

**hiccup** n dǎgérdǎ 嗝儿打

**hide** v/t & v/i cáng 藏

**high 1** adj gāo 高 **2** n MOT gāo 高; (in statistics) gāofēng 高峰

**high jump** tiàogāo 跳高

**high-level** gāo jiēcéng 高阶层

**highlight 1** n (main event) zuìjīngcǎi chǎngmiàn 最精采场面; (in hair) rǎnsè 染色 **2** v/t (with pen) tūchū 突出; COMPUT xuǎn 选

**highly** likely fēicháng 非常; **~ paid** xīnshuǐ gāo 薪水高

**high point** dǐngfēng 顶峰

**high school** zhōngxué 中学

**high tech** n & adj gāoxīn jìshù 高新技术

**highway** gōnglù 公路

**hijack** v/t: **~ a plane** jiéjī 劫机; **~ a bus** jiéchē 劫车

**hijacker** (of plane) jiéjīzhě 劫机者; (of bus) jiéchēzhě 劫车者

**hike 1** n yuǎnzú 远足 **2** v/i bùxíng 步行

**hilarious** fēicháng huájī 非常滑稽

**hill** xiǎoshānpō 小山坡; (slope) shānpō 山坡

**him** tā 他

Himalayas Xǐmǎlāyǎshān 喜
马拉雅山

himself tāzìjǐ 他自己

hinder zǔzhǐ 阻止

hint tíshì 提示

hip túnbù 臀部

his adj & pron tāde 他的

historian lìshǐxuéjiā 历史
学家

historic yǒu lìshǐ yìyi 有历
史意义

historical yǒuguān lìshǐ 有
关历史

history lìshǐ 历史

hit 1 v/t dǎ 打; (collide with)
zhuàng 撞 2 n (blow)
dǎjī 打击; MUS liúxíng
chàngpiàn 流行唱片;
(success) jùdà chénggōng
巨大成功

hitchhike miǎnfèi dāchē 免
费搭车

HIV rénlèi sàngshī miǎnyìlì
bìngdú 人类丧失免疫
力病毒

hoarse sīyǎ 嘶哑

hoax n qīpiàn 欺骗

hobby shìhào 嗜好

hog n (pig) zhū 猪

hold 1 v/t (in hands) ná 拿;
(support, keep in place)

zhīchí 支持; passport,
license chíyǒu 持有;
prisoner guānyā 关押;
(contain) chéngyǒu 盛有;
~ the line TELEC qǐng bié
guàduàn 请别挂断 2 n (in
ship, plane) huòcāng 货舱;
take ~ of zhuāzhù 抓住

holdup (robbery) qiǎngjié 抢
劫; (delay) yánwù 延误

hole dòng 洞

holiday (single day) xiūxīri
休息日; Br (period) jiàqī
假期

hollow zhōngkōng 中空

holy shénshèng 神圣

home 1 n (native
country) zǔguó 祖国;
(town, part of country)
jiāxiāng 家乡; (for old
people) lǎorényuàn 老人
院; at ~ (in my house) zài
jiā 在家; (in my country)
zài guónèi 在国内 2 adv
jiā 家; go ~ huíjiā 回家; (to
own country) huíguó 回国

homeless adj wújiā 无家

homesick: be ~ xiǎngjiā
想家

home town jiāxiāng 家乡

homework EDU zuòyè 作业

**homicide** (*crime*) móushā
谋杀; (*police department*)
míng'ànbù 命案部

**homosexual** *n & adj*
tóngxìngliàn 同性恋

**honest** chéngshí 诚实

**honesty** chéngshí 诚实

**honeymoon** *n* mìyuè 蜜月

**Hong Kong** Xiānggǎng 香港

**honor 1** *n* róngyù 荣誉 **2** *v/t*
gěiyǐ róngyù 给以荣誉

**honorable** guāngróng 光荣

**hood** (*on head*) dōumào
兜帽

**hook** (*for clothes*) guàgōu
挂钩; (*for fishing*) yúgōu
鱼钩

**hookey**: *play ~* táoxué 逃学

**hope** *n & v/t* xīwàng 希望

**hopeful** (*optimistic*) lèguān
乐观; (*promising*) yǒu
xīwàng 有希望

**hopefully** *say* bàoyǒu xīwàng
抱有希望; (*I / we hope*)
dànyuàn 但愿

**hopeless** *position etc* méiyǒu
xīwàng 没有希望; (*useless:
person etc*) méi qiántú 没
前途

**horizon** dìpíngxiàn 地平线

**horizontal** shuǐpíng 水平

**horoscope** zhānxīngshù
占星术

**horrible** zāogāo 糟糕

**horrify**: *I was horrified* wǒ
bèi xiàhuàile 我被吓坏了

**horrifying** kěpà 可怕

**horror** kǒngbù 恐怖

**horse** mǎ 马

**hose** ruǎnguǎn 软管

**hospitable** hàokè 好客

**hospital** yīyuàn 医院

**hospitality** rèqíng zhāodài
热情招待

**host** *n* (*at party*) zhǔrén 主
人; (*of TV show*) zhǔchírén
主持人

**hostage** rénzhì 人质

**hostel** (*for students*) xiàowài
jìsùshè 校外寄宿舍

**hostess** (*at party*) nǚzhǔrén
女主人; (*air ~*) kōngjiě
空姐

**hostility** díyì 敌意

**hot** rè 热; (*spicy*) là 辣

**hotel** bīnguǎn 宾馆

**hour** xiǎoshí 小时

**house** *n* fángzi 房子; *at
your ~* zài nǐjiā 在你家

**House of Representatives**
Zhòngyìyuàn 众议院

**housework** jiāwù 家务

how zěnme 怎么; ~ *are you?* nǐ hǎo ma? 你好吗？; ~ *about ... ? ...*zěnmeyàng? ...怎么样？; ~ *many?* jǐge? 几个？; ~ *much?* duōshao? 多少？; ~ *much is it?* duōshao qián? 多少钱？; ~ *funny!* duō huájī! 多滑稽！

however bùguò 不过; ~ *rich they are* bùguǎn tāmen duō fù 不管他们多富

howl v/i háojiào 嗥叫

hug v/t yōngbào 拥抱

huge jùdà 巨大

human 1 n rén 人 2 adj rénlèi 人类

human being rén 人

humane réndào 人道

humanitarian réndàozhǔyì zhě 人道主义者

human resources (*department*) rénlì zīyuán 人力资源

humble qiānbēi 谦卑; *origins* dīwēi 低微; *house* jiǎnlòu 简陋

humid shīrè 湿热

humidity shīdù 湿度

humiliate xiūrǔ 羞辱

humor (*comical*) yōumò 幽

默; (*mood*) qíngxù 情绪

hunch (*idea*) yùgǎn 预感

hundred bǎi 百

hunger jī'è 饥饿

hungry jī'è 饥饿; *I'm ~* wǒ è le 我饿了

hunt n (*for animals*) shòuliè 狩猎; (*for criminal, missing child*) xúnzhǎo 寻找

hurry 1 n cōngmáng 匆忙; *be in a ~* jímáng 急忙 2 v/i kuàidiǎnr 快点儿

♦ hurry up v/i kuàidiǎnr 快点儿; *~!* gǎnjǐn! 赶紧!

hurt 1 v/i tòng 痛 2 v/t shāng 伤

husband zhàngfu 丈夫

♦ hush up zhēyǎn 遮掩

hut péngwū 棚屋

hydraulic yèyā 液压

hydroelectric shuǐlì fādiàn 水力发电

hygiene wèishēng 卫生

hygienic wèishēng 卫生

hyphen liánzìhào 连字号

hypnotize: ~ *X* shǐ X jìnrù cuīmián zhuàngtài 使X进入催眠状态

hypocrite wěijūnzǐ 伪君子

hysterical xiēsīdǐlǐ 歇斯底里

# I

I wǒ 我

ice bīng 冰

icebox bīngxiāng 冰箱

ice cream bīngqílín 冰淇淋

I-Ching Yìjīng 易经

icon (*cultural*) shèngxiàng 圣像; COMPUT túbiāo 图标

icy *road* huá 滑

idea zhǔyì 主意

ideal (*perfect*) lǐxiǎng 理想

identical yīmúyíyàng 一模一样

identification yànzhèng 验证; (*papers etc*) shēnfen zhèngmíng 身分证明

identify jiànbié 鉴别

identity shēnfen 身分; ~ *card* shēnfenzhèng 身分证

idiot báichī 白痴

idle *adj person* lǎnduò 懒惰

idolize chóngbài 崇拜

if rúguǒ 如果

ignition MOT fādòng zhuāng-zhì 发动装置; ~ *key* dǎhuǒyàoshi 打火钥匙

ignorance wúzhī 无知

ignore hūlüè 忽略

ill yǒubìng 有病; *be taken* ~ shēngbìng 生病

illegal fēifǎ 非法

illegible biànrèn bùqīng 辨认不清

illiterate wénmáng 文盲

illness jíbìng 疾病

illogical bù hé luóji 不合逻辑

illusion huànxiàng 幻象

illustration chātú 插图

image (*of politician, company*) xíngxiàng 形象

imaginary jiǎxiǎng 假想

imagination xiǎngxiàng 想象

imaginative jùyǒu xiǎngxiànglì 具有想象力

imagine xiǎngxiàng 想象

imitate mófǎng 模仿

imitation (*copying*) mófǎng 模仿; (*something copied*) fǎngzào 仿造

immature bù chéngshú 不成熟

immediate jíkè 即刻

immediately lìjí 立即

immigrant *n* yímín 移民

immigration yímín 移民

immoral bú dàodé 不道德

immunity (*to infection*)
miǎnyì 免疫; *diplomatic*
~ wàijiāo huòmiǎnquán 外
交豁免权

impact *n* (*of missile, vehicle*)
zhuàngjī 撞击; (*effect*)
yǐngxiǎng 影响

impartial gōngzhèng 公正

impassable bùtōng 不通

impatient bú nàixīn 不耐心

imperial huángdì 皇帝

impersonal bú jù réngéxìng
不具人格性

impetuous qīngshuài 轻率

implement 1 *n* gōngjù 工
具 2 *v/t measures etc* shíshí
实施

implicate: ~ *X in Y* shǐ X
qiānshè dào Y zhōng 使
X牵涉到Y中

implication ànshì 暗示

imply ànzhǐ 暗指

import *n & v/i* jìnkǒu 进口

importance zhòngyàoxìng
重要性

important zhòngyào 重要

impossible bù kěnéng 不
可能

impression yìnxiàng 印象;
(*impersonation*) huájī de
mófǎng 滑稽的模仿

impressive gěi rén yī
shēnkè yìnxiàng 给人以深
刻印象

imprison jiānjìn 监禁

improve 1 *v/t* gǎijìn 改进
2 *v/i* (*of health*) hǎozhuǎn
好转; (*of Chinese, skills*)
tígāo 提高

improvement gǎijìn 改进

improvise *v/i* jíxìng 即兴

impulsive yì chōngdòng
易冲动

in 1 *prep* ◊ zài 在 ◊: ~ *1999*
yījiǔjiǔjiǔ nián 1999 年;
~ *two hours* (*from now*)
liǎng ge xiǎoshí yǐhòu 两个
小时以后; (*over period of*)
liǎng ge xiǎoshí nèi 两个小时; 
~ *August* bāyuè 八月 ◊:
~ *English* / *Chinese* yòng
Yīngyǔ/Hànyǔ 用英语/汉
语 ◊: *one* ~ *ten* shífēnzhīyī
十分之一 2 *adv* (*at home,
in building etc*) zài lǐmiàn
在里面 3 *adj* (*fashionable*)
liúxíng 流行

inability wúnéng 无能

inaccessible nán jiējìn 难

接近

inadequate bú shìdàng 不适当

inappropriate bú shì dàng 不适当

inaugural *speech* jiùzhí 就职

incentive dònglì 动力

incessant liánxù 连续

inch n yīngcùn 英寸

incident shìjiàn 事件

incidentally shùnbiàn shuō yíxià 顺便说一下

incite shāndòng 煽动

incline: be ~d to do X yǒu zuò X de qīngxiàng 有做 X 的倾向

include bāokuò 包括

including *prep* bāokuò 包括

inclusive *adj & prep* bāokuò zàinèi 包括在内

incoherent bù liánguàn 不连贯

income shōurù 收入

income tax suǒdéshuì 所得税

incoming *flight* jídá 即达; *president* xīnrèn 新任

incompatible bù xiāngfú 不相符

incompetent bú chènzhí 不称职

incomprehensible bùkě lǐjiě 不可理解

inconsiderate kǎolǜ bùzhōu 考虑不周

inconsistent bù yízhì 不一致

inconvenient bù fāngbiàn 不方便

increase 1 *v/t & n* zēngjiā 增加 2 *v/i* tígāo 提高

incredible (*very good*) nányǐ zhìxìn 难以置信

incurable bùkě zhìyù 不可治愈

indeed (*in fact*) shìshí shàng 事实上; (*yes, agreeing*) díquèshì 的确是; *very much* ~ fēicháng 非常

indefinitely wú xiànqī 无限期

independence dúlì 独立

Independence Day Dúlìrì 独立日

independent dúlì 独立

indicate *v/t* biǎomíng 表明

indifferent mò bù guānxīn 漠不关心

indigestion xiāohuà bùliáng 消化不良

indignant fènkǎi 愤慨

indirect ~ jiànjiē 间接

indiscriminate rènyì ér wéi
任意而为

indispensable bùkě quēshǎo
不可缺少

individual 1 n gèrén 个人
2 adj (separate) dāndú 单
独; (personal) gèrén 个人

individually gèzì 各自

indoor shìnèi 室内

indoors zài shìnèi 在室内

industrial gōngyè 工业

industry gōngyè 工业

inefficient wúxiàolǜ无效率

inequality bùpíngděng 不
平等

inevitable bùkě bìmiǎn 不
可避免

inexpensive piányi 便宜

inexperienced méi jīngyàn
没经验

infant yīng'ér 婴儿

infantry bùbīng 步兵

infatuated: be ~ with X
míliàn X 迷恋X

infect (of person) yǐngxiǎng
影响; food, water wūrǎn
污染

infection chuánrǎn 传染

infectious chuánrǎn 传染;
fig: laughter gǎnrǎn 感染

inferior quality lièzhì 劣质

inferiority complex zìbēigǎn
自卑感

infidelity bùzhōng 不忠

infiltrate v/t dǎrù 打入

infinite wúxiàn 无限

infinity wúqióng 无穷

inflammable yìrán 易燃

inflammation MED fāyán
发炎

inflation tōnghuò péngzhàng
通货膨胀

inflexible gùzhí 固执

influence n & v/t yǐngxiǎng
影响

influential yǒu yǐngxiǎng
有影响

inform v/t tōngzhī 通知

informal fēi zhèngshì 非
正式

informant tígōng xiāoxirén
提供消息人

information xìnxī 信息

informer gàofārén 告发人

infuriating lìngrén shēngqì
令人生气

ingenious jīngmíng 精明

ingredient yuánliào 原料;
fig (for success) yīnsù 因素

inhabit jūzhù 居住

inhabitant jūmín 居民

inhale 1 v/t xīrù 吸入 2 v/i

(*when smoking*) xīqì 吸气

inherit jìchéng 继承

inhibition yāyì 压抑

in-house *adj & adv* zài gōngsī nèi 在公司内

initial **1** *adj* zuìchū 最初 **2** *n* xìngmíng shǒu zìmǔ 姓名首字母

initiative zhǔdòngxìng 主动性

inject MED zhùshè 注射; *capital* tóurù 投入

injured **1** *adj leg* shòushāng 受伤; *feelings* shòushāng-hài 受伤害 **2** *n: the ~* shòushāngzhě 受伤者

injury shānghài 伤害

in-laws yīnqīn 姻亲

inner nèibù 内部

inner city jiùchéngqū 旧城区

Inner Mongolia Nèi Měnggǔ 内蒙古

innocence (*of child*) tiānzhēn 天真; LAW wúzuì 无罪

innocent *child* tiānzhēn 天真; LAW wúzuì 无罪

innovative géxīn 革新

input *n & v/t* (*to project*) tóurù 投入; COMPUT shūrù 输入

inquest shěnxùn 审讯

inquire xúnwèn 询问

inquiry xúnwèn 询问

inquisitive hàoqí 好奇

insane fēngkuáng 疯狂

insanity fēngkuáng 疯狂

inscription míngwén 铭文

insect kūnchóng 昆虫

insert *v/t* chārù 插入

inside **1** *n* (*of house, box*) nèibù 内部; *~ out* fāndào wàimiàn 翻过来到外面 **2** *prep* zài ...lǐ 在 ... 里; *~ of 2 hours* bú dào liǎng xiǎoshí 不到两小时 **3** *adv stay* zài lǐmiàn 在里面; *go, carry* lǐmiàn 里面 **4** *adj* nèibù 内部; *~ information* nèibù xiāoxi 内部消息; *~ lane* (*on road*) lǐdào 里道

insider nèibùrén 内部人

insides lǐmiàn 里面

insight dòngchá 洞察

insist jiānchí 坚持

insistent jiānchí 坚持

insomnia shīmián 失眠

inspect *work, tickets, baggage* jiǎnchá 检查; *factory, school* shìchá 视察

inspiration línggǎn 灵感

inspire respect etc yǐnqǐ 引起; *be ~d by X* cóng X dédào línggǎn 从 X 得到灵感

install ānzhuāng 安装

installment (of story) jí集; FIN yīqī fùkuǎn 一期付款

instant 1 adj lìjí 立即 2 n chànà 刹那

instant coffee sùróng kāfēi 速溶咖啡

instantly jíkè 即刻

instant noodles fāngbiànmiàn 方便面

instead dàitì 代替; *would you like X?~? *nǐ hē kāfēi xíng ma? 你喝咖啡行吗？; *~ of* ér búshì 而不是

instinct běnnéng 本能

instinctive běnnéng 本能

institute n xiéhuì 协会; (special home) yuàn 院

institution (governmental) jīgòu 机构; (sth traditional) fēngsú xíguàn 风俗习惯

instruct (order) zhǐshì 指示; (teach) zhǐdǎo 指导

instruction shuōmíng 说明

instrument MUS yuèqì 乐器;

(tool) qìjù 器具

insulation ELEC juéyuán cáiliào 绝缘材料; (against cold) gérè 隔热

insult n & v/t wǔrǔ 侮辱

insurance bǎoxiǎn 保险

insurance company bǎoxiǎn gōngsī 保险公司

insurance policy bǎoxiǎndān 保险单

insure v/t gěi ...bǎoxiǎn 给 ...保险

intact (not damaged) wèishòusǔn 未受损

integrity (of person) chéngshí 诚实

intellectual 1 adj zhìlì 智力 2 n zhīshifènzǐ 知识分子

intelligence zhìlì 智力; (news) qíngbào 情报

intelligent cōngmíng 聪明

intend (plan) dǎsuàn 打算; *~ to do X* (do on purpose) zhǐzài zuò X 旨在做X

intense jùliè 剧烈

intensive qiánghuà 强化

intention yìtú 意图

intentional yǒuyì 有意

interactive jiāohùshì 交互式

intercept ball lánjié 拦截; message jiéchá 截查

*missile* jiéjī 截击

intercom duìjiǎngjī 对讲机

intercourse (*sexual*) xìngjiāo 性交

interest 1 *n* xìngqù 兴趣; FIN lìxī 利息 2 *v/t*: ~ **X** yǐnqǐ X de xìngqù 引起X的兴趣

interesting yǒuqù 有趣

interfere gānshè 干涉

♦ interfere with *controls* nònghuài 弄坏; *plans* gānrǎo 干扰

interference gānshè 干涉; (*on radio*) gānrǎo 干扰

interior *adj & n* nèibù 内部

intermediary *n* zhōngjiānrén 中间人

intermediate *adj* zhōngjí 中级

internal nèibù 内部; *trade* guónèi 国内

international *adj* guójì 国际

Internet yīntèwǎng 因特网

interpret 1 *v/t* kǒuyì 口译; *music, comment etc* jiěshì 解释 2 *v/i* zuò kǒuyì 作口译

interpretation kǒuyì 口译; (*of music, meaning*) lǐjiě 理解

interpreter kǒuyìzhě 口译者

interrogate xúnwèn 询问

interrupt 1 *v/t* dǎduàn 打断 2 *v/i* chāhuà 插话

interruption zhōngduàn 中断

intersection shízì lùkǒu 十字路口

interstate *n* zhōujìjiān 州际公路

interval jiàngé 间隔; (*in theater*) jiànxiē 间歇

intervene (*of police etc*) jièrù 介入

interview *n & v/t* (*on TV, for paper*) cǎifǎng 采访; (*for job*) miànshì 面试

intimacy (*sexual*) qīnnì 亲昵

intimidate wēixié 威胁

into dào ...里 到 ...里; *translate ~ English* fānyì chéng Yīngyǔ 翻译成英语; *be ~ X* F (*like*) xǐhuān X 喜欢X; (*be involved with*) chīmí X rùmíxX 迷X

intolerable bùnéng rěnshòu 不能忍受

intolerant bù róngrěn 不容忍

introduce jièshào 介绍; *new technique etc* yǐnjìn 引进

**introduction** (*to person, new food, sport etc*) jièshào 介绍; (*in book*) xùyán 序言; (*of new techniques etc*) yǐnjìn 引进

**intruder** qīnfànzhě 侵犯者

**invade** qīnlüè 侵略

**invalid** *n* MED bìngruò 病弱

**invaluable** *help* wújià 无价

**invasion** qīnlüè 侵略

**invent** fāmíng 发明

**invest** *v/t & v/i* tóuzī 投资

**investigate** diàochá 调查

**investigation** diàochá 调查

**investment** tóuzī 投资

**invitation** yāoqǐng 邀请

**invite** yāoqǐng 邀请

**invoice 1** *n* zhàngdān 帐单 **2** *v/t* kāi zhàngdān 开帐单

**involve** *work, expense* xūyào 需要; (*concern*) shèjí 涉及

**inwardly** nèixīn 内心

**IQ** (= **intelligence quotient**) zhìshāng 智商

**iron 1** *n* tiě 铁; (*for clothes*) yùndǒu 熨斗 **2** *v/t* yùn 熨

**ironic(al)** fěngcì 讽刺

**irony** fěngcì 讽刺

**irrelevant** bùxiāngguān 不

相干

**irrespective:** ~ **of X** búgù X 不顾X

**irritable** fánzào 烦躁

**irritate** rěnù 惹怒

**irritating** fánrén 烦人

**irritation** fánzào 烦燥

**Islam** Yīsīlánjiào 伊斯兰教

**island** dǎo 岛

**isolate** (*separate*) gélí 隔离; (*cut off*) gūlì 孤立

**isolated** *house* gūlì 孤立; *occurrence* dānyī 单一

**issue 1** *n* (*matter*) shìqíng 事情; (*of magazine*) qī 期 **2** *v/t* fāxíng 发行

**it** tā它◊ (*not translated*): ~**'s me** shì wǒ 是我; ~**'s yellow** shì huángde 是黄的; *that's* ~**!** (*that's right*) duìle! 对了！; (*finished*) wánle! 完了！

**itch 1** *n* yǎng 痒 **2** *v/i* fāyǎng 发痒

**item** tiáo 条

**itemize** fēnxiàng lièjǔ 分项列举

**its** tāde 它的

**itself** tāzìjǐ 它自己

# J

**jacket** jiākè 茄克; (*of book*) hùfēng 护封

**jade** *n* yù 玉

**jail** *n* jiānyù 监狱

**January** yīyuè 一月

**Japan** Rìběn 日本

**Japanese 1** *adj* Rìběn 日本 **2** *n* (*person*) Rìběnrén 日本人; (*language*) Rìyǔ 日语

**jar** *n* (*container*) guàn 罐

**jasmine tea** mòlìhuāchá 茉莉花茶

**jaw** *n* hé 颌

**jazz** juéshìyuè 爵士乐

**jealous** dùjì 妒忌

**jeans** niúzǎikù 牛仔裤

**jeopardize** shǐ xiànyú kùnjìng 使陷于困境

**jerk 1** *n* měngrán yídòng 猛然一动 **2** *v/t* měnglā 猛拉

**jet 1** *n* pēnjīshì 喷气式; (*nozzle*) guǎnzuǐ 管嘴

**jetlag** shíchā fǎnyìng 时差反应

**jeweler** zhūbǎoshāng 珠宝商

**jewelry** zhūbǎo 珠宝

**jiao** (*Chinese money*) jiǎo 角

**job** gōngzuò 工作; (*task*) rènwù 任务

**jog** *v/i* mànpǎo 慢跑

**join 1** *v/i* (*of roads, rivers*) huìhé 汇合; (*become a member*) cānjiā 参加 **2** *v/t* (*connect*) liánjiē 连接; *person* yǔ…huìmiàn 与…会面; *club* cānjiā 参加

**joint 1** *n* ANAT guānjié 关节; (*in woodwork*) liánjiēchù 连接处 **2** *adj* gòngtóng 共同

**joint account** liánhé zhànghù 联合帐户

**joint venture** hézī qǐyè 合资企业

**joke** *n* gùshì 故事; (*practical ~*) xiàohua 笑话

**jolt 1** *n* (*jerk*) diānbǒ 颠簸 **2** *v/t* (*push*) tuī 推

**jostle** *v/t* tuījǐ 推挤

**journalism** (*writing*) xīnwén xiězuò 新闻写作; (*trade*) xīnwényè 新闻业

**journalist** xīnwén gōngzuòzhě 新闻工作者

**journey** n lǚxíng 旅行

**joy** kuàilè 快乐

**judge 1** n LAW fǎguān 法官; (in competition) píngwěi 评委 **2** v/t pànduàn 判断

**judgment** LAW cáijué 裁决; (opinion) kànfǎ 看法; (good sense) juéduànlì 决断力

**judo** róudào 柔道

**juice** zhī 汁

**July** qīyuè 七月

**jumble** n yìtuán 一团

**jump 1** n tiào 跳; (increase) tūzēng 突增 **2** v/i tiào 跳; (in surprise) jīngtiào 惊跳

**jumpy** jǐnzhāng 紧张

**June** liùyuè 六月

**junior** adj (subordinate) dìwèi dī 地位低; (younger) xiǎo 小

**junk**[1] fèipǐn 废品

**junk**[2] (boat) fānchuán 帆船

**junk food** lājī shípǐn 垃圾食品

**junkie** yǒu dúyǐnzhě 有毒瘾者

**junk mail** lājī yóujiàn 垃圾邮件

**juror** péishěnyuán 陪审员

**jury** péishěntuán 陪审团

**just** adv (barely) gānggāng 刚刚; (exactly) qiàhǎo 恰好; (only) zhǐshì 只是; **I've ~ seen her** wǒ gānggāng kàndào tā 我刚刚看到她; **~ about** (almost) jīhū 几乎; **~ now** (a few moments ago) gāngcái gāngcái 刚才; (at the moment) xiànzài 现在; **~ you wait!** nǐ děngzhe ba! 你等着吧!

**justice** gōngpíng 公平; (of cause) zhèngyì 正义

**justify** zhèngmíng ... shì zhèngdàng 证明... 是正当

# K

**karate** kōngshǒudào 空手道

**keep 1** v/t bǎoliú 保留; (not give back) yōngyǒu 拥有;

(in specific place) cúnfàng 存放; family gōngyǎng 供养; animals yǎng 养;

~ *a promise* bǎoshǒu
chéngnuò 保守承诺; ~ ...
*to oneself* (*not tell*) bǎ ...
bǎozhù mìmì 把...保住秘
密; ~ *X from Y* bùràng Y
zhīdào X 不让 Y 知道 X;
~ *on trying* jìxù chángshì
继续尝试 **2** v/i (*remain*)
bǎochí bǎochí 保持; (*of food,
milk*) bǎozhì bǎozhì 保质

♦ **keep down** v/t *voice*
yādī 压低; *costs* bǎochí
dīshuǐpíng 保持低水平;
*food* tūnxià 吞下

♦ **keep up 1** v/i (*when
running etc*) gēnshàng 跟
上 **2** v/t *pace, payments*
gēnshàng 跟上; *bridge*
zhīchēng 支撑; *pants* tí tí提

**ketchup** fānqiéjiàng 番茄酱

**kettle** n hú 壶

**key 1** n *yàoshi* 钥匙;
COMPUT, MUS jiàn 键 **2** adj
(*vital*) guānjiàn 关键 **3** v/t
COMPUT jiànrù 键入

**keyboard** COMPUT, MUS
jiànpán 键盘

**keyring** yàoshiquān 钥匙圈

**kick** n, v/t tī 踢

**kid F 1** n (*child*) xiǎoháir 小
孩儿 **2** v/t & v/i kāi wánxiào

开玩笑

**kidnap** n & v/t bǎngjià 绑架

**kill** v/t shāsǐ 杀死

**kind¹** adj yǒuhǎo 友好

**kind²** n zhǒnglèi 种类;
(*make*) pǐnpái 品牌; *what
~ of ... ?* shényàng-
de ...? 什么样的... ?; ~
*of sad* F yǒudiǎnr nánguò
有点儿难过

**kindness** hǎoyì 好意

**kiss 1** n & v/t wěn 吻 **2** v/i
qīnwěn 亲吻

**kit** chéngtào yòngpǐn 成套
用品; (*to assemble*) zǔ-
zhuāngjiàn 组装件

**kitchen** chúfáng 厨房

**kitten** xiǎomāo 小猫

**knack** juéqiào 诀窍

**knee** n xī 膝

**kneel** guìxià 跪下

**knife** n dāo 刀

**knock 1** n (*at door*) qiāo 敲;
(*blow*) zhuàngjī 撞击
**2** v/t (*hit*) jī 击 **3** v/i (*at
door*) qiāo 敲

♦ **knock down** (*of car*)
zhuàngdǎo 撞倒; *object,
building etc* chāichú 拆除

♦ **knock out** *boxer etc* shǐ
hūnmí 使昏迷

knot *n* jié 结

know 1 *v/t* zhīdao 知道; *person* rènshi 认识; *place* shúxī 熟悉; *language* dǒng dǒng 懂; (*recognize*) rènchū 认 出 2 *v/i*: **I don't ~** wǒ bù zhīdào 我不知道

knowhow jìnéng 技能

knowledge zhīshi 知识

Korea (*South*) Nán Hán 南 韩; (*North*) Běi Cháoxiǎn 北朝鲜

Korean 1 *adj* (*South*) Nán Hán 南韩; (*North*) Běi Cháoxiǎn 北朝鲜 2 *n* (*South*) Nán Hánrén 南韩人; (*North*) Běi Cháoxiǎnrén 北朝鲜人; (*language*) Cháoxiǎn yǔ 朝鲜语

Kowloon Jiǔlóng 九龙

kung-fu gōngfu 功夫

# L

label *n* biāoqiān 标签

labor *n* (*work*) láodòng 劳 动; (*workers*) gōngrén 工 人; (*in pregnancy*) fēnmiǎn 分娩

laboratory shíyàn shì 实 验室

Labor Day Láodòngjié 劳 动节

lace *n* (*material*) huābiān 花 边; (*for shoe*) xiédài 鞋带

lack 1 *n* quēshǎo 缺少 2 *v/t* & *v/i* quēfá 缺乏

lacquerware qīqì 漆器

ladder tīzi 梯子

ladies' room nǚcè 女厕

lady nǚshì 女士

♦ **lag behind** luòhòu 落后

lake hú 湖

lamb gāoyáng 羔羊; (*meat*) gāoyáng ròu 羔羊肉

lame *person* qué 瘸

lamp dēng 灯

land 1 *n* tǔdì 土地; (*shore*) lùdì 陆地; (*country*) guójiā 国家 2 *v/i* (*of airplane*) zhuólù 着陆; (*of ball, stone*) luò 落

landing (*top of staircase*) (lóutī) píngtái (楼梯) 平台

landlady (*of apartment etc*) fángdōng 房东

**landlord** (*of apartment etc*) fángdōng 房东

**landmark** lùbiāo 路标; *fig* lǐchéng bēi 里程碑

**landscape** *n* fēngjǐng 风景

**lane** (*in country*) xiǎoxiàng 小巷; (*alley*) hútòng 胡同; (*on freeway*) hángdào 行道

**language** yǔyán 语言

**Lantern Festival** Yuánxiāojié 元宵节

**Lao** Lǎowō yǔ 老挝语

**Laos** Lǎowō 老挝

**Laotian 1** *adj* Lǎowō 老挝 **2** *n* (*person*) Lǎowōrén 老挝人

**lap¹** *n* (*of track*) quān 圈

**lap²** *n* (*of person*) dàtuǐ 大腿

**laptop** COMPUT xiédài shì diànnǎo 携带式电脑

**large** dà 大; *sum* duō 多

**largely** (*mainly*) zhǔyào 主要

**laryngitis** hóuyán 喉炎

**laser** jīguāng 激光

**last¹** *adj* (*in series*) zuìhòu 最后; (*preceding*) shàng yīcì 上一次; ~ **but one** dàoshǔ dì'èrge 倒数第二个; ~ **night** zuówǎn 昨晚; *at* ~ zhōngyú 终于

**last²** *v/i* chíxù 持续

**lastly** zuìhòu 最后

**late** (*behind time*) chídào 迟到; (*in day*) wǎn 晚

**lately** zuìjìn 最近

**later** *adv* hòulái 后来

**latest** *news etc* zuìxīn 最新

**latter** hòuzhě 后者

**laugh 1** *n* xiàoshēng 笑声 **2** *v/i* xiào 笑

♦**laugh at** cháoxiào 嘲笑

**laughter** xiàoshēng 笑声

**launch 1** *n* (*boat*) xiǎotǐng 小艇; (*of rocket*) fāshè 发射; (*of ship*) xiàshuǐ 下水; (*of product*) fāxíng 发行 **2** *v/t rocket* fāshè 发射; *new product* fāxíng 发行

**launch pad** fāshètái 发射台

**laundromat** zìzhù xǐyī diàn 自助洗衣店

**laundry** (*place*) xǐyī diàn 洗衣店; (*clothes*) yīwù 衣物

**lavatory** (*place*) cèsuǒ 厕所

**law** fǎlìng 法令; (*as subject*) fǎlǜ 法律

**lawn** cǎopíng 草坪

**lawsuit** sùsòng 诉讼

**lawyer** lǜshī 律师

**lay** *v/t* (*put down*) fàngxià 放下; *eggs* xià 下

**layer** n céng 层

**layout** n bùjú 布局；COMPUT géshì 格式

**lazy** lǎn 懒；*day* lìngrén lǎnsǎn 令人懒散

**lead**[1] 1 v/t *party etc*, *(take)* dàilǐng 带领；*race* lǐngxiān 先 2 v/i *(in race, competition)* lǐngxiān 领先

**lead**[2] n *(for dog)* jiāngsheng 缰绳

**lead**[3] n *(substance)* qiān 铅

**leader** lǐngxiù 领袖

**leadership** *(of party etc)* lǐngdǎo dìwèi 领导地位

**leading-edge** adj *technology* lǐngxiān 领先

**leaf** yèzi 叶子

**leaflet** chuándān 传单

**leak** 1 n lòu 漏；*(to press etc)* xièlòu 泄漏 2 v/i lòu 漏

**lean**[1] v/i *(at an angle)* wāi 歪；*~ against* kàozhe 靠着

**lean**[2] adj *meat* shòu 瘦

**leap** n & v/i tiào 跳

**learn** xuéxí 学习

**learning** n *(knowledge)* zhīshì 知识；*(act)* xuéxí 学习

**lease** 1 n zūqì 租契 2 v/t zū 租

**least** 1 adv *likely etc* zuìbù 最不 2 n zuìshǎo 最少；*at ~* zhìshǎo 至少

**leather** n & adj pí皮

**leave** 1 n *(vacation)* jiàqī 假期；*on ~* fàngjià 放假 2 v/t *place* líkāi 离开；*person* yǔ...fēnshǒu 与...分手；*husband, wife* pāoqì 抛弃；*(forget, leave behind)* wàngjì 忘记；*~ X alone (not touch)* biépèng X 别碰 X；*(not interfere with)* bù dǎjiǎo 不打搅；*be left* shèngxià 剩下 2 v/i líkāi 离开

**lecture** 1 n jiǎngzuò 讲座 2 v/i *(at university)* jiāo 教

**lecturer** jiǎngshī 讲师

**ledge** *(of window)* chuāngtái 窗台

**left** 1 adj zuǒ 左 2 n zuǒbiān 左边；POL zuǒpài 左派；*on the ~* zài zuǒbiān 在左边 3 adv *turn etc* zài zuǒcè 在左侧

**left-handed** guànyòng zuǒshǒu 惯用左手

**left-wing** POL zuǒyì 左翼

**leg** tuǐ 腿

**legacy** yíchǎn 遗产

legal (*allowed*) héfǎ 合法; (*relating to the law*) fǎlǜ 法律

legality héfǎxìng 合法性

legalize shǐhéfǎ 使合法

legend chuánshuō 传说

legible yìbiànrèn 易辨认

legitimate héfǎ 合法

leisure kòngxiùsān 空闲

lemon níngméng 柠檬

lend: ~ X to Y jiègěi Y X 借给 Y X

length chángdù 长度; at ~ describe xiángxì de 详细地; (*eventually*) zuìzhōng 最终

lengthen shǐ biàncháng 使变长

lenient kuāndà 宽大

lens yǎnjìng 眼镜; (*of camera*) jìngtóu 镜头

less: eat / talk ~ shǎo chī /shuō 少吃/说; ~ interesting méi nàme yǒuqù 没那么有趣; ~ than $200 shǎoyú liǎngbǎi měiyuán 少于两百美元

lesson kè 课

let v/t (*allow*) ràng jǐ 让; ~ me go! ràng wǒzǒu! 让我走！; ~'s go wǒmen zǒu

ba 我们走吧; ~ go of (*rope, handle*) fàngkāi 放开

lethal zhìmìng 致命

letter (*of alphabet*) zìmǔ 字母; (*in mail*) xìnjiàn 信件

lettuce shēngcài yè 生菜叶

leukemia báixuè bìng 白血病

level 1 adj surface píngtǎn 平坦; (*in score*) bìngjìn 并进 2 n (*on scale*) shuǐpíng 水平; (*in hierarchy*) jíbié 级别; (*amount, quantity*) lǜ 率

lever n gànggǎn 杠杆

liable (*answerable*) fùzé 负责; be ~ to (*likely*) yǒu kě néng 有可能

◆ liaise with yǔ ... jiànlì liánxì 与 ... 建立联系

liar shuōhuǎngzhě 说谎者

liberal adj (*broad-minded*) dàfāng 大方; POL zìyóu 自由

liberate jiěfàng 解放

liberty zìyóu 自由

library túshūguǎn 图书馆

license 1 n zhízhào 执照 2 v/t xǔkě 许可

license number zhízhào hàomǎ 执照号码

license plate chēpái 车牌

**lick** v/t tiǎn 舔

**lid** gàizi 盖子

**lie¹** 1 n (untruth) huǎnghuà 谎话 2 v/i shuō huǎnghuà 说谎话

**lie²** v/i (of person: on back) tǎng 躺; (on stomach) pā 趴; (of object) píng fàngzhe 平放着; (be situated) wèiyú 位于

♦ **lie down** tǎngxià 躺下

**life** shēngmìng 生命

**life insurance** rénshòu bǎoxiǎn 人寿保险

**life jacket** jiùshēng yī 救生衣

**lift** 1 v/t jǔqǐ 举起 2 v/i (of fog) xiāosàn 消散 3 n (in car) dā biànchē 搭便车

**light¹** 1 n guāngxiàn 光线; (lamp) dēng 灯 2 v/t (fire, cigarette) diǎnhuǒ 点火; (illuminate) zhàomíng 照明 3 adj (not dark) míngliàng 明亮

**light²** adj (not heavy) qīng 轻

**light bulb** diàndēng pào 电灯泡

**lighter** (for cigarettes) dǎhuǒjī 打火机

**lighting** zhàomíng 照明

**lightning** shǎndiàn 闪电

**like¹** prep xiàng 象

**like²** v/t xǐhuan 喜欢; I ~ it wǒ xǐhuan 我喜欢; I would ~ ... wǒ xiǎngyào ... 我想要...; I would ~ to ... wǒ xīwàng ... 我希望...; would you ~ ... ? nǐyào ... ma? 你要...吗?; ~ to do X xǐhào X 喜好X; if you ~ suíbiàn nǐ 随便你

**likeable** kě'ài 可爱

**likelihood** kěnéngxìng 可能性

**likely** (probable) kěnéng 可能

**limit** 1 n xiàndù 限度 2 v/t xiànzhì 限制

**limp** n bǒxíng 跛行

**line¹** n (on paper, road) xiàntiáo 线条; (of people, trees) páibān 排; (of text) háng 行; (of business) zhíyè 职业

**line²** v/t (with material) ānchènlǐ 安衬里

♦ **line up** v/i páiduì 排队

**linger** (of person) dòuliú 逗留; (of pain) áizhe 挨着

**lining** (of clothes) chènlǐ 衬里

衬里

**link** 1 *n* liánjiē 连接; (*in chain*) yìjié 一节 2 *v/t* liánjiē 连接

**lip** zuǐchún 嘴唇

**lipstick** kǒuhóng 口红

**liqueur** lìkǒu jiǔ 利口酒

**liquid** 1 *n* yètǐ 液体 2 *adj* yèzhuàng 液状

**liquor** jiǔjīng yǐnliào 酒精饮料

**liquor store** mài jiǔdiàn 卖酒店

**list** *n* yìlán biǎo 一览表

**listen** tīng 听

♦ **listen to** tīng 听

**literature** wénxué 文学

**litter** lājī 垃圾

**little** 1 *adj* xiǎo 小 2 *n*: *a ~* yìdiǎn 一点; *a ~ wine* yìdiǎn jiǔ 一点酒 3 *adv* shāoxǔ 稍许; *~ by ~* zhújiànde 逐渐地; *a ~ better* hǎo yìdiǎn 好一点

**live**[1] *v/i* (*reside*) zhùzài 住在; (*be alive*) shēnghuó 生活

**live**[2] *adj* broadcast shíkuàng 实况

**livelihood** shēngjì 生计

**lively** huópo 活泼

**liver** MED gānzàng 肝脏;

(*food*) gān 肝

**livestock** shēngchù 牲畜

**living** 1 *adj* huóde 活的 2 *n* móushēng 谋生

**living room** kètīng 客厅

**load** 1 *n* fùdàn 负担 2 *v/t* zhuāng 装

**loaf** miànbāo 面包

**loan** 1 *n* dàikuǎn 贷款; *on* ~ jièyòng 借用 2 *v/t* jiè 借

**local** 1 *adj* dìfāng 地方 2 *n* (*person*) běndìrén 本地人

**local call** TELEC qūnèi diànhuà 区内电话

**locally** zài dāngdì 在当地

**local time** dāngdì shíjiān 当地时间

**locate** factory etc shèzhì 设置; (*identify position of*) zhǎochū 找出

**lock** *n & v/t* door suǒ 锁

**locker** yǒusuǒguì 有锁柜

**log** (*wood*) yuánmù 圆木; (*written record*) jìlù 记录

**logic** luójí 逻辑

**logical** yǒu luójí 有逻辑

**logo** biāozhì 标志

**London** Lúndūn 伦敦

**lonely** person gūdān 孤单; place jìmò 寂寞

**long**[1] 1 *adj* cháng 长;

*journey* yuǎn 远；*it's a ~ way* hěnyuǎn 很远啊 2 *adv* chángjiǔ 长久；~ *before* lǎozǎo 老早；*before ~ long* bùjiǔ 不久；*so ~ as* (*provided*) zhǐyào 只要；*so ~!* mànzǒu! 慢走！

**long²** *v/i*: ~ *for X* pànwàng X 盼望 X；*be ~ing to do X* kě wàng zuò X 渴望做 X

**long-distance** *adj phonecall* chángtú 长途；*race, flight* yuǎn jùlí 远距离

**long jump** tiàoyuǎn 跳远

**long-range** *missile* yuǎnchéng 远程；*forecast* chángyuǎn 长远

**long-term** *adj* chángqī 长期

**look 1** *n* (*appearance*) wàiguān 外观；(*glance*) kàn 看；*have a ~ at* (*examine*) kànyíkàn 看一看；*can I have a ~?* wǒ néng kàn yíxià ma? 我能看一下吗？2 *v/i kàn* 看；(*search*) xúnzhǎo 寻找；(*seem*) sìhū 似乎；*you ~ tired* nǐ kànqǐlái hěn lèi 你看起来很累

♦ **look after** zhàogù 照顾

♦ **look at** kàn 看；(*examine*)

jiǎnchá 检查

♦ **look for** zhǎo 找

♦ **look out** *v/i* (*of window*) cháowàikàn 朝外看；~! xiǎoxīn! 小心！

♦ **look up to** (*respect*) zūnjìng 尊敬

**loose** *wire, button* sōng 松；*clothes* kuānsōng 宽松；*morals* fàngdàng 放荡

**loosen** jiěkāi 解开

**lorry** Br huòchē 货车

**lose 1** *v/t object* diūshī 丢失；*game* shū 输；*I'm lost* wǒ mílù le 我迷路了 2 *v/i* SP shūdiào 输掉；(*of clock*) zǒumàn 走慢

**loser** SP shūzhě 输者

**loss** (*of object*) sǔnshī 损失；(*of loved one*) sàngshī 丧失；(*in business*) kuīsǔn 亏损

**lost** shīqù 失去

**lot**: *a ~/a ~ of* hěnduō 很多；*a ~ better* hǎo de duō 好得多

**lotion** xǐjì 洗剂

**loud** xiǎng 响

**loudspeaker** yángshēngqì 扬声器

**lousy** bù zěnme yàng 不怎

么样; *thing to do* tǎoyàn
讨厌

**love 1** *n* ài 爱; (*in tennis*)
língfēn 零分; **be in ~** zài
liàn'ài zhīzhōng 在恋爱之
中; **fall in ~ with** àishàng 爱
上 **2** *v/t* ài 爱

**love affair** fēngliú yùnshì 风
流韵事

**lovely** *face, hair* měilì 美丽;
*color* piàoliang 漂亮; *tune*
yōuměi 优美; *person, meal*
hěn hǎo 很好; *vacation,
day* lìngrén yúkuài 令人
愉快

**lover** qíngrén 情人

**low 1** *adj wall* ǎi 矮; *salary,
price, voice* dī 低; *quality*
chà 差 **2** *n* (*in statistics*) zuì
dīdiǎn 最低点

**loyal** zhōngxīn 忠心

**luck** yùnqì 运气; **bad ~** èyùn
恶运; **good ~** xìngyùn 幸

运; **good ~!** zhùnǐ zǒuyùn!
祝你走运！

**luckily** xìngyùnde 幸运地

**lucky** *person* xìngyùn 幸运;
*day, number* jíxiáng 吉祥;
**you were ~** nǐ zhēn zǒuyùn
你真走运

**luggage** xínglǐ 行李

**lukewarm** wēiwēn 微温;
*reception* bú rèqíng 不热情

**lull** *n* zànshí píngxī 暂时
平息

**lump** (*of sugar*) kuài 块;
(*swelling*) zhǒngkuài 肿块

**lump sum** zǒng'é 总额

**lunar** yuèliang 月亮

**lunatic** *n* fēngzi 疯子

**lunch** wǔcān 午餐

**lung** fèi 肺

**lung cancer** fèi'ái 肺癌

**lust** *n* xìngyù 性欲

**luxury** *n & adj* háohuá 豪华

**lychee** lìzhī 荔枝

# M

**Macao** Àomén 澳门

**machine** *n* jīqì 机器

**macho** dànánzǐ qì 大男
子气

**mad** fēng 疯

**made-to-measure** dìngzuò
定做

**madness** jīngshén shīcháng

精神失常

magazine (printed) zázhì
杂志

magic 1 n mófǎ 魔法;
(tricks) móshù 魔术 2 adj
juémiào 绝妙

magnetic yǒucíxìng 有磁性

magnificent zhuàngguān
壮观

magnify fàngdà 放大

mah-jong májiàng 麻将

maid nǔpú 女仆; (in hotel)
nǔ qīnglǐgōng 女清理工

mail 1 n yóuzhèng 邮政 2 v/t
letter yóujì 邮寄

mailbox (in street) yóutǒng
邮筒; (for house, e-mail)
xìnxiāng 信箱

mailman yóudìyuán 邮递员

main adj zhǔyào 主要

mainland dàlù 大陆

mainland China Zhōngguó
dàlù 中国大陆

mainly zhǔyào 主要

main street zhǔjiē 主街

maintain law and order
wéichí 维持; speed bǎochí
保持; machine bǎoyǎng 保
养; innocence jiānchí 坚持

major 1 adj zhǔyào 主要 2 n
MIL shàoxiào 少校

majority dàduōshù 大多数;
POL duōdéde piàoshù 多得
的票数

make 1 n (brand) páizi 牌
子 2 v/t zuò 做; ~ X do Y
(force to) pòshǐ X zuò Y 迫
使X做Y; (cause to) cùshǐ
X zuò Y 促使X做Y; ~ X
happy shǐ X gāoxìng 使
X高兴; made in China
Zhōngguó zhìzào 中国
制造

♦make out check kāichū开
出; (see) biànrèn 辨认;
(imply) ànshì 暗示

♦make up v/i (after
quarrel) héjiě 和解
2 v/t story biānzào 编
造; (constitute) zhàn 占;
be made up of X yóu X
zǔchéng 由X组成

♦make up for míbǔ 弥补

maker zhìzàozhě 制造者

make-up (cosmetics)
huàzhuāngpǐn 化妆品

Malay Mǎláixīyà rén 马来西
亚人; (language) Mǎlái yǔ
马来语

Malaysia Mǎláixīyà 马来
西亚

Malaysian Mǎláixīyà 马

来西亚

**male 1** adj nánxìng 男性；
animal xióng 雄 **2** n nánrén
男人；(animal) xióngxìng
雄性

**male chauvinist** dànánzǐ
zhǔyìzhě 大男子主义者

**malfunction 1** n shīlíng 失
灵 **2** v/i fāshēng gùzhàng
发生故障

**mall** (shopping ~) gòuwù
zhōngxīn 购物中心

**malnutrition** yíngyǎng
bùliáng 营养不良

**man** n nánrén 男人；(human
being) rén人；(humanity)
rénlèi 人类

**manage 1** v/t business
jīngyíng 经营；money guǎn
管；suitcase etc nádòng 拿
动；... **to** ... zuòchéng ... 做
成... **2** v/i (cope) yìngfu
应付

**management** guǎnlǐ 管
理；(managers) zhǔguǎn
rényuán 主管人员

**manager** jīnglǐ 经理

**managing director**
zǒngjīnglǐ 总经理

**Mandarin** Pǔtōnghuà 普
通话

**mandatory** qiángzhì 强制

**maneuver 1** n xíngdòng 行
动 **2** v/t shèfǎyídòng 设
法移动

**maniac** kuángrén 狂人

**manipulate** person bǎibù
摆布

**manner** (of doing sth)
fāngshì 方式；(attitude)
tàidu 态度

**manners**: **good** / **bad ~**
yǒu / méiyǒu lǐmào 有
/ 没有礼貌；**have no ~**
méilǐmào 没礼貌

**manpower** láodònglì 劳动力

**manual 1** adj shǒugōng 手工
**2** n book zhǐnán 指南

**manufacture** n & v/t zhìzào
制造

**manufacturer** zhìzàoshāng
制造商

**many** adj & pron xǔduō 许
多；**too ~ ...** tàiduō... 太多
...；**how ~ do you need?**
nǐ xūyào duōshao? 你需
要多少？

**mao** (money) máo 毛

**Mao Tse-tung** Máo Zédōng
毛泽东

**map** n dìtú 地图

**March** sānyuè 三月

march 1 *n* xíngjūn 行军; (*demo*) yóuxíng 游行 2 *v/i* (*in protest*) yóuxíng 游行

margin (*of page*) kòngbái 空白; COM yínglì 盈利

marine 1 *adj* hǎiyáng 海洋 2 *n* MIL hǎilùbīng 海陆兵

mark 1 *n* (*stain*) wūdiǎn 污点; (*sign, token*) biāozhì 标志; (*trace*) jìxiàng 迹象; EDU fēnshù 分数 2 *v/t* (*stain*) liú hénjì yú 留痕迹于; EDU pīgǎi 批改; (*indicate*) biāomíng 标明

market 1 *n* jíshì 集市; (*for particular commodity*) shìchǎng 市场 2 *v/t* xiā oshòu 销售

market economy shìchǎng jīngjì 市场经济

marketing tuīxiāo 推销

market research shìchǎng diàochá 市场调查

mark-up jiàgé tígāo 价格提高

marriage (*institution*) hūnyīnzhì 婚姻制; (*being married*) hūnyīn 婚姻; (*event*) hūnlì 婚礼

marriage certificate jiéhūn zhèngshū结婚证书

married yīhūn 已婚; **be ~ to X** yǔ X jiéhūn 与X结婚

marry jiéhūn 结婚; **get married** jiéhūn 结婚

martial arts wǔshù 武术

marvelous jíhǎo 极好

Marxism Mǎkèsīzhǔyì 马克思主义

mascara jiémáogāo 睫毛膏

masculine nánzǐqì 男子气

mass (*great amount*) zhòngduō众多

massacre *n* dàtúshā大屠杀

massage *n* ànmó 按摩

massive jùdà 巨大

master 1 *n* (*of dog*) zhǔrén 主人; (*of ship*) chuánzhǎng 船长 2 *v/t skill* jīngtōng 精通

masterpiece jiézuò 杰作

mastery jīngtōng 精通

match¹ (*for light*) huǒchái 火柴

match² 1 *n* (*competition*) bǐsài 比赛 2 *v/t* (*be the same as*) yǔ … yíyàng yǔ … 一样 3 *v/i* (*of colors etc*) xiāngpèi 相配

matching *adj* xiétiáo 协调

mate 1 *n* (*of animal*) ǒu 偶 2 *v/i* jiāopèi 交配

material n (fabric) bùliào 布料; (substance) cáiliào 材料

materials yuánliào 原料

maternal mǔqīn fāngmiàn 母亲方面

maternity mǔxìng 母性

math shùxué 数学

mathematical shùxué 数学

matter (affair) shìqing 事情; PHYS wùzhì 物质; **what's the ~?** zěnmele? 怎么了？2 v/i yàojǐn 要紧; **it doesn't ~** méiguānxi 没关系

mattress chuángdiàn 床垫

mature adj chéngshú 成熟

maturity chéngshú 成熟

maximum 1 adj (highest) zuìgāo 最高; (biggest) zuìdà 最大 2 n zuìduō 最多

May wǔyuè 五月

may ◊ (possibility) yěxǔ 也许; **it ~ rain** kěnéng huì xiàyǔ 可能会下雨 ◊ (permission) kěyǐ 可以

maybe kěnéng 可能

May Day Wǔyī Jié 五一节

mayonnaise dànhuángjiàng 蛋黄酱

me wǒ 我

meal cān 餐

mean[1] (with money) lìnsè 吝啬; (nasty) bēibǐ 卑鄙

mean[2] v/t (intend) yìzhǐ 意指; (signify) biǎoshì 表示

meaning hányì 含义

means (financial) cáiyuán 财源; (way) fāngfǎ 方法

meantime: **in the ~** tóngshí 同时

measure 1 n (step) cuòshī 措施 2 v/t cèliáng 测量

measurement chǐcun 尺寸; (action) cèliáng 测量

meat ròu 肉

mechanic jìgōng 技工

mechanism jīxiè zhuāngzhì 机械装置

medal jiǎngzhāng 奖章

media: **the ~** dàzhòng chuánméi 大众传媒

median strip zhōngyāng fēnchēdài 中央分车带

mediator tiáojiěrén 调解人

medical 1 adj yīliáo 医疗 2 n tǐgé jiǎnchá 体格检查

medicine (science) yīxué 医学; (medication) yào 药

mediocre píngyōng 平庸

meditate míngxiǎng 冥想

**medium 1** adj zhōngděng 中等 **2** n (in size) zhōnghào 中号

**meet 1** v/t jiàn 见; (collect) jiē jiē 接; (satisfy) dádào 达到 **2** v/i jiànmiàn 见面; (in competition) bǐsài 比赛; (of committee etc) jùhé 聚合 **3** n SP yùndònghuì 运动会

**meeting** huìyì 会议

**melon** guā 瓜

**melt** v/t & v/i rónghuà 融化

**member** chéngyuán 成员

**memo** bèiwànglù 备忘录

**memoirs** huíyìlù 回忆录

**memorable** zhídé jìniàn 值得纪念

**memorial** n jìniànbēi 纪念碑

**memorize** jìzhù 记住

**memory** jìyì 记忆; (power of recollection) jìyìlì 记忆力

**mend** v/t xiūlǐ 修理

**men's room** náncè 男厕

**mental** jīngshén 精神

**mentality** xīnlǐ zhuàngtài 心理状态

**mention** v/t tídào 提到; **don't ~ it** búyòng kèqì 不用客气

**menu** also COMPUT càidān 菜单

**merchandise** huòpǐn 货品

**mercy** réncí 仁慈

**merger** COM hébìng 合并

**merit** n (worth) jiàzhí 价值; (advantage) yōudiǎn 优点

**merry** yúkuài 愉快

**mess** n zānggluàn 脏乱; (trouble) kùnjìng 困境

**message** qǐshì 启示; **can I leave a ~?** wǒkěyǐ liúyán ma? 我可以留言吗?

**messy** room língluàn 凌乱; person lāta 邋遢

**metal** n & adj jīnshǔ 金属

**meter¹** (for measuring) biǎo 表; (parking ~) tíngchē jìshí qì 停车计时器

**meter²** (unit of length) mǐ 米

**method** fāngfǎ 方法

**methodical** yǒutiáolǐ 有条理

**metropolitan** adj dà dūshì 大都市

**microphone** màikèfēng 麦克风

**microwave** wēibōlú 微波炉

**midday** zhōngwǔ 中午

**middle 1** adj zhōngjiān 中间 **2** n zhōngyāng 中央

**middle-aged** zhōngnián 中年

**middle-class** adj zhōngchǎn jiējí 中产阶级

**Middle East** Zhōngdōng 中东

**midnight** wǔyè 午夜

**Midwest** Zhōngxībù 中西部

**might** yěxǔ 也许; *I ~ be late* wǒyěxǔ chídào 我也许迟到

**mild** wēnhé 温和

**mile** yīnglǐ 英里

**militant** n jījí fènzǐ 积极分子

**military 1** adj jūnshì 军事 **2** n: *the ~* jūnduì 军队

**milk** n nǎi 奶

**millionaire** bǎiwànfùwēng 百万富翁

**mimic** v/t mófǎng 模仿

**mind 1** n tóunǎo 头脑; *change one's ~* gǎibiàn zhǔyì 改变主意 **2** v/t (*look after*) zhàokàn 照看; (*object to*) jièyì 介意; (*heed*) liúxīn 留心; *~ your own business!* bùguān nǐ de shì! 不关你的事! **3** v/i: *~!* (*be careful*) dāngxīn 当心; *never ~!* méiguānxì! 没关系！; *I don't ~* wǒwúsuǒwèi 我无所谓

**mine**[1] pron wǒde 我的

**mine**[2] n (*for coal etc*) kuàng 矿

**mine**[3] n (*explosive*) dìléi 地雷

**mineral** n kuàngwù 矿物

**mineral water** kuàngquánshuǐ 矿泉水

**miniature** adj xiùzhēnxíng 袖珍型

**minimal** zuìxiǎo 最小

**minimum 1** adj zuìshǎo 最少 **2** n zuìdīxiàndù 最低限度

**minor 1** adj cìyào 次要 **2** n LAW wèichéngniánrén 未成年人

**minority** shǎoshù 少数

**minute**[1] n (*of time*) fēnzhōng 分钟

**minute**[2] adj (*tiny*) wēixiǎo 微小; (*detailed*) xiángxì 详细

**minutes** (*of meeting*) jìlù 记录

**miracle** qíjì 奇迹

**mirror** n jìngzi 镜子

**miscarriage** MED liúchǎn 流产

**miserable** nánguò 难过; *day* lěngrèn bùkuài 令人不快

**misfortune** búxìng 不幸

**misjudge** cuòwù gūjì 错

误估计

**misleading** shǐ rén wùjiě使人误解

**misprint** n cuòyìn 错印

**miss¹**: *Miss Wang* Wáng xiǎojiě王小姐

**miss²** v/t (*not hit*) wèijīzhòng 未击中; (*emotionally*) xiǎngniàn 想念; *bus* méigǎnshàng 没赶上; (*not notice, fail to take*) cuòguò 错过; (*not be present at*) bùchūxí 不出席

**missile** (*guided*) dǎodàn 导弹

**missing** diūshī 丢失; *be ~* xiàluòbùmíng 下落不明

**mist** bówù 薄雾

**mistake** 1 n cuòwù 错误; *make a ~* fàn cuòwù 犯错误 2 v/t:~ *X for Y* wùjiāng X rènzuò Y 误将X认作Y

**mistress** (*lover*) qíngfù 情妇; (*of dog*) nǚzhǔrén 女主人

**mistrust** 1 n búxìnrèn 不信任 2 v/t huáiyí 怀疑

**misty** bówù lǒngzhào 薄雾笼罩

**misunderstand** wùjiě 误解

**misunderstanding** wùjiě

误解

**mitt** (*in baseball*) bàngqiú shǒutào 棒球手套

**mix** 1 n (*mixture*) hùnhé 混合; (*in cooking*) hùnhéwù 混合物 2 v/t hùnhé 混合 3 v/i (*socially*) xiāngchǔ 相处

**mixed** *feelings* fùzá 复杂

**mixture** hùnhéwù 混合物; MED fùfāngyào 复方药

**moan** v/i (*in pain*) shēnyín 呻吟

**mob** n bàomín 暴民

**mobile** 1 adj kěyídòng 可移动 2 n (*for decoration*) fēngdòng shìwù 风动饰物; Br (*phone*) shǒujī 手机

**mock** v/t qǔxiào 取笑

**mockery** (*derision*) cháonòng 嘲弄

**model** 1 adj boat, plane móxíng 模型 2 n (*miniature*) chúxíng 雏型; (*pattern*) móshì 模式; (*fashion ~*) mótèr 模特儿

**modem** tiáozhì jiětiáoqì 调制解调器

**moderate** 1 adj shìdù 适度; POL wēnhé 温和 2 n POL wēnhépài 温和派

**modern** xiàndài 现代

**modernize 1** v/t shǐ xiàndàihuà 使现代化 **2** v/i xiàndàihuà 现代化

**modest** house pǔsù 朴素; (not conceited) qiānxùn 谦逊

**modify** xiūgǎi 修改

**moist** cháoshī 潮湿

**moisturizer** (for skin) rùnfūshuāng 润肤霜

**mold¹** n (on food) méi 霉

**mold²** n in muzi 模子 **2** v/t clay etc jiāozhù 浇铸

**mom** mā 妈

**moment** piànkè 片刻; at the ~ xiànzài 现在; for the ~ zànshí 暂时

**Monday** xīngqīyī 星期一

**monetary** huòbì 货币

**money** qián 钱

**Mongolia** Měnggǔ 蒙古

**Mongolian 1** adj Měnggǔ 蒙古 **2** n (person) Měnggǔrén 蒙古人

**monitor 1** n COMPUT jiānshìqì 监视器 **2** v/t jiānkòng 监控

**monopolize** lǒngduàn 垄断

**monopoly** dúzhàn 独占

**monosodium glutamate** wèijīng 味精

**monotonous** dāndiào fáwèi 单调乏味

**month** yuè 月

**monthly** adj měiyuè 每月

**monument** jìniànbēi 纪念碑

**mood** xīnqíng 心情; (bad ~) huàiqíngxù 坏情绪; be in a good / bad ~ qíngxù hǎo / huài 情绪好 / 坏

**moon** yuèliang 月亮

**moral 1** adj dàodé 道德 **2** n (of story) yùyì 寓意; ~s xíngwéi biāozhǔn 行为标准

**morale** shìqì 士气

**morality** měidé 美德

**more 1** adj gèngduō 更多; some ~ tea? zài láidiǎn chá ma? 再来点儿茶吗? **2** adv gèng (duō) 更 (多); ~ important gèng zhòngyào 更重要; once ~ zàiyícì 再一次; ~ than duōyú 多于; I don't live there any ~ wǒbúzài zhù nàrle 我不再住那儿了 **3** pron: do you want some ~? nǐ hái yàodiǎnr ma? 你还要点儿吗?

**moreover** érqiě 而且

morning shàngwǔ 上 午;
(*early*) zǎochén 早 晨;
***good*** ~ shàngwǔ hǎo 上 午
好; zǎochén hǎo 早晨好

morphine mǎfēi 吗啡

Moscow Mòsīkē莫斯科

mosquito wénzi 蚊子

most 1 *adj* duōshù 多数
2 *adv* (*very*) hěn 很; ***the*** ~
***interesting*** zuì yǒuqù 最
有趣; ~ ***of all*** zuì zhòngyào
最重要3 *pron* dàduōshù
大多数; ***at*** ~ zhìduō至多

mostly zhǔyào 主要

mother mǔqīn 母亲

mother-in-law (*of man*)
yuèmǔ岳母; (*of woman*)
pópo 婆婆

mother tongue mǔyǔ 母语

motivation dònglì 动力

motive dòngjī 动机

motor fādòngjī 发动机

motorbike mótuōchē 摩
托车

motorcyclist qí mótuōchēde
rén 骑摩托车的人

motor rickshaw bèngbèng-
chē 蹦蹦车

mountain shān 山

mountaineering dēngshān
yùndòng 登山运动

mourn *v/t* dàoniàn 悼念

mouse shǔ 鼠; COMPUT
shǔbiāo 鼠标

mouth zuǐ 嘴; (*of river*)
hékǒu 河口

move 1 *n* (*in chess*) yíbù
一步; (*step, action*)
jǔcuò 举措; (*change
of house*) bānjiā 搬家
2 *v/t object* yídòng 移动;
(*transfer*) zhuǎnyí 转移;
(*emotionally*) gǎndòng 感
动3 *v/i* dòng 动; (*transfer*)
zhuǎn 转

movement dòngzuò 动作;
(*organization*) yùndòng 运
动; MUS yuèzhāng 乐章

movie diànyǐng 电影

movie theater diànyǐngyuàn
电影院

moving (*emotionally*) gǎnrén
感人

mph (= *miles per hour*)
yīnglǐshísù 英里时速

Mr xiānsheng 先生; ~ ***Wang***
Wáng xiānsheng 王先生

Mrs tàitai 太太; ~ ***Wang***
Wáng tàitai 王太太

Ms nǚshì 女士; ~ ***Wang***
Wáng nǚshì 王女士

much 1 *adj* xǔduō 许多;

***there's not* ~ ...** méiyǒu
duōshao ... 没有多少...
**2** *adv* hěn 很; ***I don't like
him* ~** wǒ bútài xǐhuan
tā 我不太喜欢他;~
***better* hǎo** de duō 好得
多; ***very* ~** fēicháng 非常;
***too* ~** guòduō 过多 **3** *pron*
duōshǎo 多少; ***nothing* ~**
méi shénme 没什么

**mud** ní 泥

**mug¹** *n* (*for drink*) dàbēi
大杯

**mug²** *v/t* (*attack*) xíngxiōng
qiǎngjié 行凶抢劫

**multinational** *n* COM duōguó
多国

**multiple** *adj* duōgè 多个

**multiply** *v/t* chéng 乘

**murder** *n & v/t* móushā 谋杀

**murderer** xiōngshǒu 凶手

**muscle** jīròu 肌肉

**museum** bówùguǎn 博物馆

**mushroom** *n* mógu 蘑菇

**music** yīnyuè 音乐; (*written*)
yuèpǔ 乐谱

**musician** yīnyuèjiā 音乐家

**must** bìxū 必须; ***I ~n't be
late*** wǒbùnéng chídào 我
不能迟到

**mustache** bāzì hú 八字胡

**mustard** jièmò 芥末

**mutter 1** *v/i* gūnong 咕哝
**2** *v/t* dīshēng shuō 低声说

**mutual** xiānghù 相互

**my** wǒde 我的

**myself** wǒzìjǐ 我自己

**mysterious** shénmì 神秘

**mystery** mí 谜

# N

**nag** *v/i* (*of person*) láodao
bùtíng 唠叨不停

**nail** (*for wood*) dīng 钉; (*on
finger, toe*) zhǐjia 指甲

**nail file** zhǐjia cuò 指甲锉

**nail polish** zhǐjia yóu 指甲
油

**naive** tiānzhēn 天真

**naked** luǒtǐ 裸体

**name** *n* míngzi 名字; ***what's
your ~?*** nǐ jiào shénme
míngzi? 你叫什么名字？

**nap** *n* xiǎoshuì 小睡

**narrow** *street, bed etc* xiázhǎi

狭窄; *views* xiá'ài 狭隘; *victory* miǎnqiǎng 勉强

**narrow-minded** xīnxiōng xiázhǎi 心胸狭窄

**nasty** *person, remark* bēibǐ 卑鄙; *smell, weather* èliè 劣; *cut, disease* yánzhòng 严重

**nation** guójiā 国家

**national 1** *adj* guólì 国立; *newspaper, security* guójiā 国家; *pride* àiguó 爱国 **2** *n* guómín 国民

**Nationalist Party** (*KMT*) Guómíndǎng 国民党

**nationality** guójí 国籍

**nationalize** shǐguóyǒu huà 使国有化

**National People's Congress** Quánguó Rénmín Dàibiǎo Dàhuì 全国人民代表大会

**native** *adj* (*of country*) běnguó 本国; (*of place*) běndì 本地

**natural** zìrán 自然; *flavor* tiānrán 天然

**natural gas** tiānrán qì 天然气

**naturally** (*of course*) dāngrán 当然; *behave* zìrán 自然;

(*by nature*) tiānshēng 天生

**nature** zìrán 自然; (*of person*) xìnggé 性格; (*of problem*) běnzhì 本质

**naughty** tiáopí 淘气

**nausea** ěxin 恶心

**nauseous: feel ~** juéde ěxin 得恶心

**nautical** hánghǎi 航海

**naval** hǎijūn 海军

**navigate** *v/i* cèháng 测航

**navigator** (*on ship*) hánghǎi jiā 航海家; (*in airplane*) jiàshǐyuán 驾驶员

**navy** hǎijūn 海军

**navy blue** *n & adj* hǎijūn lán 海军蓝

**near 1** *adj & adv* jìn 近 **2** *prep* jiējìn 接近; **~ the bank** kàojìn yínháng 靠近银行

**nearby** *adv* zài fùjìn 在附近

**nearly** jīhū 几乎

**neat** zhěngjié 整洁; *whiskey* chún 纯; *solution* qiǎomiào 巧妙; F (*terrific*) tǐnghǎo 挺好

**necessary** bìbù kěshǎo 必不可少; **it is ~** yǒu bìyào zuò 有必要做

**necessity** bìyàoxìng 必要

性; (sth necessary) bìxūpǐn
必需品

**neck** bózi 脖子

**necklace** xiàngliàn 项链

**necktie** lǐngdài 领带

**need 1** n xūyào 需要; in ~
yǒu kùnnán 有困难 **2** v/t
xūyào 需要; **you don't ~
to wait** nǐ búbì děngzhe 你
不必等着

**needle** (for sewing) zhēn 针;
(for injection) zhēntóu 针
头; (on dial) zhǐzhēn 指针

**negative** adj GRAM fǒudìng
否定; attitude, person xiāojí
消极; ELEC fùdiàn 负电

**neglect 1** n hūlüè 忽略 **2** v/t
zhàogù bùzhōu 照顾不周

**negligence** wánhū zhíshǒu
玩忽职守

**negotiate** v/t & v/i xiéshāng
协商

**neighbor** línjū 邻居

**neighborhood** jiēqū 街区

**neither 1** adj liǎngzhě dōu
bù 两者都不 **2** pron
něige dōu bù 哪个都不;

~ **of them recognized
me** tāmenliǎ shéi dōu méi
rènchūwǒ lái 他们俩谁
都没认出我来 **3** adv: ~

**... nor ...** jìbù ... yěbù ...
既不... 也不... **4** conj yě
bù 也不; ~ **do I** wǒ yěbù
我也不

**Nepal** Níbó'ěr 尼泊尔

**Nepalese 1** adj Níbó'ěr 尼
泊尔 **2** n Níbó'ěrrén 尼泊
尔人; (language) Níbó'ěr
yǔ 尼泊尔语

**nephew** (brother's son)
zhízi 侄子; (sister's son)
wàisheng 外甥

**nerve** shénjīng 神经

**nervous** jǐnzhāng 紧张

**net** adj price chún 纯; weight
jìng 净

**net profit** jìnglì 净利

**network** liánluò wǎng 联络
网; COMPUT wǎngluò 网络

**neurotic** adj shénjīng zhì
神经质

**neutral 1** adj country zhōnglì
中立; color fēi cǎisè 非彩
色 **2** n (gear) kōngdǎng
空档

**neutrality** zhōnglì dìwèi 中
立地位

**never** (past) cónglái méi 从
来没; (present) cónglái bù
从来不; (future) juébùhuì
绝不会

**nevertheless** dànshì 但是

**new** xīn 新

**news** xīnwén 新闻; (TV, radio) xīnwén bàodǎo 新闻报导

**newspaper** bàozhǐ 报纸

**New Territories** (in Hong Kong) Xīnjiè 新界

**New Year** Xīnnián 新年; (Chinese) Chūnjié 春节; *Happy ~!* Xīnnián kuàilè! 新年快乐！

**New Year's Day** (Jan 1) Yuándàn 元旦; (Chinese) Chūyī 初一

**New Year's Eve** (Dec 31) Yuándàn Qiányè 元旦前夜; (Chinese) Chúxī 除夕

**New York** Niǔyuē 纽约

**next 1** adj (in time, space) xià yíge 下一个 ♦ **2** adv xià yíbù 下一步; ♦ **to X** (beside) zài X de pángbiān 在X的旁边; (in comparison with) yǔ X xiāngbǐ 与X相比

**next door** adj & adv gébì 隔壁

**next of kin** zuìjìnde qīnshǔ 最近的亲属

**nice** hǎo 好

**nickname** n wàihào 外号

**niece** (brother's daughter) zhínǚ 侄女; (sister's daughter) wài shengnǚ 外甥女

**night** yè 夜; **11 o'clock at ~** wǎnshàng shíyīdiǎn 晚上十一点; *good ~* wǎn'ān 晚安

**nightclub** yèzǒnghuì 夜总会

**nightdress** shuìyī 睡衣

**nightmare** èmèng 恶梦; fig kěpàde jīnglì 可怕的经历

**night school** yèxiào 夜校

**no 1** adv bù 不; *do you understand? – ~* nǐ dǒng ma? – bùdǒng 你懂吗？– 不懂 ♦ **2** adj méiyǒu 没有; *I have ~ money* wǒ méiyǒu qián 我没有钱; *~ parking* jìnzhǐ tíngchē 禁止停车

**nobody** méirén 没人

**nod** n & v/i diǎntóu 点头

**noise** shēngyīn 声音; (loud, unpleasant) zàoyīn 噪音

**noisy** xuānhuá 喧哗

**nominate** (appoint) tímíng 提名; *~ X for a post* (propose) tuījiàn X rèn mǒuge zhíwèi 推荐X任某个职位

**nonalcoholic** bù hán jiǔjīng 不含酒精

**noncommittal** bù míngláng 不明朗

**none** méiyǒu yígè 没有一个

**nonetheless** rán'ér 然而

**nonpayment** wèifù 未付

**nonsense** húshuō 胡说

**nonsmoker** bù xīyānzhě 不吸烟者

**nonstop** adj & adv zhídá 直达; chatter bùtíng 不停

**noodles** miàntiáo 面条

**noon** zhōngwǔ 中午

**nor** yòubú 又不; ~ do I wǒ yěbù 我也不

**normal** zhèngcháng 正常

**normally** (usually) yìbān de 一般地; (in a normal way) zhèngcháng de 正常地

**north 1** n běibù 北部 **2** adj běibù 北部 **3** adv travel xiàngběi 向北

**North America** Běiměi 北美

**North American 1** adj Běiměizhōu de 北美洲的 **2** n Běiměizhōu rén 北美洲人

**northern** běifāng 北方

**nose** bízi 鼻子

**nosebleed** liú bíxuè 流鼻血

**nostalgia** huáijiù 怀旧

**nosy** hàoguǎn xiánshì 好管闲事

**not** ◊ (present and future) bù 不; ~ there nàr bùxíng 那儿不行; like that bùnéng nàyàng 不能那样; ~ a lot yìdiǎndian 一点点 ◊ (past tense, and with yǒu) méi 没; we don't have a car wǒmen méiyǒu chē 我们没有车

**note** n (short letter) biàntiáo 便条; MUS (comment on text) zhùshì 注释; take ~s jì bǐjì 记笔记

**notebook** also COMPUT bǐjìběn 笔记本

**notepaper** biàntiáo zhǐ 便条纸

**nothing** méiyǒu shénme 没有什么; ~ for me thanks wǒ shénme yě búyào xièxie 我什么也不要谢谢; ~ but zhǐ 只

**notice 1** n (on bulletin board, in newspaper) tōnggào 通告; (advance warning) yùxiān tōngzhī 预先通知; (to leave job) cízhí tōngzhī 辞职通知; (to leave house)

zūlín tōngzhī 租赁通知;
*at short* ~ tūrán 突然;
*take* ~ *of X* zhùyì X 注意
X; *take no* ~ *of X* búyào
guǎn X 不要管 X **2** *v/t*
zhùyì 注意
**notify** tōngzhī 通知
**notorious** shēngmíng lángjí
声名狼藉
**nourishing** yǒu yíngyǎng
有营养
**novel** *n* xiǎoshuō 小说
**novelist** xiǎoshuōjiā 小说家
**November** shíyīyuè 十一月
**novice** xuétú 学徒
**now** xiànzài 现在; *~ and
again* yǒushí 有时; *by* ~
zhèshí 这时; *from* ~ *on*
cóng xiànzài kāishǐ 从现
在开始; *right* ~ cǐkè 此刻

**nowadays** xiànjīn 现今
**nowhere** wúchù 无处
**nuclear** yuánzǐhé 原子核
**nuclear energy** hénéng 核能
**nuclear power station**
hénéngzhàn 核能站
**nuclear weapons** hé wǔqì
核武器
**nude** *adj* luǒtǐ 裸体
**nuisance** fánrén 烦人
**number** *n* (*figure*) shùmù 数
目; (*quantity*) ruògān 若
干; (*of room, phone etc*)
shùzì 数字
**numerous** xǔduō 许多
**nurse** hùshì 护士
**nut** jiānguǒ 坚果; (*for bolt*)
luómǔ 螺母
**nutritious** yǒu yíngyǎng
有营养

# O

**oath** LAW shìyán 誓言
**obedience** fúcóng 服从
**obedient** fúcóng 服从
**obey** fúcóng 服从
**obituary** n fùgào 讣告
**object**[1] n wùtǐ 物体; (*aim*)
mùdì 目的; GRAM bīnyǔ

宾语
**object**[2] v/i fǎnduì 反对
**objection** fǎnduì 反对
**objective 1** *adj* kèguān 客观
**2** n mùbiāo 目标
**obligation** yìwù 义务
**obliterate** *city* huǐmiè 毁灭;

*memory* chúqù 除去

**obnoxious** yǐnrén fǎngǎn 引人反感

**obscene** yínhuì 淫秽

**observant** liúxīn 留心

**observation** (*of nature*) guānchá 观察; (*comment*) yìjiàn 意见

**observe** *behavior* zhùyì 注意; *people* kàndào 看到; *nature* guāncè 观测

**obsession** pǐ 癖; (*with a person, hobby*) zháomí 着迷

**obsolete** yǐfèiqì 已废弃

**obstacle** zhàng'ài 障碍

**obstinate** wángù 顽固

**obstruct** *road* zǔsè 阻塞; *investigation* zǔdǎng 阻挡

**obtain** dédào 得到

**obvious** míngxiǎn 明显

**occasion** jīhuì 机会

**occasional** ǒu'ěr 偶尔

**occasionally** ǒurán 偶然

**occupant** (*of vehicle*) chéngkè 乘客; (*of house*) jūzhùzhě 居住者

**occupation** (*job*) zhíyè 职业; (*of country*) zhànlǐng 占领

**occupy** *time, mind* zhànyòng 占用; *job* chōngrèn 充任; *country* zhànlǐng 占领

**occur** (*happen*) fāshēng 发生

**ocean** hǎiyáng 海洋

**o'clock: at five ~** wǔ diǎnzhōng 五点钟

**October** shíyuè 十月

**odd** (*strange*) qíguài 奇怪; (*not even*) jīshù 奇数

**odor** qìwèi 气味

**of: the name ~ the street** jiē de míngzi 街的名字; **five / ten minutes ~ twelve** shí'èr diǎn chà wǔ / shí fēn 十二点差五/十分; **die ~ cancer** sǐ yú áizhèng 死于癌症

**off** *adv*: **be ~** (*of light*) méi kāidēng 没开灯; (*of machine*) méikāi 没开; (*of lid, top*) méi gàizhe gàir 没盖着盖儿; (*canceled*) qǔxiāo 取消; **it's 3 miles ~** sān yīnglǐ yuǎn 三英里远; **drive / walk ~** kāizǒu / zǒukāi 开走/走开 **3** *adj*: **~ switch** guānbì jiàn 关闭键

**offend** *v/t* màofàn 冒犯

**offense** LAW zuìxíng 罪行

**offensive 1** *adj* tǎoyàn 讨

**one**

厌 **2** *n* MIL (*attack*) gōngjī
攻击; *go onto the ~*
cǎiqǔgōngshì 采取攻势

**offer 1** *n* tígōng 提供 **2** *v*/*t*
tígōng 提供; *~ X Y* gěi X
Y 给 X Y

**office** (*building*) bàngōnglóu
办公楼; (*room*)
bàngōngshì 办公室

**office block** bàngōng dàlóu
办公大楼

**office hours** bàngōng shíjiān
办公时间

**officer** MIL jūnguān 军官; (*in
police*) jǐngguān 警官

**official 1** *adj* guānfāng 官方;
(*confirmed*) zhèngshì 正式
**2** *n* guānyuán 官员

**often** jīngcháng 经常

**oil** *n* yóu 油

**oil company** shíyóu gōngsī
石油公司

**oil tanker** yóuchuán 油船

**oil well** yóujǐng 油井

**ointment** ruǎngāo 软膏

**ok** kěyǐ 可以; *are you ~?*
(*well, not hurt*) nǐ méishìr
ba? 你没事儿吧?

**old** lǎo 老; (*previous*) jiù 旧;
*how ~ are you?* nǐ duōdà
niánjì le? 你多大年纪

了?

**old age** lǎonián 老年

**old-fashioned** guòshí 过时

**omit** yílòu 遗漏

**on 1** *prep*: *~ the table* zài
zhuō shang 在桌上; *~
the bus* / *train* gōnggòng
qìchē / huǒchēlǐ 公共汽车
/ 火车里; *~ TV* / *the radio*
diànshì shang / guǎngbōlǐ
电视上/广播里 **2** *adv*:
*be ~* (*of light*) kāidēng 开
灯; (*of TV, computer etc*)
kāi 开; (*of lid, top*) gàizhe
gàir 盖着盖儿; *what's
~ tonight?* (*on TV etc*)
jīnwǎn yǒu shénme jiémù?
今晚有什么节目?;
(*what's planned?*) jīnwǎn
gàn shénme? 今晚干什
么? **3** *adv*: *~ switch* kāiqǐ
jiàn 开启键

**once** *adv* (*one time*) yīcì 一
次; (*formerly*) céngjīng 曾
经; *at ~* (*immediately*) lìjí
立即; *all at ~* (*suddenly*)
tūrán 突然; (*together*)
yìqǐ 一起

**one 1** *n* (*number*) yī 一;
(*in phone numbers*) yāo
幺 **2** *adj* yīgè 一个; *~ day*

yìtiān 一天 **3** *pron* yígè 一
个；*which ~?* nǎyíge? 哪
一个？；*the little ~s* xiǎo
péngyǒumen 小朋友们
**one child policy** jìhuà
shēngyù 计划生育
**onion** yángcōng 洋葱
**on-line** *adj* shàngwǎng 上网
**only 1** *adv* zhǐ 只；*not ~ X
but also Y* bù jǐnjǐn X,
Y yěshì 不仅仅 X, Y 也
是；*~ just* gānggang 刚
刚 **2** *adj* wéiyī 唯一；*~
son / daughter* dúzǐ / nǚ
独子 / 女
**onto:** *put X ~ Y* bǎ X
fàngdào Y shang 把X放
到Y上
**open 1** *adj* kāizhe 开着；
(*frank*) tǎnbái 坦白 **2** *v/t*
kāi 开；*book* tānkāi 摊开；
*file* dǎkāi 打开；*meeting*
kāishǐ 开始 **3** *v/i* kāi 开
**opera** gējù 歌剧
**operate 1** *v/i* MED dòng
shǒushù 动手术 **2** *v/t*
*machine* cāozuò 操作
**operation** MED shǒushù 手术
**opinion** kànfǎ 看法
**opponent** duìshǒu 对手
**opportunity** jīhuì 机会

**oppose** fǎnduì 反对
**opposite 1** *adj side of road*
duìmiàn 对面；*direction,
meaning* xiāngfǎn 相反 **2** *n*
fǎnmiàn 反面
**oppressive** *rule* bàonüè 暴
虐；*weather* chénzhòng
沉重
**optimist** lèguānzhě乐观者
**optimistic** lèguān 乐观
**option** xuǎnzé 选择
**optional** kě xuǎnzé 可选择
**or** huò 或
**orange** *n* (*fruit*) chéng 橙；
(*color*) chéngsè 橙色
**orange juice** chéngzhī 橙
汁儿
**orchestra** guǎnxián yuèduì
管弦乐队
**order 1** *n* (*command*)
mìngling 命令；(*sequence*)
cìxù 次序；(*being well
arranged*) zhìxù 秩序；
(*for goods*) dìnggòu 定
购；(*in restaurant*) dìng
càidān 定菜单；*out of ~*
(*not functioning*) shīlíng
失灵；(*not in sequence*)
cìxù diāndǎo 次序颠倒
**2** *v/t goods* dìnghuò 定 货；
*meal* jiàocài 叫菜；*~ X to*

**do Y** mìnglìng X qù zuò Y 命令 X 去做 Y **3** *v/i (in restaurant)* diǎncài 点菜

**ordinary** pǔtōng 普通

**organic** *food* tiānrán 天然

**organization** jīgòu 机构; *(organizing)* zǔzhī 组织

**organize** zǔzhī 组织

**Orient** Dōngfāng 东方

**origin** qǐyuán 起源

**original** *adj (not copied)* yuánzuò 原作; *(first)* zuìchū 最初

**originally** yuánxiān 原先

**other 1** *adj* qítā 其他 **2** *n:* **the ~s** qítāde 其他的

**otherwise** bùrán dehuà 不然的话; *(differently)* bùtóng 不同

**ought** yīnggāi 应该

**our** wǒmen 我们

**ours** wǒmende 我们的

**ourselves** wǒmen zìjǐ 我们自己

**out: be ~** *(of light)* guāndiào 关掉; *(of fire)* xīmiè 熄灭; *(of flower)* shèngkāi 盛开; *(of sun)* chūlái 出来; *(not at home, not in building)* búzài 不在; *(no longer in competition)* táotài 淘汰;

*(get)* **~!** chūqù! 出去 !

**outbreak** *(of violence, war)* bàofā 爆发

**outcome** jiéguǒ 结果

**outdoor(s)** shìwài 室外

**outer** *wall etc* wàibù 外部

**outgoing** *flight* chūháng 出航; *personality* kāilǎng 开朗

**outlet** *(of pipe)* chūkǒu 出口; *(for sales)* xiāoshòu diǎn 销售点; ELEC chāzuò 插座

**outlook** zhǎnwàng 展望

**out of** ◊ *(motion)*: **run ~ the house** pǎochū wūwài pǎo 出屋外 ◊ *(position)*: **20 miles ~ Nanjing** Nánjīng yǐwài èrshí yīnglǐ 南京以外二十英里 ◊ *(cause)*: **~ jealousy** yóuyú jídù 由于嫉妒 ◊ *(without)*: **we're ~ gas** wǒmen chēméi yóu le 我们车没油了 ◊ **5 ~ 10** shífēn zhīwǔ 十分之五

**output 1** *n (of factory)* chǎnliàng 产量 **2** *v/t (produce)* shēngchǎn 生产

**outrage** *n (feeling)* gōngfèn 公愤; *(act)* bàoxíng 暴行

**outrageous** *acts* wúchǐ 无

耻; *prices* guòfèn 过分

**outside 1** *adj* wàibù 外部 **2** *adv* wàimian 外面 **3** *prep* zài ... yǐwài 在 ... 以外

**outsider** lěngmén 冷门

**outskirts** jiāoqū 郊区

**outstanding** *quality* xiǎnzhù 显著; *writer, athlete* jiéchū 杰出; *payment etc* wèifù 未付

**oval** *adj* tuǒyuán 椭圆

**oven** kǎoxiāng 烤箱

**over 1** *prep* (*across*) guò 过; (*more than*) chāoguò 超过; (*above*) zài ... shàngfāng 在 ... 上方 **2** *adv*: *be ~* (*finished*) wánjié 完结; (*left*) shèngyú 剩余; *~ here* zài zhèlǐ 在这里; *it hurts all ~* wǒhúnshēn dōu téng 我浑身都疼; *do X ~* (*again*) zàicì zuò X 再次做X

**overcoat** dàyī 大衣

**overcome** *difficulty* zhēngfú 征服

**overdo** kuāzhāng 夸张; (*cooking*) zhǔ guòhuǒr 煮过火儿

**overdone** *meat* guòhuǒ 过火

**overdose** *n* guòliàng 过量

**overdraft** chāozhī 超支

**overestimate** guògāo gūjì 过高估计

**overhead** *n* FIN tōngcháng kāizhī 通常开支

**overhear** tōutīng 偷听

**overlook** *of tall building etc* fǔshì 俯视; (*not see*) hūlüè 忽略

**overnight** *adv* yèjiān 夜间

**overrated** guògāo gūjì 过高估计

**overseas** *adj & adv* hǎiwài 海外

**overseas Chinese** Huáqiáo 华侨

**oversight** shūhū 疏忽

**overtake** chāoguò 超过; *Br MOT* chāochē 超车

**overtime** *work* jiābān 加班

**owe** *v/t* qiàn 欠

**owing to** yóuyú 由于

**own¹** *v/t* yōngyǒu 拥有

**own² 1** *adj* zìjǐ 自己 **2** *pron*: *on his ~* tā zìjǐ 他自己

**owner** yōngyǒuzhě 拥有者

**oyster sauce** háoyóu 蚝油

**ozone layer** chòuyǎng céng 臭氧层

# P

pace n (step) bù 步; (speed) sùdù 速度

Pacific: the ~ (Ocean) Tàipíngyáng 太平洋

Pacific Rim: the ~ Tàipíngyáng quān 太平洋圈

pack 1 n (back~) bēibāo 背包; (of cereal, food) dài 袋; (of cigarettes) bāo 包 2 v/t bag jiāng dōngxi zhuāngrù 将东西装入; item of clothing etc fàngrù xíngli 放入行李; goods bāozhuāng 包装 3 v/i zhěngli xíngzhuāng 整理行装

package n bāoguǒ 包裹; (of offers etc) zhěngdài cáiliào 整袋材料

package deal (for vacation) bāobàn lǚxíng 包办旅行

packet bāo 包

paddy dàozi 稻子

page¹ n (of book etc) yè 页

page² v/t (call) chuánhū 传呼

pager chuánhūjī 传呼机

pagoda bǎotǎ 宝塔

pail tǒng 桶

pain téngtòng 疼痛

painful téngtòng 疼痛; (distressing) lìngrén tòngkǔ 令人痛苦

painkiller zhǐtòngpiàn 止痛片

paint 1 n túliào 涂料; (for artist) yánliào 颜料 2 v/t wall etc shàng túliào 上涂料; picture yòng yánliào huà 用颜料画 3 v/i (as art form) huìhuà 绘画

painter (artist) huàjiā 画家

painting (activity) huìhuà 绘画; (picture) túhuà 图画

pair duì 对; a ~ of shoes / sandals yìshuāng xié / liángxié 一双鞋 / 凉鞋

pajamas shuìyīkù 睡衣裤

pale person cāngbái 苍白

palm (of hand) shǒuzhǎng 手掌

pamphlet xiǎocèzi 小册子

pan n guō 锅

panic 1 n kǒnghuāng 恐慌 2 v/i shòujīng 受惊

**pant** v/i chuǎnxī 喘息

**panties** nèikù 内裤

**pants** kùzi 裤子

**pantyhose** liánkùwà 连裤袜

**paper** n 1 n zhǐ 纸; (news~) bàozhǐ 报纸; (academic) lùnwén 论文; (examination ~) kǎoshìjuàn 考试卷; ~s (documents) wénjiàn 文件; (identity ~s) zhèngjiàn 证件

**paperback** píngzhuāngshū 平装书

**parade** n (procession) yuèbīng 阅兵

**paradise** lèyuán 乐园; fig tiāntáng 天堂

**paragraph** duànluò 段落

**parallel** n (line) píngxíngxiàn 平行线; fig xiāngsì zhīchù 相似之处

**paralyze** tānhuàn 瘫痪; fig bù zhīsuǒcuò 不知所措

**paramedic** hùlǐ rényuán 护理人员

**paranoia** wàngxiǎngkuáng 妄想狂

**paranoid** adj duōyí 多疑

**parcel** n bāoguǒ 包裹

**pardon** v/t yuánliàng 原谅; LAW shèmiǎn 赦免; ~ me? nǐ shuō shénme? 你说

什么？

**parent** jiāzhǎng 家长

**parental** fùmǔ 父母

**park¹** (area) gōngyuán 公园

**park²** MOT 1 v/t tíngfàng 停放 2 v/i tíngchē 停车

**parking** MOT tíngchē 停车

**parking garage** shìnèi tíngchēchǎng 室内停车场

**parking lot** tíngchēchǎng 停车场

**parking meter** tíngchējìshí shōufèiqì 停车计时收费器

**parking ticket** wéizhāng tíngchē fákuǎndān 违章停车罚款单

**parliament** yìhuì 议会

**part** n (section, area) bùfen 部分; (of machine) língjiàn 零件; (in play, movie) juésè 角色; (in hair) fèng 缝; **take ~ in** cānjiā 参加

**participate** cānjiā 参加

**particular** (specific) tèbié 特别; (special) tèshū 特殊; (fussy) tiāoti 挑剔

**particularly** tèbié 特别

**partition** n (screen) píngfēng 屏风; (of country) fēnliè 分裂

**partly** bùfen 部分

**partner** COM héhuǒrén 合伙人；(in relationship) tóngbàn 同伴；(in activity) dādàng 搭档

**partnership** COM héhuǒ jīngyíng 合伙经营；(in activity) dādàng guānxi 搭档关系

**part-time** adj & adv jiānzhí 兼职

**party** n qìngzhùhuì 庆祝会；POL dǎng 党；(group) zǔ 组

**party member** dǎngyuán 党员

**pass** 1 n (for entrance) tōngxíngzhèng 通行证；SP chuánqiú 传球；(in mountains) guān'ài 关隘 2 v/t (hand) dì dì 递；(go past) jīngguò jīngùo；car, cyclist yuèguò 越过；(go beyond) chāoguò 超过；(approve) biǎojué tōngguò 表决通过；SP chuánqiú 传球；**~ an exam** tōngguò kǎoshì 通过考试 3 v/i (of time) tuīyí 推移；(in exam) jígé 及格

**passage** (corridor) tōngdào 通道；(from book) yíduàn 一段

**passenger** chéngkè 乘客

**passer-by** guòlùrén 过路人

**passion** (fervor) rèqíng 热情；(sexual) xìng'ài 性爱

**passive** adj bèidòng 被动

**passport** hùzhào 护照

**password** kǒulìng 口令

**past** 1 adj (former) yǐqián 以前；**the ~ few days** jìnjǐtiān 近几天 2 n guòqù 过去；**in the ~** zài guòqù 在过去 3 prep (in time) chíyú 迟于；(in position) jīngguò 经过；**it's half ~ two** xiànzài liǎngdiǎnbàn 现在两点半

**pastime** xiāoqiǎn 消遣

**pastry** (for pie) yóusū miàntuán 油酥面团

**paternal** relative fùxì 父系；pride, love fùqīnbān 父亲般

**paternity** fùqin shēnfen 父亲身分

**path** xiǎolù 小路

**pathetic** zhāorén liánmǐn 招人怜悯；F (bad) kěbēi 可悲

**patience** nàixīn 耐心

**patient** n bìngrén 病人 2 adj yǒu nàixīn 有耐心

**patriotic** àiguó 爱国

**patrol 1** *n* xúnluóduì 巡逻队
**2** *v/t* xúnluó 巡逻

**patrolman** xúnjǐng 巡警

**patronizing** gāorén yìděng
高人一等

**pattern** *n* (*on fabric*) tú'àn 图
案; (*for sewing*) yàngshì 样
式; (*model*) móxíng 模型;
(*in events*) fāngshì 方式

**pause 1** *n & v/i* tíngdùn 停
顿 **2** *v/t tape* zàntíng 暂停

**pavement** (*roadway*) lùmiàn
路面

**paw** *n* zhuǎzi 爪子

**pay 1** *n* xīnjīn 薪金 **2** *v/t
employee* fùqián gěi fù
钱给; *sum, bill* fù fù 付
**3** *v/i* fùzhàng 付帐; (*be
profitable*) yǒu lìrùn 有
利润

**pay check** xīnjīn zhīpiào 薪
金支票

**payday** fāxīnrì 发薪日

**payment** (*of bill*) fùkuǎn
付款; (*money*) fùchūde
kuǎnxiàng 付出的款项

**pay phone** gōngyòng
diànhuà 公用电话

**PC** (= *personal computer*)
gèrén diànnǎo 个人电
脑; (= *politically correct*)

détǐ 得体

**peace** hépíng 和平; (*quiet*)
níngjìng 宁静

**peaceful** píngjìng 平静

**peak** *n* (*of mountain*) shāndǐng 山顶; *fig* dǐngfēng
顶峰

**peak hours** gāofēng shíjiān
高峰时间

**pear** lí 梨

**Pearl River** Zhūjiāng 珠江

**peck** *n & v/t* (*bite*) zhuó 啄

**peculiar** (*odd*) qíguài 奇怪

**pedal** *n* (*of bike*) tàbǎn 踏板

**pedal rickshaw** dàoqílú 倒
骑驴

**pedestrian** *n* xíngrén 行人

**pediatrician** érkēzhuān jiā 儿
科专家

**pedicab** sānlúnchē 三轮车

**peel 1** *n* guǒpí 果皮 **2** *v/t
fruit* xiāopí 削皮 **3** *v/i* (*of
skin*) tuōluò 脱落

**peer** *v/i* níngshì 凝视; ~ *at*
zǐxìkàn 仔细看

**Peking Opera** Jīngjù 京剧

**pen** *n* (*ballpoint*) yuánzhūbǐ
圆珠笔

**penalize** bùlìyú 不利于

**penalty** chéngfá 惩罚; SP
fáqiú 罚球

**penalty clause** wéiyuē fákuǎn tiáokuǎn 违约罚款条款

**pencil** qiānbǐ 铅笔

**penetrate** chuāntòu 穿透；*market* dǎrù 打入

**penicillin** qīngméisù 青霉素

**peninsula** bàndǎo 半岛

**penitentiary** jiānyù 监狱

**pension** yǎnglǎojīn 养老金

**Pentagon: the ~** Wǔjiǎo Dàlóu 五角大楼

**penthouse** dǐngcéng gōngyù 顶层公寓

**people** rén 人；*(race, tribe)* mínzú 民族

**People's Commune** Rénmín Gōngshè 人民公社

**pepper** hújiāofěn 胡椒粉；*(vegetable)* làjiāo 辣椒

**percent** bǎifēnzhī 百分之

**perception** *(with senses)* gǎnzhī nénglì 感知能力；*(of situation)* kànfǎ 看法

**perfect 1** *adj* wánměi 完美 **2** *v/t* wánshàn 完善

**perfection** wánměi 完美

**perfectly** jíjiā 极佳；*(totally)* wánquán 完全

**perform** *v/t (carry out)* zuò 做；*(of actor)* biǎoyǎn 表演

**performance** *(by actor*

*etc)* biǎoyǎn 表演；*(of employee, company etc)* biǎoxiàn 表现；*(of machine)* xìngnéng 性能

**perfume** xiāngshuǐ 香水；*(of flower)* xiāngwèi 香味

**perhaps** yěxǔ 也许

**peril** wēixiǎn 危险

**perimeter** zhōubiān 周边

**period** yíduàn 一段；*(menstruation)* yuèjīng 月经；*(punctuation)* jùhào 句号

**perjury** wěizhèng 伪证

**permanent** *adj* yǒngjiǔ 永久

**permanently** chángqī 长期

**permission** xǔkě 许可

**permit 1** n xǔkězhèng 许可证 **2** *v/t* róngxǔ 容许

**perpetual** chíxù 持续

**persecute** pòhài 迫害

**persecution** pòhài 迫害

**persist** chíxù 持续；**~ in** zhíyì zuò 执意做

**persistent** *person* gùzhí 固执；*questions, rain etc* chíxù búduàn 持续不断

**person** rén 人；**in ~** qīnzì 亲自

**personal** *(private)* sīrén 私人；*(of an individual)* gèrén

个人

**personal computer** gèrén diànnǎo 个人电脑

**personality** gèxìng 个性; *(celebrity)* míngrén 名人

**personally** *(for my part)* jiù wǒláishuō 就我来说; *(in person)* qīnzì 亲自

**personnel** zhíyuán 职员; *(department)* rénshì bùmén 人事部门

**perspiration** hànshuǐ 汗水

**persuade** shuōfú 说服

**persuasion** quànshuō 劝说

**pessimist** bēiguānzhě 悲观者

**pessimistic** bēiguān 悲观

**pest** *(bird)* hàiniǎo 害鸟; *(insect)* hàichóng 害虫; *(animal)* hàishòu 害兽

**pester** jiūchán 纠缠

**pesticide** shāchóngjì 杀虫剂

**pet 1** *n* chǒngwù 宠物 **2** *adj* *(favorite)* zuì xǐhuān 最喜欢

**petition** *n* qǐngyuànshū 请愿书

**petrochemical** shíyóu huàxué chǎnpǐn 石油化学产品

**petroleum** shíyóu 石油

**petty** *person* xiǎoqì 小气; *details, problem* suǒsuì 琐碎

**pharmaceuticals** zhìyào gōngsī 制药公司

**pharmacist** yàoshāng 药商

**pharmacy** *(store)* yàofáng 药房

**phase** jiēduàn 阶段

**philosopher** zhéxuéjiā 哲学家

**philosophical** yǒu zhélǐ 有哲理

**philosophy** zhéxué 哲学

**phobia** kǒngbùzhèng 恐怖症

**phone 1** *n* diànhuàjī 电话机 **2** *v/t & v/i* dǎ diànhuà 打电话

**phone book** diànhuàbù 电话簿

**phone booth** diànhuàtíng 电话亭

**phonecall** diànhuà 电话

**phone number** diànhuà hàomǎ 电话号码

**phon(e)y** *adj* wěizhuāng 伪装

**photo** *n* xiàngpiàn 相片

**photocopier** yǐngyìnjī 影印机

**photocopy 1** *n* yǐngyìnběn 影印本 **2** *v/t* yǐngyìn 影印

**photographer** shèyǐngshī 摄影师

**photography** shèyǐng 摄影

**phrase** *n* piànyǔ 片语

**physical** *adj* (*of the body*) shēntǐ 身体

**physician** yīshēng 医生

**physicist** wùlǐ xuéjiā 物理学家

**physics** wùlǐ 物理

**physiotherapy** lǐliáo 理疗

**piano** gāngqín 钢琴

**pick** *v/t* (*choose*) xuǎn 选; *flowers, fruit* cǎi 采

**♦ pick up** *v/t* náqǐ 拿起; (*from ground*) jiǎnqǐ 拣起; (*collect*) qǔhuí 取回; (*from airport etc*) jiē 接; (*in car*) ràngrén dābiànchē 让人搭便车; (*in sexual sense*) gōuyǐn 勾引; *skill* xuéhuì 学会

**pick-up (truck)** qīngxíng xiǎohuòchē 轻型小货车

**picnic** *n & v/i* yěcān 野餐

**picture 1** *n* (*photo*) zhàopiàn 照片; (*painting*) huìhuà 绘画; (*illustration*) chātú 插图; (*movie*) diànyǐng 电影

**picturesque** rúhuà 如画

**pie** pài 派

**piece** (*fragment*) suìpiàn 碎片; (*component*) bùfen 部分; (*in board game*) zǐr 子儿; **a ~ of pie / bread** yíkuài pài / miànbāo 一块派/面包

**pierce** (*penetrate*) cìtòu 刺透; *ears* zhāyǎn 扎眼

**pig** zhū 猪; (*unpleasant person*) húndàn 混蛋

**pigeon** gēzi 鸽子

**pile** duī 堆

**pill** yào 药; **the ~** kǒufú bìyùnyào 口服避孕药

**pillar** zhùzi 柱子

**pillow** *n* zhěntou 枕头

**pilot** *n* (*of airplane*) fēixíngyuán 飞行员

**pilot plant** shìyàn qū 试验区

**PIN (= personal identification number)** mìmǎ 密码

**pin** *n* (*for sewing*) dàtóuzhēn 大头针; (*in bowling*) mùzhù 木柱; (*badge*) huīzhāng 徽章

**pinch** *n* niē 捏; (*of salt etc*) yìniē 一捏

**pine** n (*tree*) sōngshù 松树;
(*wood*) sōngmù 松木

**pineapple** bōluó 菠萝

**pink** fěnhóngsè 粉红色

**pinyin** pīnyīn 拼音

**pioneering** adj kāituò 开拓

**pipe** n guǎnzi 管子; (*to
smoke*) yāndǒu 烟斗

**pipeline** guǎndào 管道

**pirate** v/t software etc dàobǎn
盗版

**pistol** shǒuqiāng 手枪

**pitch** 1 n tóngqíng 同情; *it's a ~
that …* yíhàn … 遗憾 2 v/i
(*in baseball*)
tóuqiú 投球 2 v/t tent dā
搭; *ball* tóu 投

**pitcher**[1] (*in baseball*) tóushǒu
投手

**pitcher**[2] n (*container*) guàn 罐

**pitiful** lìngrén liánmǐn 令
人怜悯

**pity** n tóngqíng 同情; *it's a ~
that …* yíhàn … 遗憾

**pizza** bǐsà 比萨

**PLA** (= *People's Liberation
Army*) Jiěfàngjūn 解放军

**place** 1 n dìfang 地方; (*bar,
restaurant*) cānyǐnchù 餐
饮处; (*home*) jiā 家; (*seat*)
zuòwèi 座位; *at my / his ~*
zài wǒ / tānr 在我 / 他那
儿 2 v/t fàng 放

**plain** adj (*clear*) qīngchǔ 清
楚; (*not patterned*) méiyǒu
túàn 没有图案

**plan** 1 n jìhuà 计划;
(*drawing*) shèjìtú 设计图
2 v/t (*prepare*) zhǔnbèi 准
备; (*design*) shèjì 设计; *~
to do X* dǎsuàn zuò X 打
算做X

**plane** (*airplane*) fēijī 飞机

**planet** xíngxīng 行星

**plank** mùbǎn 木板

**planning** jìhuà 计划

**plant**[1] 1 n zhíwù 植物 2 v/t
zhòng 种

**plant**[2] n (*factory*) chǎng 厂;
(*equipment*) shèbèi 设备

**plaque** (*on wall*) shìbǎn
饰板

**plaster** n (*on wall*) huīní
灰泥

**plastic** n & adj sùliào 塑料

**plastic surgery** zhěngxíng
wàikē 整形外科

**plate** n (*for food*) pánzi 盘子

**platform** wǔtái 舞台; (*at
station*) zhàntái 站台

**platinum** n & adj bó 铂

**play** 1 n (*in theater, on TV*)
jù 剧; (*of children*) yóuxì
游戏 2 v/i (*of children*)

wánr 玩儿; (of musician) tánzòu 弹奏; (SP: perform) dǎ 打; (SP: take part) cānsài 参赛 3 v/t instrument tán 弹; music wánzòu 演奏; game wánr 玩儿; opponent yǔ... bǐsài 与... 比赛; role bànyǎn 扮演

**player** SP yùndòngyuán 运动员; (musician) yǎnzòuzhě 演奏者; (actor) yǎnyuán 演员

**playing card** zhǐpái 纸牌

**playwright** jùzuòjiā 剧作家

**plea** n kěnqiú 恳求

**plead** v/i qǐngqiú 请求; ~ for kěnqiú 恳求; ~ guilty / not guilty fú 服/ bùfú zuì 服/ 不服罪

**pleasant** lìngrén yúkuài 令人愉快

**please** 1 adv qǐng 请; more tea? – yes, ~ hái yào chá ma? – hǎode, xièxiè 还要茶吗? – 好的, 谢谢; ~ do méiwèntí 没问题 2 v/t shǐ gāoxìng 使高兴

**pleased** gāoxìng 高兴; ~ to meet you hěn gāoxìng rènshí nǐ 很高兴认识你

**pleasure** kuàilè 快乐; (as opposed to work) yúlè 娱乐

**plenty** fùzú 富足; ~ of xǔduō 许多

**plot** 1 n yīnmóu 阴谋; (of novel) qíngjié 情节 2 v/t & v/i mìmóu 密谋

**plow** 1 n lí 犁 2 v/t & v/i gēngdì 耕地

**plug** n (for bath) sāizi 塞子; ELEC chātóu 插头; (for new book etc) xuānchuán 宣传

**plum** n lǐzi 李子

**plumber** shuǐnuǎngōng 水暖工

**plumbing** (pipes) guǎndào zhuāngzhì 管道装置

**plump** adj fēngmǎn 丰满

**plunge** v/i tūrán diēluò 突然跌落; (of prices) xiàdiē 下跌

**plus** prep jiāshàng 加上

**pneumonia** fèiyán 肺炎

**poach** v/t & v/i salmon etc tōubǔ 偷捕

**poached egg** wò jīdàn 卧鸡蛋

**P.O. Box** yóuzhèng xìnxiāng 邮政信箱

**pocket** n kǒudài 口袋

**pocketbook** (woman's) xiǎo shǒutíbāo 小手提

包; (*wallet*) qiánbāo 钱包; (*book*) píngzhuāngshū 平装书

**poem** *n* shī 诗

**poet** shīrén 诗人

**poetry** shīgē 诗歌

**point 1** *n* (*of knife etc*) jiānduān 尖端; (*in contest*) fēn 分; (*purpose*) yìyì 意义; (*in discussion*) guāndiǎn 观点; (*in decimals*) diǎn 点 **2** *v/i* zhǐ 指

♦ **point at** zhǐxiàng 指向

♦ **point out** *sights* shǐ zhùyì 使注意; *advantages etc* zhǐchū 指出

**pointless** wúyìyì 无意义

**poison** *n* dúyào 毒药

**poke** *v/t* tǒng 捅; (*stick*) shēnchū 伸出

**pole** (*of wood, metal*) gān gǎn 杆杆

**police** *n* jǐngfāng 警方

**policeman** jǐngchá 警察

**police station** jǐngchájú 警察局

**policy**[1] *n* zhèngcè 政策

**policy**[2]: *insurance* ~ bǎoxiǎndān 保险单

**polish 1** *n* cāguāngjì 擦光剂 **2** *v/t* cāliàng 擦亮

**Politbureau** Zhèngzhìjú

政治局

**polite** yǒu lǐmào 有礼貌

**politeness** lǐmào 礼貌

**political** zhèngzhì 政治

**politician** zhèngzhìjiā 政治家

**politics** zhèngzhì 政治

**poll** *n* (*survey*) mínyì cèyàn 民意测验

**pollute** wūrǎn 污染

**pollution** wūrǎn 污染

**pond** chítáng 池塘

**ponytail** mǎwěifà 马尾发

**pool**[1] (*swimming* ~) chí 池; (*of water, blood*) tān 摊

**pool**[2] (*game*) pǔ'ěrdànzǐ xì 普尔弹子戏

**poor** *adj* pínqióng 贫穷; (*not good*) bùhǎo 不好; (*unfortunate*) bùxíng 不幸

**pop**[1] *v/i* (*of balloon etc*) fāchū pēngde yīshēng 发出砰的一声

**pop**[2] *n* MUS liúxíng yīnyuè 流行音乐

**Popsicle**® bàngbàngbīng 棒棒冰

**popular** shòu huānyíng 受欢迎; *belief, support* pǔbiàn 普遍

**popularity** (*of person*)

shēngwàng 声望

**population** rénkǒu 人口

**porcelain** n & adj cí 瓷

**pork** zhūròu 猪肉

**pornographic** huángsè 黄色

**pornography** sèqíng zuòpǐn 色情作品

**port** n (town) gǎngshì 港市; (area) gǎngkǒu 港口; COMPUT duānkǒu 端口

**portable** adj shǒutíshì 手提式; **~ TV** wēixíng diànshì 微型电视

**porter** (at railroad station) bānyùngōng 搬运工; (doorman) ménwèi 门卫

**portion** n (of food) fèn 份

**portrait** n xiàoxiàng 肖像

**pose** v/i (for artist) bǎi zīshì 摆姿势

**position 1** n (location) wèizhi 位置; (stance) zīshì 姿势; (in race, competition) wèi 位; (point of view) lìchǎng 立场; (situation) chǔjìng 处境 **2** v/t ānfàng 安放

**positive** attitude lèguān 乐观; response biǎoshì tóngyì 表示同意; medical test yángxìng 阳性; GRAM kěndìng 肯定; ELEC zhèngjí

正极

**possession** chíyǒu 持有; (thing owned) cáichǎn 财产; **~s** suǒyǒuwù 所有物

**possibility** kěnéngxìng 可能性

**possible** kěnéng 可能; **the best ~ ...** jìn kěnéng zuìhǎo ... 尽可能最好...

**possibly** kěnéng 可能; (perhaps) yěxǔ 也许

**post¹ 1** n (of wood, metal) gānzi 杆子 **2** v/t notice zhāngtiē 张贴

**post²** v/t guards bùzhì 布置

**postage** yóuzī 邮资

**postcard** míngxìnpiàn 明信片

**postdate** tiánwǎn rìqī 填晚日期

**poster** hǎibào 海报

**posting** (assignment) wěipài 委派

**postmark** yóuchuō 邮戳

**post office** yóujú 邮局

**postpone** tuīchí 推迟

**pot** (for cooking) guō 锅; (for coffee, tea) hú 壶; (for plant) pén 盆

**potato** tǔdòu 土豆

**potato chips** zháshǔpiàn

炸薯片

**potential 1** *adj* kěnéng chūxiàn 可能出现 **2** *n* qiánlì 潜力

**pothole** (*in road*) kēngwā 坑洼

**poultry** (*birds*) jiāqín 家禽; (*meat*) jiāqínròu 家禽肉

**pound**¹ *n* (*weight*) bàng 磅

**pound**² *v/i* (*of heart*) jùliè tiàodòng 剧烈跳动

**pound sterling** yīngbàng 英镑

**pour** *v/t liquid* dào 倒

**poverty** pínkùn 贫困

**powder** *n* fěnmò 粉末; (*for face*) fěn 粉

**powder room** nǚcèsuǒ 女厕所

**power** *n* (*strength*) lì 力; (*authority*) quánlì 权力; (*energy*) néngliàng 能量; (*electricity*) diàn 电

**power cut** tíngdiàn 停电

**powerful** qiángyǒulì 强有力

**powerless** wúlìliàng 无力量

**power station** fādiànzhàn 发电站

**PR** (= *public relations*) gōngguān 公关

**practical** *experience* shíjì 实际; *person* xiànshí 现实; (*functional*) shíyòng 实用

**practice 1** *n* liànxí 练习; (*rehearsal*) páiliàn 排练; (*custom*) chángguī 常规 **2** *v/i* xùnliàn 训练 **3** *v/t* liànxí 练习; *law, medicine* zhíyè 执业

**praise 1** *n* zànyù 赞誉 **2** *v/t* chēngzàn 称赞

**precaution** yùfáng cuòshī 预防措施

**precede** *v/t* xiānyú 先于

**precious** bǎoguì 宝贵

**precise** zhǔnquè 准确

**precisely** jīngquè 精确

**predecessor** (*in job*) qiánrènzhě 前任者

**predict** yùyán 预言

**predominant** zhàn yōushì 占优势

**predominantly** zhǔyào 主要

**preface** *n* qiányán 前言

**prefer** gèng xǐhuān 更喜欢

**preferable** gèng chènxīn 更称心

**preference** piān'ài 偏爱

**preferential** yōuxiān 优先

**pregnancy** yùnqī 孕期

**pregnant** huáiyùn 怀孕

**prejudice** *n* piānjiàn 偏见

preliminary adj yùbèixìng 预备性

premature: ~ birth zǎochǎn 早产

première n shǒucì gōngyǎn 首次公演

premises dìfang 地方

premium n (insurance) bǎoxiǎnfèi 保险费

prepare v/t zhǔnbèi 准备

prescription MED yàofāng 药方

presence zàichǎng 在场

present¹ 1 adj (current) mùqián 目前; be ~ zàichǎng 在场 2 n: the ~ xiànzài 现在; GRAM xiànzàishí 现在时; at ~ cǐkè 此刻

present² 1 n (gift) lǐwù 礼物 2 v/t award shòuyǔ 授予; program zhǔchí 主持

presentation (to audience) bàogào 报告

presently (at the moment) xiànzài 现在; (soon) bùjiǔ 不久

preserve v/t peace etc wéihù 维护; wood etc bǎohù 保护; food bǎocún 保存

presidency zǒngtǒng zhíwèi

president POL zǒngtǒng 总统; (of company) dǒngshìzhǎng 董事长

presidential zǒngtǒng 总统

press 1 n: the ~ xīnwénjiè 新闻界 2 v/t button àn 按; clothes yùn 熨

pressure n yālì 压力 2 v/t qiǎngpò 强迫

prestige wēiwàng 威望

presumably dàgài 大概

pretend v/i jiǎzhuāng 假装

pretense xūjiǎ 虚假

pretext jièkǒu 借口

pretty 1 adj piàoliang 漂亮 2 adv (quite) xiāngdāng 相当

prevent fángzhǐ 止止; ~ X (from) doing Y zǔzhǐ X zuò Y 阻止X做Y

preview n yùzhǎn 预展

previous qiányī 前一

prey n lièwù 猎物

price n jiàgé 价格

priceless wújià 无价

pride n zìháo 自豪; (self-respect) zìzūn 自尊

priest mùshī 牧师

primary 1 adj zhǔyào 主要 2 n POL chūxuǎn 初选

**prime minister** shǒuxiàng
首相

**primitive** yuánshǐ 原始；
*conditions* jiǎnlòu 简陋

**principal 1** *adj* zhǔyào 主要
**2** *n* EDU xiàozhǎng 校长

**principle** *moral* zhǔnzé 准
则；*(rule)* yuánzé 原则

**print 1** *n* *(in book)* yìnshuā
zìtǐ 印刷字体；*out of ~*
juébǎn 绝版 **2** *v/t* yìnshuā
印刷；COMPUT dǎyìn 打印

**printer** dǎyìnjī 打印机；
*(person)* yìnshuāshāng
印刷商

**prior** *adj* shìxiān 事先

**prioritize** *(order)* huàfēn
qīngzhònghuǎnjí 划分轻
重缓急；*(put first)* jǐyǔ
yōuxiān 给予优先

**priority** yàowèi 要位

**prison** jiānyù 监狱

**prisoner** qiúfàn 囚犯

**privacy** sīrén kōngjiān 私
人空间

**private** *adj* sīrén 私人

**privately** *(in private)* sīxià
私下；*owned* gèrén 个人；
*(inwardly)* nèixīn 内心

**privilege** *(special treatment)*
tèquán 特权；*(honor)*

róngxìng 荣幸

**prize** *n* jiǎngshǎng 奖赏

**prizewinner** huòjiǎngzhě
获奖者

**probability** kěnéngxìng 可
能性

**probable** hěn kěnéng 很
可能

**probably** yěxǔ 也许

**probe** *n* *(investigation)*
diàochá 调查

**problem** wèntí 问题

**procedure** bùzhòu 步骤

**process 1** *n* guòchéng 过
程 **2** *v/t food, materials*
jiāgōng 加工；*data* chǔlǐ 处
理；*application etc* shěnchá
审查

**produce 1** *n* chǎnpǐn 产品
**2** *v/t commodity* shēngchǎn
生产；*(bring about)* yǐnqǐ
引起；*(bring out)* náchū 拿
出；*play, movie* zhìzuò
制作

**producer** zhìzào chǎngjiā 制
造厂家；*(of play, movie)*
zhìpiānrén 制片人

**product** chǎnpǐn 产品

**production** chǎnliàng 产量；
*(play, movie)* zuòpǐn 作品

**productive** duōchǎn 多

产; *talks* yǒu chéngxiào
有成效

**productivity** shēngchǎnlì
生产力

**profession** zhíyè 职业

**professional 1** *adj* zhuānyè
专业; *work* yǒu jìqiǎo 有
技巧 **2** *n* zhuānyè rénshì
专业人士; *(not amateur)*
zhíyè rényuán 职业人员

**professor** jiàoshòu 教授

**profit** *n* lìrùn 利润

**profitable** kěhuò lìrùn 可
获利润

**profit margin** lìrùnlǜ 利
润率

**program** *n* jìhuà 计划;
*(radio, TV)* jiémù 节目;
COMPUT chéngxù 程序;
THEA jiémùdān 节目单

**programmer** COMPUT
chéngxùyuán 程序员

**progress 1** *n* jìnbù 进步
**2** *v/i* jìnzhǎn 进
展; *(make ~)* qǔdé jìnbù 取
得进步

**project**[1] *n* *(plan)* jìhuà 计
划; *(undertaking)* xiàngmù
项目; *(houses)* tǒngjiàn
zhùzháiqū 统建住宅区

**project**[2] **1** *v/t figures* jìhuà jì

划 **2** *v/i* *(stick out)* tūchū
突出

**projection** *(forecast)* yùcè
预测

**projector** *(for slides)*
fàngyìngjī 放映机

**proletariat** wúchǎn jiējí 无
产阶级

**prolong** yáncháng 延长

**prom** *(dance)* wǔhuì 舞会

**promise 1** *n* chéngnuò 承诺
**2** *v/t* xǔnuò 许诺

**promote** *employee* jìnshēng
晋升; COM xuānchuán
宣传

**promotion** *(of employee)*
jìnjí 晋级; COM cùxiāo
促销

**prompt** *adj* *(on time)* zhǔnshí
准时; *(speedy)* jíshí 及时

**pronounce** *word* fāyīn 发音

**proof** *n* zhèngjù 证据

**propaganda** xuānchuán
宣传

**proper** *(real)* zhēnzhèng 真
正; *(correct)* qiàdàng 恰当;
*(fitting)* shìdàng 适当

**properly** zhèngquè 正确

**property** cáichǎn 财产;
*(land)* fángdìchǎn 房地产

**proportions** miànjī 面积

**proposal** tíyì 提议; (of marriage) qiúhūn 求婚

**propose 1** v/t (suggest) jiànyì 建议; (plan) jìhuà 计划 **2** v/i (to marry) qiúhūn 求婚

**prosecute** v/t LAW tíqǐ gōngsù 提起公诉

**prosperous** xīngwàng 兴旺

**prostitute** n jìnǔ 妓女

**protect** v/t bǎohù 保护

**protection** bǎohù 保护

**protest 1** n kàngyì 抗议; (demonstration) shìwēi 示威 **2** v/i shēngbiàn 声辩; (demonstrate) shìwēi 示威

**proud** jiāo'ào 骄傲; **be ~ of** yǐ …wéi zìháo 以…为自豪

**prove** zhèngmíng 证明

**provide** tígōng 提供; **~d (that)** zhǐyào 只要

**province** shěng 省

**provisional** línshí 临时

**provoke** (cause) yǐnqǐ 引起; (annoy) jīnù 激怒

**proximity** línjìn 邻近

**psychiatric** jīngshénbìng 精神病

**psychiatrist** jīngshénkēyī shēng 精神科医生

**psychiatry** jīngshénbìngxué 精神病学

**psychoanalysis** jīngshén fēnxī 精神分析

**psychoanalyst** jīngshén fēnxīxuéjiā 精神分析学家

**psychological** xīnlǐ 心理

**psychologist** xīnlǐ xuéjiā 心理学家

**psychology** xīnlǐxué 心理学

**public 1** adj gōngzhòng 公众 **2** n: **the ~** mínzhòng 民众

**publication** (of book) chūbǎn 出版; (by newspaper) kānchū 刊出

**publicity** xuānchuán 宣传

**publicly** dāngzhòng 当众

**public relations** gōngguān 公关

**publish** chūbǎn 出版

**publisher** chūbǎnshè 出版社

**pull 1** n (on rope) lā 拉 **2** v/t (drag) lā 拉; (tug) chě 扯; muscle lāshāng 拉伤 **3** v/i zhuài 拽

♦ **pull out** v/i (of agreement, competition) tuìchū 退出

**pulse** màibó 脉搏

**pump** n bèng 泵

punch **1** n (*blow*) jīdǎ 击打
**2** v/t (*with fist*) yòng quán
jī 用拳击

punctual zhǔnshí 准时

punish chéngfá 惩罚

punishment chéngfá 惩罚

pupil (*student*) xuésheng
学生

purchase n & v/t gòumǎi
购买

purchaser mǎizhǔ 买主

pure silk chún 纯; air, water
jiéjìng 洁净; (*morally*)
chúnjié 纯洁

purely wánquán 完全

purify water jìnghuà 净化

purpose (*aim, object*) mùdì
目的; **on ~** gùyì 故意

purse n (*pocketbook*)
shǒudài 手袋

pursue v/t person zhuīzhú
追逐; course of action jìxù
jìnxíng 继续进行

pursuer zhuīgǎnzhě 追赶者

push v/t tuī 推; button àn 按;

(*pressure*) bīpò 逼迫

put fàng 放; *question* wèn 问

♦ put down fàngxià 放下;
*deposit* fù dìngjīn 付定金;
*rebellion* zhènyā 镇压

♦ put off *light, TV* guāndiào
关掉; (*deter*) shǐ rén búzuò
使人不做

♦ put on *light, TV* dǎkāi
打开; *music* fàng 放;
*jacket* chuān 穿; *make-up*
cháyòng 搽用

♦ put out *hand* shēnchū伸
出; *fire* xīmiè 熄灭; *light*
guāndiào 关掉

♦ put up v/t *hand* jǔqǐ 举起;
(*give a bed*) gōngyìng shísù
供应食宿; (*erect*) shùqǐ
竖起; *price* tígāo 提高;
*poster* zhāngtiē 张贴

♦ put up with rěnshòu 忍受

puzzle **1** n (*mystery*) mí
谜; (*game*) zhìlì yóuxì 智
力游戏 **2** v/t shǐ kùnhuò
使困惑

# Q

qualification wénpíng 文凭

qualified *nurse etc* hégé 合格

qualify v/i EDU qǔdé zīgé 取
得资格; (*in contest*) qǔdé

bǐsài zīgé 取得比赛资格

**quality** zhìliàng 质量;
  (*characteristic*) tèxìng 特性

**quantity** liàng 量

**quarrel** n & v/i chǎozuǐ 吵嘴

**quart** kuātuō 夸脱

**quarter** n sìfēn zhīyī 四分之
  一; ~ *of an hour* yīkèzhōng
  一刻钟; a ~ *of 5* wǔdiǎn
  chà yīkè 五点差一刻;
  ~ *after 5* wǔdiǎn yīkè 五
  点一刻

**quarterfinal** sìfēn zhīyī
  juésài 四分之一决赛

**quarterly** adj & adv jìdù
  季度

**query** 1 n yíwèn 疑问 2 v/t
  (*doubt*) duì... biǎoshì
  yíwèn 对... 表示疑问

**question** 1 n wèntí 问题
  2 v/t person wèn 问;
  (*doubt*) huáiyí 怀疑

**question mark** wènhào 问
  号

**questionnaire** wènjuàn 问卷

**quick** kuài 快

**quickly** kuài 快

**quiet** xiǎoshēng 小声; *street*
  ānjìng 安静; *town* píngjìng
  平静

**quit** v/t & v/i cízhí 辞职

**quite** (*fairly*) xiāngdāng
  相当; (*completely*)
  wánquán 完全; *I didn't
  ~ understand* wǒbù tài
  míngbai 我不太明白; ~!
  zhèngshì zhèyàng! 正是这
  样！; ~ *a lot* hěn duō很多;
  *it was ~ a surprise* zhēn
  jīngrén真惊人

**quiz** n wèndá bǐsài 问答
  比赛

**quota** dìngliàng 定量

**quote** 1 n (*from author*)
  yǐnwén 引文; (*price*) bàojià
  报价; (~ *mark*) yǐnhào 引
  号 2 v/t text yǐnyòng 引用;
  *price* bàojià 报价

# R

**rabbit** tùzi 兔子

**race 1** n SP jìngsài 竞赛; *the
  ~s* (*horse ~s*) pǎomǎ 跑马

**2** v/i (*run fast*) jíxíng 疾行

**racial** zhǒngzú 种族

**racism** zhǒngzú qíshì 种

族歧视

**racist** n zhǒngzú qíshìzhě 种族歧视者

**rack** n (for bikes) zìxíngchējià 自行车架; (for bags on train) xínglijià 行李架; (for CDs) chàngpiān jià 唱片架

**racket¹** SP qiúpāi 球拍

**racket²** (noise) xuānnào 喧闹; criminal piànjú 骗局

**radar** léidá 雷达

**radiator** nuǎnqì 暖气; (in car) qǔnuǎnqì 取暖器

**radical 1** adj chèdǐ 彻底; POL jījìn 激进 **2** n POL jījìn zhǔyìzhě 激进主义者

**radio** shōuyīnjī 收音机

**radioactive** fàngshèxìng 放射性

**rag** (for cleaning) mābù 抹布

**rage** n kuángnù 狂怒

**raid 1** n (MIL, by police) tūxí 突袭; (by robbers) qiǎngjié 抢劫 **2** v/t (MIL, of police) tūrán sōuchá 突然搜查; (of robbers) tūrán xíjī 突然袭击

**rail** (on track) tiěguǐ 铁轨; (hand~) fúshǒu 扶手

**railings** lángān 栏杆

**railroad** tiělù 铁路

**railroad station** huǒchēzhàn 火车站

**rain 1** n yǔ 雨; the ~s yǔjì 雨季 **2** v/i xiàyǔ 下雨; it's ~ing xià zhe yǔne 下着雨呢

**raincoat** yǔyī 雨衣

**raise 1** n (in pay) zēngjiā 增加 **2** v/t children fǔyǎng 抚养

**rally** n (meeting) jíhuì 集会

**ranch** dà mùchǎng 大牧场

**rancher** mùchǎng zhǔ 牧场主

**random 1** adj suíjī 随机 **2** n: at ~ suíbiàn 随便

**range** n (of goods) xìliè 系列; (of gun) shèchéng 射程; (of airplane) zuìdà xíngchéng 最大行程; (of mountains) shānmài 山脉

**rank** n MIL jūnxián 军衔

**ransack** xǐjié 洗劫

**ransom** n miǎnjīn 赎金; hold X to ~ bǎngjià X yǐ lèsuǒ shújīn 绑架X以勒索赎金

**rape** n & v/t qiángjiān 强奸

**rapid** kuài 快

**rapids** jīliú 急流

**rare** hǎnjiàn 罕见

**rarely** hěnshǎo 很少

**rash**¹ MED pízhěn 皮疹

**rash**² adj action lǔmǎng 鲁莽

**rat** lǎoshǔ 老鼠

**rate** n (of exchange) bǐlù 比率; (speed) sùdù 速度

**rather** (fairly) xiāngdāng 相当

**rational** hélǐ 合理

**rationalize** v/t production etc shǐ hélǐhuà 使合理化

**raw** food shēng 生; sugar, iron wèijīng jiāgōng 未经加工

**raw materials** yuán cáiliào 原材料

**ray** guāngxiàn 光线

**razor** tìxūdāo 剃须刀

**razor blade** tìxūdāo dāopiàn 剃须刀刀片

**reach** v/t city etc dàodá 到达; (go as far as) dào 到; decision dédào 得到

**react** fǎnyìng 反应

**reaction** fǎnyìng 反应

**reactionary** n & adj POL fǎndòng pài 反动派

**reactor** (nuclear) fǎnyìng duī 反应堆

**read 1** v/t dú 读; Chinese rènshi 认识 **2** v/i yuèdú 阅读

读

**reader** (person) dúzhě 读者

**readily** admit xīnrán 欣然

**reading** yuèdú 阅读; (from meter etc) dúshù 读数

**ready** (prepared) zhǔnbèi hǎo 准备好; (willing) yuànyì 愿意

**real** adj zhēn 真

**realistic** xiànshí 现实

**reality** xiànshí 现实

**realize** v/t truth yìshí dào 意识到; ideal shíxiàn 实现

**really** zhēnzhèng 真正; (very) hěn 很; ~? zhēnde ma? 真的吗?

**realtor** búdòng chǎn zhōngjiān shāng 不动产中间商

**rear** adj legs hòu 后; seats, lights hòumiàn 后面

**reason** n (faculty) lǐzhì 理智; (cause) yuányīn 原因

**reasonable** person hélǐ 合理; price gōngpíng 公平

**reassuring** lìng yǒu xìnxīn 令人有信心

**rebel** n fǎnpànzhě 反叛者

**rebellion** fǎnpàn 反叛

**recall** v/t ambassador zhàohuí 召回; (remember) jìqǐ 记起

receipt shōujù 收据; **acknowledge ~ of** quèrèn shōudào 确认收

receive shōudào 收到

recent zuìjìn 最近

recently zuìjìn 最近

reception (in hotel, company) jiēdàichù 接待处; (party) zhāodài huì 招待会; (welcome) huānyíng 欢迎; (for phone etc) jiēshōu 接收

reception desk jiēdàichù 接待处

receptionist jiēdàiyuán 接待员

recession bù jǐngqì 不景气

recipe càipǔ 菜谱

recipient (of parcel etc) jiēshōurén 接收人; (of money) shōukuǎnrén 收款人

reciprocal hùhuì 互惠

recite poem bèisòng 背诵

reckless bùgù hòuguǒ 不顾后果

reckon rènwéi 认为

recognition (of state, achievements) chéngrèn 承认

recognize person, tune rènde

认得; symptoms biànrèn chū 辨认出; POL chéngrèn 承认

recommend tuījiàn 推荐

recommendation tuījiàn 推荐

reconciliation tiáojiě 调解

recondition xiūfù 修复

reconnaissance MIL zhēnchá 侦察

reconsider v/t & v/i chóngxīn kǎolǜ 重新考虑

record 1 n MUS chàngpiān 唱片; SP jìlù 纪录; (written, in database) jìlù 记录; **~s** dǎng'àn 档案 2 v/t (on tape etc) lù lù 录

record-breaking dǎpò jìlù 打破纪录

record holder jìlù bǎochízhě 纪录保持者

recording lùyīn 录音

recover 1 v/t sth lost zhǎohuí 找回 2 v/i MED huīfù 恢复

recovery (of sth lost) zhǎohuí 找回; MED huīfù 恢复

recreation yúlè 娱乐

recruit 1 n MIL xīnbīng 新兵; (to company) xīnlái de 新来的 2 v/t new staff zhā opìn 招聘; MIL zhēngmù 征募

**recruitment** zhāopìn 招聘

**rectangle** chángfāng xíng 长方形

**recurrent** zàifā 再发

**recycle** huíshōu 回收

**recycling** huíshōu 回收

**red** hóng X

**Red Army** Hóngjūn 红军

**Red Cross** Hóngshízì 红十字

**redevelop** part of town chóngxīn fāzhǎn 重新发展

**red-handed: catch X ~** dāngchǎng bǔhuò X 当场捕获 X

**redhead** yǒu hóng tóufà de rén 有红头发的人

**red light** MOT hóngdēng 红灯

**red tape** guānliáo chéngxù 官僚程序

**reduce** jiàngdī 降低

**reduction** jiǎnshǎo 减少

**reel** (of film, thread) juǎn 卷

**refer** v/i: **~ to** tídào 提到

**referee** SP cáipàn 裁判; (for job) tuījiànrén 推荐人

**reference** shèjí 涉及; (for job) tuījiàn 推荐; (~

number) cānkǎo hàomǎ 参考号码

**refinery** tíliàn chǎng 提炼厂

**reflect 1** v/t light fǎnshè 反射 **2** v/i (think) fǎnxǐng 反省

**reflection** fǎnshè 反射; (consideration) fǎnxǐng 反省

**reflex** fǎnyìng nénglì 反应能力

**reform** n & v/t gǎigé 改革

**refreshing** drink qīngshuǎng 清爽; experience qīngxīn yuèmù 清新悦目

**refrigerate** lěngcáng 冷藏

**refrigerator** bīngxiāng 冰箱

**refuel** n & v/i jiā ránliào 加燃料

**refugee** nànmín 难民

**refund** n & v/t tuìkuǎn 退款

**refusal** jùjué 拒绝

**refuse: ~ to do X** jùjué zuò X 拒绝做 X

**regard 1** n: (kind) **~s** wènhòu 问候 **2** v/t: **~ X as Y** bǎ X kànzuò Y 把 X 看作 Y

**regardless: ~ of** bùgù 不顾

**regime** POL zhèngquán 政权

**regiment** n tuán 团

**region** dìqū 地区

**regional** dìqū 地区

**register** 1 *n* dēngjì bù 登记簿 2 *v/t* birth, death dēngjì 登记; car shàngpái 上牌; letter guàhào 挂号 3 *v/i* (for course, with police) dēngjì 登记

**regret** 1 *v/t* hòuhuǐ 后悔 2 *n* yíhàn 遗憾

**regular** 1 *adj* flights dìngqī 定期; intervals yǒu guīlù 有规律; pattern, shape yúnchèn 匀称; (normal) pǔtōng 普通 2 *n* (at bar etc) chángkè 常客

**regulate** kòngzhì 控制

**regulation** (rule) guīzhāng 规章

**rehearsal** páiyǎn 排演

**rehearse** *v/t & v/i* páiyǎn 排演

**reimburse** bǔcháng 补偿

**reinforce** structure xiūbǔ 修补; beliefs jiāqiáng 加强

**reject** *v/t* jùjué 拒绝

**relapse** MED jiùbìng fùfā 旧病复发

**related** (by family) yǒu qīnshǔ guānxi 有亲属关系; events, ideas xiāngguān 相关

**relation** (in family) qīnshǔ 亲属; (connection) guānxi 关系

**relationship** guānxi 关系

**relative** 1 *n* qīnqi 亲戚 2 *adj* xiāngduì 相对

**relatively** xiāngduì 相对

**relax** *v/i* fàngsōng 放松

**relaxation** fàngsōng 放松

**relay**: ~ (race) jiēlìsài 接力赛

**release** 1 *n* (from prison) shìfàng 释放; (of CD etc) fāxíng 发行 2 *v/t* prisoner shìfàng 释放; parking brake sōngkāi 松开; information gōngbù 公布

**relent** ràngbù 让步

**relentless** (determined) búxiè 不懈; rain etc wúqíng 无情

**relevant** yǒuguān 有关

**reliable** kěkào 可靠

**relief** kuānwèi 宽慰

**relieve** pressure, pain jiǎnqīng 减轻; be ~d (at news etc) kuānwèi 宽慰

**religion** zōngjiào 宗教

**relocate** *v/i* bānqiān 搬迁

**reluctance** miǎnqiǎng 勉强

**reluctant** miǎnqiǎng 勉强;

be ~ to do X bù qíngyuàn zuò X 不情愿做X

♦ **rely on** yīkào 依靠

**remain** (be left) shèngxia 剩下; (stay) dāizài 呆在

**remark** n huà 话

**remarkable** fēifán 非凡

**remember** v/t & v/i jìde 记得

**remind** v/t: ~ **X to do Y** tíxíng X zuò Y 提醒X做Y; ~ **X of Y** (call to mind) shǐ X xiǎngqǐ Y 使X想起Y

**reminder** tíxǐng wù 提醒物; (to pay) cuīzhàng dān 催账单

**reminisce** huáijiù 怀旧

**remnant** cánjī 残迹

**remorse** àohuǐ 懊悔

**remote** village piānpì 偏僻; ancestor jiǔyuǎn 久远

**remote control** yáokòng 遥控

**removal** yídòng 移动; (from home) qiānjū 迁居

**remove** yídòng 移动; top, lid nákāi 拿开; tumor qùchú 去除; doubt jiěchú 解除

**renew** contract etc yánqī 延期; talks chóngxīn kāishǐ 重新开始

**renounce** v/t xuānbù fàngqì 宣布放弃

**rent** 1 n zūjīn 租金; for ~ chūzū 出租 2 v/t zū (out) chūzū 出租

**rental** zūjīn 租金

**rental car** zūyòngde chē 租用的车

**reopen** v/t store chóngxīn kāizhāng 重新开张; negotiations zài jìnxíng 再进行

**repair** v/t & n xiūlǐ 修理

**repay** money chánghuán 偿还; person bàodá 报答

**repeal** v/t law fèichú 废除

**repeat** 1 v/t chóngfù 重复 2 n (TV program) chóngbō 重播

**repeated** fǎnfù 反复

**repel** v/t attack jītuì 击退; insects qūgǎn 驱赶

**repercussions** yǐngxiǎng 影响

**repetitive** chóngfù 重复

**replace** (put back) fànghuí 放回; (take place of) tìdài 替代

**replacement** dàitìrén 代替人; (thing) dàitì wù 代替物

**replica** fùzhì pǐn 复制品

**reply** n, v/t & v/i huídá 回答

**report 1** n (account) bàogào 报告; (by journalist) bàodào 报道 **2** v/t (to authorities) tōngzhī 通知

**reporter** jìzhě 记者

**represent** (act for) dàibiǎo 代表; (stand for) zhǔzhāng 主张

**representative** n dàibiǎorén 代表人; COM dàilǐshāng 代理商; POL zhòngyìyuán 众议员

**repress** revolt zhènyā 镇压; feelings yāyì 压抑; laugh rěnzhe 忍着

**reprieve** n & v/t huǎnxíng 缓刑

**reprimand** v/t shēnchì 申斥

**reprisal** bàofù xíngwéi 报复行为

**reproach** n zébèi 责备

**reproduce 1** v/t zàixiàn 再现 **2** v/i BIO fánzhí 繁殖

**republic** gònghé guó 共和国

**republican 1** n gònghé zhǔyìzhě 共和主义者; POL **Republican** Gònghé dǎngrén 共和党人 **2** adj gònghé zhǔyì 共和主义

**Republic of China** Zhōnghuá Mínguó 中华

民国

**repulsive** lìngrén yànwù 令人厌恶

**reputable** yǒu míngshēng 有名声

**reputation** míngyù 名誉

**request** n & v/t yāoqiú 要求

**require** (need) xūyào 需要

**requirement** (need) xūyào 需要; (condition) tiáojiàn 条件

**rescue** n & v/t yuánjiù 援救

**research** n yánjiū 研究

**research and development** yánjiū yǔ fāzhǎn 研究与发展

**resemble** xiàng 像

**resent** bùmǎn 不满

**reservation** (of room, table) yùdìng 预定

**reserve 1** n (store) chǔbèi 储备; SP yùbèi duìyuán 预备队员; ~s FIN chǔbèi jīn 储备金 **2** v/t room, table yùdìng 预定

**residence** (stay) jūzhù 居住

**residence permit** jūliúzhèng 居留证

**resident** n jūmín 居民

**resign** v/i cízhí 辞职

**resignation** cízhí 辞职;

(*mental*) wúkěnàihé 无可奈何

**resist** v/t dǐkàng 抵抗

**resistance** dǐkàng 抵抗

**resolution** (*decision*) juéyì 决议; (*New Year*) juédìng 决定

**resort** n (*place*) dùjià shèngdì 度假胜地

**resource** zīyuán 资源

**resourceful** zúzhì duōmóu 足智多谋

**respect 1** n for older people zūnjìng 尊敬; (*consideration*) zūnzhòng 尊重; **with ~ to** guānyú 关于 **2** v/t person, opinion, privacy zūnzhòng 尊重; law zūnshǒu 遵守

**respectable** person tǐmiàn 体面; bar xiàngyàng 象样

**respond** dáfù 答复; (*react*) zuòchūfǎnyìng 做出反应

**response** dáfù 答复; (*reaction*) fǎnyìng 反应

**responsibility** zérèn 责任

**responsible** fùzé 负责

**rest**[1] **1** n & v/i xiūxi 休息 **2** v/t (*lean etc*) kào 靠

**rest**[2] n: **the ~** yúxià 余下

**restaurant** cānguǎn 餐馆

**restore** building xiūfù 修复

**restrain** yuēshù 约束; **~ oneself** kòngzhì zìjǐ 控制自己

**restraint** (*moderation*) jiézhì 节制

**restrict** xiànzhì 限制

**restricted area** MIL jìndì 禁地

**restriction** xiànzhì 限制

**rest room** wèishēngjiān 卫生间

**result** n jiéguǒ 结果

**resume** v/t huīfù 恢复

**résumé** lǚlì 履历

**retail** adv v lìngshòu fāngshì 以零售方式

**retaliate** bàofù 报复

**retire** v/i (*from work*) tuìxiū 退休

**retirement** tuìxiū 退休

**retract** v/t claws suōjìn 缩进; statement shōuhuí 收回

**retreat** v/i MIL chètuì 撤退

**retrieve** wǎnjiù 挽救

**retrospective** huígù 回顾

**return 1** n fǎnhuí 返回; (*giving back*) tuìhuán 退还; COMPUT fǎnhuí 返回; (*in tennis*) huíqiú 回球 **2** v/t (*give back*) tuìhuán 退还;

*(put back)* fànghuí 放回; 兴; *patient* shǐ sūxīng 使
*favor, invitation* huíbào 回 苏醒 **2** *v/i (of business)* shǐ
报 **3** *v/i (go back)* fǎnhuí 返 shàngshēng 使上升
回; *(of old days, doubts)*
huífù 回复 **revolt 1** *n* fǎnkàng 反抗 **2** *v/i*
zàofǎn 造反

**reunion** tuánjù 团聚
**revolting** *(awful)* ěxin 恶心
**reunite** *v/t* tǒngyī 统一
**revolution** POL *etc* géming 革
**reveal** *(make visible)* xiǎnshì 命; *(turn)* xuánzhuǎn 旋转
显示; *secret* jiēlù 揭露
**revolutionary 1** *n* POL
**revealing** *remark* tòulù géming jiā 革命家 **2** *adj*
zhēnxiàng 透露真相 *ideas* chuàngxīn 创新

**revenge** *n* bàofù 报复 **revolutionize** chèdǐ biàngé
彻底变革
**revenue** shōurù 收入
**revulsion** fǎngǎn 反感
**reverse 1** *n (opposite)*
xiāngfǎn 相反; *(back)* **reward** *n (financial)* shǎngjīn
bèimiàn 背面; MOT 赏金; *(benefit)* bàochóu
dàodǎng 倒档 **2** *v/i* MOT 报酬
dàochē 倒车
**rewarding** zhíde zuò 值得做
**review 1** *n (of book, movie)*
pínglùn 评论 **2** *v/t book,* **rhyme** *n* yùn 韵
*movie* pínglùn 评论; **rhythm** jiézòu 节奏
*situation* shěnchá 审查;
EDU fùxí 复习 **rib** lèigǔ 肋骨

**reviewer** pínglùn jiā 评论家 **ribbon** sīdài 丝带

**revise** *v/t opinion* xiūzhèng **rice** mǐ 米; *(food)* mǐfàn
修正; *text* jiàozhèng 校正 米饭

**revision** *(of text)* jiàozhèng **rice bowl** fànwǎn 饭碗
校正
**rich 1** *adj* yǒuqián 有钱;
**revisionism** POL xiūzhèng *food* yóunì 油腻 **2** *n: the ~*
zhǔyì 修正主义 fùrén 富人

**revive 1** *v/t custom* fùxīng 复 **rickshaw** rénlìchē 人力车

**rid**: *get ~ of waste* rēngdiào
扔掉; *accent etc* bǎituō

摆脱

**ride 1** n (on horse) qímǎ 骑马; (in vehicle) chéngchējīhuì 乘车机会; (journey) lǔtú 旅途 **2** v/t horse, bike qí 骑 **3** v/i (on horse) qímǎ 骑马; (on bike) qí zìxíngchē 骑自行车; (in vehicle) chéngchē 乘车

**ridicule 1** n xīluò 奚落 **2** v/t fēngcì 讽刺

**ridiculous** huāngmiù 荒谬

**rifle** n láifú qiāng 来复枪

**right 1** adj (correct) zhèngquè 正确; (proper, just) zhèngdàng 正当; (suitable) héshì 合适; (not left) yòu 右; be ~ (of answer) zhèngquè 正确; (of person) zhèngzhí 正直; that's ~! duì a! 对啊！ **2** adv (directly) jiù 就; (correctly) zhèngquè 正确; (not left) yòu 右; ~ now (immediately) mǎshàng 马上; (at the moment) xiànzài 现在 **3** n (civil, legal) quánlì 权利; (not left) yòu 右, POL yòupài 右派; on the ~ zài yòubiān 在右边; POL zài

yòuyì nàbiān 在右翼那边

**rightful** owner etc héfǎ 合法

**right-handed** yòu piězi 右撇子

**right wing** POL, SP yòuyì 右翼

**rigid** material jiānyìng 坚硬; attitude kèbǎn 刻板

**rigorous** discipline yángé 严格; tests jīngquè 精确

**rim** (of wheel) lúnyuán 轮缘

**ring¹** (circle) yuánquān 圆圈; (on finger) jièzhi 戒指; (boxing) quánjīchǎng 拳击场

**ring² 1** n (of bell) zhōngshēng 钟声 **2** v/t bell qiāozhōng 敲钟 **3** v/i (of bell) míng 鸣

**ringleader** tóumù 头目

**rinse** n (for hair) rǎnsè 染色 **2** v/t piǎoxǐ 漂洗

**riot 1** n bàoluàn 暴乱 **2** v/i nàoshì 闹事

**rip** n & v/t (in cloth) sīliè 撕裂

**ripe** fruit shóu 熟

**rip-off** n F bōxuē 剥削

**rise** n & v/i (in price, temperature) shàngzhǎng 上涨; (in water level) shàngshēng 上升; (of sun) shēngqǐ 升起

**risk 1** *n* fēngxiǎn 风险 **2** *v/t* mào ... fēngxiǎn 冒 ... 风险

**rival** *n* duìshǒu 对手

**rivalry** jìngzhēng 竞争

**river** héliú 河流

**road** lù 路

**roadblock** lùzhàng 路障

**road map** xiànlù tú 线路图

**roadsign** lùbiāo 路标

**roam** mànyóu 漫游

**roar** *v/i* (*of lion*) páoxiào 咆 哮; (*of person*) dàshēng chǎo 大声吵

**roast** *v/t* & *v/i* kǎo 烤

**rob** qiǎngjié 抢劫

**robber** qiǎngjiézhě 抢劫者

**robbery** qiǎngjié 抢劫

**robot** jīqìrén 机器人

**robust** *health* jiànzhuàng 健 壮; *material* jiāngù 坚固

**ROC** (= *Republic of China*) Zhōnghuá Mínguó 中华 民国

**rock 1** *n* yánshí 岩石 **2** *v/i* (*on chair*) yáodòng 摇动; (*of boat*) yáohuàng 摇晃

**rocket** *n* huǒjiàn 火箭

**rock'n'roll** yáogǔn yuè 摇 滚乐

**role** juésè 角色

**role model** bǎngyàng 榜样

**roll 1** *n* (*bread*) xiǎo yuán miànbāo 小圆面包; (*of film*) juǎn 卷 **2** *v/i* (*of ball*) gǔn 滚

**roller skate** *n* hànbīng xié 旱冰鞋

**romantic** làngmàn 浪漫

**roof** wūdǐng 屋顶

**room** fángjiān 房间; (*space*) kōngjiān 空间

**roommate** shìyǒu 室友

**room service** fángjiān fúwù 房间服务

**root** gēn 根; **~s** (*of person*) gēnjī 根基

**rope** shéng 绳

**rot** *n* & *v/i* fǔlàn 腐烂

**rotate** *v/i* xuánzhuǎn 旋转

**rotten** *food, wood* fǔlàn 腐烂

**rough** *adj surface* bùpíng 不平; *voice* shāyǎ 沙 哑; (*violent*) cūbào 粗 暴; *seas* jiānnán 艰难; (*approximate*) dàgài 大概

**roughly** (*approximately*) dàyuē 大约

**round 1** *adj* yuán 圆 **2** *n* (*of competition*) chǎng 场

**round trip** láihuí lǚxíng 来 回旅行

**rouse** (*from sleep*) xǐng 醒;
(*interest*) shāndòng 煽动

**route** lùxiàn 路线

**routine** *adj & n* chángguī
常规

**row** (*line*) pái 排; (*in
spreadsheet etc*) háng 行

**rowboat** huátǐng 划艇

**royal** *adj* huángjiā 皇家

**rub** *v/t* cuō 搓

**rubber 1** *n* xiàngpí 橡皮
**2** *adj* xiàngjiāo 橡胶

**rude** cūlǔ 粗鲁

**rudeness** wúlǐ 无礼

**rudimentary** jīběn 基本

**rug** xiǎo dìtǎn 小地毯;
(*blanket*) tǎnzi 毯子

**rugged** *scenery* qíqū 崎岖;
*face* cūguǎng 粗犷

**ruin 1** *n* ~**s** fèixū 废墟 **2** *v/t*
*party, plans* pòhuài 破坏;
*reputation* huǐhuài 毁坏;
**~ed** (*financially*) pòchǎn
破产

**rule 1** *n* (*of club, game*) guīzé
规则; **as a ~** tōngcháng 通
常 **2** *v/t & v/i* (*of monarch*)
tǒngzhì 统治

**ruler** (*to measure*) chǐzi 尺
子; (*of state*) tǒngzhìzhě
统治者

**ruling** *adj* POL dāngquán
当权

**rumor** *n* yáoyán 谣言

**run 1** *n* (*on foot*) pǎobù 跑
步; (*in pantyhose*) chōusī
抽丝 **2** *v/i* pǎo 跑; (*of
river*) liú 流; (*of trains etc*)
xíngshǐ 行驶; (*of makeup*)
tǎngliú 淌流; (*of faucet*)
kāi 开; (*of play*) liánxù
yǎnchū 连续演出; (*of
engine, software*) yùnzhuǎn
运转; **~ for President**
jìngxuǎn zǒngtǒng 竞选总
统 **3** *v/t race* jìngsài 竞赛; *3
miles etc* pǎo 跑; *business*
guǎnlǐ 管理

**run-down** *person* píjuàn
疲倦; *area* pòjiù 破旧;
*building* shīxiū 失修

**runner** sàipǎozhě 赛跑者

**runner-up** yàjūn 亚军

**running dog** *pej* zǒugǒu
走狗

**running water** (*from
faucet*) zìláishuǐ 自来水;
(*flowing*) liúshuǐ 流水

**runway** pǎodào 跑道

**rural** nóngcūn 农村

**rush 1** *n* tūjī 突击 **2** *v/t
person* cuī 催 **3** *v/i* gǎn 赶

**rush hour** gāofēng shíjiān 高峰时间

**rust** *n* xiù 锈

**rusty** shēngxiù 生锈; *French etc* shēngshū 生疏

**ruthless** wúqíng 无情

# S

**sack** *n* dà kǒudài 大口袋

**sad** bēishāng 悲伤; *state of affairs* yíhàn 遗憾

**sadist** nüèdàikuáng 虐待狂

**sadly** yōuchóu 忧愁; *(regrettably)* lìngrén yíhàn 令人遗憾

**sadness** yōuchóu 忧愁

**safe 1** *adj (not dangerous)* ānquán 安全; *(not in danger)* wúwéixiǎn 无危险 **2** *n* bǎoxiǎnguì 保险柜

**safely** *arrive* píng'ān 平安; *drive* ānquán 安全

**safety** ānquán 安全

**safety pin** biézhēn 别针

**sail 1** *n* fān 帆; *(trip)* hángchéng 航程 **2** *v/i* jiàshǐchuán 驾驶船; *(depart)* qǐháng 启航

**sailboat** fānchuán 帆船

**sailing** SP fānchuán yùndòng 帆船运动

**sailor** *(in navy)* hǎiyuán 海员; SP shuǐshǒu 水手

**saint** shèngtú 圣徒

**sake:** *for my / your ~* wèile wǒ / nǐ 为了我 / 你

**salad** sèlā 色拉

**salary** xīnshuǐ 薪水

**sale** xiāoshòu 销售; *(reduced prices)* liánjià chūshòu 廉价出售; *for ~* dàishòu 待售

**sales clerk** shòuhuòyuán 售货员

**salesman** tuīxiāoyuán 推销员

**salt** yán 盐

**salty** xián 咸

**salute 1** *n* MIL jìnglǐ 敬礼 **2** *v/t & v/i* zhìjìng 致敬

**same 1** *adj* tóngyàng 同样 **2** *pron: I'll have the ~ as you* hé nǐ yīyàng 和你一样 **3** *adv: look the ~* kànqǐlái yíyàng 看起来一样

sample *n* yàngběn 样本

sanction *n* (*penalty*) zhìcái 制裁

sand *n* shā 沙

sandal liángxié 凉鞋

sandwich *n* sānmíngzhì 三明治

sane shénzhì zhèngcháng 神志正常

sanitarium liáoyǎngyuàn 疗养院

sanitary wèishēng 卫生; *installations* qīngjié 清洁

sanitary napkin wèishēngjīn 卫生巾

sanitation (*installations*) wèishēng shèbèi 卫生设备; (*waste removal*) páiwū 排污

sanity shénzhì zhèngcháng 神志正常

sarcasm jīfēng 讥讽

sarcastic jīfēng 讥讽

SARS fēidiǎn 非典

satellite wèixīng 卫星

satire fēngcì 讽刺

satirical hán fěngcì yìwèi 含讽刺意味

satisfaction mǎnzú 满足

satisfactory lìngrén mǎnyì 令人满意; (*just ok*) fúhé yāoqiú 符合要求

satisfy *customers* shǐ mǎnyì 使满意; *needs* mǎnzú 满足; *conditions* fúhé 符合

Saturday xīngqīliù 星期六

sauce jiàng 酱

saucer chábēidié 茶杯碟

sauna sāngná 桑拿

sausage xiāngcháng 香肠

savage *adj animal* yěxìng 野性; *attack* cánkù 残酷; *criticism* èdú 恶毒

save 1 *v/t* (*rescue*) jiù 救; *money* chǔcún 储存; *time* jiéshěng 节省; COMPUT cúnpán 存盘 2 *v/i* (*put money aside*) zǎnqián 攒钱 3 *n* SP jiùqiú 救球

saving (*amount*) jiéshěng 节省; (*activity*) cúnqián 存钱

savings cúnkuǎn 存款

saw *n* (*tool*) jù 锯

say *v/t* shuō 说

saying yànyǔ 谚语

scaffolding jiǎoshǒujià 脚手架

scale *n* (*size*) guīmó 规模; (*of map*) bǐlì 比例; MUS yīnjiē 音阶

scales (*to weigh*) tiānpíng 天平

scan v/t *horizon, page* sǎoshì
扫视；MED sǎomiáo 扫描；
COMPUT sōusuǒ 搜索

scandal liúyán fēiyǔ 流言
蜚语

scanner MED sǎomiáoqì 扫
描器；COMPUT sǎomiáoyí
扫描仪

scar n shāngbā 伤疤

scarce duǎnquē 短缺

scarcely jīhūbù 几乎不

scare 1 v/t jīngxià 惊吓；
*be ..d of* hàipà 害怕 2 n
*(panic, alarm)* jīngkǒng
惊恐

scarf *(for neck)* wéijīn 围巾；
*(over head)* tóujīn 头巾

scary hěn kǒngbù 很恐怖

scatter 1 v/t *leaflets, seed* sǎ
撒 2 v/i *(of crowd)* sànkāi
散开

scenario qíngkuàng 情况

scene THEA chǎng 场；*(view,
sight)* qíngjǐng 情景；*(of
accident etc)* shìfā dìdiǎn
事发地点；*(argument)*
chǎonào 吵闹

scenery jǐngsè 景色；THEA
wǔtái bùjǐng 舞台布景

scent n xiāngwèi 香味

schedule n *(of events)*

chéngxùbiǎo 程序表；*(of
work)* jìhuàbiǎo 计划表；
*(for trains)* shíkèbiǎo 时
刻表；*be on* ~ àn yùdìng
shíjiān 按预定时间；*be
behind* ~ luòhòuyú yùdìng
jìhuà 落后于预定计划

scheduled flight dìngqī
hángbān 定期航班

scheme n *(plan)* jìhuà 计划；
*(plot)* yīnmóu 阴谋

schizophrenia jīngshén
fēnlièzhèng 精神分裂症

scholarship xuéshù chéngjiù
学术成就；*(financial
award)* jiǎngxuéjīn 奖学金

school xuéxiào 学校；
*(university)* xuéyuàn 学院；
*go to* ~ shàngxué 上学

schoolchildren zhōngxiǎo-
xué xuésheng 中小学
学生

schoolteacher zhōngxiǎoxué
jiàoshī 中小学教师

science kēxué 科学

science fiction kēhuàn
科幻

scientific kēxué 科学

scientist kēxuéjiā 科学家

scissors jiǎnzi 剪子

scoff v/i jīxiào 讥笑

scold v/t zémà 责骂

scooter MOT xiǎoxíng mótuōchē 小型摩托车

scope fànwéi 范围; (opportunity) jīhuì 机会

scorch v/t tàngjiāo 烫焦

score 1 n SP bǐfēn 比分; (written music) yuèpǔ 乐谱 2 v/t & v/i SP défēn 得分

scorn n bǐshì 鄙视

scornful qīngmiè 轻蔑

scowl n nùróng 怒容

scrap 1 n (metal) fèijīnshǔ 废金属; (little bit) shǎoliàng 少量 2 v/t project etc fèidiào 废掉

scrape 1 n (on paint) guācā 刮擦 2 v/t paint guādiào 刮掉; arm cāshāng 擦伤

scratch 1 n (mark) huáhén 划痕 2 v/t guācā 刮擦; itch sāoyǎng 搔痒

scream 1 n jiānjiàoshēng 尖叫声 2 v/i jiānjiào 尖叫

screen 1 n (in room, hospital) gélián 隔帘; (protective) yǎnbìwù 掩避物; (for movie) yínmù 银幕; COMPUT píngmù 屏幕 2 v/t (protect, hide) zhēbì 遮蔽; (for security) shěnchá

审查

screw n luósīdīng 螺丝钉

screwdriver luósīdāo 螺丝刀

scribble n liáocǎode zìjì 潦草的字迹

script (for play) jiǎoběn 脚本; (writing) shūxiětǐ 书写体

scriptwriter zhuàngǎorén 撰稿人

scroll n (manuscript) zhǐjuǎn 纸卷

scrub v/t floor etc cāxǐ 擦洗

scruples gùlǜ 顾虑

scrutinize xìchá 细察

scuba diving dài shuǐfèi qiánshuǐ 戴水肺潜水

sculpture n (art) diāokè 雕刻; (object) diāosù 雕塑

sea dàhǎi 大海; by the ~ zài hǎibiān 在海边

seafood hǎiwèi 海味

seal 1 n (on document) yìnzhāng 印章; TECH mìfēng 密封 2 v/t container mìfēng 密封

sea level: above / below ~ gāoyú / dīyú hǎipíngmiàn 高于 / 低于 海平面

seam n (on garment) fèng 缝

search 1 *n* sōuxún 搜寻
2 *v/t* sōuchá 搜查
◆search for xúnzhǎo 寻找
searchlight tànzhàodēng
探照灯
search party sōusuǒduì 搜
索队
seasick yùnchuán 晕船
season *n* (*of year*) jìjié 季
节; (*for tourism etc*) wàngjì
旺季
seasoning zuóliào 作料
season ticket chángqīpiào
长期票
seat *n* zuòwèi 座位; (*of
pants*) túnbù 臀部
seat belt ānquándài 安全带
seaweed hǎidài 海带
secluded rénjīhǎnzhì 人
迹罕至
second 1 *n* (*of time*) yī
miǎozhōng 一秒钟 2 *adj*
dì'èr 第二 3 *adv* come yī
dì'èrwèi 以第二位
second best *adj* dì'èr hǎo
第二好
second class *adj* ticket
èrděng 二等
second-hand èrshǒu 二手
secondly qícì 其次
second-rate èrliú 二流

secrecy bǎomì 保密
secret *n* mìmì 秘密
secretary mìshū 秘书; POL
bùzhǎng 部长
Secretary of State
Guówùqīng 国务卿
secretive ài bǎomì 爱保密
sect pàibié 派别
section bùfen 部份
sector bùmén 部门
secure *adj* láogù 牢固;
*feeling* wú yōulǜ 无忧虑;
*job* yǒu bǎozhèng 有保证
security (*in job*) bǎozhàng
保障; (*for investment*)
bǎozhèng 保证; (*at
airport etc*) ānquán 安全;
(*department*) bǎo'ānbù
保安部
sedan xiǎo jiàochē 小轿车
sedative *n* zhènjìngyào 镇
静药
seduce gōuyǐn 勾引
see kànjiàn 看见;
(*understand*) míngbai 明
白; *can I ~ the manager?*
wǒ kěyǐ jiàn jīnglǐ ma? 我
可以见经理吗？; *~
you!* zàijiàn! 再见！
◆see off (*at airport etc*)
sòngxíng 送行

**♦ see to** (handle) chǔlǐ 处理

**seed** zhǒngzi 种子

**seeing (that)** jìrán 既然

**seek** v/t job xúnzhǎo 寻找

**seem** kànqǐlái 看起来

**seemingly** kànshangqu 看上去

**segment** bàn 瓣

**segregate** gélí 隔离

**seize** zhuāzhù 抓住;
opportunity bǎwò 把握;
(of customs, police) kòuyā
扣押

**seldom** hǎnjiàn 罕见

**select 1** v/t xuǎnzé 选择
**2** adj (exclusive) gāojí 高级

**selection** xuǎnzé 选择;
(that chosen) jīngxuǎn pǐn
精选品

**selective** tiāojiǎn 挑拣

**self-confidence** zìxìn 自信

**self-conscious** búzìrán 不
自然

**self-defense** zìwèi 自卫

**selfish** zìsī 自私

**self-respect** zìzūn 自尊

**self-service** adj zìzhùshì
自助式

**sell 1** v/t mài 卖 **2** v/i (of
products) xiāoshòu 销售

**semester** xuéqī 学期

**semi** (truck) jiǎojiēchē 铰
接车

**semicircle** bànyuánxíng
半圆形

**semifinal** bànjuésài 半决赛

**seminar** yántǎohuì 研讨会

**senate** cānyìyuàn 参议院

**senator** cānyìyuán 参议员

**send** v/t (by mail) yóujì 邮
寄; (by e-mail, fax etc) fā 发

**senile** shuāilǎo 衰老

**senior** niánzhǎng 年长; (in
rank) gāojí 高级

**senior citizen** lǎorén 老人

**sensation** (feeling) gǎnjué
感觉; (surprise event)
hōngdòng 轰动

**sensational** hōngdòng 轰
动; (very good) juémiào
绝妙

**sense** n (meaning) yìyì 意
义; (purpose, point) yìsi
意思; (common ~) jiànshi
见识; (of sight, smell etc)
guānnéng 官能; (feeling)
gǎnjué 感觉

**sensible** míngzhì 明智;
advice hélǐ 合理

**sensitive** skin jiāonèn 娇嫩;
person mǐngǎn 敏感

**sensuality** ròuyù 肉欲

sentence n GRAM jùzi 句子；
LAW túxíng 徒刑

sentimental shānggǎn 伤感

separate 1 adj dúlì 独立
2 v/t fēnkāi 分开 3 v/i (of
couple) fēnjū 分居

separated couple fēnshǒu
分手

separation fēnlí 分离；(of
couple) fēnshǒu 分手

September jiǔyuè 九月

sequel xùjí 续集

sequence n shùnxù 顺序

sergeant zhōngshì 中士

serial n liánxù gùshì 连续
故事

serial number biānhào 编号

series xìliè 系列

serious yánzhòng 严重；
(person: earnest) rènzhēn
认真

seriously yánzhòng 严重

serve 1 n (in tennis) fāqiú
发球 2 v/t food duānshang
端上；customer zhāodài
招待；the people fúwù 服
务 3 v/i (as politician etc)
gòngzhí 供职；(in tennis)
fāqiú 发球

service n fúwù 服务；(for
machine) wéixiū 维修

service charge fúwùfèi 服
务费

service industry fúwù
hángyè 服务行业

service station jiāyóuzhàn
加油站

sesame oil xiāngyóu 香油

session (of Congress etc)
huìyì 会议

set 1 n (of tools, books
etc) tào 套；(of people)
yìhuǒrén 一伙人；(for
movie) pāishè chǎngdì 拍
摄场地；(in tennis) pán盘
2 v/t (place) fàng 放；date,
time dìng 定；alarm clock
tiáo调；broken limb jiēhǎo
接好；~ the table bǎifàng
cānjù 摆放餐具 3 v/i
(of sun) luò 落；(of glue)
níngjié 凝结 4 adj views,
ideas wángù 顽固；~ meal
dìngcān 定餐

setback zǔài 阻碍

settle 1 v/i (of liquid)
chéngqīng 澄清；(to live)
dìngjū 定居 2 v/t dispute jiě
jué 解决；debts chánghuán
偿还

settlement (of claim, debt)
qīngcháng 清偿；(of

*dispute)* jiějué 解决

**sever** v/t *arm, cable* qiēduàn 切断; *relations* zhōngduàn 中断

**several** adj & pron jǐgè 几个

**severe** *illness, penalty* yánzhòng 严重; *teacher, face* yánlì 严厉; *weather* èliè 恶劣

**sew** v/t féng 缝

**sewer** wūshuǐguǎn 污水管

**sewing** féngrèn 缝纫

**sex** (*act*) xìngjiāo 性交; (*gender*) xìngbié 性别

**sexual** xìng fāngmiàn 性方面

**sexy** xìnggǎn 性感

**shabby** *coat* hánsuān 寒酸

**shade** n (*for lamp*) dēngzhào 灯罩; (*of color*) sèdù 色度; (*on window*) liánzi 帘子

**shadow** n yǐngzi 影子

**shady** yīnliáng 阴凉; *dealings* kàobúzhù 靠不住

**shake** 1 v/t yáo 摇; ~ **hands** wòshǒu 握手 2 v/i (*of hands, voice*) chàndǒu 颤抖; (*of building*) huàngdòng 晃动

**shallow** qiǎn 浅; *person*

qiǎnbó 浅薄

**shame** 1 n xiūchǐ 羞耻; *what a ~!* zhēn yíhàn! 真遗憾！2 v/t shǐ diūliǎn 使丢脸

**shampoo** n xǐfàjīng 洗发精

**Shanghai** Shànghǎi 上海

**shape** n xíngzhuàng 形状

**share** 1 n yífèn 一份; FIN gǔfèn 股份 2 v/t fēnxiǎng 分享; *opinion* gòngtóng jùyǒu 共同具有

**sharp** adj *knife* fēnglì 锋利; *mind* língmǐn 灵敏; *pain* jùliè 剧烈; *taste* xīnlà 辛辣

**shatter** v/t *glass* fěnsuì 粉碎; *illusions* pòmiè 破灭

**shattering** *news, experience* lìngrén zhènjīng 令人震惊

**shave** 1 v/t guā 刮 2 v/i guāliǎn 刮脸

**shaver** (*electric*) tìdāo 剃刀

**shawl** pījiān 披肩

**she** tā 她

**shed** [1] v/t *blood, tears* liú 流

**shed** [2] n péng 棚

**sheep** miányáng 绵羊

**sheer** adj *madness, luxury* shízú 十足; *cliffs* jìnhū chuízhí 近乎垂直

sheet (*for bed*) chuángdān 床单; (*of paper*) zhāng 张; (*of metal, glass*) bǎn 板

shelf jià 架

shell n ké 壳; MIL pàodàn 炮弹

shellfish bèilèi 贝类

shelter 1 n (*refuge*) bìhù 庇护; (*construction*) yǎnbìwù 掩蔽物 2 v/i (*from rain, bombing etc*) duǒbì 躲避 3 v/t (*protect*) bǎohù 保护

shift 1 n (*in thinking*) gǎibiàn 改变; (*switchover*) zhuǎnbiàn 转变; (*period of work*) bān 班 2 v/t (*move*) yídòng 移动 3 v/i (*move*) nuódòng 挪动; (*in opinion*) gǎibiàn 改变

shine 1 v/i zhàoyào 照耀; (*of polish*) fāguāng 发光; fig chūzhòng 出众 2 v/t light zhàoyízhào 照一照

ship 1 n chuán 船 2 v/t (*send*) yùnsòng 运送; (*send by sea*) hǎiyùn 海运

shipment huòwù 货物

shipyard zàochuánchǎng 造船厂

shirt chènshān 衬衫

shiver v/i chàndǒu 颤抖

shock 1 n zhènjīng 震惊; ELEC chùdiàn 触电 2 v/t shǐrén zhènjīng 使人震惊

shocking lìngrén zhènjīng 令人震惊; F (*very bad*) hěn zāo 很糟

shoe xié 鞋

shoot v/t shèzhòng 射中; (*and kill*) kāiqiāng jīngbì 开枪杀毙; *movie* pāishè 拍摄

shop 1 n shāngdiàn 商店 2 v/i mǎi dōngxi 买东西

shopper gòuwùrén 购物人

shopping (*activity*) gòuwù 购物; (*items*) mǎidào de dōngxi 买到的东西

shore àn 岸

short adj (*in height*) ǎi 矮; *distance, time* duǎn 短; **be ~ of** quēfá 缺乏

shortage quēfá 缺乏

shortcoming quēdiǎn 缺点

short cut jiéjìng 捷径

shorten v/t nòngduǎn 弄短; *text* biànduǎn 变短; *vacation* suōduǎn 缩短

shortfall chìzì 赤字

short-lived duǎnzàn 短暂

shortly (*soon*) bùjiǔ 不久

shorts duǎnkù 短裤; (*underwear*) sānjiǎo kù 三角裤

三角裤

**shortsighted** jìnshì 近视;
*fig* wú yuǎnjiàn 无远见
**short-term** duǎnqī 短期
**shot** shèjīshēng 射击声;
(*photograph*) jìngtóu 镜头
**shotgun** lièqiāng 猎枪
**should** yīnggāi 应该; *what ~
I do?* wǒ gāi zuò shénme?
我该做什么？; *you ~n't
do that* nǐ bù yīnggāi nàme
zuò 你不应该那么做
**shoulder** n jiānbǎng 肩膀
**shout 1** n hǎnshēng 喊声
**2** v/i jiàohǎn 叫喊 **3** v/t
mìnglìng 命令
**shove 1** n zhuàng 撞 **2** v/t tuī
推 **3** v/i jǐ 挤
**show 1** n THEA, TV jiémù 节
目; (*display*) biǎolù 表露
**2** v/t *passport* chūshì 出示;
*interest, emotion* biǎodá 表
达; *movie* diànyǐng 电影
**3** v/i (*be visible*) kàndejiàn
看得见; (*of movie*)
shàngyìng 上映
**shower 1** n (*of rain*) zhènyǔ
阵雨; (*to wash*) línyù 淋浴
**2** v/i línyù 淋浴
**show-off** ài xuànyào de rén
爱炫耀的人

**shred** v/t *paper* sīchéng
suìpiàn 撕成碎片; *food*
qiēchéng xiǎotiáo 切成
小条
**shrewd** jīngmíng 精明
**shrink** v/i suōshuǐ 缩水; (*of
support etc*) jiǎnruò 减弱
**shrug** v/i sǒngjiān 耸肩
**shudder** v/i (*of person*)
fādǒu 发抖; (*of building*)
zhèndòng 震动
**shun** duǒbì 躲避
**shut** v/t & v/i guān 关
♦ **shut up** v/i (*be quiet*)
ānjìng 安静; *~!* zhùzuǐ!
住嘴！
**shy** hàixiū 害羞
**sick** shēngbìng 生病; *I feel
~* (*about to vomit*) wǒ gǎndào
ěxin 我感到恶心; *be
~ of* gǎndào yànwù 感到
厌恶
**sick leave** bìngjià 病假
**side** n (*of box, house*) cèmiàn
侧面; (*of room, field*) biān
边; (*of mountain*) miàn 面;
(*of person*) lèi 肋; SP yìfāng
一方; *I'm on your ~* wǒ
zhīchí nǐ 我支持你; *~ by
~* bìngpái 并排
**sideboard** (*furniture*)

cānjùguì 餐具柜

**sideburns** liánbìn húzi 连鬓胡子

**side effect** fùzuòyòng 副作用

**side street** xiǎoxiàng 小巷

**sidewalk** rénxíngdào 人行道

**sigh 1** *n* tànxī 叹息 **2** *v/i* tànqì 叹气

**sight** *n* qíngjǐng 情景; (*power of seeing*) shìlì 视力; **~s** (*of city*) míngshèng 名胜

**sightseeing** guānguāng 观光

**sign 1** *n* (*indication*) jìxiàng 迹象; (*road ~*) zhǐshìpái 指示牌; (*outside store*) zhāopai 招牌 **2** *v/t* & *v/i* qiānzì 签字

**signal 1** *n* xìnhào 信号 **2** *v/i* (*of driver*) zhǐshì 指示

**signature** qiānmíng 签名

**significance** (*importance*) zhòngyàoxìng 重要性; (*meaning*) yìyì 意义

**significant** zhòngyào 重要; (*large*) dàliàng 大量

**sign language** shǒushì yǔ 手势语

**silence 1** *n* chénmò 沉默 **2** *v/t* yāzhì 压制

**silent** ānjìng 安静

**silk 1** *n* sīchóu 丝绸 **2** *adj* *shirt etc* sīzhì 丝制

**silly** shǎ 傻

**silver 1** *n* yín 银 **2** *adj* yínzhì 银制; *hair* huībái 灰白

**similar** xiāngsì 相似

**similarity** xiāngsì 相似

**simple** jiǎndān 简单; *person* tóunǎo jiǎndān 头脑简单

**simplicity** jiǎndān 简单

**simplified characters** jiǎntǐzì 简体字

**simplify** shǐ jiǎndān 使简单

**simply** (*absolutely*) juéduì 绝对

**simultaneous** tóngshí 同时

**sin** *n* zuì'è 罪恶

**since 1** *prep* zìcóng 自从; **~** *last week* zìcóng shàngzhōu yǐlái 自从上周以来 **2** *adv* zìnà yǐhòu 自那以后 **3** *conj* (*time*) cóng ... yǐlái 从 ... 以来; (*seeing that*) jìrán 既然

**sincere** chéngzhì 诚挚

**sincerity** zhēnchéng 真诚

**sing** chàng 唱

**Singapore** Xīnjiāpō 新加坡

**singer** gēshǒu 歌手

**single** n (sole) wéiyī 唯一; (not double) yígè 一个; (not married) dúshēn 独身

**single parent** dānqīn 单亲

**sinister** xié'è 邪恶

**sink 1** n xǐdícáo 洗涤槽 **2** v/i chénmò 沉没; (of sun) luòxia 落下

**sip** n yìxiǎokǒu 一小口

**sir** xiānsheng 先生

**sister** (older) jiějie 姐姐; (younger) mèimei 妹妹

**sister-in-law** (wife's elder sister) qīzǐ 妻姊; (wife's younger sister) qīmèi 妻妹; (husband's elder sister) dàgūjiě 大姑姐; (husband's younger sister) xiǎogū 小姑; (younger brother's wife) dìmèi 弟妹; (older brother's wife) sǎozi 嫂子

**sit** v/i zuò 坐

♦ **sit down** zuòxia 坐下

**sitcom** qíngjǐng xǐjù 情景喜剧

**site** n chǎngdì 场地

**sitting room** kètīng 客厅

**situated:** be ~ zuòluòzai 坐落在

**situation** xíngshì 形势; (of building etc) wèizhi 位置

**size** dàxiǎo 大小; (of jacket, shoes) hàomǎ 号码

**skate** v/i (on ice) huábīng 滑冰; (roller skating) huá hànbīng 滑旱冰

**skateboard** n huábǎn 滑板

**skeptic** huáiyílùn zhě 怀疑论者

**skeptical** huáiyí 怀疑

**skepticism** huáiyí tàidu 怀疑态度

**sketch 1** n cǎotú 草图; THEA huájī duǎnjù 滑稽短剧 **2** v/t xiěshēng 写生

**ski** n & v/i huáxuě 滑雪

**skid 1** n shāchē 刹车 **2** v/i dǎhuá 打滑

**skiing** huáxuě 滑雪

**skill** jìqiǎo 技巧

**skilled** yǒujìnéng 有技能

**skillful** shúliàn 熟练

**skin 1** n pífū 皮肤 **2** v/t qùpí 去皮

**skinny** píbāogǔ 皮包骨

**skip 1** n (little jump) bèng 蹦 **2** v/t (omit) lüèguò 略过

**skipper** NAUT chuánzhǎng 船长; (of team) duìzhǎng 队长

skirt n qúnzi 裙子

skull tóulúgǔ 头颅骨

sky tiānkōng 天空

skyscraper mótiān dàlóu 摩天大楼

slack rope sōngchí 松驰; discipline xièdài 懈怠; work cūxīn 粗心; period qīngdàn 清淡

slacken v/t rope sōngchí 松驰; pace fàngmàn 放慢

slam v/t door pēngde guānshang 砰地关上

slander n & v/t fěibàng 诽谤

slant v/i qīngxié 倾斜

slap n & v/t zhǎngjī 掌击

slash v/t n (cut) kǎnhén 砍痕; (punctuation) xiéxiàn 斜线 2 v/t cost dà xuējiǎn 大削减

slaughter n & v/t túshā 屠杀; (of people) shālù 杀戮

slave n núlì 奴隶

sleazy xiàliú 下流

sleep 1 n shuìjiào 睡觉; go to ~ qù shuìjiào 去睡觉 2 v/i shuì 睡

sleeping bag shuìdài 睡袋

sleeping pill ānmiányào 安眠药

sleepless night bùmián 不眠

sleepy town yōujìng 幽静; I'm ~ wǒ kùn le 我困了

sleeve xiùzi 袖子

slender figure xiānxì 纤细; margin wēibó 微薄

slice 1 n piàn 片 2 v/t loaf etc qiēchéng báopiàn 切成薄片

slide 1 n (for kids) huátī 滑梯; PHOT huàndēngpiàn 幻灯片 2 v/i huá 滑

slight adj person miáotiáo 苗条; (small) xiǎo 小

slightly shāowēi 稍微

slim 1 adj miáotiao 苗条; chance wēixiǎo 微小 2 v/i jiǎnféi 减肥

slip v/i (on ice etc) huá 滑; (of quality etc) xiàjiàng 下降

slipper tuōxié 拖鞋

slippery huá 滑

slit 1 n (tear) kǒuzi 口子; (in skirt) kāichà 开叉 2 v/t sīkāi 撕开

slogan kǒuhào 口号

slope 1 n pō 坡 2 v/i qīngxié 倾斜

sloppy work cǎoshuài 草率

slot n fèngxì 缝隙

slouch *v/i* lǎnsǎn 懒散

slow màn 慢

♦slow down 1 *v/t* jiǎnmàn 减慢 2 *v/i* mànxiàlái 慢下来

slum *n* pínmínkū 贫民窟

slump *n* (*in trade*) xiāotiáoqī 萧条期

slurred *speech* hánhubùqīng 含糊不清

slush bànróngxuě 半融雪

sly jiǎohuá 狡猾

small *adj* xiǎo 小

small hours língchén shífēn 凌晨时分

small talk liáotiān 聊天

smart *adj* piàoliang 漂亮; (*intelligent*) cōngmín 聪敏

smash 1 *n* MOT zhuàngsuì 撞碎 2 *v/t* (*break*) dǎsuì 打碎; (*hit hard*) zhàngjī 撞击 3 *v/i* (*break*) pòsuì 破碎

smear *n* (*of ink etc*) wūjì 污迹; (*on character*) wūmiè 污蔑

smell 1 *n* qìwèi 气味 2 *v/t* wénchū 闻出 3 *v/i* (*bad*) yǒu chòuwèi 有臭味; (*sniff*) wén 闻

smile *n & v/i* wēixiào 微笑

smirk *n & v/i* shǎxiào 傻笑

smoke 1 *n* yān 烟 2 *v/t* *cigarette* xī 吸 3 *v/i* xīyān 吸烟

smoker (*person*) xīyānderén 吸烟的人

smoking xīyān 吸烟; *no ~* jìnzhǐ xīyān 禁止吸烟

smolder (*of fire*) huǎnmàn ránshāo 缓慢燃烧

smooth *adj surface* guānghuá 光滑; *ride* píngwěn 平稳; *transition* shùnlì 顺利

smother *flames* mēnzhù 闷住; *person* shǐ zhìxī 使窒息

smug zìmǎn 自满

smuggle *v/t* zǒusī 走私

smuggler zǒusīzhě 走私者

smuggling zǒusī 走私

snack *n* xiǎochī 小吃

snake *n* shé 蛇

snap 1 *v/t* (*break*) duànliè 断裂; (*say sharply*) lìshēng shuō 厉声说 2 *v/i* (*break*) pàde zhéduàn 啪地折断

snarl *n* (*of dog*) nùhǒu 怒吼

snatch *v/t* duódé 夺得; (*steal*) tōuzǒu 偷走; (*kidnap*) bǎngjià 绑架

sneakers fānbùxié 帆布鞋

sneer *n & v/i* lěngxiào 冷笑

sneeze 1 n pēntì 喷嚏 2 v/i
dǎ pēntì 打喷嚏

sniff 1 v/i (to clear nose)
yòng bí xīqì 用鼻吸气;
(of dog) xiù x  嗅 2 v/t (smell)
wén 闻

sniper jūjīshǒu 狙击手

snob shìlì xiǎorén 势利
小人

snooty mùzhōngwúrén 目
中无人

snore v/i dǎ hān 打鼾

snow 1 n xuě 雪 2 v/i xià
xuě 下雪

snowball n xuěqiú 雪球

snowplow xuělí 雪犁

snowstorm bàofēngxuě 暴
风雪

snub n & v/t dàimàn 怠慢

so 1 adv: ~ hot tài rè 太
热; not ~ much búnàme
不那么; ~ much better
hǎo róngyile 好容易了;
~ am I / do I wǒ yě shì 我
也是; and ~ on děngděng
等 等; 2 pron: I hope ~ wǒ
xīwàng rúcǐ 我希望如
此 3 conj (for that reason)
yīncǐ 因此; (in order that)
shǐde 使得; ~ what? nà
yòu zěnmeyàng? 那又怎

么样？

soak v/t (steep) pào 泡; (of
water, rain) jìnshī 浸湿

soaked shītòu 湿透

soap n féizào 肥皂

soap (opera) féizào jù 肥
皂剧

soar (of rocket) shēngrù 升
入; (of bird, plane) áoxiáng
翱翔

sob 1 n wūyàn 呜咽 2 v/i
chōuqì 抽泣

sober qīngxǐng 清醒

soccer zúqiú 足球

sociable héqún 合群

social adj shèhuì 社会;
(recreational) shèjiāo 社交

socialism shèhuì zhǔyì 社
会主义

socialist 1 adj shèhuì zhǔyì
社会主义 2 n shèhuì
zhǔyì zhě 社会主义者

socialize shèjiāo 社交

social worker shègōng 社工

society shèhuì 社会;
(organization) shètuán
社团

sock wàzi 袜子

socket ELEC chāzuò 插座;
(of arm, eye) wō 窝

soda (~ water) sūdá 苏打

(ice-cream ~) bīngqílíng sūdá shuǐ 冰淇淋苏打水; (soft drink) ruǎnxìng yǐnliào 软性饮料

**sofa** shāfā 沙发

**soft** pillow, chair ruǎn 软; voice wēnróu 温柔; music yuè'ěr 悦耳; light, color róuhé 柔和; skin róuhuá 柔滑; (lenient) kuānhòu 宽厚

**soft drink** ruǎnxìng yǐnliào 软性饮料

**soft seat** RAIL ruǎnzuò 软座

**soft sleeping car** RAIL ruǎnwò 软卧

**software** ruǎnjiàn 软件

**soil** n (earth) tǔrǎng 土壤

**solar energy** tàiyáng néng 太阳能

**soldier** shìbīng 士兵

**sole** n (of foot) jiǎodǐ bǎn 脚底板; (of shoe) xiédǐ 鞋底

**solemn** (serious) yánsù 严肃; promise zhèngzhòng 郑重

**solid** adj (hard) yìng bāngbāng 硬梆梆; (without holes) wú kòngxì 无空隙; gold chún 纯; (sturdy) láogù 牢固; support chèdǐ 彻底

**solidarity** tuánjié yīzhì 团结一致

**solitaire** (card game) dānrén zhǐpái xì 单人纸牌戏

**solitary** life gūdú 孤独; (single) gū línglíng 孤零零

**solitude** dúzì yīrén 独自一人

**solo** 1 n dúzòu qǔ 独奏曲; (of singer) dúchàng qǔ 独唱曲 2 adj dānrén 单人

**solution** jiědá 解答; (mixture) róngyè 溶液

**solve** jiějué 解决

**somber** dark huī'àn 灰暗; (serious) yánjùn 严峻

**some** 1 adj yīxiē 一些; ~ people say ... yǒu rén shuō ... 有人说... 2 pron yīxiē 一些; would you like ~? nǐ yào diǎnrma? 你要点儿吗?

**somebody** yǒurén 有人

**someday** yǒuzhāo yīrì 有朝一日

**somehow** xiǎng bànfa 想办法; (for unknown reason) bùzhī zěnde 不知怎的

**someone** yǒurén 有人

**someplace** → **somewhere**

**something** mǒu shìwù 某事

物; *is ~ wrong?* zěnme le? 怎么了？

**sometimes** yǒushí 有时

**somewhere 1** adv mǒugè dìfāng 某个地方 **2** pron mǒuchù 某处

**son** érzi 儿子

**song** gēqǔ 歌曲

**son-in-law** nǚxù 女婿

**soon** kuài 快; *soon after* bùjiǔ zhīhòu 不久之后; *as ~ as ...* yī ... jiù 一 ... 就; *as ~ as possible* jǐnkuài 尽快

**soothe** *pain* jiǎnqīng 减轻

**sophisticated** *person* jīngtōng shìgù 精通世故; *machine* jīngmì 精密

**sordid** bēibǐ 卑鄙

**sore 1** adj (painful) téng 疼 **2** n chuāng 疮

**sorghum** gāoliáng 高粱

**sorrow** n yōushāng 忧伤

**sorry** (regretful) hòuhuǐ 后悔; (sad) nánguò 难过; *I'm ~ ...* (apology) duìbuqǐ ... 对不起...; (expressing sympathy) hěn yíhàn ... 很遗憾...

**sort 1** n zhǒng 种 **2** v/t fēnlèi 分类; COMPUT páiliè 排列

**sound 1** n shēngyīn 声音; (noise) shēng 声 **2** v/i: *that ~s interesting* tīngqǐlái hěn yǒuqù 听起来很有趣

**soundproof** adj géyīn 隔音

**soup** tāng 汤

**sour** adj suān 酸; *milk* sōu 馊; *comment* jiānsuān kèbó 尖酸刻薄

**source** n láiyuán 来源; (of river) yuántóu 源头

**south 1** adj nán 南 **2** n nánbù 南部 **3** adv wǎngnán 往南

**Southeast Asia** Dōngnán Yà 东南亚

**southern** nán 南

**souvenir** jìniàn pǐn 纪念品

**sovereignty** zhǔquán 主权

**Soviet Union** Sūlián 苏联

**sow** v/t seeds bōzhǒng 播种

**soy sauce** jiàngyóu 酱油

**space** n (beyond earth) tàikōng 太空; (area) kòngbái 空白; (room) kōngjiān 空间

**spacecraft** yǔzhòu fēichuán 宇宙飞船

**space shuttle** hángtiān fēijī 航天飞机

**spacious** kuānchang 宽敞

spade (*for digging*) qiāo 锹

spare 1 *v/t time, money*
yúnchū 匀出; (*do without*)
shěngdiào 省掉 2 *adj*
*money* duōyú 多余; (*extra*)
bèiyòng 备用 3 *n* (*part*)
língjiàn 零件

spare ribs páigǔ 排骨

spare room kèfáng 客房

spare time yèyú shíjiān 业
余时间

spare tire MOT bèiyòng lúntāi
备用轮胎

spark *n* huǒxīng 火星

spark plug huǒhuāsāi 火
花塞

sparse *vegetation* xīshū
稀疏

speak 1 *v/i* shuōhuà 说话;
**~ing** TELEC wǒshì 我是
2 *v/t language* huìjiǎng 会讲

speaker (*at conference*)
yǎnjiǎngzhě 演讲者; (*of
sound system*) yīnxiāng
音箱

special tèshū 特殊;
(*particular*) tèbié 特别

specialist zhuānjiā 专家

specialize zhuānmén
cóngshì 专门从事

specially tèbié 特别

specialty zhuāncháng 专长;
(*food*) tèsè cài 特色菜

species zhǒnglèi 种类

specific tèbié 特别

specify zhǐdìng 指定

specimen yàngpǐn 样品

spectacle (*impressive sight*)
zhuàngguān 壮观

spectator guānzhòng 观众

speculate *v/i* cāicè 猜测;
FIN zuò tóujī mǎimài 做投
机买卖

speech (*address*) jiǎnghuà
讲话; (*in play*) táicí 台词

speed 1 *n* sùdù 速度 2 *v/i*
(*drive*) jíshǐ 疾驶; (*walk*)
kuàizǒu 快走; (*drive too
quickly*) chāosù 超速

speeding *n* MOT chāosù
超速

speed limit xiànsù 限速

spell¹ *v/t & v/i* pīn 拼

spell² *n* (*period of time*)
yīduàn shíjiān 一段时间

spelling pīnxiě 拼写

spend *money* huāqián 花钱;
*time* dùguò 度过

spice *n* xiāngliào 香料

spider zhīzhū 蜘蛛

spill *v/t & v/i* sǎ 洒

spin *n, v/t & v/i* (*of wheel*)

xuánzhuǎn 旋转

spinach bōcài 菠菜

spinal jízhù 脊柱

spine jízhù 脊柱; (of book) shūjí 书脊

spin-off pàishēng chǎnpǐn 派生产品

spiral n luóxuán 螺旋

spirit n (not body) jīngshén 精神; (of dead) línghún 灵魂; (courage) yǒngqì 勇气; (attitude) tàidu 态度

spirits¹ (alcohol) lièjiǔ 烈酒

spirits² (morale) qíngxù 情绪

spiritual adj shén 神

spit v/i (of person) tǔtán 吐痰

spite n èyì 恶意

spiteful huáiyǒu èyì 怀有恶意

splash v/t person jiàn 溅; water, mud pō 泼

splendid jíhǎo 极好

splendor zhuàngguān 壮观

splinter 1 n cì 刺 2 v/i fēnliè 分裂

split 1 n (tear) lièkǒu 裂口; (disagreement) fēnliè 分裂; (division, share) fēngē 分割 2 v/t & v/i (tear) lièkāi 裂开

spoil v/t child chǒnghuài 宠坏; party, fun pòhuài 破坏; de xìngzhì 破坏 ... 的兴致; cooking, essay nòngzāo 弄糟

spoilsport F bàixìngzhě 败兴者

spokesperson fāyánrén 发言人

sponsor 1 n dānbǎorén 担保人 2 v/t dānbǎo 担保

sponsorship dānbǎo 担保

spontaneous zìfā 自发; person zìrán 自然

spoon n sháo 勺

sporadic língsǎn 零散

sport n tǐyù yùndòng 体育运动

sportscar pǎochē 跑车

sportsman yùndòngyuán 运动员

sportswoman nǚyùndòngyuán 女运动员

spot¹ (pimple) fěncì 粉刺; (from measles etc) qiūzhěn 丘疹; (in pattern) bāndiǎnr 斑点儿

spot² (place) dìdiǎn 地点

**spot**³ v/t (notice) zhǎodào 找到; (identify) biànrèn 辨认

**spot check** chōuyàng jiǎnchá 抽样检查

**spotlight** n jùguāng dēng 聚光灯

**sprain** n & v/t niǔshāng 扭伤

**sprawl** v/i shēnkāi sìzhī 伸开四肢; (of city) mànyán 蔓延

**spray** 1 n (of sea water) lànghuā làng huā 浪花; (paint) pēnqī 喷漆; (for hair) pēnfà jiāo 喷发胶 2 v/t pēn 喷

**spread** 1 n (of disease, religion etc) mànyán 蔓延 2 v/t butter mǒ 抹; news, disease chuánbō 传播 3 v/i (of fire) mànyán 蔓延; (of news, disease) chuánbō 传播

**spring**¹ n (season) chūntiān 春天

**spring**² n (device) tánhuáng 弹簧

**springboard** n tiàobǎn 跳板

**sprinkle** v/t sǎ 撒

**sprint** n & v/i bēnpǎo 奔跑

**spurt** 1 n (in race) chōngcì 冲刺 2 v/i (of liquid) pēnshè 喷射

**spy** n jiàndié 间谍

♦**spy on** ànzhōng jiānshì 暗中监视

**squalid** āngzāng 肮脏

**squander** huīhuò 挥霍

**square** 1 adj shape fāng 方; ~ mile píngfāng yīnglǐ 平方英里 2 n sìfāng xíng 四方形; (in town) guǎngchǎng 广场

**squash**¹ n (vegetable) nánguā 南瓜

**squash**² n (game) bìqiú 壁球

**squash**³ v/t yālàn 压烂

**squat** v/i dūn 蹲; (illegally) shànzì zhànyòng 擅自占用

**squeak** n (of mouse) zhīzhī shēng 吱吱声; (of hinge) zhīgā shēng 吱嘎声

**squeeze** v/t jǐ 挤; hand jǐnwò 紧握; orange etc zhà 榨

**squint** n xiéyǎn 斜眼

**stab** v/t cì 刺

**stability** wěndìng 稳定

**stable**¹ adj wěndìng 稳定

**stadium** tǐyùchǎng 体育场

**staff** n (employees) gùyuán 雇员; (teachers) jiàoyuán 教员

教员

**stage¹ 1** v/i (*in project*) jiēduàn 阶段; (*of journey*) duàn lù 段路

**stage²** n THEA wǔtái 舞台

**stagger 1** v/i diēdiē zhuàngzhuàng 跌跌撞撞 **2** v/t (*in time*) cuòkāi 错开

**stain 1** n (*mark*) wūjì 污迹; (*for wood*) rǎnsèjì 染色剂 **2** v/t (*dirty*) zhānwū 沾污; *wood* rǎnsè 染色

**stainless steel** n búxiùgāng 不锈钢

**stair** tíjí 梯级; *the ~s* lóutī 楼梯

**stake** n (*of wood*) zhuāng 桩; (*in gambling*) dǔzhù 赌注; (*investment*) gǔfèn 股份

**stale** *bread* zǒuwèir 走味儿; *air* mēn 闷; *news* guòshí 过时

**stall** v/i (*of engine*) xīhuǒ 熄火; (*of vehicle*) pāomáo 抛锚; (*for time*) tuōyán 拖延

**stamina** nàilì 耐力

**stammer** n & v/i jiēba 结巴

**stamp** n (*for letter*) yóupiào 邮票; (*on visa etc*) yìn 印

**stance** (*position*) tàidù 态度

**stand 1** n (*at exhibition*) tānzi 摊子 **2** v/i (*not sit*) zhànzhe 站着; (*rise*) qǐlì 起立 **3** v/t (*tolerate*) rěnshòu 忍受

♦ **stand by 1** v/i (*be ready*) zuò hǎo zhǔnbèi 作好准备 **2** v/t *person* zhīchí 支持; *decision* jiānchí 坚持

♦ **stand for** (*represent*) dàibiǎo 代表

♦ **stand up** v/i zhàn qǐlái 站起来

**standard 1** adj (*usual*) chángguī 常规 **2** n (*level*) shuǐzhǔn 水准; TECH biāozhǔn 标准

**standardize** v/t shǐ biāozhǔnhuà 使标准化

**standard of living** shēnghuó shuǐzhǔn 生活水准

**standby: on ~** (*for flight*) hòubǔ 候补

**standpoint** guāndiǎn 观点

**standstill: be at a ~** tíngdùn 停顿

**staple diet** zhǔshí 主

**stapler** dìngshūjī 订书机

**star 1** n xīng 星; *fig* míngxīng 明星 **2** v/t & v/i (*in movie*) zhǔyǎn 主演

stare **1** *n* níngshì 凝视 **2** *v/i* mùbù zhuǎnjīng de kàn 目不转睛地看；**~ at** dīngzhe 盯着

Stars and Stripes Xīngtiáo qí 星条旗

start **1** *n* kāitóu 开头 **2** *v/i* kāishǐ 开始；(*of engine*) fādòng 发动 **3** *v/t* kāishǐ 开始；*engine* fādòng 发动；*business* chuàngbàn 创办

starter (*food*) tóupán 头盘；MOT qǐdòng zhuāngzhì 起动装置

starvation jīè 饥饿

starve *v/i* áiè 挨饿

state¹ **1** *n* (*condition*) zhuàngkuàng 状况；(*part of country*) zhōu 州；(*country*) guójiā 国家；*the States* Měiguó 美国 **2** *adj* capital etc zhōu 州；~ *banquet* guóyàn 国宴

state² *v/t* shēngmíng 声明

State Department Guówù Yuàn 国务院

statement (*announcement*) shēngmíng 声明；(*to police*) kǒugòng 口供；(*bank ~*) jiésuàn dān 结算单

state-of-the-art *adj* zuì yōuliáng 最优良

statesman zhèngzhìjiā 政治家

station *n* RAIL huǒchēzhàn 火车站；RAD, TV diàntái 电台

stationary jìngzhǐ 静止

statistics (*science*) tǒngjì xué 统计学；(*figures*) tǒngjì zīliào 统计资料

statue sùxiàng 塑像

status dìwèi 地位

status symbol shēnfènde xiàngzhēng 身份的象征

stay **1** *n* dòuliú 逗留 **2** *v/i* dòuliú 逗留；(*in a condition*) bǎochí 保持；~ *at home* dāi zài jiā lǐ 呆在家里；~ *in a hotel* dāi zài lǚguǎn 呆在旅馆

steady *adj* (*not shaking*) píngwěn 平稳；(*regular*) yǒu guīlǜ 有规律

steak niúpái 牛排

steal *v/t money etc* tōu 偷

steam **1** *n* zhēngqì 蒸汽 **2** *v/t food* zhēng 蒸

steamed bread mántou 馒头

steamer (*for cooking*)

zhēngguō 蒸锅

steel n & adj gāng 钢

steep adj hill etc dǒu 陡

steer v/t jiàshǐ 驾驶

steering wheel fāngxiàng
pán 方向盘

stem n (of plant) gàn 干

step n (pace) bù 步; (stair)
jiētī 阶梯; (measure)
cuòshī 措施

♦step down (from post etc)
ràngwèi 让位

stereo n (sound system)
lìtǐshēng 立体声

stereotype n chéngjiàn 成见

sterilize jiézhá 结扎;
equipment xiāodú 消毒

stern adj yánsù 严肃

steroids jīsù 激素

stew n dùn shípǐn 炖食品

steward (on plane, ship)
chéngwùyuán 乘务员

stewardess (on plane, ship)
nǚ chéngwùyuán 女乘
务员

stick¹ n mùgùn 木棍; (of
policeman) jǐnggùn 警棍

stick² 1 v/t (with adhesive)
niánzhù 粘 住 2 v/i niánzhù
粘住; (jam) qiǎ zhù le
卡住了

sticky nián hūhū 黏糊糊

stiff adj brush, leather
yìng bāngbāng 硬邦邦;
muscle jiāngyìng 僵硬;
(in manner) jūjǐn 拘谨;
competition jīliè 激烈

stifle v/t yawn rěnzhe 忍着;
debate èshā 扼杀

stifling lìngrén zhìxī 令人
窒息

stigma chǐrǔ 耻辱

still¹ 1 adj píngjìng 平静
2 adv: keep ~! bié dòng!
dòngqù! 别动来动去！

still² adv (yet) hái 还;
(nevertheless) wúlùn
rúhé 无论如何; ~ more
gèngduō 更多

stimulant xīngfènjì 兴奋剂

stimulate person cìjī 刺激;
demand cùjìn 促进

stimulation jīlì 激励

stimulus dònglì 动力

sting 1 v/t of bee, jellyfish
zhē 螫 2 v/i (of eyes)
fātòng 发痛; (of scratch) gǎndào
cìtòng 感到刺痛

stipulate guīdìng 规定

stir v/t jiǎobàn 搅拌

stir-fry v/t wànghuǒ biānchǎo
旺火煸炒

**stitch 1** n (sewing) zhēnjiǎo
针脚; (knitting) yìzhēn 一
针; **~es** MED féngzhēn 缝
针 **2** v/t (sew) féng 缝

**stock 1** n (reserves) chǔcún
储存; (COM: of store) huò
货; FIN gǔpiào 股票; **in
~ / out of ~** yǒu / wúhuò
有 / 无货 **2** v/t COM bèiyǒu
备有

**stockbroker** gǔpiào jīngjìrén
股票经纪人

**stock exchange** gǔpiào
jiāoyìsuǒ 股票交易所

**stockholder** gǔdōng 股东

**stock market** gǔpiào
shìchǎng 股票市场

**stockpile** n chǔbèi wùzī 储
备物资

**stomach** n (insides) dùzi 肚
子; (abdomen) fùbù 腹部

**stomach-ache** dùzi téng
肚子疼

**stone** n shítou 石头

**stoop** v/i (bend) wānyāo 弯
腰; (have bent back) hāyāo
哈腰

**stop 1** n (for train, bus)
zhàn 站 **2** v/t (put an end
to, cease) tíngzhǐ 停止;
(prevent) zǔzhǐ 阻止

car, bus, train etc tíng 停;
**~ talking immediately!**
mǎshàng zhùzuǐ! 马上住
嘴! **3** v/i tíng 停

**stopover** dòuliú 逗留; (in
air travel) zhōngtú tíngliú
中途停留

**stop sign** tíngchē biāozhì 停
车标志

**storage** zhùcáng 贮藏

**store 1** n shāngdiàn 商
店; (stock) chǔbèi 储备;
(storehouse) cāngkù 仓
库 **2** v/t cúnfàng 存放;
COMPUT chǔcún 储存

**storm** n bàofēngyǔ 暴风雨

**stormy** yǒu bàofēngyǔ 有
暴风雨; relationship yìbō
sānzhé 一波三折

**story¹** gùshi 故事;
(newspaper article) bàodào
报道

**story²** (of building) céng 层

**stove** (for cooking) lúzi 炉
子; (for heating) jiārèqì
加热器

**straight 1** adj line zhí 直;
back bǐzhí 笔直; (honest,
direct) tǎnshuài 坦率;
whiskey chún 纯 **2** adv (in
a straight line) jìngzhí 径

直; (*directly, immediately*) zhíjiē 直接; **~ ahead be** jiùzài qiánmiàn 就在前面; *walk, drive* zhízhe zǒu 直着走; *look* xiàngqián kàn xù 向前看; **~ away** mǎshàng 马上

**straighten** *v/t* nòngzhí 弄直

**straightforward** (*honest, direct*) zhíjié tǎodàng 直截了当; (*simple*) jiǎndān 简单

**strain** *n* (*on rope, engine*) zuòyòng lì 作用力; (*on person*) zhòngfù 重负

**strand** *v/t:* **be ~ed** chǔyú kùnjìng 处于困境

**strange** (*odd*) qíguài 奇怪; (*unknown*) mòshēng 陌生

**stranger** mòshēngrén 陌生人

**strap** *n* (*of bag*) shūbāo dài 书包带; (*of dress*) jiāndài 肩带; (*of watch*) biǎodài 表带

**strategy** zhànlüè 战略

**straw** (*for drink*) xīguǎn 吸管

**strawberry** cǎoméi 草莓

**stray** *n* (*dog*) zǒushī de gǒu 走失的狗; (*cat*) zǒushī de

māo 走失的猫

**stream** *n fig* (*of people, complaints*) yìliánchuàn 一连串

**street** jiēdào 街道

**streetcar** yǒuguǐ diànchē 有轨电车

**strength** (*of person: physical*) lìqì 力气; *fig* (*strong point*) yōudiǎn 优点; (*of wind, current*) qiángdù 强度; (*of emotion, friendship*) lìliàng 力量; (*of country, currency*) shílì 实力

**strengthen** *v/t* jiāqiáng 加强

**stress 1** *n* (*emphasis*) zhòngdiǎn 重点; (*tension*) yālì 压力; **be under ~** shòudào yālì 受到压力 **2** *v/t urgency* qiángdiào 强调

**stressful** jǐnzhāng 紧张

**stretch 1** *n* (*of land, water*) piàn 片 **2** *v/t material* shēnzhǎn 伸展; *income* jiéyuē 节约 **3** *v/i* (*to relax*) shēn lǎnyāo 伸懒腰; (*to reach sth*) shēnshǒu 伸手; **~ from X to Y** (*extend*) cóng X yánshēn zhì Y 从 X 延

伸至 Y

**strict** yángé 严格

**stride** *n* dàbù 大步

**strike 1** *n* (*of workers*) bàgōng 罢工; (*in baseball*) hǎoqiú 好球; (*of oil*) fāxiàn 发现; **be on ~** zài bàgōng 在罢工 **2** *v/i* (*attack*) xíjī 袭击; (*of disaster*) jiànglín 降临 **3** *v/t* (*hit*) zhuàng 撞; *oil* fāxiàn 发现

**string** *n* xìshéng 细绳; (*of violin etc*) xián 弦; (*of tennis racket*) bēngshéng 绷绳

**strip 1** *n* chángtiáo 长条 **2** *v/t* (*remove*) chúqù 除去; (*undress*) bōguāng yīfu 剥光衣服 **3** *v/i* (*undress*) tuōqù yīfu 脱去衣服

**stripe** *n* tiáowén 条纹

**strive 1** *v/t*: **~ to do** nǔlì zuò 努力做 **2** *v/i*: **~ for** lìzhēng 力争

**stroke** *n* MED zhòngfēng 中风; (*in writing*) bǐhuà 笔画; (*in swimming*) yóufǎ 游法 **2** *v/t* fǔmō 抚摸

**stroll 1** *n* sànbù 散步 **2** *v/i* xiánzǒu 闲走

**stroller** (*for baby*) yīng'érchē 婴儿车

**strong** *person* qiángzhuàng 强壮; *structure* jiāngù 坚固; *candidate* qiáng 强; *support* jiāndìng 坚定; *wind* qiángjìn 强劲; *drink* lièxìng 烈性; *tea, coffee* nóng 浓; *taste, smell* wèinóng 味浓; *views* jiānjué 坚决; *currency* jiāntǐng 坚挺

**structural** gòujià 构架

**structure** *n* (*sth built*) jiànzhùwù 建筑物; (*way sth is built*) jiégòu 结构

**struggle 1** *n* (*fight*) zhēngdòu 争斗; (*hard time*) jiānnán 艰难 **2** *v/i* (*with a person*) gédòu 格斗; (*have a hard time*) nǔlì 努力

**stub** *n* (*of cigarette*) yāndì 烟蒂; (*of check, ticket*) cúngēn 存根

**stubborn** gùzhí 固执; *defense* wánqiáng 顽强

**stuck-up** F bǎi jiàzi 摆架子

**student** xuésheng 学生; (*at college, university*) dàxuésheng 大学生

studio (*of artist*) gōngzuòshì 工作室; (*recording ~*) lùyīnpéng 录音棚; (*film ~*) shèyǐngpéng 摄影棚; (*TV ~*) yǎnbōshì 演播室

study 1 *n* (*room*) shūfáng 书房; (*learning*) xuéxí 学习; (*investigation*) yánjiū 研究 2 *v/t* (*at school*) gōngdú 攻读; (*examine*) zǐxì chákàn 仔细察看 3 *v/i* xuéxí 学习

stuff *n* dōngxi 东西; (*belongings*) suǒyǒuwù 所有物

stuffing (*for turkey, in chair etc*) tiánliào 填料

stuffy *room* mèn 闷; *person* gǔbǎn 古板

stumble *v/i* bànjiǎo 绊脚

stumbling block zhàng'ài 障碍

stun dǎhūn 打昏; (*of news*) dàchīyìjīng 大吃一惊

stupid yúchǔn 愚蠢

stupidity yúchǔn 愚蠢

stutter *v/i* jiēbā 结巴

style *n* fēnggé 风格; (*fashion*) liúxíng kuǎnshì 流行款式; (*elegance*) gédiào 格调

subconscious: *the ~* qiányìshì 潜意识

subcontract *v/t* fēnbāo hétóng 分包合同

subcontractor fēnbāorén 分包人

subdued *lights* róuhé 柔和; *voice* dīluò 低落

subject 1 *n* (*topic*) zhǔtí 主题; (*of learning*) kēmù 科目; GRAM zhǔyǔ 主语 2 *adj*: *be ~ to X* yǒu X de qīngxiàng 有 X 的倾向

subjective zhǔguān 主观

submarine qiántǐng 潜艇

submissive shùncóng 顺从

submit *v/t plan* chéngjiāo 呈交

subordinate *n* xiàshǔ 下属

♦ subscribe to *magazine etc* dìngyuè 订阅

subscription dìng 订

subside (*of flood*) tuìqù 退去; (*of building*) xiàxiàn 下陷

subsidiary *n* fùshǔ gōngsī 附属公司

subsidy bǔzhù 补助

substance (*matter*) wùzhì 物质

substantial xiāngdāng dà 相当大

相当大

substitute 1 n dàitìpǐn 代替品; SP tìhuànzhě 替换者 2 v/t: **X for Y** yòng X qǔdài Y 用 X 取代 Y

subtitle n zìmù 字幕

subtle qiǎomiào 巧妙

subtract v/t jiǎnqù 减去

suburb jiāoqū 郊区; **the ~s** shìjiāo 市郊

subway dìtiě 地铁

succeed 1 v/i chénggōng 成功 2 v/t (come after) jìrèn 继任

success chénggōng 成功

successful chénggōng 成功

successive jiēlián búduàn 接连不断

successor jìrènrén 继任人

such 1 adj (of that kind) zhèyàng 这样; **~ a** (so much of a) nàme 那么 2 adv zhème 这么; **~ nice** ... zhème hǎode ... 这么好的...

suck shǔnxī 吮吸

sudden yìwài 意外

suddenly tūrán 突然

sue v/t kònggào 控告

suffer 1 v/i shòukǔ 受苦 2 v/t loss zāoshòu 遭受

sufficient zúgòu 足够

suffocate v/i zhìxī ér sǐ 窒息而死

sugar n táng 糖

suggest v/t jiànyì 建议

suggestion jiànyì 建议

suicide zìshā 自杀

suit 1 n xīzhuāng 西装 2 v/t (of color etc) shìhé 适合

suitable shìyí 适宜

suitcase shǒutí yīxiāng 手提衣箱

suite (of rooms) tàojiān 套间; (furniture) yītào jiājù 一套家具

sulk shēng mènqì 生闷气

sum (total) zǒngshù 总数; (amount) shùmù shùzì 数目 (in arithmetic) suànshù 算术

summarize v/t gàikuò 概括

summary n gàiyào 总结 总结

summer xiàtiān 夏天

summit shāndǐng 山顶; POL zuì gāojí huìyì 最高级会议

summon staff zhàojí 召集; meeting zhàokāi 召开

sun tàiyáng 太阳; **in the ~** zài yángguāng xià 在阳光下

sunbathe shài tàiyáng 晒

太阳

**sunblock** fángshàigāo 防
晒膏

**sunburn** shàibān 晒斑

**Sunday** xīngqīrì 星期日

**sunglasses** mòjìng 墨镜

**sunrise** rìchū 日出

**sunset** rìluò 日落

**suntan** shàihēi 晒黑

**superb** bàngjíle 棒极了

**superficial** fūqiǎn 肤浅；
*person* qiǎnbó 浅薄

**superintendent** (*of
apartment block*)
guǎnlǐyuán 管理员

**superior 1** *adj* gènghǎo 更
好；*attitude* yǒu yōuyuègǎn
有优越感 **2** *n* (*in
organization*) shàngjí 上级

**supermarket** chāojí shìchǎng
超级市场

**superpower** POL chāojí
dàguó 超级大国

**superstitious** *person* míxìn
迷信

**supervise** jiāndū 监督

**supervisor** (*at work*)
zhǐdǎozhě 指导者

**supper** wǎnfàn 晚饭

**supplier** COM gōngyìngshāng
供应商

**supply 1** *n* gōngyìng 供应
**2** *v/t goods* tígōng 提供

**support 1** *n* (*for structure*)
zhīzhù 支柱；(*backing*)
zhīchí 支持 **2** *v/t
structure* zhīchēng 支撑；
(*financially*) yuánzhù 援
助；(*back*) zhīchí 支持

**supporter** yōnghùzhě 拥护
者；SP zhīchízhě 支持者

**supportive** zhīchí 支持

**suppose** (*imagine*) liàoxiǎng
料想；*be ~d to ...* (*be
meant to*) yīnggāi ... 应该
...；(*be said to be*) jùshuō ...
据说...；*you are not ~d to
...* (*not allowed*) nǐ bùgāi ...
你不该 ...

**suppress** *rebellion* zhènyā
镇压

**Supreme Court** Gāojí Fǎtíng
高级法庭

**sure** *adj*: *I'm ~* wǒ néng
quèdìng 我能确定；*make
~ that ...* chámíng ... 查明
...；*~!* dāngrán! 当然！

**surely** yídìng 一定；(*gladly*)
dāngrán 当然

**surf 1** *n* (*on sea*) jīlàng 激浪
**2** *v/t the* Net sōuxún 搜寻

**surface** *n* biǎomiàn 表面；

(*of water*) shuǐmiàn 水面

**surfing** chōnglàng yùndòng 冲浪运动

**surge** n (*growth*) jīzēng 激增

**surgeon** wàikē yīshī 外科医师

**surgery** shǒushù 手术

**surname** xìng 姓

**surplus 1** n guòshèng 过剩 **2** adj shèngyú 剩余

**surprise 1** n jīngqí 惊奇 **2** v/t shǐ ... jīngqí ... 吃惊; **be ~d** chīle yìjīng 吃了一惊

**surprising** lìngrén jīngyà 令人惊讶

**surrender** n & v/i MIL tóuxiáng 投降

**surround** v/t bāowéi 包围

**surroundings** huánjìng 环境

**survival** xìngcún 幸存

**survive 1** v/i (*of species*) cúnhuó 存活; (*of patient*) yòuxìng cúnhuó 有幸存活 **2** v/t accident xìngcún 幸存

**survivor** xìngcúnzhě 幸存者

**suspect 1** n xiányífàn 嫌疑

犯 **2** v/t person huáiyí 怀疑; (*suppose*) juéde 觉得

**suspend** (*from office*) lèlìng tíngzhí 勒令停职

**suspense** jǐnzhānggǎn 紧张感

**suspicion** huáiyí 怀疑

**suspicious** (*causing suspicion*) kěyí 可疑; (*feeling suspicion*) yǒu yíxīn 有疑心

**swallow** v/t yàn 咽

**sway** v/i yáobǎi 摇摆

**swear** v/i zhòumà 咒骂; LAW xuānshì 宣誓

**swearword** màrénhuà 骂人话

**sweat 1** n hànshuǐ 汗水 **2** v/i chūhàn 出汗

**sweater** máoyī 毛衣

**sweatshirt** wúlǐng chángxiùshān 无领长袖衫

**sweep** v/t floor sǎo 扫

**sweet** adj taste tián 甜

**sweet and sour** adj tángcù 糖醋

**swell 1** v/i (*of limb etc*) zhǒngzhàng 肿胀 **2** adj F (*good*) jíhǎo 极好

**swelling** n MED zhǒngkuài 肿块

肿块

swerve v/i tūrán zhuǎnxiàng
突然转向

swim n & v/i yóuyǒng 游泳

swimming pool yóuyǒngchí
游泳池

swimsuit yóuyǒngyī 游
泳衣

swindle n piànjì 骗计

swing 1 n zhuǎnbiàn 转
变; (child's) qiūqiān 秋
千 2 v/t huīdòng 挥动
3 v/i bǎidòng 摆动; (turn)
zhuǎndòng 转动; (of
opinion) biàndòng 变动

switch 1 n (for light) kāiguān
开关 2 v/t (change) huàn
换 3 v/t (change) gǎihuàn
改换

♦ switch off v/t & v/i lights
etc guāndiào 关掉

♦ switch on 1 v/t lights etc
kāi 开 2 v/i kāijī 开机

swollen zhǒngzhàng 肿胀

syllabus dàgāng 大纲

symbol (written) fúhào 符
号; (poetic etc) xiàngzhēng
象征

symbolic yǒu xiàngzhēng-
xìng 有象征性

symmetric(al) duìchèn 对称

sympathetic (showing pity)
biǎoshì tóngqíng 表示同
情; (understanding) lǐjiěrén
理解人

sympathizer POL yōnghùzhě
拥护者

sympathy (pity) tóngqíngxīn
同情心; (understanding)
lǐjiě 理解

symphony jiāoxiǎngyuè
交响乐

symptom MED zhèngzhuàng
症状; fig zhēngzhào 征
兆

synthetic rénzào 人造

syringe zhùshèqì 注射器

system (method) xìtǒng 系
统; (orderliness) chéngxù
程序

## T

table n zhuōzi 桌子; (of
figures) biǎo 表

tablet yàopiànr 药片儿

table tennis pīngpāngqiú

兵乓球

**tact** jīzhì 机智

**tactful** détǐ 得体

**tactics** cèlüè 策略

**tactless** bù détǐ 不得体

**tag** (label) biāoqiān 标签

**tai chi** tàijíquán 太极拳

**tail light** wěidēng 尾灯

**tailor** cáiféng 裁缝

**tailor-made** dìngzuò 定做; solution shìdàng 适当

**Taiwan** Táiwān 台湾

**Taiwanese** 1 adj Táiwān 台湾 2 n Táiwānrén 台湾人; (dialect) Táiyǔ 台语

**take** v/t (remove) ná 拿; (transport) sòng 送; (accompany) péi 陪; (accept: credit cards) jiēshòu 接受; photograph zhàoxiàng 照相; exam, degree kǎo 考; (endure) rěnshòu 忍受; (require) xūyào 需要; how long does it ~? yào duōcháng shíjiān? 要多长时间？; I'll ~ it (when shopping) wǒ mǎi le 我买了

♦ **take out** (from bag) náchū 拿出; appendix shānchú 删除; (to dinner etc) dài

... chūqù 带 ... 出去; insurance policy bànlǐ 办理

♦ **take over** 1 v/t company etc jiānbìng 兼并 2 v/i (of new management etc) jiēguǎn 接管

♦ **take up** carpet etc jiēqǐ 揭起; (carry up) ná shàngqù 拿上去; judo, new language kāishǐ xuéxí 开始学习; space, time zhànqù 占去

**takeoff** (of plane) qǐfēi 起飞

**takeover** COM jiānbìng 兼并

**talented** yǒu tiānfù 有天赋

**talk** 1 v/i tánhuà 谈话 2 v/t English etc shuō 说 3 n (conversation) jiāotán 交谈; (lecture) yǎnjiǎng 演讲

**talk show** tánhuà jiémù 谈话节目

**tall** gāo 高

**tame** animal xùnfú 驯服

**tampon** yuèjīng shuān 月经栓

**tank** chúshuǐ chí 储水池; MOT xiāng 箱; MIL tǎnkè 坦克

**tanker** (ship) yóuchuán 油船; (truck) guànchē 罐车

**tanned** shài hēi 晒黑

Tao Dào 道

tap 1 n lóngtóu 龙头 2 v/t (knock) qīngqiāo 轻敲; phone qiètīng 窃听

tape 1 n (for recording) cídài 磁带; (sticky) jiāodài 胶带 2 v/t conversation etc lùyīn 录音; (with sticky tape) zhān 粘

tape measure juǎnchǐ 卷尺

tape recorder lùyīnjī 录音机

target 1 n mùbiāo 目标 2 v/t market bǎ ... zuòwéi mùbiāo 把 ... 作为目标

tart n guǒxiàn bǐng 果馅儿饼

task rènwù 任务

taste 1 n wèidao 味道; (in clothes, art etc) pǐnwèi 品味 2 v/t food cháng 尝

taunt n & v/t cháoxiào 嘲笑

taut jǐn 紧

tax n shuì 税

tax-free miǎnshuì 免税

taxi chūzūchē 出租车

tax payer nàshuìrén 纳税人

tax return (form) nàshuì dān 纳税单

tea chá 茶; black ~ hóngchá 红茶; green ~ lǜchá 绿茶

teach 1 v/t jiāo 教 2 v/i jiāoshū 教书

teacher lǎoshī 老师

teacup chábēi 茶杯

team zǔ 组

teamwork pèihé 配合

teapot cháhú 茶壶

tear[1] n (in cloth etc) lièkǒu 裂口 2 v/t paper, cloth sī 撕 3 v/i (go fast) jí bēn 急奔

tear[2] (in eye) lèi 泪

tearful yǎnlèi wāngwāng 眼泪汪汪

tear gas cuīlèi qì 催泪气

tease v/t dòunòng 逗弄

technical jìshù xìng 技术性

technician jìshùyuán 技术员

technique fāngfǎ 方法

technological jìshù 技术

technology jìshù 技术

teenager qīngshàonián 青少年

telecommunications diànxìn 电信

telephone 1 n diànhuà 电话 2 v/t & v/i dǎ diànhuà 打电话 → phone

telephoto lens shèyuǎn jìngtóu 摄远镜头

television diànshì 电视;

(*set*) diànshìjī 电视机

**television program** diànshì jiémù 电视节目

**tell** *v/t story, lie* jiǎng jiǎng 讲; *difference* qūfēn 区分; **~ X Y** gàosù X Y 告诉 X Y; **~ X to do Y** jiào X zuò Y 叫 X 做 Y

**teller** (*in bank*) chūnàyuán 出纳员

**temp** *n* (*employee*) línshígōng 临时工

**temper** (*bad ~*) píqì 脾气; **keep one's ~** nàzhe xìngzi 捺着性子; **lose one's ~** fā píqì 发脾气

**temperamental** (*moody*) yì jīdòng 易激动

**temperature** wēndù 温度; (*fever*) fāshāo 发烧

**temple** REL miàoyǔ 庙宇

**temporary** zànshí 暂时

**tempting** yǒu xīyǐnlì 有吸引力

**tenant** fángkè 房客; (*of land*) diànhù 佃户

**tendency** qīngxiàng 倾向

**tender**[1] *adj* (*sore*) xūruò 虚弱; (*affectionate*) wēnróu 温柔; *steak* ruǎn 软

**tender**[2] *n* COM tóubiāo 投标

**tennis** wǎngqiú 网球

**tense** *adj muscle* jǐn 紧; *voice, moment* jǐnzhāng 紧张

**tension** (*of rope*) lālì 拉力; (*in atmosphere, voice*) jǐnzhāng 紧张; (*in movie*) jǐnyào guāntóu 紧要关头

**tent** zhàngpeng 帐篷

**tentative** yóuyù 犹豫

**term** (*time*) shíqī 时期; EDU xuéqī 学期; (*condition*) tiáojiàn 条件; **long / short ~** cháng / duǎnqī 长 / 短期

**terminal 1** *n* (*at airport*) chūrùjìng kǒu 出入境口; (*for buses*) zhōngdiǎnzhàn 终点站 **2** *adj* MED wǎnqī 晚期

**terminate** *v/t contract* zhōngzhǐ 终止; *pregnancy* liúchǎn 流产

**terminus** zhōngdiǎnzhàn 终点站

**terracotta warriors** bīngmǎyǒng 兵马俑

**terrain** dìshì 地势

**terrible** kěpà 可怕

**terrific** liǎobuqǐ 了不起

**terrify** kǒnghè 恐吓

**terrifying** kěpà 可怕

**territory** lǐngtǔ 领土; *fig* lǐngyù 领域

**terrorism** kǒngbù zhǔyì 恐怖主义

**terrorist** kǒngbù fènzi 恐怖分子

**terrorize** kǒnghè 恐吓

**test 1** *n* (*scientific*) cèyàn 测验; (*exam*) kǎoyàn 考验 **2** *v/t machine, theory* cèyàn 测验; *student* kǎo 考

**testify** *v/i* LAW zuòzhèng 作证

**text** yuánwén 原文

**textbook** kèběn 课本

**textile** fǎngzhī 纺织

**texture** zhìdì 质地

**than** bǐ 比; *bigger ~ me* bǐ wǒ dà 比我大

**thank** *v/t* xiè 谢

**thanks** gǎnxiè 感谢; *~!* xièxie 谢谢

**thankful** gǎnjī 感激

**Thanksgiving (Day)** Gǎn'ēn jié 感恩节

**that 1** *adj* nàge 那个; *~ one* nàge 那个 **2** *pron* nà 那; *what's ~?* nàshì shénme? 那是什么？; *I think ~ ...* wǒ xiǎng ... 我想 ...; *the person ~ you see* nǐ

kànjiànde nàge rén 你看见的那个人

**thaw** *v/i* huà 化

*the no translation*

**theater** jùchǎng 剧场

**theft** tōuqiè 偷窃

**their** tāmende 他们的; (*his or her*) tā / tāde 他 / 她的

**theirs** tāmende 他们的

**them** tāmen 他们; (*him or her*) tā / tā 他 / 她

**theme** zhǔtí 主题

**themselves** tāmen zìjǐ 他们自己

**then** (*at that time*) nàshí 那时; (*after that*) érhòu 而后; (*deducing*) nàme 那么

**theory** lǐlùn 理论

**therapist** zhìliáo xuéjiā 治疗学家

**therapy** liáofǎ 疗法

**there** nàr 那儿; *~ is / are ...* yǒu ... 有 ...; *~ is / are not ...* méiyǒu ... 没有 ...; *~ you are* (*giving*) gěinǐ 给你

**therefore** yīncǐ 因此

**thermometer** wēndùjì 温度计

**thermos flask** bǎowēnpíng 保温瓶

**these** *adj & pron* zhèxiē

这些

they tāmen 他们; (he or
she) tā 他 / 她

thick hair mì 密; soup chóu
稠; fog duō 多; wall hòu 厚

thief xiǎotōu 小偷

thigh dàtuǐ 大腿

thin hair xī 稀; coat
báo 薄; line xì 细; person
shòu 瘦

thing dōngxi 东西; ~s
(belongings) suǒyǒuwù
所有物

think xiǎng 想; I ~ so wǒ
rènwéi rúcǐ 我认为如此;
what do you ~? nǐ shuō
ne? 你说呢?

Third World Dìsān Shìjiè 第
三世界

thirst kě渴

thirsty: be ~ kě渴

this 1 adj zhège 这个; ~ one
zhège 这个 2 pron zhège
这个; ~ is ... (introducing)
zhèshì ... 这是...; TELEC
wǒshì ... 我是...

thorough search chèdǐ 彻
底; person búyànqífán 不
厌其烦

those adj & pron nàxiē 那些

though 1 conj (although)

jǐnguǎn 尽管; as ~
hǎoxiàng 好象 2 adv
(however) rán'ér 然而

thought xiǎngfǎ 想法;
(collective) sīxiǎng 思想

thoughtful chénsī 沉思;
(considerate) xìxīn 细心

thoughtless cūxīn 粗心

thousand qiān 千; ~s of
wúshù 无数; ten ~ wàn 万

thread n xiàn 线

threat wēixié 威胁

threaten wēixié 威胁

thrill 1 n xīngfèn 兴奋 2 v/t:
be ~ed gāoxìng 高兴

thriller (movie) jīngxiǎn
diànyǐng 惊险电影;
(book) jīngxiǎn xiǎoshuō
惊险小说

thrilling lìngrén máogǔ
sǒngrán 令人毛骨悚然

thrive (of plant) zhuózhuàng
shēngzhǎng 茁壮生长;
(of economy) fánróng 繁荣

throat hóulóng 喉咙

throb n & v/i (of heart etc)
tiàodòng 跳动

through 1 prep (across)
chuānguò 穿过; (during)
zài ... qījiān 在 ... 期间;
Monday ~ Friday xīngqī yī

zhì wǔ 星期一至五 **2** *adj*:
**be ~** *(of couple)* wánle
完了; **I'm ~ with X** *(with
person)* wǒ yǔ X juéjiāo
我与 X 绝交; *(with task)*
wǒ wánchéng le X 我完
成了 X

throw **1** *v/t* rēng 扔;
*(disconcert)* shǐ ... cāng-
huáng shīcuò shǐ ... 仓皇
失措 **2** *n* tóuzhì 投掷
◆ **throw out** rēngdiào 扔掉;
*husband, drunk* niǎnzǒu
撵走

thumb *n* mǔzhǐ 拇指
thumbtack túdīng 图钉
thump **1** *(blow)* zhòngjī 重
击; *(noise)* pēng 砰
thunder *n* dǎléi 打雷
thunderstorm léiyǔ 雷雨
Thursday xīngqī sì 星期四
thwart héngxiàng 横向
Tiananmen *(incident)* liùsì
shìjiàn 六四事件; *(square)*
Tiān'ānmén 天安门
Tibet Xīzàng 西藏
Tibetan **1** *adj* Xīzàng 西藏
**2** *n* Xīzàngrén 西藏人;
*(language)* Xīzàng yǔ 西
藏语
ticket piào 票

ticket machine shòupiàojī
售票机
ticket office shòupiàochù
售票处
tickle *v/t* gēzhi 胳肢
tidy *person* zhěngjié 整洁;
*room* zhěngqí 整齐
◆ **tidy up** *v/t* shōushi 收拾
tie **1** *n (necktie)* lǐngdài 领
带; *(SP: even result)* píngjú
平局 **2** *v/t knot* dǎjié 打结;
*hands* jì 系
tight **1** *adj clothes, (hard
to move)* jǐn 紧; *security,
windows* yán 严; *(not
leaving time)* jǐncòu 紧凑
tighten *screw* shǐ ... biànjǐn
使 ... 变紧; *control* shǐ ...
yángé 使 ... 严格; *security*
shǐ ... yánjǐn 使 ... 严谨
time shíjiān 时间; *(occasion)*
cì 次; **have a good ~!** wánr
kāixīn diǎnr! 玩儿开心
点儿！; **what's the ~?**
jǐdiǎnle? 几点了?; **all
the ~** yìzhí 一直; **in ~** jíshí
及时; **on ~** ànshí 按时; **in
no ~** lìkè 立刻
time limit qīxiàn 期限
timetable shíjiān biǎo 时
间表

**time zone** shíqū 时区

**timid** miàntiǎn 缅腆

**timing** shíjiān xuǎnzé 时间选择; (*of actor, dancer*) shíjiān fēncùn 时间分寸

**tinted** *eyeglasses* fǎnguāng 反光; *paper* zháosè 着色

**tiny** jíxiǎo 极小

**tip¹** *n* (*of stick, finger*) jiānjiān 尖; (*of cigarette*) yānzuǐ 烟嘴

**tip²** *n* (*piece of advice*) quàngào 劝告; (*money*) xiǎofèi 小费

**tippy-toe:** *on* ~ yòng jiǎojiān 用脚尖

**tire¹** (*on wheel*) chētāi 车胎

**tire²** *v/i* láolèi 劳累

**tired** lèi 累; *be* ~ *of X* duì X yànjuàn 对 X 厌倦

**tissue** ANAT zǔzhī 组织; (*handkerchief*) zhǐjīn 纸巾

**title** piānmíng 篇名; (*of person*) tóuxián'r 头衔儿

**to 1** *prep* dào 到; ~ *China* dào Zhōngguó 到中国; *give X* ~ *Y* jiāng X gěi Y 将 X 给 Y; *from Monday* ~ *Wednesday* cóng xīngqīyī dào xīngqīsān 从星期一到星期三 **2** *with verbs:*

*learn* ~ *drive* xuéxí jiàshǐ 学习驾驶; *nice* ~ *eat* hǎochī 好吃 **3** *adv:* ~ *and fro* láihuí 来回

**toast 1** *n* kǎo miànbāo 烤面包; (*drinking*) gānbēi 干杯 **2** *v/t* (*when drinking*) wèi ... gānbēi 为 ... 干杯

**tobacco** yāncǎo 烟草

**today** jīntiān 今天

**toe** *n* jiǎozhǐ 脚指

**together** yìqǐ 一起; (*at the same time*) tóngshí 同时

**toilet** cèsuǒ 厕所

**toilet paper** wèishēngzhǐ 卫生纸

**toiletries** wèishēngjiān yòngpǐn 卫生间用品

**token** (*sign*) xiàngzhēng 象征

**tolerant** kuānróng 宽容

**tolerate** *noise* róngxǔ 容许; *person* róngrěn 容忍

**toll** (*for bridge, road*) tōngxíng fèi 通行费)

**toll-free** TELEC miǎnfèi diànhuà fèi 电话费)

**toll-free** TELEC miǎnfèi diànhuà 免费电话

**tomato** (*in northern China*) xīhóngshì 西红柿; (*in southern China*) fānqié

蕃茄
**tomato ketchup** fānqiéjiàng
蕃茄酱
**tomorrow** míngtiān 明天；
*the day after ~* hòutiān 后
天；*~ morning* míngchén
明晨
**ton** dūn 吨
**tone** (*of color*) fēnggé 风
格；MUS yuèyīn 乐音；*~ of
voice* shēngdiào 声调
**tongue** n shétou 舌头
**tonic** (*water*) tānglìshuǐ 汤
力水
**tonight** jīnwǎn 今晚
**tonsillitis** biǎntáoxiàn yán 扁
桃腺炎
**too** (*also*) yě 也；(*excessively*)
tài 太；*me ~* wǒ yě wǒ 我也；*~
much* tàiduō 太多
**tool** gōngjù 工具
**tooth** yáchǐ 牙齿
**toothache** yáténg 牙疼
**toothbrush** yáshuā 牙刷
**toothpaste** yágāo 牙膏
**top** 1 n (*of mountain, tree*)
dǐng 顶；(*upper part*)
shàngbù 上部；(*lid: of
bottle etc*) gài 盖；(*of class,
league*) zuì yōuxiù 最优
秀；(*clothing*) shàngyī 上

衣；(MOT: *gear*) zuì gāodǎng
最高档；*on ~ of* zài … zhī
shàng 在 … 之上；*at the ~
of* zài … zhīshàng 在 … 最
上 2 adj *branches* zuìdǐng
最顶；*floor* zuìgāo yìcéng
最高一层；*management*
gāojí 高级；*speed, note*
zuìgāo 最高
**topic** tímù 题目
**torment** n & v/t zhémo 折磨
**torture** n & v/t zhémo 折磨
**toss** v/t *ball* zhì zhì 掷；*~ a coin*
zhìbǐ 掷币
**total** 1 n zǒngshù 总数 2 adj
*amount* zǒng 总；*disaster*
juéduì 绝对；*stranger*
wánquán 完全 3 v/t F *car*
zálàn 砸烂
**totally** wánquán 完全
**touch** 1 n chùmō 触摸；
(*sense*) chùjué 触觉；SP
biānxiàn wài 边线外；*lose
~ with X* yǔ X shīqù liánxì
与 X 失去联系；*keep in
~ with X* yǔ X bǎochí liánxì
与 X 保持联系 2 v/t
chùmō 触摸；(*emotionally*)
shǐ gǎndòng 使感动 3 v/i
mō 摸
**touching** adj gǎnrén 感人

**touchy** *person* mǐngǎn 敏感

**tough** *person* jiānqiáng 坚强; *meat* bùyì jǔjué 不易咀嚼; *question* nán nàn 难; *material* jiānrèn 坚韧; *punishment* wúqíng 无情

**tour** 1 *n* lǚyóu 旅游 2 *v/t area* cānguān 参观

**tourism** lǚyóu yè 旅游业

**tourist** lǚyóuzhě 旅游者

**tourist information office** lǚyóu zīliàochù 旅游资料处

**tour operator** lǚyóu gōngsī 旅游公司

**tow** *v/t* zhuài 拽

**toward** *prep* xiàng 向

**towel** máojīn 毛巾

**town** zhèn 镇

**town hall** zhèn zhèngfǔ dàlóu 镇政府大楼

**toxic** yǒudú 有毒

**toy** wánjù 玩具

**trace** 1 *n* (*of substance*) wēiliàng 微量 2 *v/t* (*find*) xúnzhǎo 寻找

**track** *n* (*path*) xiǎojìng 小径; (*for racing*) pǎodào 跑道; RAIL guǐdào 轨道

**tractor** tuōlājī 拖拉机

**trade** 1 *n* màoyì 贸易;

(*profession*) hángyè 行业 2 *v/i* (*do business*) jīngyíng 经营 3 *v/t*: **~ X for Y** yòng X huàn Y 用 X 换 Y

**trade fair** màoyìhuì 贸易会

**trademark** shāngbiāo 商标

**tradition** chuántǒng 传统

**traditional** chuántǒng 传统

**traditional characters** fántǐzì 繁体字

**traffic** *n* jiāotōng 交通; (*in drugs*) fànmài 贩卖

**traffic circle** huánxíng jiāochā 环形交叉

**traffic cop** F jiāotōng jǐng 交通警

**traffic jam** jiāotōng dǔsè 交通堵塞

**traffic light** hónglǜdēng 红绿灯

**tragedy** bēijù 悲剧

**tragic** búxìng 不幸

**trail** 1 *n* (*path*) xiǎojìng 小径 2 *v/t* (*follow*) gēnzōng 跟踪; (*tow*) tuōlā 拖拉

**trailer** tuōchē 拖车; (*mobile home*) pénghchē 篷车

**train¹** *n* huǒchē 火车

**train²** *v/t & v/i* SP xùnliàn 训练; (*of teacher etc*) péixùn 培训

**treacherous**

**trainee** shíxí shēng 实习生

**trainer** SP jiàoliànyuán 教练员

**training** SP xùnliàn 训练; (of new staff) péixùn 培训

**train station** huǒchēzhàn 火车站

**traitor** pàntú 叛徒

**tranquilizer** zhènjìngjì 镇静剂

**transaction** jiāoyì 交易

**transfer 1** v/t diàodòng 调动; passengers zhuǎnjī 转机, **2** v/i (when traveling) qiānyí 迁移 **3** n (move, of money) diàodòng 调动; (in travel) diàohuàn 调换

**transform** v/t gǎibiàn 改变

**transformer** ELEC biànyāqì 变压器

**transfusion** shūxuè 输血

**transition** guòdù 过渡

**transitional** guòdù 过渡

**translate** fānyì 翻译

**translation** fānyì 翻译

**translator** fānyì 翻译

**transmission** (of program) bōfàng 播放; (of disease) chuánrǎn 传染; MOT biànsùqì 变速器

**transmit** program bōfàng 播

放; disease chuánrǎn 传染

**transpacific** kuàyuè Tàipíngyáng 跨越太平洋

**transparent** tòumíng 透明

**transplant** v/t & n MED yízhí 移植

**transport** v/t & n yùnshū 运输

**trap 1** n (for animal) xiànjǐng 陷阱; (question etc) quāntào 圈套 **2** v/t: be ~ped xiànrù quāntào 陷入圈套

**trash** (garbage) lājī 垃圾; (poor product) fèipǐn 废品

**trashy** lièzhì 劣质

**traumatic** chuàngshāngxìng 创伤性

**travel 1** n lǚxíng 旅行; ~s lǚtú 旅途 **2** v/i & v/t lǚxíng 旅行

**travel agency** lǚxíng shè 旅行社

**traveler** lǚxíngzhě 旅行者

**traveler's check** lǚxíng zhīpiào 旅行支票

**travel expenses** jiāotōng fèiyòng 交通费用

**travel insurance** lǚxíng bǎoxiǎn 旅行保险

**tray** tuōpán 托盘

**treacherous** bùzhōng 不忠

**tread** *n* zúyīn 足 音; (*of tire*) tāimiàn 胎 面 **2** *v/i* zǒuguò 走 过

**treason** pànguó zuì 叛 国 罪

**treasure** *n* cáifù 财 富

**Treasury Department** Cáizhèng Bù 财 政部

**treat 1** *n* kuǎndài 款 待 **2** *v/t materials* chǔlǐ 处 理; *illness* zhìliáo 治 疗; (*behave toward*) duìdài 对 待

**treaty** tiáoyuē 条 约

**tree** shù 树

**tremble** fādǒu 发 抖

**tremendously** (*very*) hěn 很; (*a lot*) hěnduō 很 多

**tremor** (*of earth*) zhèndòng 震 动

**trend** qūxiàng 趋 向; (*fashion*) cháoliú 潮 流

**trendy** xīncháo 新 潮

**trial** LAW shěnpàn 审 判; (*of equipment*) shìyàn 试 验; **on ~** LAW shòushěn 受 审

**triangle** sānjiǎo xíng 三 角 形

**trick 1** *n* jìmóu 计 谋; (*knack*) jìqiǎo 技 巧 **2** *v/t* qīpiàn 欺 骗

**trigger** *n* bānjī 扳 机

♦ **trigger off** chùfā 触 发

**trim** *v/t hair, hedge* xiāo 削; *costs* xuējiǎn 削 减

**trip 1** *n* (*journey*) lǚxíng 旅 行 **2** *v/t & v/i* (*~ up*) bàndǎo 绊 倒

**triumph** *n* shènglì de xǐyuè 胜 利 的 喜 悦

**trivial** suǒsuì 琐 碎

**troops** jūnduì 军 队

**trophy** jiǎngbēi 奖 杯

**tropical** rèdài 热 带

**trouble 1** *n* (*difficulty*) kùnnan 困 难; (*inconvenience*) máfan 麻 烦; (*disturbance*) sāoluàn 骚 乱; **no ~** méi wèntí 没 问 题 **2** *v/t* (*worry*) dānyōu 担 忧; (*bother, disturb*) máfan 麻 烦; (*of back, liver etc*) shǐ bù shūfu 使 不 舒 服

**troublemaker** dǎoluànzhě 捣 乱 者

**trousers** Br kùzi 裤 子

**truce** xiūzhàn 休 战

**truck** kǎchē 卡 车

**truck driver** kǎchē sījī 卡 车 司 机

**true** zhēn 真; *friend* gòu 够; **come ~** shíxiàn 实 现

**truly** zhēnde 真 地; *Yours ~*

cǐzhì 此 致

**trunk** (*of tree*) shùgàn 树干;
(*of elephant*) xiàngbí 象鼻;
(*large case*) dà píxiāng 大
皮箱; (*of car*) xínglǐ xiāng
行 李箱

**trust** n & v/t xìnrèn 信任

**trustworthy** zhídé xìnrèn 值
得信任

**truth** shìshí 事实

**truthful** chéngshí 诚实

**try 1** v/t chángshì 尝试; LAW
shěnpàn 审判 **2** v/i shìshi
试试

**T-shirt** yuánlǐng shān 圆
领衫

**tub** (*bath*) yùgāng 浴缸; (*for
yoghurt, ice cream*) hé box 盒

**tube** (*pipe*) guǎndào 管道;
(*of toothpaste, ointment*)
guǎn 管

**Tuesday** xīngqī èr 星期二

**tug 1** n NAUT tuōchuán 拖船
**2** v/t (*pull*) lā 拉

**tuition** fǔdào 辅导

**tummy** dùzi 肚子

**tumor** zhǒngliú 肿瘤

**tune** n qǔdiào 曲调

**tunnel** n suìdào 隧道

**turbulence** (*in air travel*)
tuānliú 湍流

**turkey** huǒjī 火鸡

**turn 1** n (*rotation*)
zhuǎndòng 转动; (*in road*)
zhuǎn 转; **it's my ~** gāi wǒ
le 该我了; **do X a good ~**
wèi X zuò hǎoshì 为 X 做
好事 **2** v/t wheel zhuàn 转;
*corner* guǎiwānr 拐弯儿
**3** v/i zhuàn 转

♦ **turn down** v/t offer
jùjué 拒绝; *volume, heat*
guānxiǎo 关小

♦ **turn off 1** v/t TV, engine
guān 关 **2** v/i (*of driver*)
xià 下

♦ **turn on** v/t TV, engine kāi
开; (*sexually*) cìjī 刺激

♦ **turn up 1** v/t collar fānqǐ
翻起; *volume, heat* kāidà
开大 **2** v/i (*arrive*) lòumiàn
露面

**turnover** FIN chéngjiāo liàng
成交量

**turnpike** gāosù gōnglù 高
速公路

**turnstile** ràogān 绕杆

**tuxedo** lǐfú 礼服

**tweezers** nièzi 镊子

**twice** liǎngcì 两次

**twin** shuāng bāo tāi 双胞胎

**twin beds** liǎng zhāng

chuáng 两张床

**twinge** (*of pain*) cìtòng 刺痛

**twist 1** *v/t* cuō 搓; **~ *one's
ankle*** niǔle jiǎohuái 扭了
脚踝 **2** *v/i* (*of road, river*)
pánxuán 盘旋

**two** èr 二; (*with measure

*words*) liǎng 俩

**tycoon** jùtóu 巨头

**type 1** *n* (*sort*) zhǒnglèi
种类 **2** *v/t & v/i* (*with
keyboard*) dǎzì 打字

**typical** diǎnxíng 典型

**tyrant** bàojūn 暴君

# U

**ugly** chǒulòu 丑陋

**ulcer** kuìyáng 溃疡

**ultimate** (*definitive*) zuìhǎo
最好; (*final*) zuìhòu 最后

**ultimatum** zuìhòu tōngdié 最
后通牒

**umbrella** sǎn 伞

**umpire** *n* cáipànyuán 裁
判员

**UN** (= *United Nations*)
Liánhéguó 联合国

**unanimous** yízhì tóngyì 一
致同意

**unassuming** qiānxùn 谦逊

**unavoidable** bùkě bìmiǎn 不
可避免

**unaware: be ~ of** méiyǒu
chájuédào 没有察觉到

**unbalanced** bù pínghéng
不平衡; PSYCH shīcháng

失常

**unbearable** nányǐ rěnshòu
难以忍受

**unbelievable** nányǐzhìxìn
难以置信; F *heat, value*
jíduān 极端

**uncertain** *future* kěnéng
gǎibiàn 可能改变; *origins*
bú quèdìng 不确定

**uncle** (*mother's brother*)
jiùjiu 舅舅; (*father's
elder brother*) bóbo 伯伯;
(*father's younger brother*)
shūshu 叔叔; (*mother's
sister's husband*) yífu 姨父;
(*father's sister's husband*)
gūfu 姑父; (*to older non-
related men*) shūshu 叔叔

**uncomfortable** bù shūshì
不舒适

**unconditional** wú tiáojiàn 无条件

**unconscious** MED shīqù zhījué 失去知觉; PSYCH xiàyìshí 下意识

**uncontrollable** kòngzhì bùliǎo 控制不了

**uncover** jiēkāi 揭开; *plot* jiēlù 揭露

**undeniable** bùkě fǒurèn 不可否认

**under** *prep* zài ... xiàmian 在 ... 下面; (*less than*) bú dào 不到

**underage**: *be* ~ wèi dào fǎdìng niánlíng 未到法定年龄

**undercarriage** qǐluòjià 起落架

**undercut** *v/t* COM xuējià qiǎng ... shēngyì 削价抢 ... 生意

**underdog** chǔyú lièshì de yìfāng 处于劣势的一方

**underdone** bù shútòu 不熟透

**underestimate** *v/t* guòfèn dīgū 过分低估

**undergo** *treatment* jiēshòu 接受; *experience* jīngshòu 经受

**underground** *adj also* POL dìxià 地下

**undergrowth** guànmùcóng 灌木丛

**underline** *v/t text* xià huàxiàn 下划线

**underlying** *problems* gēnběn 根本

**underneath 1** *prep* zài ... dìxià 在 ... 底下 **2** *adv* xiàngxià 向下

**underpants** nèikù 内裤

**underskirt** chènqún 衬裙

**understaffed** rényuán bùzú 人员不足

**understand 1** *v/t* lǐjiě 理解; *language* dǒng 懂 **2** *v/i* (*see the reason*) míngbai 明白

**understandably** kě lǐjiě 可理解

**understanding 1** *adj person* tōngqíng dálǐ 通情达理 **2** *n* (*of situation*) lǐjiě 理解; (*agreement*) xiéyì 协议

**understatement** zhòngshì qīngshuō 重事轻说

**undertaking** (*enterprise*) shìyè 事业; (*promise*) xǔnuò 许诺

**underwear** nèiyī 内衣

**underworld** (*criminal*) hēi

shèhuì 黑社会

**undisputed** wúkě zhēngbiàn
无可争辩

**undress** v/i tuō yīfu 脱衣服

**unearth** remains fājué 发掘

**unemployed** shīyè 失业;
(from state enterprise)
xiàgǎng 下岗

**unemployment** shīyè 失业

**uneven** quality bù yízhì 不
一致; surface bù píng
不平

**unexpected** chūhū yìliào 出
乎意料

**unfair** bù gōngpíng 不公平

**unfaithful** bù zhōng 不忠

**unfavorable** report fùmiàn
负面; conditions bùlì 不利

**unfit** (physically) bú jiànkāng
不健康; (morally) bú
shìhé 不适合

**unforeseen** wèi yùjiàn dào
未预见到

**unforgettable** nánwàng
难忘

**unforgivable** bù kě ráoshù
不可饶恕

**unfortunately** búxìng de shì
不幸的是

**unfriendly** lěngmò 冷漠

**ungrateful** bù lǐngqíng 不

领情

**unhappiness** bù yúkuài
不愉快

**unhappy** bù yúkuài 不愉
快; customers bù mǎnyì
不满意

**unharmed** píng'ān wúyàng
平安无恙

**uniform 1** n zhìfú 制服 **2** adj
yízhì 一致

**unify** tǒngyī 统一

**uninhabited** huāng wú rén-
yān 荒无人烟

**unintentional** fēi gùyì 非
故意

**union** POL liánméng 联盟;
(labor ~) gōnghuì 工会

**unique** dúyīwú'èr 独一
无二

**unite 1** v/t tǒngyī 统一;
family members tuánjù 团
聚 **2** v/i tuánjié 团结

**United States (of America)**
Měiguó 美国

**unity** tǒngyī 统一

**universal** pǔbiàn 普遍

**university** n dàxué 大学

**unkind** kèbó 刻薄

**unleaded** adj wúqiān 无铅

**unless** chúfēi 除非

**unlikely** bú dà kěnéng 不

大可能
**unload** xiè 卸

**unlucky** dǎoméi 倒霉;
*person* búxìng 不幸

**unmistakable** juéwú jǐnyǒu
绝无仅有

**unnatural** fǎncháng 反常

**unnecessary** bú bìyào 不
必要

**unofficial** fēi zhèngshì 非
正式

**unpack** *v/t* dǎkāi 打开

**unpaid** *work* wúcháng 无偿

**unpleasant** shǐ rén bù
yúkuài 使人不愉快

**unpopular** *person* bú shòu
huānyíng 不受欢迎; *step*
bùdé rénxīn 不得人心

**unpredictable** fǎnfù
wúcháng 反复无常

**unproductive** *meeting*
méiyǒu jiéguǒ 没有结果;
*soil* bù féiwò 不肥沃

**unprofessional** bú jìngyè
不敬业; *workman* zāogāo
糟糕

**unrealistic** bú xiànshí 不
现实

**unreasonable** bù hélǐ 不
合理

**unreliable** bù kěkào 不

可靠

**unrest** dòngluàn 动乱

**unruly** bù guījù 不规矩

**unsatisfactory** bùnéng
lìngrén mǎnyì 不能令
人满意

**unscrew** xuánsōng 旋松;
*top* nǐngkāi 拧开

**unsettled** *weather, stock
market* yìbiàn 易变;
*lifestyle* bù wěndìng 不
稳定

**unskilled** wú tèshū jìnéng 无
特殊技能

**unsuccessful** bù chénggōng
不成功; *candidate, attempt*
shībài 失败

**unsuitable** bù héshì 不合适

**untidy** língluàn 凌乱

**until** *prep* zhídào 直到; *not
~ Friday* zhídào xīngqī wǔ
cái 直到星期五才

**untiring** *efforts* bújuàn 不倦

**untrue** bù zhēnshí 不真实

**unusual** bùtóng xúncháng 不
同寻常

**unusually** yìcháng 异常

**unwell** bù shūfu 不舒服

**unwilling: be ~ to do X**
búyuàn zuò X 不愿做 X

**up 1** *adv* xiàngshàng 向上;

*~ on the roof* zài wūdǐng shang 在屋顶上; *be ~* (*out of bed*) qǐchuáng 起床; (*of sun*) shēngqǐ 升起; (*of prices, temperature*) shàngshēng 上升; *what's ~?* zěnmele? 怎么了?; *be ~ to something* (*bad*) méi zuò shénme hǎoshì 没做什么好事; *it's ~ to you* nǐ lái juédìng 你来决定 **2** *prep: ~ the mountain* zài wǎng shānshàng yìxiē 再往山上一些 **3** *n: ~s and downs* gānkǔ 甘苦

**upbringing** jiàoyǎng 教养

**update** *v/t file, records* xiūdìng 修订

**upheaval** (*emotional*) jùbiàn 剧变; (*physical*) biàndòng 变动; (*political, social*) dòngluàn 动乱

**uphold** *rights* wéihù 维护; (*vindicate*) zhèngshí 证实

**upkeep** *n* bǎoyǎng 保养

**upmarket** *adj restaurant, hotel* gāojí 高级

**upper** *part* shàngbù 上部; *stretches of a river* shàngyóu 上游; *deck* shàngcéng 上层

**uprising** qǐyì 起义

**uproar** (*loud noise*) xuānxiāo 喧嚣; (*protest*) kàngyì 抗议

**upset 1** *v/t glass* nòngfān 弄翻; (*emotionally*) shǐrén nánguò 使人难过 **2** *adj* (*emotionally*) nánguò 难过; *have an ~ stomach* gǎndào chángwèi bùshì 感到肠胃不适

**upstairs 1** *adv* zài lóushàng 在楼上 **2** *adj room* lóushàng 楼上

**up-to-date** *data* zuìxīn 最新; *fashions* xīnshì 新式

**upturn** (*in economy*) hǎozhuǎn 好转

**uranium** yóu铀

**urban** dūshì 都市

**urge 1** *n* yùwàng 欲望 **2** *v/t: ~ X to do Y* jiélì cuīcù X zuò Y 竭力催促 X 做 Y

**urgency** jǐnjí 紧急

**urgent** *job* jíjí 急; *letter* jǐnjí 紧急

**us** wǒmen 我们

**US(A)** (= *United States* (*of America*)) Měiguó 美国

**use 1** *v/t* shǐyòng 使用;

*skills, knowledge* yùnyòng 运用; *car* yòng 用; *pej: person* lìyòng 利用 **2** *n* shíyòng 使用; **be of no ~ to X** duì X méiyǒuyòng 对 X 没有用; **it's no ~** méiyòng 没用

used¹ *car etc* yòngguòo 用过

used²: **be ~ to X** duì X xíguàn 对 X 习惯; **get ~ to X** duì X zhújiàn shìyìng 对 X 逐渐适应

useful yǒuyòng 有用

useless *information* méiyòng 没用; F *person* chàjìn 差劲; *machine* bùnéng yòng 不能用

user yònghù 用户

user-friendly yònghù yǒuhǎo 用户友好

usual tōngcháng 通常; **as ~** xiàng wǎngcháng yíyàng 像往常一样

usually tōngcháng 通常

U-turn U xíngwān X 形弯; *fig* zhuǎnxiàng 转向

# V

vacant *building* kōng 空; *look* mángrán 茫然

vacate téngchū 腾出

vacation *n* xiūjià 休假; **be on ~** dùjià 度假

vacationer dùjiàzhě 度假者

vaccinate jiēzhòng yìmiáo 接种疫苗

vaccine yìmiáo 疫苗

vacuum **1** *n* PHYS zhēnkōng 真空 **2** *v/t floor* xīchén 吸尘

vacuum cleaner xīchénqì 吸尘器

vague bù mínglǎng 不明朗; *feeling* móhu 模糊

vain **1** *adj person* zìfù 自负 **2** *n*: **in ~** bái fèilì 白费力

valid *passport* yǒuxiào 有效; *reason* yǒu gēnjù 有根据

valuable **1** *adj* yǒu jiàzhí 有价值 **2** *n*: **~s** guìzhòng wùpǐn 贵重物品

value **1** *n* jiàzhí 价值 **2** *v/t* zhēnshì 珍视

van huòchē 货车

vanilla xiāngcǎo 香草

vanish xiāoshī 消失

**vapor** qì 汽

**variable** adj kěbiàn 可变；
moods duōbiàn 多变

**variation** biànhuà 变化

**varied** quality bùtóng 不同；
range gèzhǒng gèyàng 各
种各样；diet fēngfù 丰富

**variety** biànhuà 多样
化；(type) zhǒnglèi 种类

**various** (several) jǐgè 几个；
(different) bùtóng 不同

**varnish 1** n qīngqī 清漆；
(for nails) zhǐjiǎ yóu 指甲
油 **2** v/t tú 涂

**vary** v/i biànhuà 变化；it
varies bù yíyàng 不一样

**vase** huāpíng 花瓶

**vast** jùdà 巨大；knowledge
yuānbó 渊博

**VCR** (= video cassette
recorder) lùxiàngjī 录
像机

**veal** xiǎo niúròu 小牛肉

**vegetable** shūcài 蔬菜

**vegetarian** n sùshízhě 素
食者

**vehicle** chēliàng 车辆

**vending machine** zìdòng
shòuhuòjī 自动售货机

**venereal disease** xìngbìng
性病

**ventilation** tōngfēng 通风

**venture** n (undertaking)
màoxiǎn 冒险；COM tóujī
huódòng 投机活动

**venue** dìdiǎn 地点

**verb** dòngcí 动词

**verdict** LAW cáijué 裁决；fig
dìnglùn 定论

♦**verge on** jiējìn 接近

**verify** (check out) héshí 核
实；(confirm) zhèngmíng
证明

**vermin** hàichóng 害虫

**versatile** person duōcái
duōyì 多才多艺；gadget
duō gōngnéng 多功能

**verse** (poetry) shī 诗；(part
of poem, song) jié 节

**versus** SP, LAW duì 对

**very** adv hěn 很；was it
cold? – not – lěngbùlěng?
– bù zěnme lěng 冷不冷
？– 不怎么冷；the ~
best zuìhǎo 最好

**vessel** NAUT chuán 船

**veteran 1** n tuìwǔ jūnrén 退
伍军人 **2** adj (old) lǎoshì
老式；(experienced) lǎoliàn
老练

**veterinarian** shòuyī 兽医

**via** jīngguò 经过；(by means

*of*) tōngguò 通过

**viable** *plan* qièshí kěxíng 切实可行

**vibrate** *v/i* zhèndòng 振动

**vice** èxí 恶习

**vice president** fù zǒngtǒng 副总统

**vice versa** fǎnzhī yìrán 反之亦然

**vicinity** dìdiǎn 地点

**vicious** *dog* xiōnghěn 凶狠; *attack, temper* èdú 恶毒

**victim** shòuhàizhě 受害者

**victory** shènglì 胜利

**video** *n & v/t* lùxiàng 录像

**video camera** shèxiàngjī 摄像机

**video cassette** lùxiàng dài 录像带

**video recorder** lùxiàngjī 录像机

**Vietnam** Yuènán 越南

**Vietnamese 1** *adj* Yuènán 越南 **2** *n* Yuènánrén 越南人; (*language*) Yuènán yǔ 越南语

**view 1** *n* fēngjǐng 风景; (*of situation*) guāndiǎn 观点; **in ~ of** jiànyú 鉴于 **2** *v/i* (*watch TV*) kàn看

**viewer** TV guānzhòng 观众

**viewpoint** guāndiǎn 观点

**vigor** huólì 活力

**village** cūnzhuāng 村庄

**villager** cūnlǐrén 村里人

**vindictive** yǒu bàofù xīn 有报复心

**vine** pútáo 葡萄

**vintage 1** *n* (*of wine*) shēngchǎn niánfèn 生产年份 **2** *adj* (*classic*) jīngdiǎn 经典

**violate** *rules, sanctity* wéifàn 违犯; *treaty* wéibèi 违背

**violation: traffic ~** wéifàn jiāotōng fǎguī 违反交通法规

**violence** bàolì 暴力

**violent** bàolì 暴力; *gale* měngliè 猛烈

**VIP** (= **very important person**) zhòngyào rén 要人

**viral** *infection* bìngdú 病毒

**virtual** shízhì 实质

**virtually** (*almost*) jīhū 几乎

**virus** MED, COMPUT bìngdú 病毒

**visa** qiānzhèng 签证

**visibility** néngjiàn dù 能见度

**visible** *object* yìjiàn 易见; *difference* míngxiǎn 明显;

*anger* yì chájué 易察觉

**vision** shìlì 视力; REL *etc* yōulíng 幽灵

**visit** n & v/t bàifǎng 拜访; (*to place, country*) yóulǎn 游览

**visitor** kèrén 客人; (*to museum etc*) cānguānzhě 参观者; (*tourist*) yóukè 游客

**visual** shìjué 视觉; *arts* zhíguān 直观

**visualize** xiǎngxiàng 想象; (*foresee*) shèxiǎng 设想

**vital** (*essential*) bìbù kěshǎo 必不可少

**vitamin** wéitāmíng 维他命

**vitamin pill** wéitāmíng yàopiàn 维他命药片

**vivid** *color* xiānyàn 鲜艳; *imagination etc* huóyuè 活跃

**vocabulary** cíhuì 词汇

**voice 1** n shēngyīn 声音 **2** v/t *opinions* biǎodá 表达

**voicemail** diànhuà dálùjī 电

话答录机

**volcano** huǒshān 火山

**voltage** diànyā 电压

**volume** (*of container*) róngliàng 容量; (*of work, liquid*) liàng liàng; (*of business*) é 额; (*of book*) cè 册; (*of radio etc*) yīnliàng 音量

**voluntary** adj *helper* zhìyuàn 志愿; *work* yìwù 义务

**volunteer 1** n yìgōng 义工 **2** v/i zhìyuàn 志愿

**vomit** v/i ǒutù 呕吐

**voracious** *appetite* lángtūn hǔyàn 狼吞虎咽

**vote 1** n xuǎnpiào 选票 **2** v/i POL tóupiào 投票; ~ *for* / *against* tóu zànchéng piào / fǎnduì piào 投赞成票 / 反对票

**voucher** piàoquàn 票券

**voyage** hánghǎi 航海

**vulgar** cūsú 粗俗

**vulnerable** (*to attack*) bóruò 薄弱

# W

**wad** n (of absorbent cotton etc) tuán 团; (of bills) dá 沓
**wade** báshè 跋涉
**wag** v/t tail, finger yáodòng 摇动
**wage** n gōngzī 工资
**wagon** RAIL chǎngpéng huòchē 敞篷货车
**wail** v/i (of person, baby) tòngkū 恸哭
**waist** yāobù 腰部
**waistline** yāowéi 腰围
**wait 1** n děngdài 等待 **2** v/i děng 等
**waiter** nán fúwùyuán 男服务员
**waiting list** děnghòuzhě míngdān 等候者名单
**waiting room** děnghòushì 等候室
**waitress** nǚ fúwùyuán 女服务员
**wake 1** v/i: ~ (up) xīnglái 醒来 **2** v/t huànxǐng 唤醒
**wake-up call** huànxǐng diànhuà 唤醒电话
**walk 1** n bùxíng 步行; go

for a ~ qù sànbù 去散步 **2** v/i zǒu 走; (as opposed to taking the bus etc) zǒulù 走路; (hike) chángtú túbù lǚxíng 长途徒步旅行
**wall** qiáng 墙
**wallet** qiánbāo 钱包
**wallpaper** n bìzhǐ 壁纸
**Wall Street** Huá'ěrjiē 华尔街
**wander** v/i (roam) mànbù 漫步; (of attention) zǒushén 走神
**want 1** n (need) xūyào 需要 **2** v/t yào 要; (need) xūyào 需要; ~ to do X xiǎngzuò X 想做 X; he ~s a haircut tā děi jiǎn tóufa 他得剪头发
**want ad** suǒqiú guǎnggào 索求广告
**wanted** (by police) bèi tōngjí 被通缉
**war** n zhànzhēng 战争
**warden** (of prison) jiānguǎnrén 监管人
**warehouse** cāngkù 仓库

**warfare** zhànzhēng 战争

**warhead** dàntóu 弹头

**warm 1** adj nuǎnhuo 暖和; welcome rèqíng 热情 **2** v/t shǐ nuǎnrè 使暖热

**warmhearted** rèxīncháng 热心肠

**warmth** wēnnuǎn 温暖; (of welcome) rèqíng 热情

**warn** jǐnggào 警告

**warning** n jǐnggào 警告

**warped** fig fǎncháng 反常

**warrant** n xǔkězhèng 许可证

**warranty** bǎodān 保单

**warship** jūnjiàn 军舰

**wartime** zhànshí 战时

**wary: be ~ of** jǐnfáng 谨防

**wash 1** n xǐdí 洗涤 **2** v/t & v/i xǐ 洗

♦ **wash up** xǐyíxǐ 洗一洗

**washbasin** liǎnpén 脸盆

**washer** (for faucet etc) diànquān 垫圈

**washing machine** xǐyījī 洗衣机

**Washington** Huáshèngdùn 华盛顿

**washroom** guànxǐshì 盥洗室

**waste 1** n làngfèi 浪费; (industrial) fèiwù 废物 **2** adj fèiqì 废弃 **3** v/t làngfèi 浪费

**waste basket** fèizhǐlǒu 废纸篓

**watch 1** n (timepiece) shǒubiǎo 手表 **2** v/t movie, TV kàn 看; (spy on) jiānshì 监视; (look after) zhàokàn 照看 **3** v/i kàn 看

**water 1** n shuǐ 水; **~s** NAUT lǐnghǎi 领海 **2** v/t plant jiāo 浇 **3** v/i (of eyes) liúlèi 流泪

**water chestnut** gāncǎo lìzi 甘草栗子

**watermelon** xīguā 西瓜

**waterproof** adj fángshuǐ 防水

**wave**[1] n (in sea) bōlàng 波浪

**wave**[2] n (of hand) zhìyì 致意 **2** v/i (with hand) huīshǒu 挥手 **3** v/t flag huīwǔ 挥舞

**way 1** n (method) fāngfǎ 方法; (of behaving etc) fāngshì 方式; (route) lùxiàn 路线; **this ~** (like this) zhèyàng 这样; (in this direction) zhètiáolù 这条路; **by the ~** shùnbiàn 顺便

wènyīxià 顺便问一下；
*lead the* ~ yǐnlù 引路；*lose
one's* ~ mílù 迷路；*be in
the* ~ (*obstruct*) dǎnglù 挡
路；*no* ~! juéduì bù! 绝
对不！2 *adv* F (*much*)
yuǎnyuǎn 远远

**way in** rùkǒu 入口
**way of life** shēnghuó fāngshì
生活方式
**way out** n chūkǒu 出口；*fig*
(*from situation*) chūlù 出路
**we** wǒmen 我们
**weak** *coffee* dàn 淡；
*government, currency* bóruò
薄弱；(*physically*) xūruò
虚弱；(*morally*) ruǎnruò
软弱
**weaken 1** *v/t* xuēruò 削弱
**2** *v/i* biànruò 变弱
**wealth** cáifù 财富
**wealthy** fùyǒu 富有
**weapon** wǔqì 武器
**wear 1** n: ~ (*and tear*)
sǔnhào 损耗 **2** *v/t* (*have
on*) chuān 穿
♦ **wear out 1** *v/t* shǐ pífá 使
疲乏；*shoes* yònghuài 用
坏 **2** *v/i* (*of shoes, carpet*)
yòngjiù 用旧
**weary** kùnfá 困乏

**weather** n tiānqì 天气
**weather forecast** tiānqì
yùbào 天气预报
**web** (COMPUT, *of spider*)
wǎng 网
**web site** wǎngzhǐ 网址
**wedding** hūnlǐ 婚礼
**wedding ring** jiéhūn jièzhǐ
结婚戒指
**Wednesday** xīngqīsān 星
期三
**weed** n zácǎo 杂草
**week** xīngqī 星期；*a* ~
*tomorrow* xiàyīzhōude
míngtiān 下一周的明天
**weekday** xīngqī yī dào wǔ 星
期一到五
**weekend** zhōumò 周末；*on
the* ~ zhōumò 周末
**weekly** *adj* & *adv* měizhōu
yícì 每周一次
**weep** kūqì 哭泣
**weigh 1** *v/t* chēng ... de
zhòngliàng 称 ... 的重量
**2** *v/i* cèchū zhòngliàng 测
出重量
**weight** zhòngliàng 重量
**weird** guàiyì 怪异
**welcome 1** *adj* shòu huānyíng 受欢迎；*you're* ~!
biékèqì! 别客气！**2** n

(*for guests etc*) huānyíng
欢迎 **3** *v/t guests* yíngjiē
迎接; *decision etc* duì ...
gǎndào yúkuài 对 ... 感
到愉快

**welfare** jiànkāng 健康;
(*financial assistance*) fúlì
jiùjì 福利救济

**well**[1] *n* (*for water, oil*) jǐng 井

**well**[2] **1** *adv* hǎo 好; *as ~*
(*too*) yě 也; *as ~ as* (*in
addition to*) hái 还; *very
~* (*acknowledging*) shì 是;
(*reluctance*) hǎoba 好吧;
*~, ~ !* (*surprise*) yōu, yōu!
呦, 呦！; *~ ...* (*uncertainty,
thinking*) ai ... āiyōu 哎 ... 哎呦;
*be ~* jiànkāng 健康

**well-behaved** xíngwéi guījù
行为规矩

**well-dressed** yīzhuó zhěngjié 衣着整洁

**well-known** zhòngsuǒ
zhōuzhī 众所周知

**west 1** *n* xīmiàn 西面; *the
West* Xīfāng Guójiā 西
方国家 **2** *adj* xī 西 **3** *adv*
xiàngxī 向西

**West Coast** (*of USA*) Xī
Hǎi'àn 西海岸

**western 1** *adj* zài xībù 在西

部; *Western* Xīfāng guójiā
西方国家 **2** *n* (*movie*)
xībùpiàn 西部片

**Westerner** Xīfāngrén 西
方人

**wet** *adj* shī 湿; (*rainy*) duōyǔ
多雨

**what 1** *pron* shénme 什么; *~
is it?* (*what do you want*)
zěnmele? 怎么了？; *~
about ...?* ... zěnmeyàng?
... 怎么样? **2** *adj*
shénme 什么; *~ color?*
shénme yánsè? 什么颜
色？

**whatever 1** *pron* búlùn
shénme 不论什么;
(*regardless of*) bùguǎn
shénme 不管什么 **2** *adj*
rènhé 任何

**wheat** xiǎomài 小麦

**wheel 1** *n* lúnzi 轮子 **2** *v/t
bicycle* tuī 推

**wheelchair** lúnyǐ 轮椅

**when 1** *adv* shénme shíhòu
什么时候 **2** *conj* dāng ...
de shíhòu 当 ... 的时候;
*~ I was a child* dāng wǒ shì
ge háizi de shíhòu 当我是
个孩子的时候

**whenever** wúlùn shénme

shíhou 无论什么时候
**where** 1 *adv* nǎr 哪儿;~
*should I put this?* wǒ bǎ
zhèige fàng nǎr? 我把这
个放哪儿? 2 *conj: this
is ~ I used to live* zhè shì
wǒ céngjīng zhùguò de
dìfang 这是我曾经住过
的地方

**wherever** 1 *conj* wúlùn nǎlǐ
无论哪里 2 *adv* dàodǐ zài
nǎlǐ 到底在哪里

**whether** shìfǒu 是否

**which** 1 *adj* nǎyíge 哪一个
2 *pron* (interrogative) nǎge
哪个; (relative): *the book
~ I bought* wǒ mǎide nèibě
n shū 我买的那本书

**whichever** 1 *adj* rènhé 任
何 2 *pron* wúlùn nǎge 无
论哪个

**while** *conj: ~ ...* zài ... shíqī
在 ... 时期

**whip** 1 *n* biānzi 鞭子 2 *v/t*
(beat) biānda 鞭打; *cream*
jiǎodǎ 搅打

**whirlpool** xuánwō 旋涡;
(for relaxation) ànmó yù-
gāng 按摩浴缸

**whiskey** wēishìjìjiǔ 威士
忌酒

**whisper** 1 *n* ěryǔ 耳语 2 *v/i*
qièqièsīyǔ 窃窃私语 3 *v/t*
dīshēng shuō 低声说

**whistle** 1 *n* (sound)
kǒushàoshēng 口哨声;
(device) shàozi 哨子 2 *v/i*
fā xūxūshēng 发嘘嘘声

**white** 1 *n* báisè 白色;
(person) báirén 白人 2 *adj*
cāngbái 苍白; *person*
báirén 白人

**White House** Bái Gōng
白宫

**who** ◊ (interrogative) shéi 谁;
*~'s that?* nà shì shéi? 那是
谁? ◊ (relative): *the man
~ taught me* jiāoguò wǒ
de nèige rén 教过我的
那个人

**whoever** wúlùn shì shéi 无
论是谁

**whole** 1 *adj* zhěngge 整个
2 *n* zhěngtǐ 整体

**wholesale** 1 *adj* pīfā 批发
2 *adv* yǐ pīfājià 以批发价

**wholesome** cùjìn jiànkāng
促进健康

**whose** *pron & adj* shéide
谁的;~ *is this?* zhè shì
shéide? 这是谁的?

**why** wèishénme 为什么

**wicked** xié'è 邪恶

**wicket** (*in station, bank etc*) guìtái 柜台

**wide** *adj* kuānkuò 宽阔; *experience* fēngfù 丰富; *range* guǎngfàn 广泛

**widely** *used, known* guǎngfàn 广泛

**wide-open** dàkāi 大开

**widespread** biànbù 遍布

**widow** guǎfu 寡妇

**widower** guānfū 鳏夫

**width** kuāndù 宽度

**wife** qīzi 妻子

**wild** *adj animal, flowers* yě shēng 野生; *applause* rèliè 热烈

**wildlife** yěshēng niǎoshòu 野生鸟兽

**will**[1] *n* LAW yízhǔ 遗嘱

**will**[2] *n* (*willpower*) yìzhì 意志

**will**[3] ◊ (*future*) huì 会 ◊: *the car won't start* chē qǐdòng bù liǎo 车启动不了 ◊: ~ *you tell her that ...?* nǐ kě yǐ gàosù tā ... ma? 你可以告诉她 ... 吗?

**willing** lèyú 乐于

**willingly** gānxīn qíngyuàn 甘心情愿

**win 1** *n* shènglì 胜利

**2** *v/t* huòshèng 获胜 **3** *v/i* yíngdé 赢得

**wind**[1] *n* fēng 风

**wind**[2] **1** *v/i* (*of path etc*) wānyán 蜿蜒 **2** *v/t cloth etc* chánrào 缠绕

**window** chuānghu 窗户; COMPUT shìchuāng 视窗

**windowsill** chuāngtái 窗台

**windshield** dǎngfēng bōli 挡风玻璃

**wine** pútáojiǔ 葡萄酒

**wing** *n* chìbǎng 翅膀; SP biāncè 边侧

**wink 1** *n* zhǎyǎn 眨眼 **2** *v/i* (*of person*) shǐ yǎnsè 使眼色

**winner** huòshèngzhě 获胜者

**winnings** yíngdéde qián 赢得的钱

**winter** *n* dōngtiān 冬天

**winter sports** dōngjì yùndòng 冬季运动

**wipe** *v/t* cā 擦; *tape* mǒdiào 抹掉

**wire** jīnshǔsī 金属丝; ELEC diànxiàn 电线

**wiring** ELEC xiànlù 线路

**wisdom** zhìhuì 智慧

**wise** yīngmíng 英明

**wish 1** n yuànwàng 愿望；
***best~es*** zhùhǎo 祝好
**2** v/t: **I ~ that ...** yàoshì ...
jiù hǎo le 要是 ... 就好了
**3** v/i: **~ for** qídǎo 祈祷

**wit** (humor) jīzhì yōumò 机
智幽默

**with** ◊ (accompanied by,
proximity) hé ... yìqǐ 和
... 一起；***she came ~ her
sister*** tā hé tāde mèimei
yìqǐ láide 她和她的妹妹
一起来的；***a meeting ~
the President*** yǔ zǒngtǒng
huìmiàn 与总统会面；
**~ no money** méiyǒu qián
没有钱；(agency) yòng
用；***write ~ a brush*** yòng
máobǐ xiězì 用毛笔写
字 ◊ (cause) yóuyú 由于；
shivering ~ fear yóuyú
kǒngjù ér chàndǒu 由于恐
惧而颤抖 ◊ (possession)
yǒu 有；***the house ~ the
red door*** yǒu hóng mén de
nèige fángzi 有红门的那
个房子

**withdraw** v/t complaint
chèxiāo 撤消；money tíqǔ
提取；troops chèhuí 撤回

**withdrawn** adj person gūpì
孤僻

**wither** diāoxiè 凋谢

**within** prep (distance) bù
chāoguò 不超过；(inside)
zài ... lǐmiàn zài ... 里面；
(in time) zài ... zhīnèi 在
... 之内

**without** méiyǒu 没有；**~
looking** méi kàn 没看

**withstand** jǐndézhù 禁得住

**witness** n (at trial) zhèngrén
证人；(of accident, crime)
mùjīzhě 目击者

**witty** jīzhì 机智

**wok** guō 锅

**woman** nǚrén 女人

**women's lib** fùnǚ jiěfàng 妇
女解放

**wonder 1** n (amazement)
jīngqí 惊奇 **2** v/i gǎndào
jīngyà 感到惊讶

**wonderful** jíhǎo 极好

**wood** mù 木；(forest) shùlín
树林

**wooden** mùzhì 木制

**wool** yángmáo 羊毛

**woolen** adj yángmáozhì 羊
毛制

**word** n cí 词；(promise)
nuòyán 诺言

**wording** cuòcí 措辞

**word processing** wénzì chǔlǐ
文字处理

**work 1** n gōngzuò 工作
**2** v/i gōngzuò 工作; (of
machine) yùnzhuǎn 运转;
(succeed) zòuxiào 奏效

♦ **work out 1** v/t solution
zhǎochū 找出 **2** v/i (at
gym) dàliàng yùndòng 大
量运动; (of relationship
etc) qǔdé chénggōng 取
得成功

**workaholic** n F gōngzuò-
kuáng 工作狂

**worker** gōngrén 工人

**work day** gòngzuòrì 工作
日; (not a holiday) fēi
xiūxīrì 非休息日

**workmanship** jìyì 技艺

**work of art** jīngzhìde wùpǐn
精致的物品

**work permit** gōngzuò xǔkě
工作许可

**world** shìjiè 世界

**worldwide** adj biànjì shìjiè
遍及世界

**worn-out** pòjiù 破旧; person
jīnpílìjìn 筋疲力尽

**worried** dānyōu 担忧

**worry 1** n dānyōu 担忧
**2** v/t dānxīn 担心; (upset)

shǐrén yōuchóu 使人忧愁
**3** v/i dānyōu 担忧

**worse 1** adj gènghuài 更坏
**2** adv gèng bǔhǎo 更不好

**worsen** v/i biàndé gènghuài
变得更坏

**worst 1** adj zuìhuài 最坏
**2** adv zuìzāo 最糟

**worth** adj: be ~ ... FIN zhí ...
值...; be ~ seeing zhídé
kàn 值得看

**worthless** wú jiàzhí 无价
值; person méiyǒng 没用

**worthwhile** cause zhídé zuò
值得做

**would:** ~ you like to ...? nǐ
xiǎng ... ma? 你想 ...吗?
~ you tell her that ...? qǐng
nǐ gàosù tā ... hǎoma? 请
你告诉她 ... 好吗?

**wound** n shāng 伤

**wrap** v/t gift bāo 包; (wind)
chánráo 缠绕

**wrapping paper** bāozhuāng-
zhǐ 包装纸

**wreck 1** n cánhái 残骸 **2** v/t
huǐhuài 毁坏; plans huǐmiè
毁灭

**wreckage** cánhái 残骸

**wrecker** tuōchē 拖车

**wrench** n (tool) bānzi 扳子

**wriggle** *v/i* niǔdòng 扭动

**wrinkle** *n* zhòuwén 皱纹

**wrist** shǒuwàn 手腕

**wristwatch** shǒubiǎo 手表

**write 1** *v/t* xiě 写; *check* kāi
开 **2** *v/i* xiě 写; (*of author*)
xiězuò 写作; (*send a letter*)
xiěxìn 写信

**writer** zuòzhě 作者

**writing** (*as career*) xiězuò
写作; (*hand-writing*) zìjì
字迹; (*words*) wénzì 文
字; (*script*) shūxiě tǐxì 书
写体系

**writing paper** xìnzhǐ 信纸

**wrong 1** *adj* cuòwù 错误;
**be ~** (*of person*) cuòle 错
了; (*morally*) bú duì 不对;
*what's ~?* zěnmee? 怎么
了？; *there's something
~ with the car* chē yǒu diǎn
máobìng 车有点毛病
**2** *adv* cuòwù 错误; *go ~*
(*of person*) fàn cuòwù 犯
错误; (*of plan etc*) chūxiàn
wèntí 出现问题 **3** *n* bù
gōngzhèng de shì 不公
正的事

**wrong number** bōcuòle
hàomǎ 拨错了号码

# XY

**X-ray** *n* X guāng zhàopiàn
X 光照片

**yacht** yóutǐng 游艇

**Yangtze River** Chángjiāng
长江

**Yank** F Měiguó Lǎo 美国佬

**yard**[1] (*of institution*) fàngfēng
chǎng 放风场; (*behind
house*) yuànzi 院子; (*for
storage*) duīchǎng 堆场

**yard**[2] (*measurement*) mǎ 码

**yawn 1** *n* hēqiàn 呵欠 **2** *v/i*

dǎ hēqian 打呵欠

**year** nián 年

**yearly** *adj & adv* měinián
每年

**yell 1** *n* jiàohǎn 叫喊 **2** *v/i*
rāngrang 嚷嚷

**yellow 1** *n* huángsè 黄色
**2** *adj* huáng 黄

**yellow pages** huángyè 黄页

**yes** shìde 是的 ◊ (*repetition
of verb etc*): *are you
cold? – ~* nǐ lěng bu lěng?

– lěng 你冷不冷？– 冷
◊ (agreeing) duì 对; **he
should go** – tā yīnggāi
qù – duì 他应该去 – 对
◊ (accepting suggestion)
xíng 行

**yesterday** zuótiān 昨天;
**the day before ~** qiántián
前天

**yet** adv: **as ~** dàocǐ wéizhǐ
到此为止; **is he here ~?
– not ~** tā láile ma? – hái
méine 他来了吗？– 还
没呢

**yield 1** v/t harvest chūchǎn 出
产; interest shēngxī 生息
**2** v/i (to enemy) tóuxiáng 投
降; (of traffic) rànglù 让路

**yogurt** suānnǎi 酸奶

**you** (singular) nǐ 你; (plural)
nǐmen 你们; (polite) nín

您; (polite plural, rare)
nínmen 您们

**young** person niánqīng 年
青

**your, yours** (singular) nǐde
你的; (plural) nǐmende
你们的; (polite singular)
nínde 您的; (polite plural)
nínmende 您们的

**yourself** nǐ zìjǐ 你自己

**yourselves** nǐmen zìjǐ 你
们自己

**youth** qīngchūn niándài 青
春年代; (young man) xiǎo
huǒzi 小伙子; (young
people) qīngshàonián 青
少年

**youth hostel** qīngnián zhā
odàisuǒ 青年招待所

**yuan** (Chinese money)
yuán 元

# Z

**zap** v/t COMPUT (delete)
xiāochú 消除

**Zen Buddhism** Chánzōng
Fójiào 禅宗佛教

**zero** líng 零

**zip code** yóuzhèng biānmǎ
邮政编码

**zipper** lāliàn 拉链

**zone** qū 区

**zoo** dòngwù yuán 动物园

# Numbers

| | | | | |
|---|---|---|---|---|
| 0 | ○ líng | | 20 | 二十 èrshí |
| 1 | 一 yī | | 30 | 三十 sānshí |
| 2 | 二 èr *or* liǎng* | | 40 | 四十 sìshí *etc* |
| 3 | 三 sān | | | |
| 4 | 四 sì | | 21 | 二十一 èrshíyī |
| 5 | 五 wǔ | | 35 | 三十五 sānshíwǔ |
| 6 | 六 liù | | 99 | 九十九 jiǔshíjiǔ |
| 7 | 七 qī | | | |
| 8 | 八 bā | | 100 | 百 bǎi |
| 9 | 九 jiǔ | | 105 | 一百零五 yìbǎi líng wǔ |
| 10 | 十 shí | | | |
| 11 | 十一 shíyī | | 300 | 三百 sānbǎi |
| 12 | 十二 shí'ér | | 350 | 三百五十 sānbǎi wǔshí |
| 13 | 十三 shísān *etc* | | 356 | 三百五十六 sānbǎi wǔshíliù |

| | | |
|---|---|---|
| 1,000 | 千 qiān | |
| 1,005 | 一千零五 yìqiān líng wǔ | |
| 1,050 | 一千零五十 yìqiān líng wǔshí | |
| 5,300 | 五千三百 wǔqiān sānbǎi | |

| | | |
|---|---|---|
| 10,000 | 万 wàn | |
| 65,300 | 六万五千三百 liùwàn wǔqiān sānbǎi | |
| 100,000 | 十万 shíwàn | |
| 1,000,000 | 百万 bǎiwàn | |
| 10,000,000 | 千万 qiānwàn | |
| 100,000,000 | 万万 wànwàn | |

| | | |
|---|---|---|
| 100,000,000 | 亿 yì | |

The following more complex characters are also used on bills, checks etc.

| | | | | | |
|---|---|---|---|---|---|
| 0 | 零 líng | | 7 | 柒 qī |
| 1 | 壹 yī | | 8 | 捌 bā |
| 2 | 貳 èr | | 9 | 玖 jiǔ |
| 3 | 叁 sān | | 10 | 拾 shí |
| 4 | 肆 sì | | 100 | 佰 bǎi |
| 5 | 伍 wǔ | | 1,000 | 仟 qiān |
| 6 | 陆 liù | | | |

## Ordinal numbers

Ordinal numbers are formed by putting **dì** in front of the cardinal numbers:

| | | | |
|---|---|---|---|
| 1 | 一 yī | 3 | 三 sān |
| 1st | 第一 dìyī | 3rd | 第三 dìsān |
| | | | *etc* |
| 2 | 二 èr | | |
| 2nd | 第二 dì'èr | | |

\* **liǎng** is used when the number two is used in combination with a measure word.